IT GETS B
C.

Trudy Culross was born and brought up
in Dundee, Scotland. For the past 20
years she has lived in London and
worked as a journalist, both writing features and editing a number of women's
magazines.

She lives in Maida Vale, North London,
with her faithful dog, Angus.

Trudy Culross

It gets better after Cairo

Mandarin

For my father,
who worried but tried not to show it
and my mother, who blessed me and sent me on my way.
Without their encouragement, I wouldn't have
started the journey. Without their support, I couldn't
have finished this book.

With special thanks
to my friend Nadia, for her endless patience and
valid criticisms and Yvonne, my editor,
who burned much midnight oil
on my behalf.

And for Martin . . .
a kiss, wherever you may be.

A Mandarin Paperback

IT GETS BETTER AFTER CAIRO

First published in Great Britain 1988
by Ebury Press
This edition published 1990
by Mandarin Paperbacks
Michelin House, 81 Fulham Road, London sw3 6RB

Mandarin is an imprint of the Octopus Publishing Group

Copyright © Trudy Culross 1988

A CIP catalogue record for this book
is available from the British Library

ISBN 0 7493 0096 5

Phototypeset by Input Typesetting Ltd, London
Printed and bound in Great Britain by
Cox & Wyman Ltd, Reading

Contents

Prologue

This book won't reveal much about the art of travel. I can't tell you the cost of a second class rail ticket from Rangoon to Mandalay, or the proper way to eat fried grasshopper, or how to recognize the early symptoms of typhoid fever. I'll leave that to the professionals. But I *am* an expert on what a levelling and humbling experience travelling can be – and how much it can teach us. I *can* tell you about freedom – what a rare thing it is, how easy to abuse, how difficult to fully enjoy. Ironic, isn't it, that total freedom should require complete self-discipline.

A few years ago, I was the sad remains of someone's wife. Confused, afraid, bitter, vengeful. But it wasn't too late to change. The world was full of women like me, who had to pick up the pieces and start over. Only I went one better. Not content to merely rebuild my life, I redesigned it at the same time – completely remodelling myself along what I fancied were sleeker, more stylish lines. For a time I was quite pleased with the finished product. I saw myself as a woman of the Eighties – divorced, childless, financially independent, emotionally self-contained, sexually aggressive. But as a model of new womanhood I had some serious defects which gradually came to light. And almost before I knew what was happening, I began to fall apart at the seams.

Of course, I laid the blame on outside influences – the pace of London life, the pressure of work, superficial friends – and figured that a change of scene was all that was needed to put things right. So I set off on a haphazard journey and unwittingly took with me the only real problem I had – my new 'improved' self.

The woman who left London had all the functions necessary for city living. She knew how to treat head waiters, where to find late night cabs, when to get tough at business meetings, what to say at dinner parties. She could just as easily emasculate a man as seduce him, and took malicious pleasure in doing both. But outside of her territory none of that counted for much, and she seemed to have nothing to offer in its place. She never could have survived the journey – her sort don't last long in the real world. But for all that, she was part of me, and, in trying to eliminate her, I nearly destroyed both of us.

So many stupid decisions, so much unnecessary risk-taking . . . why had my attempt at travel turned into such a death-defying trip? The answers, when they came, were shocking. They were nothing to do with being an amateur globetrotter but everything to do with being divorced, rejected, angry and vengeful . . . and having no self-esteem. And the truth, when it finally hit me, knocked me for six.

If you've ever wanted power, if you've ever longed for freedom, I can tell you how exciting – and dangerous – these things are. So difficult to enjoy, so easy to abuse.

If you've ever dreamed of a new identity and a different way to live your life, then you can share my experience. Hop over my side of the fence and see for yourself that the grass isn't greener. Just longer. But as the world opened, so did I. The less I tried to impress, the more response I got. The more vulnerable I grew, the less threatened I felt. Once I learned to trust, I met with endless kindness. As my affection for people and my pleasure in them grew, I found I began to like myself more, too. And so my inner journey became as magical as the trip itself.

I never intended to write this book this way, never dreamed I would admit so many painful things to perfect strangers. It's all about having the opportunities, getting the breaks – and still making mistakes. But if it makes *you* a little less afraid, leaves you feeling a little less alone, that's good. If my story shows you that, in the end, all you need do is learn to trust yourself, then the years of work, the massive overdraft, shattered social life and tears (lots of these) will all have been worthwhile.

Trudy Culross

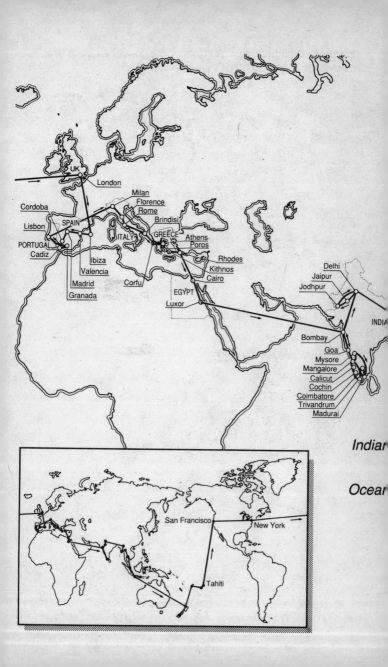

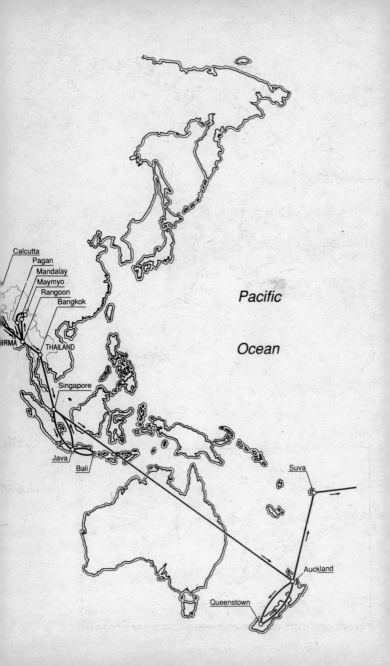

PART ONE

My time to cry

Chapter One

Take me to bed and show me that you care

I used to think that those first seconds after making love – as Rui's body slipped away from mine, his breathing already shallow in sleep – were the saddest moments of all. Our lovemaking did nothing for me, meant nothing to me. But if he sensed that, he didn't seem to care. My bed became the loneliest place in the world, filled with the smell and the warmth of a slumbering stranger I once knew so well.

I also used to think the emptiness of being with him was more bearable than being by myself; that *feeling* lonely in our shared bed sure as hell beat *being* lonely in an empty one.

Once, when I really loved him, I used to think I would die for him. Even when I loved him less, I used to think I would surely die without him. I used to think a lot of things I don't think now, but on that summer evening six years ago, while I waited for my husband to come home, I was thinking about things even more than usual.

How *do* you pull the plug on twelve years of marriage? I wondered, as I let myself into our silent home and mechanically went about the evening's chores. I was just hours away from doing precisely that, yet I didn't know where I would begin, when Rui came home. *If* Rui came home. . . .

It was just after eight o'clock and the rooms were still flooded with daylight as I moved through them, wondering what he was up to. Drinks with the boys in El Vino's probably – their Porsches, parked ostentatiously at the door, guaranteed to draw in a steady stream of females, eager to be chatted up over free champagne. From Bexleyheath and Bromley by way of Selfridges lingerie department and Dickins & Jones cosmetics counters, these carefully made up salesgirls vied with sloe-eyed language students and the odd Swedish nanny for the attentions and the part-time affections of my husband and his cronies.

Sporting expensive suits and expansive charm, their Portuguese accents lending a romantic lilt to even the most mundane remark, Rui's mob ruled El Vino's, running up horrendous bar bills and taking it in turns to placate their wives on the manager's office phone, while adoring temp secs and shoe shop girls dangled, dreaming, from their arms, enjoying the sense of danger. I could quite understand that, for hadn't I once been an arm-dangler, a naïve young dreamer, myself – sensing that Rui was trouble and loving the thrill of it all?

I'd been just twenty-one when I met him and already, for me, it was the year of living dangerously. A rank amateur at the game of life, I'd recently moved down from Dundee and was sharing a flat in London with ten crazy girls, who impressed me half to death with their posh accents and even posher clothes. I was heady with the excitement of my new job on a teenage magazine – disappointed that they wouldn't let me answer the telephone until I had toned down my broad Scottish brogue but thrilled to be surrounded by people who called each other 'love' and 'darling' and met each other for 'lunch'.

Although I'd been a late starter in the sexual stakes, I liked to think I was making up for lost time since arriving in the city and already I could boast a tiny potted sexual history of my own. True, the inadequate fumblings I'd experienced at the hands of my first *real* boyfriend had left little impression since, on the only occasion that son of Cyprus had attempted to make love to me, a combination of fear and 'flu had rendered me a most uncooperative partner.

Boyfriend Number Two had been a young and macho mounted policeman who, while every bit as curious about sex as I was, knew even less about it. So instead of coupling, our evenings were mostly spent grappling, as he initiated me into the art of judo. The bruises I sported after a session of holds and throws made me the envy of my flatmates, who never doubted that the bumps and thumps they could hear through

4

my bedroom door were the shorthand of sex. And who was I to gainsay them?

Boyfriend Number Three was a different story altogether – suave and stylish, lovely to look at, and South American. (Already I was developing a taste for foreign men.) I'm sure there was a lot he could have taught me and God, knows, I still had everything to learn. But by the time he'd talked me out of my clothes, parted me from my long acrylic hairpiece to reveal the perm-gone-wrong beneath and presented me with a bright pink pregnancy-stopping pessary, which I'd no idea where or how to insert, I was beyond being laid. Or at least, beyond enjoying the experience. Too embarrassed, too inhibited, too distressed by the knowledge that I knew so little. Two weeks later, I was on the Pill. Boyfriendless again, yet a little more prepared for whoever should become Encounter Number Four.

Then, suddenly, it was summer. I celebrated twenty-one-ness and, although the world wasn't yet my oyster, Portugal was certainly within my reach. My very first trip abroad – my first sun, sea and sex vacation. Brandishing everything but a 'kiss me quick' hat, I headed for the Algarve and a deserted, picturesque little fishing village called Albufeira. This is where I met Rui and grew up overnight.

I'd known him for forty-eight hours when I went to bed with him. I'd known him for six days when I realized I was desperately in love. I'd known him for eight days, when I discovered he was married. On that particular morning, we'd managed to stagger out of bed (sex was finally beginning to make sense) and were having breakfast at a streetside café when one of Rui's friends wandered by with the news that there was a telegram waiting for him at the post office.

He treated me to one of those wide smiles I had come to adore and assured me it was 'probably notheeng'. And then, his eyes full of mischief, 'Eet is probably from my wife – with news of the baby. . . .'

I don't suppose he noticed the smile fade from my face as he stood up with a shrug and headed across the road to the post office while, speechless, I stared after his slight figure – taking in the arrogant swagger, the confident set of the shoulders which said he didn't give a sod about anything. Or anyone. That was when the little voice inside my head said, 'Watch him, girl. Whatever happens next, you mustn't trust him.' It was the first good piece of advice I'd given myself in years – typical of me to ignore it.

The telegram was from his mother – his son was now ten days old and both mother and baby were doing well. When was he coming home, she wanted to know. While I wanted to know a whole helluva lot more than that. And over breakfast, I heard it all.

Rui had made Annabella's acquaintance under a table in a smart Lisbon nightclub. (You see, I really had *no* idea how the other half lived.) From there, the association had continued at a cracking pace – so much so, that they were married a matter of weeks later. A mistake Rui never would have made, he assured me, if his parents and brother hadn't tried so hard to break up the relationship on the grounds that she was 'unsuitable'.

Now, however, he was forced to agree they'd been right. For she was a girl whose beauty had far exceeded her brains, though she'd turned out to have more than her share of animal cunning. Still, she was great in the sack for all her faults and it was too bad she'd immediately become pregnant, he mused, as he toyed with his coffee. The lovely Annabella, no doubt anticipating her new husband's sudden change of heart, had obviously taken out the best kind of insurance – a baby.

While she had gestated in the comfort of his parents' house, Rui had continued to rattle around the Lisbon bars and nightclubs and, although he had promised to be with her when their son was born, he'd had a good run at the tables that evening and gambled the night away. A celebration breakfast had followed that run of luck, over which his friends (all of whom were as wealthy and spoiled as he was himself) had insisted he'd never survive without his parents' money.

Never one to resist a challenge, Rui had set out at dawn from the outskirts of Lisbon, hopefully thumbing a lift north to the sunlit beaches of the Algarve and totally unconcerned about his impending fatherhood.

6

And now, here he was – crazy Rui, divested of all his cash and left to make his way without so much as a change of clothes. All for a drunken bet. Of course, now that his long-suffering family had traced him, he would go home and face the music, he insisted. But since I was heading home in a few days myself and since we were having such a great time together . . . wouldn't it be better if he stayed on just a little longer?

That was the moment, of course – when I realized for the second time he was *trouble*. And if I had backed off then, I wouldn't have been pacing around our London home now, wondering how the hell to back off, twelve long years later. But I'd never been so excited about a man before and who could blame me for wanting more? Instead, like the little arm-danglers down at El Vino's, I hung on to some other woman's husband and willed him to be mine. You see, I'd never met anyone like Rui – and was amazed that someone so flamboyant, so funny, so full of tireless energy and good humour, could even exist outside of my imagination.

He was always ready to laugh, so easy to please – always telling hilarious stories in which he was the butt of the joke. He was the water skier who nearly drowned in three feet of water . . . the son who pawned all his parents' silver to settle a gambling debt . . . the fighter pilot who crashed three planes and had his private parts painted as a punishment . . . the airforce officer who was usually too drunk to go on parade, kept his own pet goat and his own pet whore on the base, had his uniforms tailor-made in the finest materials. He was the grade A university student who'd been declared schizophrenic by military psychiatrists; the national rock'n'roll champion; the poor little rich kid, who'd crashed his father's Porsche Spider when he was twelve, laid his first girl when he was fourteen, was running up bar bills and gambling debts when he was hardly into his seventeenth year; never shaved himself (his barber did that), never ran his own bath (his maid did that) and, at twenty-five, had never done a day's work in his life.

To say he turned my head would be an understatement. Rui nearly blew my mind. Twenty years spent steeped in the

7

work ethic, the scrimp-and-save-for-a-future-and-no-sex-till-you're-married (and maybe not even then) ethic had pickled my brain nicely. Obey your parents, save your money, be grateful you have a job, keep fun for Friday nights and sex for Saturdays (assuming you are lucky enough to have a husband). For years, I'd lived by the rules unquestioningly, keeping my legs and my mind pretty much closed to any new experience . . . but all the time sensing that there might be another side to the story.

And now there was Rui – living proof of a lifestyle practically the opposite of my own and apparently thriving on it. For him, there was no point in existing if you couldn't have fun. No point in making money if you didn't know how to spend it. No sense in being ambitious, if it gobbled up your energy and ruled your life. Just as it made no sense to show anger, when smiles and cajoling brought higher returns; made no sense to argue, when saying 'yes' to everything (even when you really meant 'no') could confuse the opposition long enough to let you have your own way.

It seemed an unworkable credo, but giving life the old two-fingered sign seemed to work for Rui. While I – who'd been taking life seriously and playing by the rules – was twenty-one going on forty and long overdue for fun. So for those last two days of my Portuguese holiday, we'd hardly moved out of bed, making love in ways I'd never dreamed of and positions previously unknown. And all the time he would murmur endearments in a language I couldn't understand; stroking my hair, caressing my back, kissing my eyes, my ears, singing to me. Making me cry with laughter, when I wasn't crying with happiness. Showering me with affection and teaching me how to respond. All the affection, the tenderness, the humour, the optimism and excitement . . . all the love I'd ever dreamed of. It was here in one man and I didn't see how I could live without him.

At least, that's what I told myself that lifetime of summers ago. Now, of course, I know that I had other, less noble reasons for falling in love with Rui. The man oozed self-confidence, he was utterly self-centred and selfish and without doubt a law unto himself; all the things I had never dared to be. He was also sophisticated, stylish, worldly, arrogant and superior – the result of careful breeding and a terrific education. The by-product of money and privilege.

I saw all of these characteristics as enviable 'qualities', instead of the flaws they actually were. And the working-class girl in me, anxious to shake off her modest background, craved Rui's identity, almost as much as she wanted the man himself. For back then, I had a real craving to be *somebody* who was *going places* and Rui, with his love of the good life, certainly fitted into my scheme of things. From him, I could learn the art of having a good time and sod everyone else.

When I think back to my childhood, and my mother's before that, I realize that there was a definite pattern to it all, that this longing to 'better' myself, to add up to more than the sum of my boring little parts, was almost as old as I was – instilled in me by a woman who'd spent her life trying to escape the disadvantages of her own birth. . . .

My mother was illegitimate, a fact of which she was blissfully unaware until she was fourteen and went to work as a weaver in the local jute mill, where her employers asked for her birth certificate. She mentioned their request when she got home that night. Then the truth came out and my mother's world caved in. After fourteen years of being called 'Frances', she discovered that her name was really 'Sylvia'.

Sylvia Buchan Lawrence.

Imagine being told across the tea table that you don't belong. That the kids scrapping over the bread and jam aren't your brothers and sisters after all; aren't even related to each other. My mother was just one more in a household of unwanted children. Waifs and strays who later died off one by one of tuberculosis, while only the girl's dogged instinct for survival kept her going.

Later it was replaced by a grim determination to succeed, as she grew into a pretty eighteen-year-old who joked and jived her way through the end of the war, and her green eyes and dark curly hair soon turned Walter's head. He was one of the 'overpaid, oversexed and over here' brigade – a young doctor who was going back to Idaho to start up a medical

9

practice and saw in my mother the kind of intelligent, alert young woman that ambitious doctors' wives are made of. Well, he proposed, my mother said 'yes' and she would have married him, too – thinking she was in love and never realizing that Walter's attraction lay in the respectability of his name and the status of his profession, while Idaho promised an escape from the mean tenement streets she'd grown up in.

But then she met my father, home on leave, sporting his dress naval uniform and gliding around the Palais dance floor in true Gene Kelly style.

On the face of it, he was no one, with nothing to offer. A soon-to-be-demobbed sailor with just the slimmest chance of a job working in a slaughterhouse. Moody and uncommunicative – the runt in a litter of twelve kids, raised on large helpings of salted porridge and the Bible. His father was a mild-mannered lay preacher, while his daunting mother had a tongue like a whiplash and a temper to match. Still, quite apart from loving him, Frances saw something in this man; an outlet for her energy, a channel for her burning ambition . . . who knows?

What I *do* know, because she has recently admitted it to me, is that my mother had no intention of ever having children. She was determined to be upwardly mobile, long before the phrase was coined, and broods of children are a barrier to that kind of progress. A big house on the hill in the posh part of town, a nice little car and a dog were the sum total of what she promised my father. But six weeks into her marriage, she discovered she was pregnant. Three more children followed closely on my heels.

For most women, that would have been the end of the Grand Plan but my mother was made of sterner stuff. And although she woke to the sound of the factory's whistle and dutifully answered its summons – scurrying to the mill in the dawn light with hundreds of other weavers – she spent all her energy proving what she always knew to be the case; that she was somehow different, special. Better than the others. My dad, a hardworking, unassuming man, backed her all the way. Not for him the odd pint after work or Saturday mornings spent down at the betting shop, misappropriating the

10

housekeeping money. While other dads swanned around in new cars, wearing posh clothes and talking about their holidays in some faraway place called Spain, my dad was cycling to work in all weathers, with cardboard cutouts lining the worn-out soles of his shoes. Yes, my mum was a woman with a mission and she'd married a man in a million. Until, that is, he lost his temper. Until some secret button was pressed, some terrible switch was pulled and this quiet, self-effacing man turned into a raging bull. Then our house became a battleground as he lashed out at everything in his path. Kids and pets would scatter for cover, while my mother alone stood her ground – defiant and almost taunting; meeting his physical violence with a verbal barrage of her own as I watched from behind the scullery door, utterly terrified.

No matter how many times it happened, I couldn't believe the depth of anger and the very real sense of hatred which seemed to possess them both at these times. And even on calm days, I kept a weather eye open for the slightest wind of change between my parents. Constantly sniffing the air for the first sign of squalls, I was still caught unawares every single time the storm broke, still frightened long after it had abated. I couldn't handle violence then and I still can't deal with it today.

Too much work, too little money. Too many kids, not enough time or privacy or fun. The pressures are so easy for me to understand now. But as an eight-year-old, then a ten-year-old, then a fourteen-year-old, I knew only that the kids were somehow to blame. And, as the eldest, I figured mine was the main burden of guilt. Now I know I grew up with a rather warped sense of 'self' and I think this is where it began.

Inevitably, I was left in charge of their brood. The minder, the sheepdog and, frequently, the bully. Cleaning up after them, watching over them and keeping them in line, I grew to resent them. Washing shitty nappies, cooking meals, helping them with their homework and lying for them in an effort to keep the fragile peace, I finally grew to dislike my sister and my two brothers. A feeling I didn't bother to hide when the folks weren't around. When they were on hand, though, I was on my best behaviour. The little mother, the silent helper

11

– I played my part to the hilt. I became what they needed, a sensible, dutiful eldest child who could be trusted to perform all kinds of tasks. Outwardly quiet and studious, while inwardly the resentment grew and grew.

Now, I wonder why my memories of growing up are, for the most part, depressing to recall, since my upbringing wasn't particularly hard. In the world I knew, most of us were latchkey kids and, as families go, I suppose ours was closer and happier than most. But when I think about those days, everything is overshadowed by a sense of anxiety. When I recall my childhood, the overwhelming emotions are those of jealousy and anger. And an enormous feeling of . . . deprivation, I guess.

My father isn't a demonstrative man and talk of love embarrasses him. So my mother, a passionate woman by nature, soon learned to curb her girlish displays of affection. Not that there's anything unusual in that; I'm more likely to see purple rain than I am to see two people kiss each other in greeting on a Scottish High Street. But I wanted to be kissed – a lot. I wanted to be held and hugged and *shown* that I was loved.

Inevitably, of course, I've been asking men to show me ever since: *Take me to bed and show me that you care.* It's only now that I realize I've spent my womanhood confusing sex with love.

All I know is that, as a little girl, I owed it to myself to find a reason why I wasn't getting the hugs and kisses. And the answer was obvious. There were too many kids in the house, all demanding the same thing. And so began the jealousy and, with it, the need to possess. Elements which I have fought so hard to control that the adult in me has feigned indifference in the face of my man's infidelities – my need to possess being so repressed that I appear downright casual. When, in fact, I am filled with a jealous rage.

And all of this – all of it, I know – stems from the child in me who still pretends not to feel these things which hurt her most. The young girl who sussed that it was all to do with being broke and having babies and promised herself that neither of these dreadful fates would befall her.

So, while the family limped from crisis to crisis – my father constantly caving in under the pressure and my mother finding ever more ingenious ways of saving the day – I got serious about my studies and sailed through my exams. Partly in this tired old effort to please the folks and thereby curry favour but partly because I sensed that, if my mother had benefited from the education I was getting, her life might have been very different.

I'd learned from her mistakes and now there was no way I was going to live out my days in a dead-end town, forever being dragged down by too little money and too many ungrateful kids. Financial independence meant freedom and 'A' levels were my passport out. My mother said that to me often enough and I believed her, although neither of us knew exactly where 'out' might eventually lead me.

Not that her own Grand Plan had worked out too badly. She did achieve the house on the hill, the nice car *and* the dog. She was still working hard in yet another factory but she looked in her prime, that autumn of my fifteenth year – slim and trim and as attractive as ever.

Happy, too. It was obvious to my expert eye that my folks were getting along well. *Too* well, as it turned out. For one Sunday afternoon, as we were washing dishes together, she announced that there was shortly to be another addition to the family.

I couldn't even pretend to be pleased, as visions of a baby-filled future danced before me. It spelled more sleepless nights, more frayed tempers, more strain on the finances. More pressure, more worry, more trouble. Not to mention acres of shitty nappies for me to wash, countless bottles to mix, endless time spent babysitting . . . and sharing my parents even more. There never was going to be an end to it, I could see that now.

Sensing my resentment, my mother tried to include me in the preparations for the home birth of this newest arrival and the morning finally came when I woke to find I had another brother. Sensing my displeasure, the midwife lifted young Colin from the wicker laundry basket which now served as his bed, placed him in my arms and watched carefully while

I gave him his first bath – something I could do with practised ease.

But nothing about this baby could soften my mood. Not his tiny pink, silky feet or his white blond curls, his blue eyes or his vacant smile. I wasn't to be won over so easily, for by now I was permanently immune to babies. All babies. Every single baby that might ever be born, including my own. And as for *this* baby . . . well, this bloody baby was the last straw.

For two more years, I rubbed along with my family. Tolerated my sister and two brothers, steadfastly ignored the new baby and single-mindedly planned my escape; just as, twenty years before, my mother had planned hers. By my seventeenth birthday, I'd passed my exams and got myself a job in a small publishing house. Suddenly I had some money in my pocket and – totally disillusioned with family life and the whole idea of sharing – I began to glimpse that there was a whole world outside my home. A place where I could dictate my own terms and surround myself with people who might give me the undivided love and attention I craved.

It took one more row (by now there were a lot of these). One more screaming match, during which the house erupted and the aftermath – all cold war and icy silences – was more than usually unbearable. One morning, after my mother had stormed out to work and my father had marched out stony-faced behind her, I waited until the kids had gone to school, then resolutely packed my bags.

Slamming the front door shut behind me for the last time, I tossed my key defiantly through the letterbox and went off in search of that place my mother had dreamed about for so long. 'At last,' I thought, 'I'm really getting out. . . .'

'Out' was a tiny flat on the other side of town where I happily settled down for the next couple of years, coming and going as I pleased and pretty much suiting myself. I took a fancy to a tall, lanky local who was much more into football than fornication and dated him for the prerequisite fifteen months before we announced the inevitable engagement.

By this time, the rift had been healed with my folks and I made dutiful daughter visits most Saturdays – that's when my fiancé and I weren't out flat-hunting for a little box to call

14

our own. My wedding was in the offing – I'd even started to put together a bottom drawer – when I was sent to London on business. Four days spent whizzing around the Strand and Piccadilly, breathing in the sights and sounds of that city, and life would never be the same for me again.

True, I'd been temporarily sidetracked by the idea of wife-dom. But the thought of having to raise a tiny football team had always slightly marred my dreams of domestic bliss. Now, though, the lure of London proved irresistible, so I handed back my engagement ring, gave in my notice and packed all my worldly goods into a battered blue metal trunk.

My folks saw me off on the London-bound train on a chilly October morning and, as Dad humped my luggage up into the carriage, Mum and I just looked at each other. Both of us knowing it was finally happening . . . that at last one of us was making a real bid for freedom.

For the first three hours of the journey, I was too self-conscious to sit down amongst so many strangers. So I stood in the gangway, glancing down at my trunk for reassurance. Then I fingered the money in my jacket pocket – twenty quid. Twenty quid between me and whatever was coming next. Twenty quid with no job, no flat and no idea what would happen when I reached my destination. That was a thought . . . and by the time the train pulled into Carlisle, I'd begun to feel just a little bit afraid.

I needn't have worried, though. London in the early Seventies was a place where everything was happening and soon I was running with the pack. Enjoying my job writing for a teenage magazine and my new friends. Enjoying my life. And looking, always looking, for ways to improve it. No wonder Rui had proved so attractive.

Still, when I'd been back from Portugal for a few days and the graphic details of my holiday romance had become old news amongst my flatmates, I did begin to think that Rui might not after all have done much for the quality of my life. Okay, so I'd gone into orbit with a half-mad married Latin but I'd safely re-entered the atmosphere again. And I was just settling gently back to earth, warming to that same old work-until-you-drop, save-to-the-grave, no-sex-on-the-sofa ethic, when the half-mad married Latin telephoned in the middle of the night.

It was the first of many phone calls during which we discussed why we *shouldn't* do it; how, practically speaking, we *couldn't* do it and he promised he *wouldn't* do it. However, when he turned up on my doorstep three weeks later, I'd never been so ecstatic about anything in my whole boring life. With his pedigree (such style and panache) and my tireless drive and fierce ambition, I figured we'd be a formidable team.

And, for a while, that's exactly what we were. . . .

The sudden ringing of the telephone shattered the silence and I slowly got to my feet, aware that the daylight had gone and the still living-room was now shrouded in darkness. I didn't bother to switch on the table lamp as I picked up the receiver, knowing Rui would be at the other end.

''Ello, pretty girl!' he yelled above the wall of sound. He'd obviously moved on from El Vino's. 'Don't worry about dinner. I forgot to tell you, I'm eating out. That boreeng business with the fly-drive crowd . . . I must get sometheeng on paper tonight. Okay?' he added as an afterthought. Knowing it would be, since it always was.

Slowly, I put the receiver back on its rest. So he had to get something down on paper, did he? That probably meant his dinner date worked in John Lewis's stationery department. Some little thing who usually sold white envelopes by the dozen and thought she'd died and gone to heaven now that she'd met Rui. He liked his little joke, you see – always giving me clever clues, so that I could read him like an open book. If I cared – if I dared – to look between the lines.

'Ah, well, it looks like dinner for one,' I remarked to Angus. My little West Highland terrier, who'd seen it all before, trotted matily at my heels as I wandered into the kitchen, flicking all the switches and flooding the rooms with light as I went.

'How *do* you pull the plug on twelve years of marriage?' I found myself wondering again, as I grabbed a tin of something and jabbed it with a can opener.

Well, first, you wait . . . and wait . . . and wait, until your two-timing bloody husband decides to come home.

And then?

'And then you sock it to the bastard!' I yelled at the half-opened can of tuna fish, as, finally, the tears began.

Chapter Two

Mistress of the cold kiss

You know what they say – about how all the world loves a lover? Well, mostly I think that's a load of crap. My observation is based on personal experience, for when the world and most of the people we knew in it weren't being plain old-fashioned, disapproving of our love affair, they were being downright bloody obstructive.

Maybe I'm taking it too personally. Maybe xenophobia was rampaging through Europe that particular October when Rui arrived in London and we were just two more casualties. But my flatmates, who'd regarded my whirlwind affair as a necessary ingredient of foreign holidays, were altogether more sceptical when we began to resuscitate this romance in my little attic bedroom.

Even my closest male friends – a couple of young Welshmen who lived on the other side of the block – asked me what I was doing with 'that shaggy haired wop', when both of them had been offering to service me for the longest time. Mark you, when I looked at Rui through their eyes, I realized they had a point; the slight figure huddled beneath its large navy overcoat bore little resemblance to the arrogant, tanned Romeo who had reigned supreme in Albufeira.

Instead, Rui's skin looked yellow in this cold, northern light, his large brown eyes looked dull and listless in what was fast becoming a pinched little face and even his mane of blue-black hair had lost its sheen. Not only that, but Rui was losing weight. Already the effort of shaving himself and running his own bath each day was taking its toll and it was questionable whether his stamina would actually stretch to holding down a job.

And that was *another* problem – work. Although Rui spoke very good French and more than passable Italian, his English was halting and heavily accented – particularly when he spoke on the telephone. Until that improved, the only work he was likely to get was the sort of work he would die rather than do. He just wasn't the stuff of the mini cab driver, waiter or barman.

So he took to lying around in bed all day, while I headed off into commuterland each morning. By now, I was the assistant editor on the magazine, an editorship was in the offing and it was time to get serious in the world of journalism. Yet I couldn't afford to get too enthusiastic about that around Rui, since he viewed my thrusting ambition with a mildly jaundiced eye. Here was a man with time hanging heavily on his hands – a man with energy to spare. He'd enjoyed the marathon bedroom sessions we'd had in Portugal and, now that he was in London, he wanted a rematch, since there wasn't much else to occupy his mind.

But now that I was a working girl again, trying to make enough money to keep two of us, I was up against the harsh reality of life. My body couldn't take the strain and neither could my bank balance and all this extra work and worry meant willing flesh, weak spirit and all that. To put it bluntly, going home meant getting laid – usually even *before* I'd managed to start cooking the evening meal and it would probably happen again after we ate and before I got started on the washing up. (I see you've already noticed and you're right: Rui wasn't the kind of man who did chores about the house.)

If he was feeling particularly frisky, the sex might go on for most of the night and, while I really revelled in all this attention, even I had a cut-off point, beginning to see the attraction in staying late at the office. In other words, I wasn't nearly as much fun as I had been in the summer, while Rui, a long way from home and friends, was broke and getting bored. The situation was dire and other people didn't help matters.

Take my folks, who certainly would never be founder members of Rui's fan club. I dragged him off to Dundee, where my dad shook him solemnly by the hand and offered to take him out for a pint (usually a treat reserved for high days and holidays) *provided* he got his hair cut. Then, handing me a pair of sharp scissors, Dad motioned towards the bathroom, while I meekly led Rui off there and proceeded to make a dog's dinner of his head.

Mum, meanwhile, had been doing one of her silent, split-second appraisals, while Rui tried to conduct a conversation with a boisterous, six-year-old Colin and neither of them understanding a bloody word. She collared me upstairs a few minutes later, her eyes bright with anger as she hissed, 'He's married, isn't he?' She never, ever missed a trick. 'Are you mad?' she rushed on through my silence. 'Bringing him to this house! God help you if your father finds out – ' And she made up the bed in a flurry of crisp, cold sheets while I stood helplessly by, wondering what she'd say if she ever got to hear about the child.

We were, of course, bedded down in separate rooms. Rui spent the next few days fielding all kinds of potentially explosive questions, like what he did for a living, and the weekend was not a resounding success. We limped dejectedly back to London; Rui nursing severe indigestion from a surfeit of mince and tatties and warm beer, while my mother's dire warnings about workshy, married foreigners rang in my ears.

The Portuguese Connection did its best to come between us as well, as odd acquaintances of Rui's, passing through London on business trips or shopping expeditions, would ring him up to remind him painfully of all the fun he was missing. Sometimes they even came by to look me over. And one of them even thought he'd sort me out.

Paulo was an old gambling buddy of Rui's, who mourned the fact that one of Lisbon's best poker players had deserted the fraternity. I remember, we were having a big party at the flat on that particular Saturday and, as I flew around with bottles of this and plates of that, I noticed that Paulo had arrived with a very pretty girl in tow. It soon became obvious that she wasn't Paulo's girlfriend but it took me a little longer to work out that she was bait – brought here to remind Rui of how the other half were still living.

Feeling threatened and possessive but determined not to show it, I ignored the well-meaning warnings from the other girls and decided to give Miss Lisbon and my man lots of space. Not that they needed much for, by now, the girl had practically grafted herself to Rui's trouser leg and her arms were entwined, snakelike, about his neck. And although his glance my way said how embarrassing it all was, the smile he gave her said something quite different.

'They look well together, my two friends – don't you think?' asked the oily Paulo and the truth was, they did. Like twins, with their olive skins, flashing eyes and shiny black hair gleaming in the candlelight. Hmmmm. . . .

Moving the candle closer was simple enough. Then I watched her flirt with Rui and, as she tossed back her thick dark mane, I waited patiently as it narrowly missed the flame. When, finally, her lacquered hair made contact with the candle, the burst of light was glorious and my quick-witted action real medal-winning stuff. The best part of a bottle of crimson plonk poured over the head is guaranteed to quench fires – particularly those of a sexual nature. And that was the last I saw of the singed and sorry Miss Lisbon.

Much later, as I lay wakeful beside a drunken and snoring Rui, I wondered at myself, letting jealousy finally get the upper hand. But when I was around him, I was constantly surprised by the depth of passion I was capable of and now I wondered what else I might discover about myself, if we continued to live together.

I knew our future looked bleak and his penniless, friendless existence was making Rui more and more unhappy. I couldn't bear the thought that he might leave me and head for home, but soon, neither of us would have a roof over our heads. The other girls, who were fairly relaxed about boyfriends staying overnight, were understandably weary of having a man permanently draped about the house and broad hints were being dropped almost daily. And I was just wondering what else could possibly go wrong when, of course, something did.

A week or so later, I was passing the telephone in the hallway when it rang out shrilly. I could hear strange whirs and clicks on the line and then a woman's voice, soft and low, asked to speak to Rui. Instinctively, I knew it was his mother and, when he came off the phone, it was with a bemused expression on his face and the news that his family wanted him home again.

He'd been gone for four months and in that time they'd had a change of heart. Now they were more than willing to settle his outstanding debts, use their influence to get him the 'right' kind of job. They would even entertain the idea of me muscling in on the act, once he'd got his life (and his wife?) sorted out. A ticket was already waiting for him at Heathrow, all he had to do was catch the plane.

I wanted to talk him out of leaving but, with a growing sense of helplessness, I realized that this was one decision he would have to make completely by himself. We discussed it, of course, but much later that evening, I went to bed alone, while Rui stayed downstairs thinking things over.

When he slipped into bed around three in the morning, I clung to him not knowing what to say. But even as he planted stray kisses in my hair, he held back from me and there was no need to ask which way the decision had gone.

You might wonder why the thought of losing him hurt so much when all we'd brought each other was trouble. But there was another side to the miserable months we'd spent together. Endless silly games and private jokes. So much shared laughter. Furious, colourful rows, which were actually enjoyable because violence – that element I'd come to fear – never once raised its ugly head.

And then there was the affection. The hugs and kisses and gentle words I'd yearned for came as naturally to Rui as breathing. I had an abundance of affection permanently on tap, which I didn't have to earn and wasn't obliged to share with anyone else. And let's not forget about the sex; ever since Rui had unlocked the mysteries of that particular pastime, the pleasure really had been all mine.

What's more, loving him gave me an outlet for my only natural talent – looking after people. My childhood had left me with a finely honed maternal instinct and Rui never tired of all the fuss and attention as I washed his hair, bathed him, stroked him to sleep, cooked his favourite meals, mended his clothes. Tasks which pleased me as much as they suited him.

In the early hours of the morning, I felt him easing his warm body away from mine; felt the springs sigh in the bed, as he quietly swung his weight to the floor. Heard faint scuffling as he wriggled into his trousers, then the slight creak of hinges as he opened the wardrobe, stealthily took out his few clothes, lifted down his travelling bag. Rui was leaving, without saying goodbye, and I knew it would be less painful all round if I just pretended to go on sleeping.

Moments after he left the room, I got up and crept over to the window. Down in the lamplit street, snow fluttered aimlessly and lay, coldly yellow, on the pavements. And suddenly there he was, his slight form hunched up against the wind and the bag bouncing against his legs, as he hurried up the avenue. Then he disappeared behind a curtain of snow and I knew that, with him, the laughter had gone out of my life.

Just after eight o'clock that evening, the doorbell jangled frantically. I was coming out of the kitchen with a cup of coffee when Alison opened the front door . . . and Rui blew in on a blast of icy wind, his navy overcoat dusted with a fine powdering of snow which drifted around the warm hallway.

Unable to believe he was actually standing there, I moved towards him and his icy hands fastened greedily around the cup. Enjoying my confusion, he drained it and said, 'Well, pretty girl – give me a kiss. I have a job, you see, so I think I deserve one.'

Holding me tightly, he sat in the crowded kitchen regaling everyone with a hilarious account of his visit to an employment agency, his trek to a grubby guest house on the Cromwell Road and his first lesson in making beds and frying eggs. For Rui, one-time drinker, gambler and gentleman of leisure, had joined the ranks of the capital's domestics, just hours after his mother had offered him a face-saving way out of his exile. And while the girls heaped congratulations upon him, I just sat there, loving him more in that moment than I've ever loved a man since.

February slid into March and on a morning filled with cold

23

sunshine, Rui got a mysterious phone call, asking him to present himself at the Portuguese airline office for an interview. Had his family finally realized that he meant to make a success of his life in London and had strings finally been pulled back in Lisbon? We never could say for sure. But suddenly Rui had a smart job in Regent Street, in an office where everyone spoke his language and he was able to wear a nice suit and have clean nails again.

We were still recovering from that stroke of luck, when a girlfriend rang to offer us the tiny second bedroom in her smart Chelsea basement flat and, as we settled into King's Road life with soft-hearted Maureen, her two cats and her wealth of Beatles music, we knew we were the two luckiest people in the whole world.

That first night, we lay down together in the tiny cramped room and whispered far into the night. About how lucky we were to be so young, so happy, so much in love. Could we ever dare hope it would last?

Which was when we made the promise. Vowed that, for the sake of the love we felt now, we would never let ourselves go the way of other couples we'd seen. The moment it no longer worked – the moment we were no longer happy together and knew the magic had gone – we would let each other go. Not for us the desperate clinging, the endless punishing battles, the destruction so many people inflicted on partners they claimed to love.

It was a promise sincerely made and one neither of us ever forgot. A promise I never dreamed I would one day have to keep. The question now was, could we still take our leave of each other without causing too much pain? Or had the destruction already begun . . . was the damage already done?

I pondered the question as I ran a bath, took off my clothes, studied my face in the mirror. I was worried and it showed. As I slid wearily into the warm water, my thoughts began to wander again and the same old questions began to race around in my head.

Where had our marriage gone wrong and why? And when?

I suppose a washing machine, a car, even one's body, sends

out distress signals when it's in trouble. So does a relationship. But often, it's only when the bloody thing breaks down completely that you wish you'd paid closer attention to all those clunks and thumps and coughs you'd chosen to neglect.

Ours, I realize now, was ailing from the start, only I was too infatuated with my image of Rui to consider that perhaps I was suffering from tunnel blindness where he was concerned. And that just beyond my limited field of vision there were whole aspects of this man which I had yet to see.

I got my first fleeting glimpse of that when his parents invited us to Portugal for a visit. Rui was delighted at the prospect of seeing his friends again, visiting the clubs, the old haunts. While I was thrilled at the thought of flying, of visiting a foreign city, of finally being acknowledged by his family – of seeing another side of this man who was still such a mystery to me.

The 'other side' began to manifest itself literally as we were walking down the aircraft steps. I'm not exaggerating when I say that a change came over Rui before we'd even cleared Customs. But there was something intangible in the air – something in the heat or the blast of strange language which met us on all sides. Whatever it was, it brought the old Rui swimming up from the depths and by the time he'd tumbled out of the taxi into the waiting arms of Luis, his super-cool brother, my Rui had been replaced by a swaggering, scoffing, elegantly bored Latin, who fascinated and frightened me at the same time.

I don't remember much about that first visit, except for a few brief moments, frozen in time.

A child with the face of an angel sleeps in his tiny bed, his golden forehead plastered with dark curls, while Rui bends over the still form and smugly shows off his eighteen-month-old son.

Maids giggle and the plump young cook blushes furiously, as Rui charms some morsel of food from her. Up to his old tricks again and teasing his way into their simple, country girl hearts.

Our bedroom door creaks around dawn, as Rui creeps home after a night spent carousing with his brother . . . Rui slipping into bed to hold me, oblivious to the fact that I'm rigid with disapproval. For, while he's been acting the Lisbon playboy, I've been sitting on the sofa all evening, making small talk with his mother.

And, the worst memory of all, Rui escorting me on a tour of his favourite haunts. An evening of shuffling, obsequious head waiters and club managers. A night of sultry Lisbon ladies, who peck my cheeks with cool indifference and teach me how much calculated insult there can be in a kiss. While a Rui I hardly recognize introduces them all as ex-girlfriends, ex-lovers, ex-mistresses.

I remember the tension which filled that night. How, as we moved from place to place, we seemed to walk in on the tail end of something. Or as we were about to leave, something seemed to be about to happen. And there was a constant flurry around me – as if the 'something' should be kept from me at all costs.

It was years before I learned that Annabella was also out on the town that night. I'd been told she was in Brussels visiting friends but she had shadowed us for most of the time – either appearing at a nightclub just ahead of us or swanning in with her retinue as we were leaving.

How many times had they sidled past each other, husband and wife, as I struggled to make conversation with Rui's party crowd? How many times had their eyes met as they shared this deliciously bad joke – while I tried to cope with the insincere flattery, the noise, the language and the sheer foreignness of it all?

So many images . . . and Rui a stranger in every one. Standing back to watch as I thrashed around, almost as if he enjoyed my discomfort. I should have read the warning he was sending out – that when the going got rough, I would always be left to fend for myself. But it had come too late, for I was already hooked on the stylishness, the easy sophistication, the smart talk, the glamour and the leisurely decadence of it all. All the things that Rui had symbolized for me on that summer holiday were here, wrapped up in his Lisbon life. And I wanted more of it.

It was, for me, the adult version of dressing up and being

someone else. This was my chance to be another kind of woman, moving in exotic circles with the smart set – the realization of all my girlish fantasies and a game I was sure I would soon learn to play. It took me a long time to discover that it wasn't a game for Rui. He really was all the things a person had to be to survive in this society – and none of them were very commendable.

Rui's 'friends' thrived on gossip and intrigue, scandal, thinly-veiled deceit and frequently flaunted infidelities. And, to be fair to him, he never claimed to be any different from the rest. But I really thought he had turned over a new leaf. And anyway, surely living in London we would be safe from the worst elements of his old life? Which is where I made my mistake. Because he hadn't . . . and we weren't.

Now I know he was a ladies' man in the real sense of the word. Charming and witty, extravagant and devil-may-care, it was a seductive combination which made him the stuff of lovers. The perfect man with whom to have an outrageous, whirlwind affair. And I suppose I had more fun with him than I've known with any other man.

But when the going got tough, when life went wrong and other qualities were needed – like resilience, patience, under-standing, sympathy or even just the odd flash of sheer practi-cality – then Rui wasn't the man for the job. And he most certainly was *not* the stuff that husbands are made of.

Since I'd suspected this from the first, I often wonder now why we bothered to get married at all. We'd been living together happily enough for three years by the time his di-vorce came through and, after all the paperwork and endless haggling, it had almost been an anti-climax when he sug-gested we should get married.

But the truth was that my so-called 'sophistication' was a paper thin layer. Underneath it, I was still a girl who needed the respectability of a wedding ring. I wouldn't admit that, though, so instead, I told myself that I had accepted his proposal because it was a compliment – that it was flattering to have him still love me this much after three years.

Rui, however, was just going through the motions – making vows which, although they weren't exactly sacrosanct for me, actually meant less than nothing to him. Married or not, his level of commitment would always remain the same. Married or not, he would still screw around and simply move on, when the mood took him.

Holiday lovers to respectably married couple. Love triumphing over all the odds. (By this time, even my folks had warmed to my man.) Really, that should have been the end of the story and, I suppose, for a while, it was. The next few years slipped by, much as they do in any marriage, and I'd have to say that we seemed to be as content as most couples around us since, in our own selfish and self-indulgent way, we were both getting what we thought we wanted out of a relationship.

Rui was becoming more and more successful, both professionally and financially, while I'd started up my own business, a publishing consultancy, and my career was forging ahead, too. By now, we'd moved from our first home purchase – a modest little London flat – into a spacious house, the sports car stood in the drive and our weekends were taken up with stylish invitations and smart friends. Yet almost without my noticing it, a spark had gone out of my life and although I sensed what it was that had died, for a long time I wouldn't admit it, even to myself.

Oh, once in a while, I would think back with longing to those early days. Sundays spent curled up in bed, feeding each other toast and marmalade; nights when we used to seek each other out, even in sleep, to kiss and touch and make love. Mornings on the Underground, arms protectively around each other as we fended off the rush hour crowds. Hours spent walking to no particular place, talking of nothing very much but just content to be together. We'd been so close then – almost inside each other's skins. And I was sad that this closeness had gone.

But then I would remind myself that there was more to a relationship than *romance* and I would catalogue our achievements. In spite of the odds, we were married. And *happy*, I would keep reminding myself. Happy because of the things we had in common – our love of the good life, our hot pursuit of fun, our ability to party endlessly, our similar clever, if cruel, wit. And surely now we were a stylish couple, envied by many of our friends. We had money in the bank, holidays abroad and the freedom to do whatever we fancied, whenever we felt like it. And, even more important than the things we both wanted, were the things we agreed we *didn't* want, at any price. Like responsibility, in any shape or form. Or – God forbid – children.

For of all the things I dreaded, being a mother was what I still dreaded most. All those tears and tantrums, all those nappies and that mindless conversation with toddlers. The dreadful business of mother and baby groups and over-dinner talk of what little Johnny said or did or sicked up today. Not to mention the dramatic cut in income, the solitude of my days . . . and my inability to keep pace with Rui.

I mean, whoever heard of a man-about-town fixing baby feeds? Whoever heard of a playboy pushing a pram? Whoever heard of Peter Pan becoming a dad? No, Rui was living life in the fast lane; he wouldn't slow down for a baby *or* its mother. And I was damned if I was going to be left behind.

You're right. We were a selfish pair who more than deserved each other. But back in my twenty-ninth year, I was still trying to congratulate myself on my shrewd choice of a mate and refusing to acknowledge just how superficial our relationship was becoming.

By now, of course, the twenty-year-old who had dragged her old battered blue trunk out of King's Cross station was outwardly no longer visible. Now I dressed stylishly, expensively – parting with vast sums of money for the privilege of having French and Italian designer labels tucked into my dresses, the insteps of my shoes, even my knickers.

Rui had taught me how to treat head waiters (disdainfully); figures of authority (disparagingly); business associates (deprecatingly); other women and all social acquaintances (distantly). Thanks to him, I could find my way around a menu in French, Portuguese or Italian and I no longer glazed over with panic when presented with a wine list.

I'd learned the art of tipping, the correct way to pour champagne, swallow oysters and cook crabs. I read the *Guardian* on weekdays and waded through the *Sunday Times* and the

Observer on Sundays, all the better to indulge in sophisticated smalltalk. I'd even been talked into bridge lessons, all the better to partner Rui at his boring bloody bridge parties.

No longer was I thrown into a flat spin when he brought home business contacts, sundry relatives and foreign friends unexpectedly, for the guest room was always ready and waiting. I had a constant supply of ice in the fridge, booze in the cupboard and enough food to feed an army. In other words, I was pretty much the ideal wife for Rui's London life; but it was in Lisbon that I excelled myself as the perfect mate. Simply because I'd become almost as Portuguese in my outlook as Rui himself.

As time had passed, I had grown very fond of Rui's family but, if I was comfortable with them, I was distinctly ill at ease with the social whirl which had once fascinated me.

Little by little, I *had* learned to play their nasty little games; now I too was mistress of the cold kiss, delivering bitchy little remarks just as devastatingly in English or Portuguese. But we hadn't after all managed to escape the Lisbon malady, for Rui had long ago given up any pretence at being faithful to me; and I added to the deception by pretending he wasn't having affairs.

Really, I'd become more Portuguese than he could have hoped for. I'd joined the ranks of bored, bitchy women who condoned unfaithful husbands – even socialized with their mistresses – because anything else was looked upon as uncool, unsophisticated behaviour. I'd long ago realized that the pretty 'cousins' Rui introduced me to at parties and night-clubs were, in fact, no relation to him at all. The word was a euphemism for 'mistresses' and these were women he flirted with openly, knowing I valued my hard-won sophistication too much to ever make a vulgar fuss. Gone were the days of setting fire to the competition. Now, I smiled and pretended not to see.

Part of me even understood his outrageous behaviour. After all, he'd come from a society where, for generations, any wealthy successful self-respecting husband kept a mistress. While a wife – happy enough with her husband's name, his children, his money and prestige – was quite glad to have some other woman take over the often tedious task of bed-room duty.

If he'd been faithful to me during our first years together in London, that was only because he'd lacked the money, the time and the opportunity to screw around. Not because he'd lacked the inclination. In other words, Rui was reverting to type and, short of leaving him, there wasn't a single bloody thing I could do about it.

Hardly surprising, then, that Lisbon life no longer held any attraction for me. Instead, Rui's frequent business trips to Portugal were mostly made without me and his long list of conquests was steadily being added to. Not only over there but on the home front, too. For Lisbon life had finally infiltrated London and El Vino's was a continuing source of nubile young things.

And yet, you know, even then I loved him. Oh, maybe not as fiercely and foolishly as in the early days . . . but there were moments when we really seemed to be happy. Moments when I convinced myself he loved me as much as he could love anyone. And at times like these, I really thought we might pull through.

Mornings when we'd be driving home after a party, the roof pulled back on our red sports car as we flew up Park Lane with Dire Straits blaring out of the stereo to add to the dawn chorus, as London's birds woke up. Then Rui would slam through the gears, laughing as the car practically took wing, and I would laugh, too, as his hand slid across my thigh and into my crotch, promising all kinds of shenanigans before we finally got to sleep.

Evenings when I'd collect him at one of his usual haunts, walking coolly into the bar to find him standing with nothing more suspicious than a group of his drinking cronies and not a single pretty girl in sight. His smile would say he was genuinely pleased to see me, as he slipped his arm around my waist to draw me possessively into the crowd.

Sunday afternoons when he would lie along the sofa in his tatty old dressing gown – his hair standing on end, the beard showing blue against his sallow, unshaven skin. Rui with a hangover – not a pretty sight. Yet still that boyish grin and

31

those mischievous eyes would have me tousling his head as I walked past or running him a life-saving bath. For at these moments, he was the old Rui. My Rui. The man I would do anything for. And I couldn't imagine being happy anywhere different with anyone else.

But then there were the times when he would fly off on yet another of his 'business trips' and, even as I pressed his shirts and packed his case, I would know that the only business on his mind was another woman. Or the times when he would make love to me without any desire to get really 'close' to the person I was – without even the slightest pretence at caring or tenderness.

These were the times when I knew what it was to be sad and empty and afraid. That's when I discovered that a bed – especially a shared one – can be the loneliest place in the world. After years of striving, I had all the things the child in me had thought I needed to make me happy but somewhere along the line, I had made a terrible mistake.

Too late, I tried to put it right. Went to work on the house and called in an army of builders, plumbers and electricians who began to pull it apart, while I made over the garden, stripped years of varnish from the doors, painted and papered and lavished lots of attention on this shell I wanted to turn into a home.

I had some sad little idea that all we needed to bring us together again was a more stable, orderly, *ordinary* life. Maybe if we saw less of other people and spent more time with each other. . . .

Cosy domesticity was what I had in mind, I guess. Just the two of us watching TV, cooking supper, entertaining a few close friends. I wanted that more and more and I hoped that he might want it too. But my change of heart came about far too late. Because the man who had happily shopped and cooked with me once, the one who'd cuddled me in the launderette and told me funny stories in the middle of the night . . . well, that man had left home a long time ago and the drinking, womanizing, Lisbon version was now permanently in residence.

Home for Rui was now just a place to rest up when he

32

wasn't having a good time outside. And I was just someone who made sure he hit the streets well fed and neatly turned out, each day.

All his other requirements were being met elsewhere; while what *I* needed, I couldn't quite define just then. But the truth is, I was getting older and I was looking for some peace and order in my life – some point to it all. And the more confused and insecure I felt, the more I wanted a husband I could rely on; a man I could trust and confide in.

After nearly thirty years of being fiercely proud of the way I could take care of myself, I was getting weary of the battle and I wanted someone to hold my hand. Someone who would sustain me emotionally, even if I continued to financially support myself. It was crazy of me to think I could ever cast my husband in that role, but the more Rui refused to take responsibility for me, the more I tried to foist it on him. And it was around this time that a whole chain of weird events occurred, which gave me the perfect excuse to lean on him for all I was worth.

First I got hepatitis. Or, rather, Rui infected me with the virus which he contracted. Any faint hope that he might have nursed me through it the way I'd so recently nursed him were dashed when – just as soon as I was no longer contagious – he packed me off to Lisbon to recuperate. Which meant he'd failed Test Number One.

Test Number Two presented itself shortly after my return from his parents' house since, while languishing in Lisbon, I'd somehow managed to pick up typhoid fever. Then followed a nightmarish period of confinement in a top security hospital in north London. One long month of isolation, during which Rui made it plain that he hated visiting hospitals by simply not showing up, more often than not.

Still, any doubts that I'd had about how depressed my absence had made him were dispelled when I was finally released from that particular hellhole. One glance at our bank statement was enough to reassure me that my husband had been nursing real sorrow, which he'd tried manfully to drown . . . spending more than one thousand pounds in bars, clubs and restaurants around town, while I'd been incarcerated, the poor soul. Touching, don't you think?

Then there was the hole. Without going into too much detail (most of which you'd have trouble believing anyway) can I say that I ended upside down in it and suspended by one ankle? Since it was a February night and I was naked at the time (no, really – don't ask), and since the only person who could rescue me was Rui and he was watching *The Big Match* on telly (England v. Portugal, with no score and extra time) you can understand why, by the time he missed me, found me and eventually saved me, my left leg was all but destroyed and I was in shock and suffering from severe exposure.

The morning after I was taken into hospital, he was off on another 'business trip'. So excited by this unexpected chance of freedom that he quite forgot to visit my sick-bed to say goodbye. It was left to friends to trundle me out of hospital, arrange a rota for feeding me and keeping me company, while I perfected ways of getting into and out of bed, the loo, the bath, with this plaster-of-Paris limb.

Two weeks later, Rui arrived home to find me and my cast (ankle to ass) propped up on the sofa, a sight which so aroused him, he promptly jumped on me and screwed me with gusto. A horribly mechanical effort which afforded me much more pain than pleasure and reminded me yet again that there really was no end to the bugger's selfishness.

It had been the latest in a long line of tests and he'd failed me miserably. That's what I was thinking a couple of weeks later, as I lay along the back seat of a black cab on my way to work. Rui couldn't provide transportation since his car, a long, low sports job – while it might be perfect for ferrying secretaries, make-up salesgirls, trainee hairdressers and any other of the women he swanned around town with – wasn't really designed for a wife with a crook leg.

It was while I was lurching from taxi to office one day that I met Peter. Well, I stepped on his foot, actually, while I was trying to manoeuvre my plaster-of-Paris up and over the snowy kerb. And, standing there, apologizing to his all-but-

34

broken toes, I never dreamed that this man would one day become so important in my life.

Peter became a real mate as winter turned into spring and I shed my cast to discover that my leg hadn't healed properly. A locked knee-cap and a bad limp meant a summer of daily therapy and a lot of pain and frustration. A problem Rui either couldn't or wouldn't deal with, so chose instead to ignore.

Peter didn't. Every single lunchtime, he collected me from my office and walked me around sunny, bustling streets – forcing me to exercise a leg about which I had become extremely self-conscious and embarrassed. And on the days when it all got too much for me and I whined self-pityingly, Peter did me the great favour of giving me a verbal boot up the backside.

Peter didn't mind that I sometimes worried and showed my fear. He wasn't disappointed when I panicked and he didn't get impatient when I was reduced to hopeless tears. Peter didn't even mind that I was relying on him more and more. In fact, Peter liked it. And, almost without realizing it, I was getting to like Peter.

Things might have carried on like this forever, with me living with one man and depending on another, and I might never have faced the truth about my marriage and my husband. If it hadn't been for the baby. . . .

Chapter Three

How do you wind up twelve years of marriage?

I'd never had much interest in biology, and at school, I'd doodled my way through lessons about what frogs did when they got together. Still, I *had* been fascinated to learn that conception didn't take place during intercourse and that hopeful little eggs might have to wait for a couple of days before they got acquainted with a wriggling spermatozoa. For a long time afterwards, I'd watched women posting letters, peeling potatoes or queuing for buses, wondering which of them was actually getting pregnant while I looked on. I know *I* got pregnant on my thirty-first birthday – during lunch, to be precise – just as I was polishing off an avocado stuffed with crab.

I was celebrating without Rui, who'd flown off to Portugal again, having already attended to my coming birthday needs. But I'd been unimpressed by the gifts, since the half-hearted, early-morning screw and the dismal brown leather shoulder bag (definitely chosen by his secretary) were both lacking in originality and presentation.

All that morning, I'd been feeling weird, somehow uncoordinated and strangely detached from my surroundings, as I slumped in the front seat of my girlfriend's car, gazing dully out at the passing countryside. Lesley was taking me to one of her favourite restaurants for a birthday lunch and it was while we were eating at the lovely old inn that I began to feel really odd. As I mindlessly fed my face, I grew aware of Lesley studying me and my neglected Bloody Mary appraisingly.

'God, now I've seen everything!' she remarked when I

passed up the wine. 'You – on the wagon? If I didn't know better, I'd say you were preggers!'

In the instant she said it, I knew she'd hit the nail on the head. And, although it would be a couple of weeks before I would know for certain, the strange behaviour of my body left me in no doubt that I'd signed on at the baby factory – and the thought terrified me.

For the next few days I moped about the house, trying to come to terms with impending motherhood, but, no matter how I looked at it, it wasn't an attractive prospect. I knew that kids could be a challenge to even the most stable, loving relationship. So what might they do to an already strained and uneasy one like ours?

Was I ready to stay at home and busy myself with babies? The answer was a resounding 'no', the prospect frightening me as much at thirty-one as it ever had at sixteen. I realized the only way I could ever attempt motherhood was if the man I was living with was desperate for fatherhood and I was desperate to make him happy.

Such a man *might* have talked me into it, if he had enough patience for both of us. If I trusted him completely and knew he could be relied upon when the going got tough.

But *Rui* . . . well, he just wasn't that man. Something he left me in no doubt about when I broached the subject over dinner, the evening he flew back home.

Almost as if he'd expected this to happen sooner or later and had long ago decided how he would handle it, Rui summed up *his* feelings in an instant. He was thirty-five; he had nothing to prove (his exact words) since he already had a son. He wasn't wild at the prospect of having more kids, but he realized I was at that age when lots of women feel broody. So if I *was* pregnant and I wanted to have it, then he would do his duty by both of us.

These last words chilled me, since El Vino's was crammed with friends of his who 'did their duty' by their wives, women who raised the kids – and knew better than to raise objections – when their menfolk came and went as they pleased. Women whose husbands were completely out of control.

Well, *my* husband was already on a pretty loose rein; I was only just managing to keep him in line. And as I considered what he'd just said, I realized that having a baby would mean I would lose my grip on our relationship completely. So . . .

'Rui – how would you feel about it if I had an abortion? That's if I *am* pregnant, of course – and I'm sure it's a false alarm,' I lied through my teeth.

'Well, that's your decision, pretty girl,' he replied, pouring himself more wine. 'I've told you how *I* feel about it so, if you don't want the baby, getting rid of it would be the sensible thing.'

There it was – the death sentence. And so easy, so easy to pronounce.

'You know, there is absolutely nothing wrong with this baby – it appears to be perfectly healthy.' The doctor gazed dispassionately down at me as I lay on her table, the sheet of hygienic paper crinkling under my backside, my legs hiked up above me in the cold stirrups.

'How old are you?'

'Thirty-one,' I replied, surprised by how quiet and serious my voice was.

'Well, in that case, it's the healthiest baby *you're* ever likely to have. Are you quite certain you want to go on with this termination?'

'Quite certain,' I answered in the strongest voice I could muster. Reminding myself how difficult it had been to get this far – how many doctors had refused to help. For Rui and I were apparently the stuff of happy families – married, moneyed, mature and halfway intelligent. Perfect parents, our GP had concluded – together with members of the Harley Street mob and various family planning clinics who had washed their hands of me.

Our insistence that neither of us wanted the baby had fallen on deaf ears – until recently, when my illogical anger and severe depression began to be apparent to all. I felt betrayed by my body, which was happily storing water, swelling and expanding – turning its nose up at food it used to love and throwing up morning, noon and night. And my emotional instability was growing at the same fantastic rate as this tiny threat inside me.

They would make me wait until I was into my ninth week before they would operate. Nine weeks, during which the clinic hoped I might change my mind; that I might somehow grow protective and tender towards this handful of pink flesh which was growing inside my womb.

Was such a change of heart possible for a woman like me? I honestly don't know to this day. Perhaps if I'd given myself even a moment to think about the baby's existence in a softer light, that might have opened the door to a whole flood of warmer, gentler – altogether more natural feelings.

But I had divorced my mind from my body, hardened my heart against this child, and I got up from the examination table that morning, determined to deny its existence as much as I was able. From that moment on, there was no hope for my baby. And not much hope for me.

From the street it looked just like any other expensive private house, set discreetly back behind a high wall and shaded by tall trees, but it was the sort of expensive private clinic which dealt with expensive people's ailments.

'Terminations', as the staff preferred to call them, were carried out at the rear of the house in what appeared to be a pre-fabricated annexe. I arrived at nine on the dot on the appointed day – outwardly calm and in control, but scared witless inside.

Rui had picked up on how afraid I was and, unable as usual to deal with problems – especially the ones which had me spinning out – he was quiet and distant as we drove through the morning rush hour.

By the time we'd parked the car and shuffled into the reception room, I thought I might faint with nerves and he was like a cat on hot bricks – especially since he was the only man in the room.

I could tell by just a glance that the women were all 'terminations'; the same wide-eyed fear and weary determination was written on every face. Rui's startled gaze took in the bowed heads and, when he glanced at me, his eyes were almost pleading. 'You know I hate hospitals – ' he faltered, desperate to leave.

'So – what's keeping you?' I asked coldly. 'Unless you were thinking of having the abortion *for* me?' Which was all the excuse he needed to turn and run – dodging the last arrival, as he dived through the swing doors.

Mary was her name. Thirty-two, Irish, with six kids and a drunken, out-of-work husband. Mary, who was taking her doctor's sensible advice about the wisdom of avoiding a seventh pregnancy – but who couldn't quite believe that, in the next hour or so, she was going to lose her child.

Poor Mary was even more distraught than I was – and even more alone, since she hadn't dared tell her husband that she was pregnant. So we sat together in the brown leather chairs – me with everything to offer a child *except* love and Mary with nothing to offer *but* that – unlikely partners in crime.

She chattered on nervously and I let her talk as, one by one, the other women disappeared into another room to undress, don gowns, have blood pressure and weight checked . . . and settle their bills, I was soon to discover. For even in expensive establishments such as this one, they like to see the colour of your money before they clinch the deal. And as Mary went in before me, I was left alone in the dim room to ponder my fate – little realizing that it was about to make yet another interesting loop.

My turn. And sitting in a white cotton gown and coarse blue bathrobe, my business suit folded neatly at my side, I answered lots of questions while a lanky nurse fitted a white plastic bracelet to my wrist. I could see it bore my surname and a lot of reference numbers, written in bright blue felt-tipped pen.

It was when they suddenly asked for money – all two hundred and fifty pounds of it – that I realized with a shock that I'd left home without any cash or even my cheque book. I had no credit cards with me – no identification of any kind – since it just hadn't occurred to me they would ask for the money up front. Surely my husband could settle the bill when he came to collect me? But although the facts were put to me very diplomatically, the bottom line was simple enough. No money – no abortion.

Dazed, I climbed back into my clothes, knowing I had to

get the money somehow, if they would just hang on for a while. Laughable, really, that I was afraid they would start without me – like a curtain going up on the first act, while I was still buying my ticket. But that wasn't so far from the truth. They had to get through nine terminations before lunch and it was already ten o'clock. If I wasn't there when my turn came, that would be just too bad.

Rui was out of the office when I tried to call him, back in the reception room. I was half-tempted to ring Peter, knowing I could rely on him to lay hands on some money and get it over to me. But it wasn't fair to involve him in this. Not when my bloody husband should have stayed near the phone – today of all days.

Five minutes later, I was on the other side of the high wall and making for the High Street, too distressed and panicked even to cry and without any clear notion of what I was doing. The welcome sight of my banking sign above one building brought a ray of hope and, swanning into the bank, I asked to see the manager, who listened sympathetically as I explained how I'd left home without any money or identification, only to find the most *darling* old rocking chair in a nearby antique shop. The sort of thing I'd been looking for for ages.

Would it be asking too much . . . could he call my bank manager in Fleet Street and arrange for some cash to be made available on the spot? And I smiled winsomely across the expanse of leather-topped desk, as the accommodating gent called his opposite number and then passed the receiver to me for the voice test.

'Well, what kind of mischief are you up to *this* time?' my long-suffering bank manager's voice came down the line and I went into my act for the second time.

Moments later, I had two hundred and fifty quid tucked into my bag, as the manager escorted me to the front entrance. It was only when I glanced down to return his firm handshake that I saw my plastic hospital bracelet shining blindly up at me – at *us*; my name and all the other details screaming out in their bright blue ink.

I think I deserved a medal for not passing out with sheer

embarrassment at that moment. As it was, I knew my face was scarlet as I said goodbye. Probably the clinic was a local landmark and distraught women wandering around with tell-tale bracelets on their wrists were an everyday occurrence. God, it was humiliating. But then I remembered what I had to endure next and suddenly, the manager's good opinion of me began to matter less.

Clothes off, gown on – blood pressure by now soaring through the roof – I sat quietly while the money was carefully counted and a receipt came sliding across the desk at me. The transaction completed, I stood up wearily, looking faintly ridiculous, I'm sure, in my black leather high heels. Hadn't I brought any slippers, the rosy-cheeked woman behind the desk enquired solicitously and I would have been touched by her concern, had she not been more than ready to send both my lump and me packing, less than an hour before.

It was with something akin to joy that I found I was sharing a room with Mary and, once we'd been visited by the anaes-thetist, we tried to relax in our narrow beds and take each other's minds off what was about to happen. How much was it likely to hurt, we both couldn't help wondering, as our eyes strayed up to the ceiling. (Mary had worked out that the operations took place on the floor above.) We could hear some evil sounding machinery which kept starting and stopping, then whirring into life again with a sickening screech. It sounded for all the world like a drill and I shuddered to think how exactly they might be employing it. But then, I happened to glance out of the window just above my head and there he was – a carpenter working away happily with his Black and Decker, quite unaware that he'd been elevated to the status of surgeon in our lurid imaginations.

Mary had grown silent – became quite still and almost drowsy. By the time two nurses came to collect her, she was barely able to walk and, shoring her limp form up between them, they spoke to her as you would to a sleepy five-year-old. Left alone in the room, I dwelt morbidly on what lay ahead and, if I'd thought the previous nine weeks had been the longest of my life, they were as nothing compared to the next fifteen minutes or so. Then the nurses were breezing through the door again – talking to me as if I too was recovering from a frontal lobotomy and slightly disconcerted to find I could step into my high heels and navigate the narrow flight of stairs outside my room unaided. At the top of which I walked into a room – and into a scene I don't think I'll ever be able to forget.

Everything was white, the walls, the floor – giving an impression of light and space – while sunshine bounced off the metallic chrome of tables, medicine cabinets, machinery and row upon row of surgical instruments. One or two nurses busied themselves about the place while the anaesthetist advanced on me with a troubled expression. But it was the sight on the far side of the room which caught my attention.

There was a long, low metal table, hung about with shining metal and leather stirrups. At the foot of this table, sitting on a small stool with his knees almost touching his chin and his arms stretched out before him – elbows bent and palms turned inwards – was the man.

He was wearing green overalls, a gauze face mask and a white skull cap on his head, while his arms were encased from fingertips to elbows in long, rubber gloves. He looked for all the world like a catcher, just waiting to intercept a throw at an American baseball game. But he was waiting for me and the sight was very frightening indeed.

The anaesthetist and I realized in the same moment what had gone wrong – I hadn't been given a pre-med. While I'd been out raising money, everyone else had been given a dartful of whoopee-juice; no wonder Mary was so dopey. By the time she'd reached this room, the lucky bitch hadn't known whether she was on her ass or her elbow. But here I was – stone cold sober, as it were – witnessing something I really would rather have been spared.

The catcher miraculously disappeared from sight while I stepped out of my shoes and climbed on to the bed. The last thing I remember was the anaesthetist's anxious face, hovering above my own, his kind voice counting backwards with me, while the sunlight glinted on the stirrups above me. And then I closed my eyes.

Coming to, I sat up suddenly to find that I was lying under

43

a blue sheet on a metal trolley, surrounded by other still forms and a nurse, who had been patiently waiting in a corner for this morgue to come to life, helped me back to my room.

Once in bed, I burrowed down beneath the bedclothes and realized that I'd been strapped into a sanitary towel. Well, I was bleeding but not too much and I had cramps but they weren't too bad and I was just thanking my lucky stars that it was all over, when a nurse came by and offered me the use of a portable telephone. Almost before I realized what I was doing, I'd dialled the number of the person I most wanted to talk to – the one who was uppermost in my mind. Peter's voice came on the line immediately. Gentle and sympathetic and soothing, all at the same time. And it was only after I had spoken to him that I thought of ringing Rui at all. I have to admit, *his* voice was nice too, but a little awkward and embarrassed and it hinted at none of the real concern or closeness I'd heard in Peter's voice. And if I sensed the distance between us on the phone, it was even more apparent when Rui visited me that evening.

He sat gingerly on the edge of my bed and I remember we laughed a lot. Too much. I recounted the drama about the money, reducing the whole awful experience to the level of black comedy, the better to be able to deal with it, I suppose. But underneath all the joking, I was angry with Rui. Angry and incredibly bitter, yet too weary to begin to work out why.

After all, I had wanted this abortion. I'd engineered it and fought tooth and nail for it and I couldn't, in all honesty, say that I was sad about losing the baby. So why did I dislike my husband so, as we sat there, laughing together?

Now I think I was angry with him because, deep down, I sensed that if he'd really loved me and cared for me at all, he would have realized it was high time I got to grips with my problem. Even as I'd always insisted I didn't want children, I think I'd hoped he might manage to change my mind – persuade me that it wouldn't ruin my life.

I guess I'd wanted – needed – him to override my decision. Because, on the subject of motherhood, I really didn't know what was best for me and it would have been a relief to have been told what to do. The way a child, overtired and fractious, might insist on staying up late – but easily falls asleep when her no-nonsense mother packs her off to bed.

If only Rui had been a more caring, more sensitive kind of man. If only I'd been a less inadequate woman. If only. . . .

Poor Mary couldn't afford the luxury of an overnight stay, knowing that already her unsuspecting husband would be wondering where the hell she'd got to. We said our goodbyes – difficult when two strangers have been through so much together in just a few hours. Then she turned back to me as she walked to the door and said: 'He's so handsome, that man of yours. Lovely eyes he has – and him so funny. My, you *are* a lucky girl.'

I just smiled and said nothing. For wasn't that what I'd been telling myself for years now? Didn't I know better than anyone that it just wasn't true any more?

A couple of weeks later, my waistline and my life had returned to normal. I'd swapped my useless diaphragm for the IUD, thrown out all the clothes I'd been forced to wear during my weight gaining days and gone back to work as if nothing had happened. In fact, everything was just as it had been before I got pregnant. Except between Peter and me. And it was almost a relief to stop the self-delusion – that he was just a man I knew – and start the affair.

Oh, we led up to it very slowly. Carefully. Almost regretfully. Because in gaining a short-term lover, there was always the risk that we would lose a long-term friend. And I needed Peter's friendship more than ever.

So, although the looks, the smiles, the glances which had earlier passed between us had long been provocative on my part and full of meaning on his; although our conversation had slipped from being mildly flirtatious to just plain steamy on occasions . . . always our lunches and after-office drinks had ended in chaste hugs and kisses and vague promises to meet again soon.

But now, we were meeting every day and when I was finally persuaded to go round to Peter's company flat, where we shared a bottle of wine before strolling into the bedroom and slipping into the bed, it seemed to both of us that the

45

visit was long overdue. One more neglected husband and one more resentful wife drifted into an affair.

If they are honest, most women will admit they would rather put up with a difficult marriage, than have no marriage at all. For there's something very comforting about having a man around the house. A husband is someone who can answer the door to late-night callers, make the car start on cold mornings and keep the bed warm on even colder nights. He can perform brilliant feats of engineering with bits of twisted coathanger, bent hairgrips and elastic bands and he can even be persuaded to nip out and buy a box of Tampax when disaster strikes.

A husband can row with you when the telly's boring, zip you into your dresses, escort you to the firm's dance, pay the milkman if you happen to be in the bath. He provides you with an extra source of income and he always, always gives you something to moan to your girlfriends about.

Really, every home should have one, we tell ourselves on these occasions when being married starts to seem too much like hard work. Which is why, even when kids aren't around to complicate the issue, most women put up with their men and just *dream* about escaping from it all.

That's what I'd often done when things went wrong between Rui and me – dreamed of walking out if things got worse, all the time telling myself that they weren't really so bad. Our relationship was coughing and spluttering – it was really getting sick. Yet I refused to deal with the symptoms and pretended that our marriage was perfectly healthy, while the disease slowly spread.

Even after the abortion, I'd stayed with Rui, kidding myself it was the right thing to do; all the time meeting Peter and kidding myself that was okay, too. Talk about living dangerously! Yet for a while, I thrived on this double life and congratulated myself on being able to hold it all together. I didn't tell a soul what was going on, because the last thing I wanted was for Rui to find out.

Not that Peter had stolen me from my husband. Rather, Rui had practically given me away to someone who treated me as if I really mattered. A man who was very comfortable to be around, simply because he saw straight through me from the first.

The co-director of a large and thriving advertising agency, Peter was a big, bluff sort who carried his success and affluence lightly, because he knew they didn't mean much at the end of the day. He was a Lancashire lad through and through – a small town boy made good, who never forgot his origins and had no time for people like me, who put on airs and graces. So every time I tried, he smartly took me down a peg or two – which did me the world of good, since I was fast turning into the worst kind of snob.

Sixteen years older than me, he had already raised two kids – a son who was studying at university in the States and a daughter who still lived at home and was training to be a dancer. I'd seen his wife only once, from a distance – an attractive blonde in her early forties – and I'm sure he loved her a lot. So why did he run risks to be with me? I never thought to ask him at the time but I've often wondered since. I suppose he felt he was being taken for granted at home, in that big old rambling Kensington house. He'd been around for so long – the breadwinner, the rock, the calm, steadying influence on his household – that they'd begun to treat him like part of the furniture.

When he wasn't being ignored at home, he was being constantly pressured at work and undermined by a business partner who had long ago stopped taking the business seriously. So, what with one thing and another, big, blond, bluff, mustachioed Peter, of the lazy grey eyes and droll sense of humour, was beginning to feel put upon and quietly resentful, as he contemplated his fiftieth year. Which is when I happened along. Young, passably pretty, reasonably bright – and desperately looking for someone to lean on.

Amazing, now, to think that he filled up my life for the best part of the next two years and appalling to think I let it go on for so long. But Peter gave me all the things my husband couldn't and, between them, they made me whole. At the end of the day, though, he was another woman's husband and eventually he had to decide where his loyalties lay.

It was the burglaries which brought things to a head – three of them in as many weeks. Each time, we were broken into and vandalized so that, by the end of that dreadful month, my house was all but taken apart, with everything of any value either stolen or destroyed. And the experience had wrought its own destruction on me.

The first time I arrived home to the sickening sight of drawers upended, plates and glasses smashed and clothes strewn everywhere, I immediately rang round all Rui's favourite haunts until I found him. He was devastated by the news that his new stereo system had been half-inched but, although he promised to come home straight away, it was nearly two in the morning before he finally turned up. His excuse being, that since the damage was already done, there was no point in rushing home. The practical aspects of clearing up the mess had never occurred to him, any more than the possibility that I might be a bit unnerved, dealing with the police and sitting amidst this chaos, all by myself.

Two more burglaries later, my nerves were in shreds and I point-blank refused to step inside the front door at night, unless Rui either picked me up at work or arrived home ahead of me. Well, he played the good shepherd for a week or so, until the lure of El Vino's proved too great and I was told to 'get a hold of myself', as he resumed his evenings with the boys.

And that's how it came about that Peter began to bring me home each evening – opening the front door himself to check that the place was deserted. Once or twice, he even had a drink before he left and I stopped worrying that Rui might come home early and find us there. Because what he might say or do in such a situation really didn't matter to me any more.

It was on one of these evenings – when Peter was doing my husband's job and making sure that I was safe – that someone burgled *his* home and his wife was left to deal with it alone, since she couldn't contact her husband. I was sad when Peter rang to tell me about it next day, knowing it was my fault she couldn't reach her husband when she needed him.

Slowly I began to realize that, in trying to give me the

attention I craved, Peter had probably been neglecting his wife in all sorts of ways – that he'd slowly been turning into the sort of deceitful, unreliable husband that Rui had become. I was almost relieved when Peter went on to explain that he couldn't see me for a while, since he felt he ought to be at home with his wife.

Maybe, after all, it wasn't too late for Peter. At least he still had his priorities right. That's what I thought as I put down the phone, finally admitting to myself that I'd depended on another woman's husband for far too long. It was time to sort out my messy marriage and my hopeless husband. But where would I begin, I wondered.

Another week had passed. Seven long days of fretting and worrying, as most of me tried desperately to settle for what I had with Rui and some small, determined part of me insisted it was time to get out. And now there I was, curled up on the bed, watching the hands of the clock as they slid from one, to one-thirty, to two – prepared to stay awake all night, now that I knew what I had to do.

Angus gave a low growl and shifted on the bed, as he recognized the sound of Rui's car further up the hill. For an instant, the bedroom was bathed in light, as the car swung into the drive. Then Rui's footsteps crunched up the gravel path. By the time he'd managed to find his key and put it in the lock, I was opening the front door to my slightly inebriated mate. Carefully, purposefully, I wound my arms about his neck, while he cocked his head back at an angle and gazed down at me – his look wary, as he waited for a rebuke.

'Are you *very* pissed?' I asked him. 'Or do you feel up to a chat?'

'Nearly three o'clock in the morneeng and my wife wants to *chat*,' he laughed mirthlessly. Then: 'So – what do you want to chat *about*?' he asked, his voice guarded.

'US, Rui,' I replied, leading him slowly up the stairs to our bedroom. 'I really want to talk about us . . .'

In the end, it was Rui himself who broached the subject – almost as if he'd been waiting for ages to get it off his chest. Told me he knew he didn't make me happy any more and admitted he wasn't happy either. Finally levelling with me

49

about the kind of life he wanted for himself – and it bore no comparison to the life I wanted for both of us.

'All this domesticity – ' he began, shaking his head despairingly. 'I am not cut out for eet, I want to enjoy myself, play around – perhaps do more travelling, I want to suit myself for a change – spend my money how I like, without having to consider someone else all the time. I just can't do that and stay married. And you . . .'

'I want to settle down. I want you to grow up and you never will, will you? I'm sick of the parties and that awful crowd you mix with. I'm sick of never being able to rely on you. And I'm sick to death of looking the other way, while you screw around with everything in skirts!' I finished – uttering the words I thought I would die rather than admit, as my voice, and my cool, finally broke.

Which is when the row broke out and the house rang with claims and counter-claims, vicious insults and wild accusations. I got to hear about all the women I *didn't* know about, as well as the ones I did. And I hit back murderously with all kinds of slights – ranging from his lack of sexual prowess to his arrogance. That arrogance which had assumed I'd been faithful to him all this time. THAT stopped him in his tracks and sure as hell upped the ante. By which time the whole street was being treated to a screaming match about how I'd killed his baby and I'd retaliated that it probably wasn't even his . . . when we both stopped short. Shocked into silence by the dreadful thing we were doing to each other.

I was fighting to stem my tears and somehow get my emotions back under control, when Rui's expression changed and he slowly said, 'Do you remember, years ago, we made a promise? That when things went wrong between us, we would try not to hurt each other too much?'

So. He'd remembered . . .

I sat there, unable to utter a sound, while the tears slid down my cheeks and my eyes fastened on his troubled face. 'Well, pretty girl – I think it might be time to keep that promise . . .'

And then he smiled a little crookedly. 'But we have had some good times, haven't we? Don't worry, I'll move out tomorrow.' And then he walked through to the bathroom while, totally exhausted, I crawled sobbing into bed.

The next morning, subdued and withdrawn, Rui left for the office. I stayed home and spent the day laundering his shirts, his underwear, pressing his clothes and packing his cases. When I left the house late that same afternoon, they stood, bathed in sunlight, in the middle of the hallway. I don't remember much about where I went or what I did – wandered unseeing through department stores; ate somewhere. And when I staggered home around midnight, after having spent a long, lonely evening propped up at some strange bar, I opened the door to find the house deserted. The suitcases had gone. And so had my husband.

How *do* you wind up twelve long years of marriage?

Painfully . . . *that's* how.

Chapter Four

Who said there was life after divorce?

Of course, a woman doesn't stop being married the day she walks out on her husband or he walks out on her. Or when she slips her wedding ring off or even when she slips into another man's bed. A woman doesn't stop being married until she starts feeling whole again. Sometimes that takes years. Sometimes it never happens and women spend the rest of their lives nursing this strangely 'empty' area somewhere between their stomachs and their bowels – for it's a sensation which is almost physical. Losing John or Bill or Fred is 'like losing an arm or a leg', some women will go so far as to say, as they try to deal with the sudden disability. Amazed at how much they depended on this limb, even when it appeared to be pretty useless.

For some, it's easier to pretend the loss is temporary, the way I once did. Injecting the magic words 'my husband' into every conversation, I rescued my wedding ring from the bottom of a drawer and jammed it defiantly on my finger, although I hadn't thought to wear it in years. Referring to myself as 'Mrs', I signed everything from cheques to letters with that coveted title, though I'd always insisted on using my maiden name before. Oh, I'd been *so liberated*, when I was married! Maybe I didn't actually have a husband, but I was still married. In some ways, more married than I'd ever been before, now that I began to realize how much weight the title carried. Marriage gives us women much needed status. Being someone's wife, like being someone's mother, pinpoints our position in life – our place in the scheme of things. As long as I was Rui's wife, I knew who I was. So did everyone else, for that matter.

Talk to any wife about the prospect of being single again and she'll rabbit on for hours about how marvellous it would be. Imagine the luxury of being able to paint finger and toe nails, pluck eyebrows, slap on face packs, without being interrupted. Fancy being able to turn off the TV when the noise got too much and using all the bath water without so much as a by-your-leave or a thank you. Think about staying in bed all Sunday when it rains and cooking pasta every night of the week, if you felt like it.

And then there would be the men . . . you could change them as often as you changed your underwear. Each one would be different, exciting – a new challenge. A new sexual experience every time – instead of good old Harry, who thinks foreplay is something to do with football, likes the missionary position, since it means he can fall comfortably asleep afterwards (or even during) and only attempts it from behind or underneath when the barmaid down at the local strikes a match against his imagination. (Too much to hope that she could set it on fire.)

Oh yes, we married women tell a good story, weave a beautiful fantasy around living by ourselves, knowing we'll probably never have to cope with the harsh reality of the situation. But suddenly, that's what I was doing – and it was no joke.

I didn't like having to worry alone over unpaid bills or the dog running off, the Mormons who hung around my front door for hours, trying to convert me, or the damp patch which appeared on the bathroom ceiling.

I didn't like the way the next door neighbour called by 'to see how I was' whenever his wife went shopping, making me wilt under his beery breath and suggestive gaze. No, I didn't like that, any more than I liked the way 'friends' excluded me from their gatherings – some seeing me as single and a threat, while others just hated odd numbers. (And I didn't like being one of *those*, either.)

I didn't like lying alone in bed, trying to ignore the wind in the trees or the creaks and groans of an empty house.

Didn't like eating by myself or sleeping by myself – and certainly didn't like it when I started talking to myself, to break the endless silence.

And as for getting laid every night of the week, now that I had the opportunity, I'd lost the inclination. Which was maybe just as well, since I didn't know where to begin looking for all those different, exciting, challenging men the married me had dreamed about.

If *this* was what it meant to be single, I wanted no part of it, I decided. And although I pretended to be self-sufficient (unblocking the drains, zipping up my own dresses and taking myself off to the works dance) and went through the motions of starting over (opening a new bank account, buying a new bed, getting my hair cut), I knew I was just marking time.

I loved Rui – there was no doubt about it now – and I refused to believe he'd stopped loving me. Okay, so he was pissed off. His pride was hurt and it might take months for him to calm down and see reason. Well, I could wait as long as I had to – the break might even do us good. And I didn't even mind that he was living with another woman. After all, someone had to look after him, until he came back to me – and he would, sooner or later. We'd been through too much together. He was bound to me by twelve long years – that made him *my* man.

If I just lived quietly – going to work each day and coming straight home each evening – and if I was a good girl and behaved myself, surely he'd give us another chance? All I had to do was wait and be patient. I'd keep everything exactly as it was. Especially our home.

By now, the house had become for me a symbol of our marriage and the only thing which still held us together. As long as we had that, we still had a chance, I convinced myself, as weeks slid into months. So I went on mowing the lawns, stocking the cupboards with groceries – even redecorating our bedroom – in preparation for his return. All the time telling myself it was love that kept me hanging on to Rui, when really, it was the fear of being alone that stopped me from letting go.

So there I was, minus my husband and my lover, discovering the hard way that divorce is a lot like 'flu. It strikes everywhere and seems almost commonplace – until it hits you. And then you're painfully reminded of how miserable it can be and how much it bloody well hurts. My life was in a mess and I was getting by, one day at a time. But five hundred miles to the north, another member of the Culross family was coping with a major setback of his own. . . .

My little brother, Colin, now an eighteen-year-old, had just had his dreams of a naval career shattered and, laid low by this first ever real disappointment, he'd opted to spend the rest of his life locked up in his bedroom. I'd probably laid eyes on him no more than a dozen times since I'd left Scotland. Each time, he must have grown a bit taller and had a bit more to say for himself, I guess. But I can't honestly say that I'd been aware of his existence, as I'd made my yearly lightning visits home. And then, just as my world was tumbling about my ears, my mother rang to say that she was very worried about her son's state of mind and could he stay with me for a few days, while he sorted himself out?

Well, I tried to tell her it wasn't a good idea, since I was in no state to babysit a still-wet-behind-the-ears teenager. But my mother was nothing if not smart and she knew the best thing for me right then was to have someone other than myself to worry about and fret over. So she insisted and I was too weary to argue, figuring as I waited for this stranger's arrival that, if the worst came to the worst, we could always OD together.

He stood there uncomfortably in the doorway – a hulking great six foot two specimen who still had some growing to do – his hair chewed up like Rod Stewart's, his impossibly tight jeans stretched over impossibly long legs, his face an expression of misery masked with a scowl, which told me clearly that being here was definitely *not* his idea.

For the first couple of days, he simply locked himself away in one of my bedrooms – same death wish, different venue. I understood his feelings very well, locked up as I was in my own bedroom, most of the time, so I left him to get on with it. As you might expect, hunger forced him out on the third day and he staggered downstairs in search of the fridge which

I'd stocked up with the sort of food I'd guessed a boy might like – just in case he called off his fast unto death.

On the evening of the fourth day, I couldn't find Angus anywhere and, after searching the house from top to bottom, I sneaked into Colin's room to find them curled up together, fast asleep beneath the duvet. Well, any boy who liked dogs couldn't be all bad . . . I found myself warming to this truculent youngster and stood there watching him as he slept. Amazed that the tiny baby should have grown into such a massive man.

By the fifth day, Colin had begun to talk to me and I found to my delight that he had a wonderful sense of humour – witty and pithy and dourly Scots. And when he smiled, he had nice teeth, while his eyes, steely blue and deep-set, missed nothing. In fact by the sixth day, I'd decided he was quite companionable and lively – and even quite handsome, in a rough and ready kind of way. Now, if only he would do something about that awful hairstyle . . . and if I could persuade him to get out of these terrible 'small town' clothes. . . . And the dull, heavy fog which had numbed me for so long began to lift imperceptibly as I studied my new project.

At the end of that first week, I laid my cards on the table. Colin didn't know me very well – didn't know me at all, in fact. But my marriage was finishing and my life was likely to become pretty strange and unpredictable in the coming months. Did he know enough to understand I was referring to the possibility of whisky and men and wild, wild living? Probably. But, looking at me, he probably dismissed the idea as highly unlikely. I thought it was fairly far-fetched myself. But you never can tell.

So, he could stay with me if he wanted to – but not if the strait-laced Protestant in him was going to disapprove of everything I might say or do. We'd have our own rooms, live our own lives – do our own thing – and it might even turn out to be fun. But there was one other condition – Colin would have to get a job. There were to be no free-loaders on this trip.

I don't know how he viewed the idea of living with me, but the alternative was going back to that miserable town with its vast unemployment, where he'd hang around the street corners with his mates until, sooner or later, he got into some kind of trouble. We both knew this was his only chance.

Once he'd agreed the terms, we scanned the evening paper and wrote off for dozens of job vacancies – everything from bar work to part-time baseball training. At one point Colin admitted he thought he'd cut quite a dash in uniform, so we wrote off to the Army Information Office, the headquarters of the Metropolitan Police, the St John Ambulance – even the London Fire Brigade. Knowing it would take a couple of weeks for any replies to arrive, he returned to Scotland to say goodbye to family and friends – to wrap up his old life.

The house was horribly empty again once he'd gone and, automatically, I began tidying up – stripping the sheets from his bed and rinsing the stubble and dollops of shaving foam from the washbasin. Gratefully, I was slipping back into my old role – a provider of creature comforts – and it hardly mattered that I was doing it for another man. I was just thinking that life wasn't so bad – that at least, now, I had some company while I waited for my husband to make an appearance. Then Rui rang me at the office and shattered my illusions. The last thing he wanted to do was come home. He wanted to put our house up for sale.

A couple of mornings later, I was wakened by lots of banging and thumping outside and I watched from the bedroom window with a sinking heart, as a couple of lads anchored a big, ugly estate agent's board to the garden wall. Still, I took comfort from the fact that the house belonged to me, too, and I'd demanded a high price for it – knowing that the property market was depressed. With luck, we'd fail to find a buyer, before Rui had a change of heart.

Even so, I realized it wouldn't do any harm if I chatted to a solicitor – just to find out where I stood. And maybe I ought to look at some flats. Not that I would ever need one. . . .

The solicitor knew that time was money and he didn't bandy words. I was the deserted wife. He held up his hand as I began to say there had been faults on both sides, his smile brooking no argument. I was the poor, wronged woman, he insisted, putting careful emphasis on the words, and he was going to set himself up as my white knight. The question wasn't *if* Rui would suffer – it was for how long and how much. Should we go straight for the jugular or just hack away at him, little by little? Did I have a preference or would I be happy to leave the whole messy business in the capable hands of my white knight?

'Too bad there aren't any kids . . .' I could almost see him thinking, as he rested his chins on his dumpy little fingers. Come to that, I suppose it was a pity Rui hadn't been in the habit of beating me every Saturday night. Shame, really, that I wasn't blind or confined to a wheelchair. Paralysed mother of three deserted by callous Latin womanizer. Oh, we could have bled the bugger then!

'Ah well, never mind,' the solicitor quipped brightly as he ushered me out. 'We have ways of dealing with your husband, never fear. That's why we're here – to help damsels in distress. Er – talk to my secretary about a second appointment, will you – ?'

But this damsel didn't trouble to call again. Divorcing Rui was one thing. Destroying him, quite another. For the first time, I began to see how sordid the end of love was. Rui and I had made a promise not to hurt one another – it might not, after all, be easy to keep.

My first attempts at flat-hunting were just as disastrous. I rang the number which was painted in six-inch-high letters at the foot of my garden and spoke to a Mr Batt, who seemed even less enthusiastic than I was at the prospect of finding me a new home. Still, he called back, once he'd arranged three viewing appointments for the following morning – and I would have made it to every one, if it hadn't been for the fact that I took Angus for a quick rock around the block, before I locked him up for the day. Only to discover when we bounded back to my front door that I'd locked us both out.

No chance of climbing in windows or forcing doors – my thrice burgled house was now as impregnable as Fort Knox. 'So, I miss the appointments,' I thought, as I sat on the doorstep waiting for the locksmith. 'So what? I don't want to buy a bloody flat anyway . . .'

By then, I was operating out of a large bustling cooperative. Here hundreds of self-employed people just like me sat around in large, open-plan rooms, trying to make an honest buck. Privacy was impossible and everyone knew everyone else's business. But I welcomed the company, the laughter and the good-natured rivalry.

In this public setting, my impending divorce was just another open secret and, on the morning after I'd locked myself out, I was sitting at my desk suffering a lecture on what I was doing wrong, delivered by a divorcee who seemed to be doing all right.

'You'll get nowhere, staying home and moping every night,' she insisted. 'You've been out of circulation too long – now you've got to put yourself about a bit, have some fun for a change. Once you've met a few men . . .' On and on she droned and I listened, more out of politeness than any real interest. I'd seen that hard, defiant look in many a divorcee's eye and listened to lots of this brittle talk. She was telling me what a great time I could be having – but I sensed the words were more for her benefit than my own. If she said she was having fun often enough, maybe she would even begin to believe it herself.

On the other hand, she did have a point. I couldn't stay locked away at home for ever. I might not fancy her life much, but I wasn't too thrilled with my own. But surely there must be an alternative, I was thinking – almost relieved when the phone rang to interrupt my thoughts. I picked it up to find an irate Mr Batt on the other end of the line and, before I knew what was happening, I was getting a lecture in stereo.

Mr Batt was furious. I'd missed the appointments, hadn't called to cancel or apologize. And my excuse, delivered haltingly over the phone now, did nothing to improve his humour. In long-suffering tones, Mr Batt went on to say that he'd made the appointments all over again for the next morning and would I please have the goodness to turn up? There was an icy silence when I explained that I'd changed my mind and no further appointments were necessary.

Then: '. . . You do realize the time and trouble I have taken on your behalf?' came the weary voice down the line and again my apologies were ignored as he drawled on. 'Under the circumstances, I think the very least you could do – is to take me to dinner.'

'Take you to *dinner*, Mr Batt?' I almost shrieked, astounded by his nerve. 'Oh – but I *can't*. I couldn't possibly,' and then, laughably, 'I'm a married woman!' I spluttered. Even as I said it, I caught sight of the divorcee's long-suffering expression and I realized that maybe she was right. Maybe it *was* time for me to get back into circulation. And now was as good a time as any. So I added defiantly, 'Dinner's definitely out of the question, but I'd be happy to buy you a drink.'

'Yes, well, that would be a beginning – ' he said, quite unruffled. 'So, I'll pick you up this evening. Shall we say around eight?' and he hung up before I could change my mind. Like it or not, my first blind date ever was a matter of hours away.

Well, I was ribbed to death for the rest of that afternoon. Fancy agreeing to a date with a total stranger – a voice on the phone! the other girls shrieked. Some oily Jewish estate agent who'd turn out to be in his fifties, with a hair transplant, a Volvo, a wide striped suit and a hundredweight of gold jewellery draped about his dumpy body. Bound to be someone pretty ugly, they patiently pointed out when I baulked at this description. Why else would a man be at a loose end at four-thirty on a Friday afternoon? And they smiled at me – sympathetic yet enjoying my discomfort. They were bound to be right, of course. When it came to men, I was a raw recruit with a helluva lot to learn. Chastened, I went back to my desk, realizing with a chill that, while he might have sounded youngish – even nicish – Mr Batt was bound to be wimpish. And the evening ahead was guaranteed to be hellish.

By seven-thirty, I'd changed my clothes a dozen times in an effort to look married without looking matronly, attractive without being suggestive. I'd thought of pretending to be out – and switched off all the lights to complete the deception. Then switched them all on again as I realized that blind dates

– like dental appointments – were something you were obliged to keep. I'd poured myself a drink to steady my nerves, yet I'd been much too nervous to drink it and I was just about to rush upstairs to change yet again, when the doorbell rang – and it was only quarter to eight!

I rushed to the door and opened it to find a tall young man on the doorstep. My heart dropped as I realized it was probably one of Colin's new drinking friends from the pub around the corner. Talk about bloody awful timing.

'Look, I'm awfully sorry – but Colin's gone up to Scotland for a few days and I'm in the most awful rush. So if you could give him a ring, perhaps next week . . ?' and I smiled apologetically as I began to close the door. Then I stopped in my tracks as a deep, faintly amused, instantly recognizable voice said, 'I'm sorry – I hope I'm not too early?' and visions of paunches and loud striped suits faded, as probably the only nice estate agent in the world stepped across my threshold.

For Mr Batt – sorry, Simon – was easily six feet two, with eyes of proverbial blue and a smile to warm the heart of even the most iced-over divorcee.

I'm sure I gaped with shock as he strode past me and into the living room, taking the place in with a practised eye, while Angus tumbled around his ankles, delighted to have a man about the house again. I wasn't so sure. Then he rolled the dog over with the toe of his shoe, fondled his ears and made a friend for life and I noticed how his presence seemed to fill the room as he proceeded to make himself at home.

I couldn't take my eyes off him as he settled comfortably on the sofa, his long legs, sheathed in navy corduroy, stretched out in front of him. His white shirt was casually opened at the neck, the sleeves rolled up over strong forearms which casually draped themselves along the back of the seat. There wasn't a trace of gold in sight.

'God – to think I almost killed the lights and pretended to be out!' I thought, hardly able to believe my good luck – while Simon smiled as if he knew exactly what I was thinking.

He kept on smiling as I fumbled with our drinks, surreptitiously checking myself in the mirror over the drinks cupboard and cursing myself for having worn such a – such a *discouraging* outfit, I thought, amazed at my own reaction. But unfortunately, I'd more than achieved the effect I'd aimed for and, in my black dress with its long, tight sleeves and its discreet side-slit, I looked pretty daunting. And every sodding minute of thirty-three, dammit.

'Christ, how old's *he*?' I wondered as I put the drink in his hand, noticing the fresh young complexion, and the hair falling over eyes which were completely unlined. I decided not to think about how young he might be, as I perched self-consciously on a seat as far away from him as possible, wondering how to open the conversation. But I needn't have worried – Mr Batt had the whole thing under control.

Two hours later, he was still smiling and affable as, in a complete daze by now, I let him talk me into making us some supper. I was glad to have something to do, for the conversation between us had completely unnerved me. Unabashed, Simon had admitted that, while I'd been psyching myself up for our blind date, he had been acting on information received. Which, to put it bluntly, was: not bad-looking, thirtyish, she's getting divorced and she's got big tits.

Too late, I remembered the man who had called round from the same agency to value the house. Busily showing him around bathrooms and bedrooms and cupboard space, I hadn't realized he'd been looking me over as well. But the description he'd carried back to the office had been one that Simon had been more than willing to check out for himself.

Hoping that he wasn't disappointed – amused with myself for thinking he might be – I set about slicing tomatoes and opening tins of tuna, blushing like a schoolgirl as he leaned against the doorframe and watched me lazily – every so often stretching out to steal an olive or a sliver of tomato. 'Boy, does he ever have me at a disadvantage!' I thought, strangely excited by the idea that any man could have the edge on me.

After supper, I sat next to him on the sofa, as we polished off the best part of two bottles of wine. I began to relax as Simon told me lots of things about his family and his many girlfriends and himself, while I glossed over the last twelve years with Rui almost as if they'd been of no consequence, even though the opposite was the case.

So it was well after midnight when I suggested that perhaps it was time for him to leave. I think he would have gone too, because – quite apart from being handsome and amusing and incredibly sure of himself – Simon was also a real gentleman. But when I began to uncurl myself from the sofa he smiled, placed his empty wine glass on the coffee table and bent to kiss me very gently – something I'd been willing him to do nearly all evening – and my hands, unbidden, reached up around his neck and lost themselves in his hair. Lovely thick, dark hair, so much like Rui's. If I closed my eyes, I could almost pretend this stranger *was* Rui. . . .

Realizing how my mind was working, I was saddened by the self-deception – knowing it was time to put some distance between myself and my husband. And what better way than with another man? Allowing myself no time to think about what I was doing, I took Simon's hand and led him upstairs to my bedroom – glad of the dark as I let him undress me. Marvelling at how very different his hands felt from Rui's or Peter's and feeling very small now that I stood so close to him, I buried my face in his shoulder as his arms slipped about me and he lifted me onto the bed. I had the oddest idea that I was doing something bad. 'I'm going to cheat on Rui,' I thought, over and over – breathless at how deliciously 'wrong' it felt. Forbidden. Somehow, lovemaking had never felt illicit with Peter. Why not? I wondered. And then I stopped wondering about anything as I touched Simon's skin – so surprisingly soft. Felt the unexpected weight of him, so new and exciting. Even as part of me was sad at what was happening, another part of me revelled in the warm sensations.

Was Simon smiling still, as we made love in that big new bed – in the room I'd so carefully redecorated for Rui's return? Perhaps. All I know is, when we'd finished making love and I lay there, calm and satisfied, one arm thrown across his broad chest and my legs warmly imprisoned beneath his thigh, I think I was probably smiling too.

'Simon . . .' I whispered into the darkness, 'd'you do a lot of this – seducing your married clients, I mean?' knowing very well that bed had been my idea.

'All the time . . .' he sighed contentedly, knowing it, too. And then he fell asleep.

I swam up from the depths of a lovely dream and woke to blinding sunlight in my face. For a second, I couldn't think why I'd left the curtains open last night – and then I remembered, there hadn't been time to close them. And I turned over, faintly shocked to see the tufts of dark hair which sprouted from beneath the duvet. Simon was almost hidden beneath the quilt, and my heart sank as I imagined the awful embarrassment we'd both feel when he woke up.

Then I panicked as I suddenly realized I must look awful. Partly because I always do, even on good mornings – and partly because I'd wept long after this boy had fallen asleep. Cried because things were changing and I didn't really understand. Now, my face was bound to be puffy, my eyes redrimmed and my mascara streaked. It was one thing to be embarrassed in the cold light of day, another to be undignified. So, slipping out of bed, I crept into the bathroom to survey the damage. Surprisingly, I didn't look too bad. My mascara was splodged, yes, but that took a moment to fix. Yet my face looked somehow rested . . . and then I realized I'd slept through the whole of a night. Precious, unbroken sleep. I hadn't had that for a long time.

I combed my hair and brushed my teeth, then carefully applied a little more mascara and kohl to make my morning eyes seem a little more alive. Then I stepped back and checked my body in the mirror, trying to see it with his eyes.

Well . . . ? My look challenged the mirror, but really, I wasn't too bad. I certainly couldn't pass for twenty but I looked pretty good for thirty-three. And if I kept my shoulders back and held my stomach in and walked on tiptoe – I really looked quite slender, I reassured myself. Then, deciding I was better safe than sorry, I wrapped my questionable attributes in a fluffy towel and padded back to the room.

Simon was still asleep, breathing easily and lightly, although now he was lying on his back and his face was uncovered. He looked just as appealing in the morning light. Just as young. And then, unable to stand it any longer, I climbed back into bed beside him, jiggled him awake. No sooner had one eye blinked open to fasten upon me blearily than I said, 'How old are you?' Not even *good morning* or *would you like some tea* – but suddenly, his age had become horribly important.

I almost passed out with shock when he said 'twenty-three' and I rolled away from him, embarrassed by this inexcusable ten year age gap. Something he'd been expecting, because he pulled me straight back and hugged me, saying: 'But I'm very mature for my age!'

I laughed then, knowing it was a little late to do anything else, and we made love again, since it seemed a shame to waste such a perfect opportunity. Afterwards, I was dumbfounded when Simon insisted on making breakfast and I lay in bed with my hands folded behind my head and Angus sitting companionably on my bed, deciding I was very impressed with the younger generation (Colin also knew his way around the kitchen and made incredible soufflés), while Simon whistled tunelessly and clattered around downstairs.

The omelette was delicious, the toast golden-brown and still hot, the tea strong and aromatic, and I wolfed it down, conscious of Simon's eyes upon me and wondering how I looked to him in the cold, unkind light of day. But he didn't seem in any hurry to rush off and, breakfast over, I took him off to the bathroom and together we climbed into the big bath I'd never shared with Rui, where we splashed around like a couple of kids.

Afterwards, this big, smiling, friendly hulk insisted on drying me off and I stood there obediently while he briskly rubbed me down. 'No man's ever done this for me before . . .' I remember thinking, recalling how I'd always been the one to dry Rui off and discovering how pleasant it was to be administered to, for a change. And as for breakfast in bed – !

So I stood there, enjoying the morning light and Simon's hands and the faint perfume from the towel. Never dreaming that Simon and I were setting a pattern – that we'd be sharing breakfasts and bathtimes and whole lots of things besides for a very long time to come.

The news that I'd a twenty-three-year-old lover soon got around. Most of my girlfriends said they'd give a lot for half my chances and only one or two of them seemed disapproving. All of them figured it was a phase I was going through. Trudy was kicking over the traces – and why not?

As for myself – well, sometimes I went up in my own estimation, since an energetic young lover was every married woman's fantasy. At other times, I was sad to think I needed to prove that I wasn't 'past it'. Mostly, though, I worried about what would happen when Colin came back. After all, there were only five years between them and I didn't think my baby brother would ever understand or approve. And if he so much as breathed a word to my folks . . . at the thought of their horrified reaction, the old childhood anxiety returned. They'd been very understanding about the separation, although I'm sure they'd have died if they'd known the gory details. There was no way they could deal with their daughter getting divorced *and* having a lover ten years her junior.

Colin's steely blue eyes grew even colder when I introduced him to Simon. He'd just arrived off the night coach from Scotland, tired and surly – and his mood wasn't improved when he saw Simon's open, honest, *English* face and heard his 'posh' accent. For Colin was still out of his depth with southerners. And Simon was the kind of southern toff he was instinctively hostile towards – the soft job and the soft hands and the soft smile getting a definite thumbs-down in any self-respecting Scotsman's opinion.

But Simon wasn't an estate agent for nothing and his friendly, unassuming manner and his amusing conversation soon relaxed my brother's guard. Then I produced the clincher – an official-looking letter from the Metropolitan Fire Brigade – and Colin's face creased into a smile as he read out the date and time of his interview. Simon congratulated him hugely and they went off to celebrate at the pub, while I prepared lunch for all three of us – relieved the meeting had gone so well.

Three weeks later, Colin was a fireman cadet – officer number 64923. And as he paraded smartly around the living room, looking taller than ever in his navy uniform with its gilt buttons and impressive crested metal belt, I laughed and applauded – all the time thinking that this long-lost brother of mine was turning out to be quite a find. He was thrilled with himself; thrilled with his uniform, his job and its generous salary; thrilled to be living in London. So overjoyed with his good luck that he didn't mind a bit when I told him that Simon would be moving in with us.

I liked Simon the moment I met him – and I like him to this day – but I never loved him. So why did I let him live with me? you might ask. Because I was lonely, would be one answer. Because it soothed my battered ego. Because I knew Rui would get to hear about it and it might make him sit up and take notice. Because it was comforting to have a man about the house and Simon was everything and more that men are supposed to be.

But most of all, having Simon – and Colin – to look after, gave me back my identity. I was now sister and girlfriend and these were roles I understood. Now I had a reason to rush home after work. I had someone to shop and cook for – someone to tidy up behind and generally fuss over. The house was lively and full, life seemed almost normal again – routine and domestic and comfortable. And I settled back into it to wait patiently once more for Rui's return – however long that might take!

While I waited, I had fun. Impossible not to, with two overgrown schoolboys cluttering up the place, and I was forever getting caught up in water fights and pillow fights and midnight feasts, when we all three raided the fridge.

Of course, neither of my new men had money to spare but that didn't seem to hamper their enjoyment at all and gradually, in their company, I found myself doing the kind of things I'd once done with a penniless Rui and enjoying them just as much the second time around. There were rowdy evenings in the pub, when I rediscovered the pleasure of drinking cheap plonk and arguing about the state of the world; long walks in Richmond Park when, dressed in Simon's spare wellies and his old windcheater, we'd stalk the scattered herds of deer. Dressed in jeans and a big old sweatshirt, with my hair piled up on my head, I'd spend whole mornings peering deep into the stomach of his ancient car, while he enlightened me on carburettors and spark plugs.

Simon was even persuaded to part with his top-secret recipe for the perfect omelette when, in my kitchen one evening, I offered him the kind of trade-off that no healthy young man could refuse. And all the time, my expensive clothes hung neglected in the wardrobe, no longer necessary. Ditto my smart manners and my sophisticated talk and my talents for deception and game playing and pretending to be what I wasn't. For these were the stock-in-trade of Rui's wife. And, whether I liked it or not, I wasn't Rui's wife any more.

Mostly, I didn't let myself dwell on that fact but, once in a while, I'd hear some news of him – and his former secretary, now the new woman in his life – and I'd be thrown into deep depression. Other times, my misery would be triggered off by something much more subtle – the sight of Simon bounding through the front door one evening or watching his reflection in the bathroom mirror as he shaved. Or even, sometimes, when we made love. For an instant, the scene I was witnessing (or taking part in) would freeze, while I would come to life to stare aghast at this man who wasn't Rui and wonder what the hell I thought I was playing at.

At times like these, Simon pretended not to notice the sudden icy drop in temperature. Just as he pretended to sleep through those nights when I slipped out of bed to wander around in the dark downstairs, crying helplessly. Surely I couldn't be suffering this alone, I would think then, praying that Rui was feeling the same sense of loss. Now, I think he must have, for he has since admitted that he often drove past his old home, letting the car purr to a halt in the deserted street, as he sat outside our front gate, smoking a cigarette and watching the darkened windows for any sign of life. But Simon's old jalopy was permanently standing guard and, noting its presence, Rui would always slide off again into the night.

Still, these black moods of mine always lifted sooner or later and it would be monkey business as usual, as winter came and brought with it heavy snows. One evening we watched it drifting lazily past the window until, just after midnight, the snow finally died on the wind, leaving behind a silent, glittering carpet which shone blue in the light of a full moon.

Perfect sledging weather, Colin announced, and, without further ado, he and Simon bundled me into several jerseys, filled up some old jam jars with brandy, pinched the lids from my plastic dustbins and we three headed out to a magically altered Hampstead Heath, where we swooped and slipped and yelled our way down the slopes for hours.

Sitting on the upturned dustbin lid, cradled in Colin's massive arms, I felt the night wind whipping past my frozen face and my cries of thrilled terror echoed on the air, as we sped along and tumbled into deep, white drifts. Colin dug me out and I laughed uproariously, unable to remember when I'd last felt so wonderfully alive.

Then the dreaded Christmas festivities came and went and I held on grimly through the New Year celebrations – hoping and praying Rui might choose this time to make peace. He didn't.

Spring came early that year, the garden looked glorious and we threw lots of parties. The boys filled the house with their friends – none of whom were older than twenty-five but all of whom accepted me easily enough. So that, after a while, I stopped feeling 'old' when I was around them and before too long I'd even stopped feeling 'older'. Age was a state of mind, I began to realize, discovering with a mixture of surprise and amusement that, if the truth be told, Simon was a whole lot 'older' than me. Cautious and sensible, amazingly conservative and conventional beneath his youthful exterior, he had an overwhelming desire to settle down and hatch a batch of little estate agents. He craved domesticity and a stable home life even more than I did. I became uncomfortably aware that settling down figured more and more in our discussions and slowly I began to realize that, although I was happy for our present arrangement to go on indefinitely, both Colin and Simon had different ideas.

Chapter Five

I'm free – so what now?

My little brother had changed dramatically in the year we'd lived together and he was now quite unrecognizable as the surly, uncertain youth who'd glared at Simon on that first meeting. As I'd suspected, he'd been only too eager to adopt that same easy, confident manner which he'd detected in my boyfriend, and he'd been a willing pupil as I'd introduced him to restaurants, clubs and a new way of life. I suppose I'd tried to do for him what Rui had once done for me – smoothed off the rough edges – and I have to say, I was very pleased with my handiwork. Colin was a fully-fledged fireman now, with money to burn, you might say. Money which he spent on the steady stream of pretty girls who moved through the house. Sometimes staying for the night or the weekend – and always, always hogging the bathroom as they primped and preened themselves, all the more to please this very eligible young man.

Life in the fire brigade had filled Colin out – leaving him not only physically strong but emotionally very mature. Now easily six feet four inches tall (and still growing), he looked very impressive in clothes which were stylish, well-cut, fashionable. His once unruly mop was swept sleekly back and wherever he went, he left behind the lingering, pleasant aroma of expensive aftershave.

Comfortable and relaxed in any company, his natural friendliness and easy laughter never failed to charm – or even appease, when the sarcastic edge to his humour found its mark. For we had that malicious trait in common, my brother and I – the ability to wound with innocent-sounding phrases

– and we both enjoyed the edge it gave us. By now, we were very close, almost telepathic in our ability to share private jokes or suss out people and situations, one for the other.

Yes, I was proud of Colin, knowing that, with him, I'd come as close to having a son as I was ever likely to get. Glad to have had a hand in his development and grateful for this chance to get to know and love at least one of my brothers. But Colin was all grown up now. There was nothing else I could teach him. And he'd decided it was time for him to find a flat of his own. As if to prove the point, Colin came home one evening with the kind of look on his face which told me he had something on his mind.

No sooner had he announced his decision to move on, than someone put in an offer for my house. It had been on the market for a year and I knew I did not dare refuse the offer or stall the sale in any way. Yet, when our home went, so did any chance of saving our marriage, I was certain of that. And as the prospect of divorce loomed large and threatening at last, I began to look for a flat in earnest. It was in the middle of this sudden upheaval that Simon confessed. He'd fallen in love with me and he wanted us to get married. . . .

By now it was July. Rui and I had been apart for almost exactly a year and I decided it was time to see how the land lay. So I had my first anniversary lunch with my husband. Sitting there, pretending to eat, I digested the unpalatable facts – his new woman was here to stay, our house would be sold, divorce proceedings were beginning. I seemed to take all this in calmly enough but I left the restaurant in a daze. For as I'd studied Rui across the table, I'd been forced to admit one more distressing fact. I was still in love with my husband and, knowing that, I could never, ever marry Simon. Or anyone else.

A gentle breeze stirred the leaves of the old apple tree above my head and carried the sweet smell of roses to where I sat quietly in a wicker chair. Refilling my glass from the bottle at my feet, I tried to ignore the sounds which floated up the garden from the house, but indoors the sale was well under-way and, for the umpteenth time, I told myself it had been the only thing to do. For my new home – a tiny one-bedroomed flat – could never accommodate all my furniture.

The ads I'd placed in the local paper had brought a whole flock of inquisitive neighbours to the door, and now, a steady stream of them bobbed along the other side of the garden wall, as they carried off chairs and coffee tables, blankets, flower pots and table lamps – all at bargain-basement prices.

Knowing I couldn't bear to watch this devastation of my home, Colin and Simon had banished me to the garden with a fortifying bottle of wine and when, at the end of the afternoon, I wandered back indoors, it was to find the rooms bare – unfriendly and unwelcoming.

Simon's eyes smiled encouragement and his voice echoed strangely around the empty living room as he said, 'I'd say it was pretty successful, sweetheart. We made more than I expected – 'and he held out a fat wad of grubby notes. Just over a thousand pounds. Remembering how every lamp, every vase, every print had been carefully chosen over a long period of time, I knew I'd lost a lot more than furniture that afternoon. I'd lost a piece of history – Rui's and mine. Twelve years of planning and dreaming and collecting. And all I had to show for it was a pile of grubby fivers.

That same evening, Colin moved out to live every young man's fantasy of flat-sharing with three girls and I spent my last night, alone, in my strangely bare bedroom. Rising before dawn after a sleepless night, I hoovered carpets, washed windows and dusted woodwork one last time. Then I strolled through the empty rooms, feeling sad and angry at what was happening to my life.

Closing the front door behind me for the last time, I locked it and threw the keys through the letterbox, watching as they landed with a dull clink on the tiled floor of the porch to lie there, winking up at me. I gazed at them for a long time, remembering how the seventeen-year-old me had once tossed away a similar set of keys, before leaving home and setting out for the unknown. But I'd been young and energetic and full of hope then, and now, sixteen years later, I was facing the unknown again. And dreading the prospect.

By mid-morning, I was standing in the living room of my

new basement flat, the bedroom window facing onto the street and the narrow hallway opening out to a small living room. French windows led to a tiny patio, while another door opened onto a fairly large kitchen. Although the place was dark and cramped, Simon had assured me it was a good buy.

'And now, you're home – whether you like it or not,' I thought as I surveyed the faded walls, the scarred parquet floor, the filth ingrained in the kitchen units, the stained bath and lavatory – finding something at last on which to vent my anger. So I scrubbed and I scraped and I disinfected, my hands moving automatically over floors and walls, while my mind raced, and my fury mounted.

'Twelve years of working hard and look where it's got you!' I goaded myself. 'Here you are, stuck in a tiny fucking basement, with only a bloody dog for company . . . thirty-three and going nowhere fast!'

'And whose fault's *that*!' I demanded, rushing to my own defence. Well, it was Rui's, of course. For hadn't I given him the best years of my life – taken him on when he was a useless, careless spendthrift and helped him on the bloody road to success? Christ, there wouldn't have been a house to sell, if it had been left to Rui. He'd never have saddled himself with a mortgage – he'd far rather have pissed the money away! But all my planning had shown a profit and now, of course, some other woman would reap the benefits of all my hard work. Oh, wasn't she the lucky one – inheriting my man, now that he was making a fantastic salary, while I had to watch every penny I spent.

'Funny,' I thought as I scrubbed on, 'I've never felt angry before.' Well, I'd never felt threatened until then, had I – knowing now that he probably wouldn't be satisfied until he got himself married and I lost him for good.

'Just watch it, sweetheart!' I hissed, as I sploshed water over windows and woodwork. 'We're not divorced yet!'

Working and worrying and whipping up my anger, I hardly noticed as the light faded from the sky and darkness pressed against the bare windows. But finally I ground to an exhausted halt – my body slicked with stale sweat, my nails broken and dirty, my hair limp and tangled. Without even bothering to undress, I lay down on my bed and wrapped my arms around a confused, nervous Angus, glad at last to be free of the white hot fury which had driven me all day. But of course it hadn't left me – it had simply burned deep into my being. For a long time, I'd kept it at bay, but now, my anger had swamped me. And it would rule my life for the next two years, spoiling any chance I had of becoming whole again as I nursed that empty, almost physical ache.

Looking back on it now, I think it's fair to say that the change in me began that night. I grew sullen and moody – always ready with a bitchy comment and impossible to please – and poor Simon bore the brunt of my anger. Suddenly, nothing he could say was right, nothing he could do was good enough. I was bored when we went to the cinema, bored if we watched TV. Bored if we didn't make love, bored when we did. And I counteracted any mention of marriage with a mocking remark and a cold stare. Eventually, Simon got the message and wisely stopped calling round at the flat, stopped ringing me. Stopped loving me.

I was free . . . to do what? Well, to put my life back together, naturally, I'd have said to anyone who asked me then. Free to enjoy for a while all those much publicized advantages of being single – the no-strings-attached sex, the looking-after-number-one lifestyle. Then, once I'd had a fling, I'd be free to find the right man – not some idealistic twenty-three-year-old, with romantic notions of 'love'.

Yes, that's what I'd have said back then, because I hadn't the first idea of what freedom meant. Now that I've begun to understand the word at last, I'm amazed by the interpretation I put on it five years ago. But it was one that a lot of women shared.

For this was the age of equality – and didn't that mean we were allowed (nay, *obliged*) to think, feel and act like the men who'd had the upper hand for so long? Now was a time for settling old scores and getting even and, not content with squaring up to men in the work-place and in the home, we were also beginning to undermine them in the sexual arena.

Any woman who doubted there was change in the air, only

had to tune into the radio or television, pick up a newspaper or a magazine and there it was – irrefutable proof that women were on the warpath and men were on the run. 'Two out of three marriages end in divorce!' screamed the headlines (and they weren't all being wound up by men), while Greenham Common was awash with those of us who had deserted homes, hearths and hubbies for something much more important. More and more of us were contemplating mother-hood, without the benefit of live-in fathers. For were men really necessary, once they'd impregnated us? Women were flying for commercial airlines, fighting fires – even storming the doors of the Roman Catholic church to terrify the pre-viously all-male priesthood.

Women everywhere seemed to be muscle-flexing and attacking men with the very weapon which had once made them so vulnerable – their sexuality. Vengeful mistresses spilled their secrets to the newspapers, destroying the careers of business magnates and cringing politicians, while nubile sixteen-year-olds brandished their tits from the depths of Page Three, scornful of their panting male readership, even as they pocketed vast sums of money and went on to open res-taurants, pubs and clubs with their easily gotten gains.

Everywhere I looked the message seemed to be the same. We were living in an age where women could grab men by the short and curlies. And it was time for me to join the movement.

It was easy to convince myself that this was how I should behave. That there were no such things as 'good guys' and all men were shits. I was miserable. And I had a man to thank for that. I'd brought it on myself by loving Rui but I wouldn't make the same mistake twice. Maybe I couldn't get even with *him*, but there were loads of men around – and what did it matter *who* paid the price since all bloody men were the same.

'Christ help the next one who tangles with me,' I vowed, fuelled by my anger and fear. 'Get the bastards before they get you.'

Well, men were bastards – Rui had proved that much. And I was out to get as many of them as I could, with the only weapon I had.

75

Oliver picked me up in Hampstead High Street while I was waiting for a taxi. Pretending to concentrate on the flow of traffic, I watched him striding towards me out of the corner of my eye. Tall and broad-shouldered, he had dark curly hair greying at the temples, a luxuriant moustache and heavy eyebrows which met over dark brown eyes. He was classically handsome, his features chiselled and strong. And as he paused next to me, smiling, with one hand thrust casually into the pocket of his immaculate suit, sheer masculine strength seemed to ooze out of his frame.

'Taxis at this time of day – always frightfully scarce, don't you find?' he commented in resonant BBC tones to no-one in particular. Then, still smiling, he dodged through the traffic and stepped off smartly along the road.

A couple of minutes later, I was still waiting patiently on the pavement when a beautiful maroon limousine purred to a halt before me. The car turned out to be a vintage Rolls-Royce. The driver turned out to be Oliver.

He introduced himself as he drove me to St John's Wood. And by the time we'd reached my flat, I'd discovered that Oliver was a city financier and chairman of a successful company. The only son of a Russian-Polish marriage and due to inherit even more money than his expensive appearance alluded to, this bachelor owned a house nearby and an elegant apartment in Kensington. I discovered all of this in less than fifteen minutes. It took me a while longer to discover he was gay.

We had our first date that evening – nice Indian food in a rather 'pukka' restaurant. And for the occasion, I was wearing one of my Rui-inspired ensembles. Oliver seemed suitably impressed.

He invited me to his place for dinner on our second date and I sat in his futuristic white and chrome kitchen, impressed by his mansion, his culinary skills, his technique with a cocktail shaker. By now, my appetite had been whetted – and for more than just food. But I thought it politic to refuse a second helping of the delicious lobster Mornay. Ditto his whimsical offer of dessert . . . something light and fluffy, which he'd intended to serve up in bed, by all accounts. For it doesn't do to appear too hungry too soon.

Our third date was spent on board a yacht owned by one of his clients – a streamlined effort with a professional crew (referred to as Number One, Number Two and Number Three). Ours was a luxurious circular bedroom which was built into the prow and I eyed the bed appraisingly from the narrow doorway, wondering what the trip would bring.

Slipping through bright waters, headed for the Isle of Wight, I watched through half-closed eyes, as Oliver played sailors, his strong legs and his powerful arms promising all sorts of delights, once we'd berthed for the night. Except . . . something about Oliver wasn't quite right, I mused, as I sipped my vodka tonic and contemplated the vast expanse of sea, trying to put my finger on the problem.

Yes, we made love that night – a task Oliver executed as skilfully as everything else he attempted, I'm sure. But that was just it – I'd been a task. Professionally executed. And as Oliver had disappeared topside almost immediately afterwards, he had seemed almost – *relieved*.

If I'd cared for him, I might have been hurt by this reaction. But I felt nothing for Oliver at all, apart from the most passing physical attraction. And now there was mild curiosity as to what lay behind his self-controlled sexual performance and his need for distance.

A few evenings later, I was invited to his house again and this time, I allowed myself to be led to that holy of holies – the master bedroom. Carefully understated cream linen walls served as a backdrop for a gallery of prints and charcoal sketches – the human form in all its glory, tastefully displayed. Dozens and dozens of male nudes, gazing down upon his immense mahogany bed.

There it stood on a dais in the centre of the room, the headboard a solid wall of dark, carved wood and the mattress strewn about with plump pillows and draped with the finest lawn sheets – everything starkly, blindingly white. A room at once impressively spartan and threateningly male – and it was here that Oliver professionally executed me again. Slowly, painstakingly, expertly. Coldly. And then, when he had finished and limbs had been disentangled, Oliver asked me if I would mind leaving.

'I know you won't take this amiss, my dear Trudy. But I find I sleep so much better when I'm alone. Surely you find this, too?' And he settled back comfortably against the pillows while I showered.

Was I devastated? No. Perhaps momentarily offended – and then hugely intrigued. Okay, so at the moment my sex life had consisted of one-night stands – but even then, part of the pleasure lay in the closeness partners enjoyed afterwards. And frankly, even after the most horrendous drilling and filling sensation, I've often felt closer to my bloody dentist than I felt to Oliver just then. So it was with genuine indifference that I flicked back his sheets and, in dulcet tones, informed my icy lover that I would happily head home – but he was driving me there.

And so our association (you could hardly call it a relationship) continued while I tried to fathom what made Oliver tick. And all the time, he was applying himself to the *real* job in hand – that of finding a suitable wife to breed the offspring necessary for this forty-two-year-old only son of ageing, wealthy parents.

For this honour, Oliver was considering me, repulsive though tits and fannies and cunts were – repugnant as women might be to this careful, calculating gay. I was to be his willing smokescreen, while our children would still the wagging tongues and give him a cloak of respectability. In return, Oliver had steeled himself to screw me rigid as often as was necessary to get me pregnant and keep me quiet.

I'd like to be able to say I'd deduced all this by myself. But I turned up at Oliver's place unexpectedly one morning to find him having breakfast with a man I'd never seen before – but one who obviously knew Oliver well and who couldn't hide his loathing for me. And any lingering doubts I might have had were dispelled the very next night, when he tried to oust me from his bed yet again. Flouncing out of his bedroom, I whirled round in the doorway and said, 'I'm going! But I've got to hand it to you – you put up a pretty good show for a queer. It's real Oscar-winning stuff, Ollie. But next time, *try* to look as if you're enjoying it, huh?'

I kept an image of his stricken face in my mind's eye, as I sauntered home in the dead of night. Triumphant, now that I'd pieced it all together and knew that, while his home, his car, his clothes, his clever pose all shrieked masculinity, Oliver himself didn't merit the label. Now I didn't mind that he'd tried to manipulate me – all the time despising me for being the very thing he needed. A female. Really, he'd done me a favour, for hadn't he confirmed my worst opinion of men? They were takers and users, every bloody one!

I was still congratulating myself on unmasking Oliver when Alan crossed my path. In his fifties, small and stockily built, he liked to throw his weight around and was a pig to do business with. I dealt with his company on behalf of one of my clients, and people in his office were always gossiping about how he'd reduced this girl to tears and fired that one on the spot. While, according to the switchboard girls (always a wonderful source of gossip), his poor, downtrodden wife was forever crying on the telephone while he delivered one of his endless broadsides. Alan might have remained forever his wife's problem if I hadn't happened to cross his line of fire myself. I'd been complaining about a missed deadline (their fault, not mine), insisting that, since I'd ended up out of pocket as a result, they should be prepared to shoulder some of the blame and the loss.

While I was discussing this with his manager in the front office, Alan walked by and immediately waded in, heavy-handed and foul-mouthed. Suddenly, I was experiencing his bully-boy tactics at first hand and I could hardly believe the viciousness of his assault as he berated me in front of every-one. I suppose if he'd confined his remarks to business, I might have survived it. But in chauvinistic fashion, he went on to decry 'these bloody silly bitches who should stay home and leave the real work to men'.

Then, satisfied he'd annihilated me, he steamed off self-importantly towards his office and left me standing in the middle of his employees, my face on fire and my eyes brimming with furious tears. Blindly, I picked up my briefcase and left the office with as much dignity as I could muster. I knew that, somehow, I would make him pay. Still, I couldn't inflict any damage on Alan personally, I had to admit, as I charged along the street, trying to regain my composure. The man was beyond my reach. But his son wasn't, I suddenly realized – the thought cheering me up no end.

Jamie was only twenty-one. A fresh-faced lad who'd just begun a promising career as a print buyer. Already he was highly thought of and people in the business liked him almost as much as they disliked his father. Not only was Jamie a regular nice guy, he was in love and engaged to be married to a real sweetie. I suppose, really, he was the model son and it was hardly surprising that he was the apple of his father's eye. Such a wholesome, rounded apple – and so easy to take a bite out of. . . .

So when I 'accidentally' met Jamie in a local wine bar, I smiled a lot and flirted a little – much to his friends' mirth and his embarrassment. The next time I saw him, in a restaurant, he was lunching with an older man – obviously business. I sent a bottle of good wine to his table, which impressed his companion, heightened young Jamie's feeling of self-importance and increased his interest in me.

A few days after that, I bumped into him in the street and whisked him off to lunch myself. And across (and under!) the table, I gave him The Treatment, being outrageously suggestive, touching him up, oh, so subtly and firing his boy's mind with all kinds of sexual nonsense.

A week later, I had Jamie just where I wanted him – tucked up in my bed. And before too long, his car was parked outside my flat at all hours. Did I fancy Jamie? Not a bit – although I said I did. Was the sex good? Actually, it was bloody awful, although I pretended to be transported with delight. Was he hard work? Every sodding minute. But he left me each time, thinking he was wonderful and convinced that next to his first love – which was cricket – I was the most fantastic thing in his life.

Slowly, slowly, Jamie fell under my influence. When he should have been rushing off to important appointments, he was in my bed; while he was supposed to be reporting at sales meetings, he was in my bath. While he should have been taking his fiancée to lunch or collecting her from her office, he was in my clutches. And I didn't let go until his job was on the line, his engagement was all washed up . . . and his poor old Dad was completely distraught by the change I'd wrought in his son.

For, of course, the whole firm was talking about Jamie's infatuation with me – and the rumours finally reached Alan. Oh, what a row they had (the switchboard operator told me all)! Father and son at loggerheads with Alan trying to bully the boy into backing off me – employing his usual knock-down, drag-out tactics, which had Jamie storming out of his office, more determined than ever to stick to me like glue.

For the first time ever, Alan had lost control of a situation. He could see his boy was heading for disaster – knew I was behind it – and he could only stand helplessly by. It's a wonder he didn't have a heart attack, as he vented his fury on everyone in the office. And when he wasn't airing his anger and frustration down the phone to his poor wife, Jamie's ex was bending Alan's ear – beseeching him to '*Do* something! He's your son. Can't you talk any sense into him?'

Ah, what a glorious mess.

What happened to Jamie? I don't really know, for I lost interest at that point, took my business elsewhere, stopped returning Jamie's calls and stood him up once or twice, until he got the message. Doubtless he patched up his broken engagement and forgot all about me eventually. But as for Alan . . . well, I understand that, even now, the mere mention of my name is enough to send his blood pressure soaring.

By this time, *lovemaking* – that subtle expression of caring and needing and wanting to share – had all but ceased for me. Now, I was caught up in a world where sex was a useful weapon, nothing more and nothing less. I learned to be unemotional about its use, as I gradually learned to master it.

I was still in the throes of dampening Jamie's ardour, when Ron took me to task over 'the whole shoddy business', as he called it. Ron was the junior partner of a printing firm and his work often brought him into contact with Alan. He'd even met Jamie once or twice.

We bumped into each other at the promotional launch of a new magazine when, standing by the bar, glass in hand, I saw him elbowing his way through the crowd towards me. Seeing him always gave me a little thrill of pleasure, for Ron was the kind of man every woman would love to get her hands on. He was good-looking in that understated way that you'd hardly notice at first. And then, just when you were about to dismiss his face as pleasant and nothing more, you would notice the startling blue of his eyes and how well-shaped and sensual his mouth was. And then, just as I did, you might begin to study him closer, noticing the cleft in his chin when he smiled, the warm richness of his laugh and his endearing habit of tugging the blond curls which clung to his well-shaped head.

Oh, yes – he was divine. Sexy. The kind of easy, natural man who makes a wonderful lover. (And in between Simon and Oliver and Jamie, I'd had enough of these to know what I was talking about.) And the nicest thing about Ron was that he had no idea how devastating he was – which is always the biggest turn-on.

But (and isn't there always a 'but' with nice men?) Ron was married. HAPPILY married. Frantically in love with his pretty wife and in raptures over their eighteen-month-old daughter. Ron was a man who was still celebrating his good fortune and even the most predatory of us women at the party hung back in the face of Real Love. Each of us remembered in her own way how marvellous that kind of relationship can be and none of us wanted to spoil it for Ron.

So, even though he was a strictly 'hands off' acquaintance, I was pleased to see Ron heading my way. He soon wiped the welcoming smile from my face though as, trying hard not to be too disapproving, he pointed out what everyone knew. That I'd used Jamie to get even with Alan. Bravely he told me what other people would only say behind my back – that I was turning into a hard, cynical bitch.

All this I listened to attentively, my eyes wide and a well-practised smile hovering about my lips. But inside I was a hotch-potch of hurt, embarrassment and shame. Ron was right, of course, but it might have been easier to bear if he'd heaped scorn on my carefully coiffed head. *That* I could have shrugged off since, these days, I almost enjoyed courting disapproval. But Ron chose to be sympathetic – the one thing I couldn't deal with. He gave me the benefit of the doubt – refusing to believe I was beyond the pale. Alluded to my unhappy personal life, the trauma of my separation, how lonely I must feel and, understandably, upset.

'But you're such a lovely girl, Trudy – I hate to see what you're doing to yourself. You mustn't let this divorce make you so bitter.' And then, smiling at me kindly, 'We've known each other for years, haven't we? We're friends, eh? And I've always thought you were super.'

'How dare you! How fucking *dare* you lecture me! You patronizing son of a bitch!' I screamed inside, as I smiled and nodded. 'Call yourself my friend! You're worse than all the rest, you arrogant, complacent bastard . . . ' And the poison seeped through me as he went on.

'Things'll start working out for you soon – you'll see. You're too attractive to be alone for long. In fact,' he added, hoping to console me, 'if I wasn't a happily married man, you're the kind of woman I'd be making a beeline for.'

That's what put the thought of seducing Ron into my mind. He gave me the weapons and I used them – played on his genuine concern for me, together with the fact that he found me attractive. Harness that to his need to be protective and sympathetic and kind, knowing that – unless I was very wrong about men – just a little flattery on my part would do the rest. Warm and snug (and, as I saw it, 'smug') with his brat, and his wife and his happy, well-ordered life, he'd dared to point out the meaninglessness of my existence, the emptiness of my world.

'You've got a few things to learn, my boy,' I thought as, head bowed, seemingly abject and penitent, I allowed him to break me down and build me up. His arm slipped comfortingly about my waist, as I shed a regretful tear and he pecked my cheek encouragingly, saying, 'Come on, luvvy. It's not the end of the world. Alan and Jamie will soon patch up their quarrel. I just thought that – well, someone ought to tell you what's being said.' And then, 'Look – we haven't had a drink together for ages. Howzabout lunch, one day next week? The firm can pick up the tab!'

And I smiled gratefully at him, thinking how easily dreams could be shattered, how quickly life could spin out of kilter. *I* knew that and soon, Ron would, too. Oh sure, we'd have lunch. But he would be picking up the tab himself. . . .

I had to summon all my powers of seduction – all my new-found guile – to get the better of Ron. For he really was in love and he really did want to be faithful. 'But men are all the same, aren't they?' I smiled to myself as, a few weeks and a lot of hard work later, I ushered a slightly inebriated Ron along my narrow hallway and into my little basement living room, where I plied him with generous brandies and even more generous compliments, as I divested him of his jacket, loosened his tie, slid my hand inside his shirt. And then, once he'd lost sight of everything and everyone but me, I took him off to bed.

His lovemaking was as tender and gentle, as caring and as naturally sexy as Ron was himself and afterwards, when he dozed fitfully against my bare shoulder, I stroked his blond curls and kissed his sleeping eyes. I realized as I held him, that Ron was the kind of man I ached to have for my own. So I lay there, watching the afternoon shadows creep along my bedroom ceiling, knowing that the battle for Ron's peace of mind had been hard fought, yet my triumph, somehow empty. Really, I wouldn't have hurt him for the world. But he'd taunted me with his clean, honest love, riled me with his complacency – and I couldn't let him get away with that.

We never went to bed again. Didn't have to, for he'd learned his lesson – that happiness is a precious thing. Fragile and easily destroyed. Now Ron knew how suddenly any one of us could fall from grace, I hoped he'd think twice before delivering any more lectures. I needn't have worried though, for Ron hasn't even spoken to me since that day.

'Ah, well,' I thought. 'You win some, you lose some.' And I went in search of new prey.

Chapter Six

Meet my friends The Stormtroopers

As it turned out, there was a lot of easy prey. And even when there weren't fatalities like Ron, Alan and Oliver, I inflicted a lot of damage on men, stalking them in bars, at parties, through business. Men who were constantly outmanoeuvred (and fascinated) by my blatant, no-nonsense approach to sex and the fact that, while they were wondering how to get me into bed, I'd already turned down the sheets and put the wine on ice, in anticipation of dragging home my latest conquest for some fun and games.

Perhaps 'fun' isn't the right word to describe how I felt about sex. For, although I was gaining confidence around men all the time – sure of my sexual prowess and enjoying the power it gave me over all kinds of males, young and old – the sexual act never brought me much satisfaction. No matter how acrobatic or prolonged the session was – no matter how much energy I expended on a demanding partner – that sleepy, satisfied sensation which used to follow *lovemaking* always eluded me now.

No matter how expert my lovers – for me there was never any release. No moment when I slipped over the edge and lost myself in the smell and the taste and the heat of the man I was with. Sex was a contest, after all – and I was determined to be the victor, not the vanquished. Not for me the subjugation, the surrender or the vulnerability which ensues when you give yourself up completely to pleasure. I denied myself that – forfeited the luxury of being all woman to any man.

But even if I hadn't been intent on swapping roles – on trying to think and act as aggressively as a man – satisfying sex would still have eluded me because all sorts of things combine to make sex pleasurable. Things like a bond of trust, a sense of caring and a need to share. In other words, lovemaking only begins to come alive when two people have some genuine feeling for each other – even though the feeling might fall short of love.

Yet I was incapable of feeling *anything* very much – except bitterness and a desire to hurt men. Especially the ones who were stupid enough to actually *care* about me.

Really, I was too damaged to be of value to any man, yet I desperately needed a companion. The gods must have realized this, which is why they sent Hannah to me.

Even now, I cringe when I think back to the night we met. One of my periodic bleak moods had descended. I was sitting in the office, knowing I should head home yet dreading the prospect. What I really wanted was to escape for a little while – and the easiest way to do that was to get blind drunk, I decided.

Hannah walked by my desk just then. Tall and cool-looking, with shoulder length dark hair which was sometimes left loose and sometimes fashionably plaited. I'd noticed her around the place – a new addition to our thriving cooperative. And now, on impulse, I smiled, introduced myself, and suggested meeting for a drink after work.

Standing shoulder to shoulder in the noisy pub, we shouted over the babble of other drinkers as we hogged our precious few inches of bar space. To begin with, we indulged in the usual small-talk of strangers, but as one large vodka after another slid down my throat, Hannah dropped all pretence at conversation. Instead, she stood quietly by and listened to my monologue on men and marriage and loneliness. Her green eyes never leaving my face, her sombre expression never altering, as I slid quickly, effortlessly, into drunken self-pity.

And then, when I was completely legless – my vision dancing, my body swaying and my speech slurred – I welcomed the release of tears. Crying there, in the crowded bar, I ignored the curious stares of strangers, while Hannah wheedled my address out of me, then walked me round in the fresh cold air, before bundling me into a taxi.

Back home she carefully removed the contact lenses from my sightless eyes, before dragging me, fully clothed, into the shower cubicle and turning the cold spray full on – turning away as I threw up and slid down the cold, tiled walls.

That was the only time I'd let my self-control slip I tried to tell Hannah the next day.

'God knows what you must think, but I don't usually behave like that. Or drink like that,' I added, clutching my pounding head. 'It's just that a lot's been happening lately and I needed to let go for a bit. But I shouldn't have involved you. I'm sorry.'

'Been there, done that,' said her smile, as she promised me I hadn't made a spectacle of myself and she hadn't been embarrassed. 'So, you felt like tying one on – that's okay. I'm glad you invited me along,' she said airily. 'Maybe you can return the favour, one day!'

And as we laughed together, neither of us realized how close we would become. Or that, one day, *I would* return the favour.

Stepping into the black satin G-string, I pulled the thong up between my legs and laced it high on my hips. Suspender belt anchored comfortably about me, I worked the seamed mesh stockings up over my thighs and clipped them in place, before slipping my feet into pointed leather stilettos and adding a good three inches to my height.

Then came the black T-shirt, with its deeply scooped neckline, and the tight black leather skirt, which strained across my belly and buttocks. I girded a heavy chain belt around my waist, fastened more chains tight around my wrists and neck, attached nuggets of metal to my ears.

My hair teased out to a fiery halo around my head, I leaned forward into the mirror to put the finishing touches to heavily made up eyes, added a slash of brilliant scarlet lipstick – and stepped back, to grimace at my reflection. I wanted my appearance to be alluring but threatening, exciting but dangerous. 'The ball-buster' look, I suppose you could call it – and one I'd achieved with little or no effort. I congratulated myself. More than satisfied with the cold, predatory image which stared boldly back at me.

Now, on with the heavy leather jacket, its shoulders outrageously padded, its waistline cinched in with a broad leather strap. Black leather gloves, black leather shoulder bag bristling with metal studs – one last glance and I was ready for the fray. Almost. Striding over to the cluster of bottles on the side table, I poured a large vodka – straight, no ice – and downed it in one gulp, sighing appreciatively as it burned its way down into my stomach. 'Now I'm ready for anything,' I told myself, as I headed out into the dark. Knowing that, on this Saturday night, as on every other, anything *could* happen. And probably would.

The place was dimly lit, crowded, noisy, but Bruno the barman smiled when he saw me and motioned me to my usual place in the far corner of the U-shaped bar. Bruno always reserved this spot for Hannah, Amy and myself – and no matter how packed the bar became, none of the regulars would dare to appropriate our stools. For this was our second home, our playground, our battlefield – the place where we three women practically lived, when we weren't actually working.

I was early. There was still no sign of the girls and I pushed my way through the mostly male throng. Then, as Bruno automatically placed glasses and my usual bottle before me, I took in the punters.

Alex was on the other side of the bar, deep in conversation with his live-in girlfriend. He was pretending he hadn't seen me, but it was obvious from the way he kept his back to me and his gaze firmly fixed on his lady that he didn't want to meet my eye. Probably remembering what we two had been getting up to, just a few evenings before, while his unsuspecting girlfriend was up North on business – and praying I wouldn't give him away, now that sanity prevailed once more.

Well, I probably wouldn't. But, then again, I just might . . . I deliberated, as my gaze travelled on through the crowd.

Ah, there was Art. He glanced up, smiled and waved across. I waved back, remembering the night I'd been sitting alone on this self-same stool. Bored, as usual. Yet as usual, reluctant to go home. Around ten-thirty, he had strolled in with another man and they'd leaned against the bar, deep in conversation. I'd watched him for a few minutes, letting my gaze burn into him. Knowing that, eventually, he would feel the eyes and turn to check out the source. It was an old trick, this unwavering stare. One I'd discovered accidentally and now used all the time. It hardly ever failed, yet it didn't seem to work on Art that evening and, if I hadn't been so bored, I might well have lost interest at that point.

As it was, I felt Bruno's gaze on me and glanced away from my prey long enough to see that my favourite barman was watching me in action again. Bruno had seen us perform here a hundred times. Watched the objects of our attentions go down like ninepins and knew that we rarely failed to get our man. His thin smile was what had goaded me then and, casually, I'd strolled along the bar, coming to rest gently against Art's elbow.

'Excuse me . . . ' I'd begun, as both men broke off their conversation to turn and look. And then, in the tone of voice one might employ to ask for a match or the time or directions to the loo, I said, 'I'm sorry to interrupt your conversation . . . but I was just wondering if perhaps you might fancy a fuck a little later?' And I smiled sweetly at my victim, waiting for the look of shock/horror and the blustering which usually followed this remark. I'd played this game lots of times before.

But Art was wonderful. His long, lugubrious face never altered as he studied me carefully. Then he slowly smiled, showing excitingly long, white teeth and, with a little nod of his head, flicked back unusually long, sleek dark hair. 'Anything's possible . . . ' he conceded, gazing at me, while his dumpy friend stood by, his eyes darting between us.

'Why don't you join us for a drink, while I give it some consideration?'

Oh yes, Art had turned out to be full of surprises and I'd even had fun for a while. Until I got bored again. Now he gave a last wave and elbowed his way out of the bar. Art had been one of the few men who hadn't been afraid of me, I admitted now.

Not like Rick, who stood quietly just a few feet away, watching me and wondering. Wondering if I'd ever make a move in his direction. Hoping I might, yet scared that I would. Because, of course, he'd heard the stories about me and he'd wanted to find out for himself if they were true.

'Now, *that's* the way I like my men!' I mused, enjoying his uncertainty. Their gut reaction was to leave me alone, yet they ignored that and kept on coming. It had happened with men like Rick time and again. Repelled yet fascinated – disliking the kind of woman I was, yet wanting to sleep with me, just the same. Until eventually, they discovered that I was even better – and so much worse – than they'd ever imagined.

It often occurred to me as I went down on a man like that, that he'd never know what it was I had in mind – the best blow-job ever or sudden, excruciating private-part surgery. Frankly, until the last moment, I often didn't know myself, so great was my desire to emasculate the whole bloody lot of them.

'Ho, hum!' I thought, as I continued to survey the crowd. 'Sorting out all these men could be a lifetime's work.' Then I straightened up on the stool and my eyes narrowed, all the better to see the man who had just walked in. Michael. Exotic and beautiful, his tight curls close-cropped to his neat head, his large eyes curiously slanted towards his temples, his lips full and generous – his exotic features, wide shoulders and slim hips a pleasure to contemplate.

But as usual, Michael gave me a wide berth. I'd been stalking him all year but he hadn't wanted to play any of my games. At least, not so far. And I wondered if and when I'd rise to that particular challenge. . . .

'God, it's foul out there!' Hannah suddenly said at my elbow, shaking drops of rain from her mane of wavy hair. I watched, feeling oddly possessive and proud of her as she tugged on the large silver zip and slid out of her biker's jacket, its gleaming black leather cunningly cut and stitched to look both threatening and sexy. Beneath it, she wore skin-tight leggings tucked into ankle-length, heavily buckled booties. And (the master stroke) the softest pink, cuddly mohair sweater which beautifully confused the signals she was giving

90

out and forced admiring men nearby to ask themselves yet again: was she – were we – just nice girls dressed up to look dangerous? Or were we, in truth, ball-breakers, disguised as girls?

She sat opposite me, her lovely green eyes edged with darkest kohl, her complexion a subtle blend of pink and pale, her lips perfectly outlined – enjoying my admiration and complimenting me in turn. Then her haughty stare cruised the bar, while Bruno silently filled her glass.

It had been nearly two years since I'd first got drunk in Hannah's company and, although we'd stayed in contact with each other, nearly another year had passed before she and I really became friends. I had turned into a real loner. Married girlfriends – busy with their own lives – couldn't fill my need for a real *friend*. Someone I could trust and confide in. Someone I could lavish affection on – the affection I flatly refused to squander on men. Hannah was the obvious choice and, as I got to know her better, I discovered her story was eerily similar to my own.

Two years younger than me, she fell in love at eighteen with gorgeous, talented Tony. Married him at twenty and blindly followed him halfway round the world, leaving friends and family in New Zealand to be with this man in his quest for fame and fortune. Stuck by him in the early years of his search – earning the lion's share of their income at a job she hated, encouraging him through his initial failures, shoring him up when he felt like quitting. Loving him and willing him on, wanting him to succeed. Until finally he did – and the money, the success, the prestige were his for the asking. Together with the fast cars, the slick friends and the women.

After years of waiting in the wings, Tony was now centre stage. Unfortunately, he still had a wife in the audience and she was suddenly an encumbrance, standing between him and the adulation of his new following. So, knowing she would lose him sooner or later, Hannah's fierce pride had forced her to fade from the scene. Turning her back on her old life, she'd begun to build a new one. Determined to be financially independent, she'd moved into the cooperative and set up a small company and I'd admired the quiet, dignified way she'd dealt with all the problems of a new business and a dying marriage. So, little by little, we'd confided in each other. Both wary of getting too close to anyone – even another woman.

For a lark, we'd gone to a make-up artist's studio for a 'makeover' and we sat side by side, giggling at our grotesquely painted reflections in the mirror. The upward tilt of Hannah's eyes and the paleness of her complexion had been exaggerated, so that she looked weirdly Japanese, while I resembled an overblown Madame, with my vulgar gold eyes and red lips.

Suddenly, a photograph tucked into the mirror caught Hannah's eye and, following her gaze, Sheila the make-up artist said, 'Ah, that's Mandy. Definitely top model material – her agent's getting her some good work. And she's got amazing bone structure – great for make-up.'

Hannah's eyes never left the picture, but her expression was weird.

'Some bloody women have all the luck!' I quipped, to fill the sudden deathly silence.

'I'll say!' Sheila laughed as she bent to paint Hannah's white lips. 'And Mandy's got more than her share. You should see the bloke she's shacked up with – gorgeous!' and she rolled her eyes comically.

The smile died on my face as, tearing the towel from her neck, Hannah threw it onto the worktop, scattering the bottles and jars, as she dived off the chair and headed for the door. I sat there for a second, frozen with shock, and by the time I reached her, she was struggling into her coat, her fingers trembling, her shoulders shaking as she fought to control herself.

She went clattering down the stairs with me hard on her heels, clutching her bag, her umbrella and all the other things she'd forgotten in her haste. Then, reaching the street, she hissed: 'I need a bloody drink!' and headed off along the pavement, while I loped at her side, knowing that, somehow, this 'Mandy' was behind it all.

'She's beautiful – isn't she!' Hannah grated, suddenly rounding on me. 'Top model material!' and she mimicked Sheila's Liverpudlian accent. Then, exasperated by the blank look on my face, she wailed at last, 'She's the one!' and the tears began to stream from her oddly Japanese eyes. 'She's living in my sodding house – with my bloody husband!

'And I'm off to get drunk!' she challenged. 'So, are you coming, or aren't you?' And tearing her belongings from my hands, she began to stalk off again, without waiting for an answer.

'Okay – so you want to get drunk?' I asked, catching her sleeve. 'Fine. But let's do it at my place. The booze is cheaper,' I added, as she hesitated.

And my place was much more private, she agreed next morning, when she woke up. Her head was pounding, her breath was foul and her eyes were tiny and bloodshot. But her dignity – that thing Hannah valued above all else – was still intact.

I'd been impressed by the amount of cognac she'd poured down her throat as we'd curled up together on my sofa. Cursing and burping and sobbing – ruining her carefully painted face – she'd polished off nearly a whole bottle of Courvoisier. While I'd cried too, in sympathy, topping up her glass, stroking her hair and giving her the odd hug, until she was blind drunk and incapable of speech. Then I'd made up a bed on the sofa, helped her out of her crumpled clothes and left her, sobbing herself to sleep like any child.

Next morning, she lay in a hot bath while I fixed breakfast and, by the time she'd washed her hair, made her face up and borrowed one of my outfits, no one looking at her would ever have guessed that Hannah had 'tied one on' or that I'd gone along for the ride. But the favour had been returned and our friendship had been cemented.

Now, Hannah's divorce was well underway, although, like me, she hadn't quite accepted that she'd lost her husband. Still in love with him, still feeling cheated and discarded, her anger was as real as my own. Yet, while she sometimes felt a need to even the score, she wasn't driven by it as I was. Didn't gloat over her conquests as I did.

And that, I guess, is where we differed. Hannah man-baited half-heartedly and without malice, while I was a one-woman crusade. Still, if she sometimes questioned my tactics and my motives, her friendship was unwavering, her loyalty fierce, and when my mouth got me into tricky situations with men, I knew I could rely on her to back me up.

That's what I was thinking as the third member of our trio sauntered into the bar. Amy – our secret weapon. Amy with her 'butter wouldn't melt in my mouth' look, her face devoid of cosmetics, her eyes wide and clear, intelligent arcs for eyebrows and a permanent, dimpled smile. Her healthy strawberry blonde hair hung loose in a classic bob, her figure was unfashionably yet excitingly curvaceous, while her bright laugh and beautiful Stateside drawl proclaimed her the healthy, outdoor, clean living type. The innocent, all-American Miss. But lovely Amy was much more than she seemed.

For her wit was caustic, her mind cunning, her manipulation of people and situations almost an art form. She could sum up a man in a moment, pinpointing his strengths and weaknesses – tying him up in wordy knots with her golden tongue, while she deftly attacked his Achilles heel. That's if she didn't like him.

But if she did – ah, then she divined his ideal woman and became that self-same creature in the twinkling of an eye. Seductive, world-weary, wise – she was all of these. Intellectual, analytical, calculating – she was that, too. Girlish, temperamental, giggly – Amy could be all those things and more. Or maybe, in reality, none of them. With her, it was difficult to know. Which made her fascinating, if unpredictable.

She swooped down on us in a flurry of hugs and kisses, her cheeks wet with rain, her lips cold, her eyes sparkling. And the temperature in the bar rose a degree or two, as her warmth and vitality flowed through it.

Unwrapping herself from her voluminous leather greatcoat, she immediately began to tease Bruno and hurled a couple of ribald remarks at two men standing just behind her. 'Trouble, looking for somewhere to happen,' I concluded, finally recognizing which version of Amy had come out to play.

She began to describe her encounter with an old boyfriend, reducing us to helpless laughter as she described his pathetic attempts to rekindle something approaching desire in her, while they strap-swung together on the packed Underground and vastly entertained the rush-hour crowds.

I laughed at her hilarious story, reflecting that I'd never even heard her mention this man's name before. But then, there was so much I still didn't know about Amy.

She'd strolled into the cooperative some time before, a Southern Belle on a three-week visit to London, having dropped by to see one of our 'inmates'. Or so she'd informed Hannah and me when we made her acquaintance in the canteen. We were both drawn to her immediately and soon we became a threesome. Now, it was nearly Christmas and Amy still had no plans to move on. Her past was shrouded in mystery, her life story, as she told it, fragmented and sketchy. And her present was equally mysterious, since she didn't work, had no visible means of support and even lacked a permanent base – moving 'twixt Hannah's flat and my own, then disappearing at a moment's notice to stay with 'friends'. Maybe she had money stashed away in the bank. Maybe she was an heiress or a dope dealer. Who could say? With Amy, anything was possible and we'd simply learned to accept her, no questions asked.

Hannah and Amy – my new family. My sisters. The thought of them made me strong as I sat there, flanked by the two pretty women. Comforted by the knowledge that, if a man tried to pull a number on any one of us, the other two would jump on him from a great height. For we three were inseparable.

Stepping out arm in arm – aware that in appearance and personality, we complemented each other perfectly – we'd haunted London's wine bars and jazz clubs. Always careful to make an entrance – and always dressed to kill. Barmen brightened visibly when we appeared and managers smiled and winked and ushered us to the best tables, while other regulars waited eagerly for the fun to begin. We'd been nicknamed The Stormtroopers and we did our best to live up to the title.

Employing the same bully-boy tactics that men had used against women for years, our favourite pastime was to swoop on some unsuspecting male – separating him from his cronies, as one stood to the left of him, one stood to the right of him and the third planted herself inches from his face. Thereafter the tactics varied. Sometimes we'd be quite gentle, dusting him down, brushing imaginary threads from his jacket, smoothing down his collar, his hair (his ruffled feathers), cooing and blowing into his ear and fluttering our eyelashes as we, oh, so subtly rubbed up against him.

Other times we'd be more aggressive – Hannah rolling lewd eyes and Amy making lewd comments, while I would slip my hand under our victim's jacket to rake my nails down his back or casually feel his bottom.

Oh, their embarrassment was sweet. Their panic amused us no end, while our efforts were redoubled if we sensed outrage or anger. Or fear. Oh, dear, oh dear, oh dear . . . we *were* bad girls. Lethal as a team – and every bit as deadly when approached individually. My heavy sarcasm, Amy's probing mind and Hannah's haughty demeanour were more than a match for any man.

Yet in the end, it *was* a game and Hannah would only take it so far. And, although Amy could, on occasion, be persuaded to take it a little further – *I* was the only one who took it to the limit, every single time.

So I was all talk and no action, was I? Just another prick tease, eh? Time and again, men accused me of that, only to learn that I was capable of everything I threatened and more besides. Eventually, my reputation preceded me and nervous glances and hostile remarks greeted me, everywhere I went.

Chapter Seven

Empty sex. Dangerous sex. And bad for me

Power over men. Suddenly I had it. It hardly mattered that they feared me – even loathed me. At last, I was in control. I congratulated myself on the fact that now no man ever made the mistake of treating me gently or dismissing me lightly. And, while they might deal with me on the most basic sexual level, none of them were stupid enough to entertain the idea of becoming seriously involved. That suited me for a while and then it began to slowly dawn on me, that I was taking part in a contest which offered no prize.

Say I *did* manage to earn the universal dislike and distrust of men – what then? What would I do, once I'd achieved my life's ambition – retire to a convent? Slit my throat? This was a no-win situation and sooner or later, I would be the loser. I began to come to terms with that fact one Friday night when Amy and I had taunted and teased – and then gone home with – John and Gerry. And Rick and Tommy and Paul. Five of them – and not one a day over twenty. Swaggering and arrogant and amusing and pretty – but just boys, for all that. And I should have left them alone. But a year of bedding blokes had left me terminally bored. Jaded. Growing quite perverse.

Making love to one of them – was it Tommy or Paul? – I could make out Amy's form on the other bed. Was she with John or Gerry? Or both? It hardly mattered as we moved around, casually swapping partners the way other women swap smalltalk. I could tell the boys couldn't believe their luck – I was even mildly excited myself. But when I woke and stared around the room in the grey dawn light, I was suddenly horribly depressed.

I soon overcame that, of course. Extricated Amy from beneath the slumbering bodies, put on all my clothes (except my G-string, which I gently wound around Paul's big toe) before we crept out of the flat.

Wasn't that wild! We congratulated each other, as we sat in a taxi, laughing about the event. Thrilled with ourselves as we sped back to my flat through the deserted city. Wolfing down breakfast in my kitchen later, remarking on what group sex did for our appetites, we were interrupted by the shrill scream of the telephone. Paul was on the line. Then Tommy. (How had they found my number?) Amy listened in on my bedroom extension while we agreed it had been a gas – and why didn't we do it all again?

Four of them arrived later that afternoon (Rick had chickened out) weighed down with bottles of booze and they all sat around my living room, while Amy and I told them stories which left them in no doubt about our wealth of 'experience' – scaring them witless and exciting them half to death at the same time. Part of me was heady with the power of it all and the other half wanted to throw up, as the whole bizarre sexual performance started up again, and I spent that night, and a good part of the next day, wandering from bed, to sofa and back to the bed. By the Sunday evening, we'd screwed ourselves to a standstill and all six of us were piled into my bed, talking quietly now and, believe it or not, getting to know each other at last.

Then Paul remembered it was Mother's Day and we'd lain there quietly while he'd called his mum and apologized for not sending flowers. Then Gerry rang his mum and John rang his and I realized with a shock that their mums were probably only a couple of years older than me. . . .

Monday morning came and the boys had jobs to go to. Amy and I stood together in the bedroom doorway, fascinated as they tumbled around like puppies, naked and searching for Y-fronts, odd socks, trousers and shoes. I had to admit, they were a beautiful sight – every one tall and good-looking, with strong young bodies which gleamed in the morning light.

Yet part of me was sickened by the sight.

I reminded myself that they were basically nice lads – all friends since their schooldays and just out for experience, whenever and wherever they could get it. No one had been hurt, it was just a bit of harmless fun. I told myself all that, but it didn't make me feel any better about how I'd spent the last forty-eight hours.

For days afterwards, I was depressed. Trying to dispel the shadowy images of sweating bodies and excited young faces and greedy, exploring hands. Trying to forget the sounds – the soft sighing and scuffling, the smirking and whispering which had filled the endless nights.

Hannah had heard about our bizarre weekend – listening gravely as I'd described the events. I'd told it juicily, wickedly, and laced with a humour I was far from feeling – pretending I'd enjoyed it all. But Hannah wasn't fooled and her still, calm face told me better than words could that I'd set foot in a strange land which she didn't want to explore. Set out on a journey she would never make.

'You can still turn back – ' her eyes said. Although we both knew I wouldn't. Not yet. For I had to take everything to the limit – and that included feeling bad about myself.

Now it was that Hannah took a small, deliberate step back from me, wanting no part of whatever 'adventure' I might embark upon next. I could hardly blame her, for I sensed I was turning into the kind of woman the married me had always pitied. The type of callous, sneering, burned-out divorcee I'd promised myself I would never become. I was still angry, still vengeful, yet sad that I'd lost an important part of myself. The feminine part.

The girl Simon had wanted to settle down with and poor Ron had tried to save – she was fading fast. And the girl Rui married had completely disappeared.

That's what he'd thought when we met for our second lunch. I know, because I read it in his startled eyes, as I sauntered into our usual restaurant – my leather gear squeaking ominously and my metal bits jangling defiantly, as I'd sprawled in the chair opposite him. It was a few weeks after THAT weekend that he'd rung to suggest a meet. He'd wanted to discuss the final details of our divorce and, once that was dealt with, he'd made the mistake of asking me how things were.

I'd enjoyed telling him, leaving out none of the sordid details – and was rewarded by the fleeting expressions of incredulity, disappointment and even disgust which had appeared on his face.

'Why am I cheapening myself like this?' some small part of me wondered as I'd described the seediness of my life. But of course, I wanted him to know what *he* had turned me into and, as I'd hoped, he was saddened by how I looked, hurt by what I said and offended by the woman I'd become.

It was quite a performance and I'd kept it up until we'd said goodbye and I'd walked slowly off into the crowd. Then suddenly I'd been enveloped by a wave of exhaustion as I realized how much emotional energy I'd spent, trying to hurt this man I still claimed to love. And, for the first time, I'd asked the question: was there a chance that, in trying to get even with Rui and every other man, I could somehow be inflicting damage on myself? I'd dismissed the idea as crazy. Why should I want to hurt myself more than I'd been hurt already? It didn't make any sense. But, just in case it was true, I'd tried to mend my ways, for a while.

Tried going straight home after work, instead of heading for the wine bar. Watching telly, cooking supper, reading books – cooped up alone, I'd tried to occupy myself with all sorts of things. But sooner or later, the silence and the emptiness got to me – while the mere thought of having to spend the rest of my life like that, 'in solitary', was enough to send me scurrying to the nearest bar. There I would sit, my eyes boring into yet another unsuspecting male, until finally, he would notice me and buy me a drink. Hopefully, one drink would lead to another. And another. (For by this time, I could only entertain the thought of sex when I was more than halfway drunk.) And enough drinks would eventually lead to bed.

Crazy, wasn't it? I couldn't bear them, yet I still needed

men in my life. Knowing that, without them, I'd be reduced to sleeping and waking and living alone. A prospect I just couldn't handle, although I didn't understand why.

Now I know that living alone is easy – even a pleasure – once you're comfortable with yourself. Once you recognize – and like – who and what you are. But during that year of living lasciviously, I didn't like myself at all.

October came and went. Then November. The most miserable year of my life was drawing wearily to a close. December was just around the corner and London started tarting herself up for the festivities. By now, the talk was all of Christmas in New York – Amy's bright idea, since she had to fly out there on some more of her mysterious 'business' and wanted us to join her for the celebrations.

Hannah loved the idea and I went along with the plans half-heartedly, since the thought of pulling crackers and men no longer held the same appeal for me and it hardly mattered whether I did it in Maida Vale or Manhattan. In fact, that December, I was allergic to the very thought of celebrating Christmas anywhere, since it was fraught with memories of better times. Just as I loathed the prospect of New Year, with all its empty promise of better things to come.

The days passed in a flurry of parties and dinners, drunken nights and dismal mornings, when I woke to find myself in bed with yet another man about whom I knew little and cared even less. Still I kept on, a bright smile pasted to my face as I tried to ignore the warnings of that small, sane part of me which knew I was heading for disaster. Praying that something would stop me in my tracks – yet hardly able to believe it, when that finally happened. . . .

Saturday night again – and no sign of my playmates. Amy was coming down with the cold Hannah was just shaking off, so both of them were staying home. I'd have quite enjoyed staying home myself – if I'd had some company to get me through the night. As it was, I headed for Bruno and my usual bar stool and, sitting there, watching the same old crowd, I got chatting to a woman I'd met there a few times before.

Angie was in her late twenties, blonde and quite pretty,

although her face wore a slightly vacuous expression and her conversation, I soon discovered, was limited to clothes, money and men. Still, I'd long ago learned not to be too choosy about drinking partners and the evening passed painlessly enough, as we wandered from bar to bar, half-heartedly searching for talent.

It was around midnight, in a jazz club I never frequented, that we got caught up in a fairly boring conversation with an equally boring man.

Jeff, I could tell at a glance, was one of life's grunts. Dull body, dull clothes, dull voice lecturing us about his appallingly dull job, while a smug expression played about his instantly forgettable face.

Why did I agree to go back to his place for coffee? Boredom, I guess. And to please Angie, who actually seemed to be enjoying his mindless conversation – now that he'd moved onto clothes, holidays and his new compact disc player. Ugh! But it was either coffee at his place – which might kill another deadly hour – or straight home to bed – alone. Put that way, the choice was easy.

Grimly amused I realized once we'd reached his bedsit that Jeff was a man of his word. 'Coffee,' he said. And that was exactly what he meant, as he proudly started up his compact disc machinery and left us slumped on his floor cushions, while he disappeared into the kitchen. Sex was obviously the last thing on his mind – something the old me would have found oddly touching. But *this* me knew I was dealing with yet another wimp – and I could never resist making short work of these.

'Pathetic!' My eyes telegraphed the word to Angie, who smiled and shrugged good-naturedly, and, as I sat there, idly studying her, Malice took my hand and walked me into alien territory.

I can honestly say I wasn't attracted to her sexually as I took in her half-closed eyes and her shoulders, swaying rhythmically to the music. We were strangers, but I liked her well enough, since she seemed pretty game. Almost ready for anything . . . I realized, as I stepped into a strange land I'd visited once before. Then it had been six boys. Now it was a man and a woman. Empty sex. Pointless sex. And dangerous for me. Yet defiantly I would see it through. I smiled at Angie and she read the challenge in my eyes.

Wordlessly, she stood up and began to undress, while I did the same – a pulse beating slowly in my forehead and my movements effortless yet mechanical, as I left my clothes in a heap on the floor.

Humming and bumming his way backwards through the door, his eyes riveted on the piled up tray he carried, Jeff swivelled round to face us and all thought of coffee fled his dull brain, as he gaped open-mouthed at two naked women in his bed.

So it began all over again, that slow-motion, film-reel feel, as my world was reduced to sound and smell, softness and shadow, movement and heat. The strange sensation of a woman's arms about me and a woman's sweet breath on my cheek . . . the comforting weight of a man's leg and the salt of his sweat. Lips caressing my shoulder and hands caressing my lips . . . and my hands and lips with a life and a will of their own . . . the taste and aroma of skin wherever I turned . . . sinew and muscle and velvet soft curves. Then his eyes, unblinking . . . and hers, heavy-lashed. So close to me – and so far away. . . .

Part of me urgent and fearful, floating free to hover near the ceiling, watching me. Us. Knowing, yet not believing what I did and frantic to escape. Then, numbed by the many sensations, that part of me grew still and quiet. Settled down to wait and left the rest of me to my fate. . . .

I was lying on the outside of the bed. Angie slept soundly next to me, propped against my shoulder, while Jeff snored faintly, trapped between Angie's warm body and the wall. Neither of them moved as I got up and padded around in the dark, looking for my clothes – most of which I found. Two minutes later, I'd sneaked out of the flat, pausing just inside the front door to pull on my boots, and wind my coat closer about me. Then I checked the time – nearly four o'clock.

Outside it was raining – a fine drizzle which gleamed on the pavements and hung in misty rings around the street lamps. I welcomed the cold slick on my face as I walked. My footsteps echoing hollowly, I headed up Tottenham Court Road, along Marylebone and towards Regent's Park, my hair plastered to my head and my collar turned up. And I walked.

Every so often, tyres would hiss wetly, as a car or a taxi slid by, their passengers staring out at me, wraithlike, through misted windows. Once or twice, I saw another scurrying figure and once I heard voices raised in anger and a woman sobbing. And I walked.

Near the mosque, a black cab cruised by, its for hire sign a gold beacon in the night as its driver peered hopefully out at me. But I waved it on – and I kept on walking.

Walked and talked to myself – telling myself what I'd lacked the courage to admit before. That my life was a mess. And I was well and truly fucked up.

How long had it been since I'd got any pleasure out of doing simple things or had any innocent fun? How long since I'd felt interested in my business or satisfied with my work? When did I last wake up in the morning, looking forward to the day and knowing it was great to be alive? Come to that, how long had it been since I'd felt good about myself – or anyone else? How long since I'd felt capable of love – or worth loving?

The truth was, I was incapable of feeling *anything* like tenderness or kindness, sympathy or understanding. These were qualities I no longer possessed, I admitted. I hardly noticed which way I went, so deep was I in thought.

Then an image of the slumbering Angie filled my mind, and I realized with a chill that I couldn't even summon up a sense of shame or regret about that room and these people I'd just left. That's how far I'd slipped into the muck of my terrible, malicious anger.

Sex? You couldn't call it that – not what I'd just been doing. And it had been *my* idea! Maybe, if I'd really fancied Angie – if I'd felt even the most lukewarm attraction for Jeff – I might have been able to excuse myself. But I didn't even like them. No, we three had ended up in bed because I was terminally bored.

Or was it even worse than that? I wondered as I walked. Had we ended up together because I wanted sex to be sordid?

Wanted to destroy any idea that it might be beautiful – special? All the things I knew it was for *other people*.

But *why*? Why would I want to spoil something which used to give me so much pleasure?

Lovemaking . . . odd now to think how good it had made me feel, once. The thrill of being possessed by someone I cared for. The ecstasy of losing myself in a man who adored me. 'But baby, look at you now!' I said aloud, seeing myself for the first time the way other people probably saw me. Dried up and iced over, but my face, my clothes, my body, all still yelling defiance. I'd been sticking two fingers up at a world which remained indifferent in the face of my wrath, and blithely unconcerned about my fate. Dimly, I realized I'd boxed myself into a corner and now, I'd nowhere to go but down and nothing to look forward to. Except, maybe, more nights like tonight. My eyes filled with frightened tears at the thought. Hellbent on diminishing men – trying to offend their pride and hurt their dignity – I'd only succeeded in wounding myself. And, as I slipped through familiar streets and walked the last few yards to my flat, I was aware of an overwhelming sense of despair.

I was thirty-five, supposedly with my whole life ahead of me, yet I had programmed myself to self-destruct. And I'd thought *I* was getting even!

My mind raced as I let myself into the flat and I realized that, now I'd finally confronted myself, there was no way I could back off. I had some serious thinking to do and, knowing sleep was beyond me, I ran a bath instead – suddenly feeling grubby and desperate to rinse away all trace of Angie and Jeff.

I lit the bathroom with candles and the warm, enveloping glow calmed me a little, as I relaxed in the water and tried to work out how I really felt about myself. Confused, basically – because I seemed to be two different women at the same time.

All my life, I'd pretended to be In Charge and My Own Boss. But always, always, I'd wanted someone to hold my hand when the going got tough. Something Rui had never been able to do, although Simon tried. And now, Amy and Hannah were doing the hand-holding.

Was *that* it? Was I afraid of being alone, because it meant standing on my own two feet? Well, perhaps the time had come for me to prove to myself that I could do it, after all. But I'd *never* learn to cope alone here in London. Whenever things got difficult, I knew I'd leg it back to the girls and sooner or later, I'd be up to my old tricks again – cruising the bars and dragging home whatever company I could find. The bad bitch in me would always end up calling the shots and the rest of me was no match for her.

No – if I wanted to shake her off – and clean my act up – I was going to have to get the hell out of town. And stay away, until I'd learned how to take care of myself.

That was the answer. Simple. I'd have to close down my business, get rid of my flat and cut myself off from everyone and everything. The immensity of it made me catch my breath for a second, then I released it in a long, low incredulous whistle.

Could I really turn my back on my life – just walk away from *everything*? Then I thought of that tatty scene with Angie and Jeff; the weekend locked up with John and Gerry and Tommy and Paul. Remembered how I'd cheapened myself with Ron and Jamie. Thought of all the shits who were lining up to try their luck – and all the nice guys who would never give me the time of day.

Until finally I accepted it – the game was up and London was finished for me. Leaving might turn out to be disastrous, but I would surely be destroyed if I stayed.

It's strange how, once you make a decision to change your life, your life begins to change, almost of its own volition. How, once you stop looking for it, the thing you think you most want suddenly drops right into your lap.

What my days lacked right then was quality, while what *I* lacked was a sense of purpose and direction. What I missed most (although I wouldn't even admit it to myself) was the love and respect of a man I could genuinely care about. All of it beyond my reach, I was sure. Yet after that long night of self-appraisal in the bath, surprising things started to happen.

106

My dread of Christmas all but disappeared and I began to enjoy the festivities; getting a real kick out of our planned expedition to New York. Suddenly, I could hardly wait for New Year's Eve, since for me, it offered the chance of a fresh start – this miserable present would soon be a thing of the past.

Although I didn't let myself think about it too much (mainly because it scared me witless) I held on to the idea of getting the hell out of London. Suddenly I had something, somewhere, to aim for. Something new to think about. I stopped dreaming about the thing which, deep down, I wanted most. And wouldn't you know, that's the time it walked straight into my life!

I'd no sooner stopped looking for a man, when a man – in the uncompromising bulk of Henry C. Stone Jnr – found me. And for once, I was completely unprepared.

It was Christmas Eve and Manhattan lay under a blanket of snow. The roads were eerily deserted as a very few cars, their wheels bound up with chains, crept silently along Fifth Avenue and skated nervously down Park. The streets were another story – alive with New Yorkers hoofing it from this bar to that party – and the air was filled with laughter and good-natured chatter, as complete strangers wished each other 'Merry Christmas' in passing.

Although darkness had fallen, the scene was brilliantly illuminated by ribbons of electric colour which garlanded the street lamps, a whole army of winking Christmas trees and the glow from dozens of sumptuously decorated shop windows. Light spilled over the crisp, snowy pavements in rainbow-hued pools and caught the movement of a million softly falling snowflakes, as they dipped and swirled out of an icy sky. Grimy old Manhattan had turned into a winter wonderland and arm in arm, we three slipped and slithered our way downtown, like excited kids just out of school.

We'd been in Manhattan for four days and already I felt a little bit like I belonged there – yet another wide-eyed immigrant in the land of opportunity. Amy's quaint little Greenwich Village apartment had been welcoming, if cramped. On the second floor of a brownstone building, it was a monument to her ability to do a lot with nothing at all – its walls and floorboards painted matt white, its overstuffed chairs piled high with colourful cushions. The bathroom led off the kitchen, which meant that conversations could easily be conducted between bather and chef – the former frequently being called upon to taste a little of this and check the salt in that, as she worked up a lather in the big old Victorian tub.

The central heating system was ancient – the water rumbling, sighing and squeaking all night long as it gushed through the ornate radiators which Amy had sprayed a glittering gold. She'd also lacquered a couple of the doors and most of her plants with the stuff, presumably making full use of her bargain-sized paint can. The oddly iridescent hues of the resident roaches indicated that even they had fallen victim to her festive spruce up.

This latest insight into Amy's lifestyle was interesting; a tantalizing mixture of the genteelly shabby, yet stylishly chic. There might be nothing edible in the fridge but just one phone call had a uniformed Adonis on the doorstep in five minutes with a perfectly chilled bottle of wine. The front door might be sagging under the weight of endless bolts and chains, since Amy lived like one under siege but her answering machine poured forth a wealth of invitations from chic people to appear at smart places. Now, it suited her to look like a bag lady, her apparel consisting mostly of our cast-offs. Yet her wardrobe yielded up stylish evening dresses and cashmere coats – all the necessary accessories for some of her expensive past lives. And, doubtless, some of her future ones.

Her bedroom was dominated by a king-sized bed and a queen-sized telly. Each morning, the thin, silvery light of another Manhattan day would filter through her large, rain streaked windows onto the three of us tucked up together in her bed, laughing uproariously at any one of a dozen naff quiz games or talent shows.

Warm as toast beneath layers of T-shirts and ankle socks, sweaters and scarves, we'd pass most of the mornings gossiping under her duvet, while Johnny Carson strutted his stuff and the snowstorms rattled the window panes. Each day, one of us would wriggle into my mink coat and leg it off down to the steamy little Italian caff at the end of the block, where we'd order up double cappuccinos and freshly baked croissants to go. I, for one, would stand there waiting to be served – getting endless pleasure from the thought that, beneath the fur and the black leather boots, I was near as dammit naked.

The days were filled with sight-seeing and shopping, the evenings spent in smoky clubs or dimly lit wine bars where we put on our same old act for a new and appreciative audience. Oh, we really turned it on for New York – insisting it was our debut performance Stateside, yet each of us knowing this was probably the Stormtroopers' swansong. I wasn't the only one who was growing weary of the game.

Still, we put everything we had into our last public appearance and that Christmas Eve, decked out as usual in leather everything, we stormed our third bar in as many hours. Moments after arriving, Amy had found some old friends, Hannah had found the loo . . . and I had found Henry C. Stone Jnr.

Standing at the crowded bar, waiting to order up drinks, I hadn't even noticed him, so much was my technique slipping. Then I became aware of eyes – appraising and almost insolent as they slid over me, daring me to return the look. 'MY trick . . . ' I remember thinking, as I stared back defiantly. And there he was, draped across a bar stool, propping up his few inches of marble counter top. Massive. Immaculately dressed. Bored and staring at my legs.

'I like your shoes . . . ' he began, looking down at my high heels. I acknowledged the casual compliment with a curt nod. 'Like your stockings . . .' he continued, as he eyed my seamed mesh legwear. 'And your skirt . . . ' he added in a low, lazy drawl, his gaze travelling slowly upwards. 'Like that, too . . .' he went on, as his examination reached the level of my breasts. 'I presume you are referring to my shirt,' I commented haughtily. 'But of course,' he replied, finally making eye contact.

The first time ever I saw his face. Well, it was all there in Henry's face. Intelligent, arrogant, clever, youthful, sexy. Quite beautiful. Yet ancient, lonely, private, closed, selfish.

Utterly cold and beyond reach. 'Keep Off' was clearly etched on his smooth, high forehead, reflected in his huge, dark almond eyes. Written on his confident mouth and oozing from his smile. So the only person I can blame is me; for looking and choosing not to see that I'd encountered a layer and slayer of the opposite sex; highly sexual, highly sociable, yet highly suspicious: the irresistible challenge. A human being who couldn't love and wouldn't be loved. An emotional retard in a six-hundred-dollar suit. On Christmas Eve, in downtown Manhattan, I thought I'd met the man of my dreams.

And that's how it began. Badinage over the ice bucket led to smart quips over shared champagne, while I took in *his* nice shoes, *his* beautifully tailored suit, *his* flamboyant scarlet braces, *his* understated, heavy gold cufflinks. Mr Wall Street, by way of Harvard; and special, from his closely cropped head to his brightly polished toe caps. Expensive, smart-mouthed . . . and single. By the time the girls bundled me out of there an hour later, en route for the next bar, I'd certainly got Henry's number. And I'd made sure he'd got mine – although I wasn't convinced that he would really call. (Note the refreshing lack of self-confidence.)

It wasn't until the disapproving Southern Belle in Amy commented on it with a knowing wink that I registered the most surprising fact of all. That Henry C. Stone Jnr was completely and utterly – and no doubt *hugely (really*, Amy!) – black.

Until then, black men hadn't been on my list of things to do, for the simple reason that the possibility hadn't occurred. I'd never given them more than a passing glance or paused to contemplate the beauty of dark skin. In fact, until the evening I met Henry, I guess I hadn't been colour prejudiced so much as colour blind. For sure, I didn't fall for him because he was black, I fell for black because it was Henry.

A couple of days later he did phone and invited me to a party. I spent the evening listening to conversations rich in political satire, laced with wicked ethnic jokes and embroidered in a wealth of informed opinion. The assembled company – fairly reeking of success and awash with street cred – was

110

black. And it meant business. Overwhelmed by this whole new angle on life as I had known it and discrimination as I had understood it, I hardly cared that Henry, unlike most of my previous escorts, seemed to have more on his mind than bedding me and was rather intrigued when, at the end of it all, he deposited me back on Amy's doorstep and disappeared into the snowy Manhattan night.

Our second date, forty-eight hours on, proved just as stimulating. On that occasion, I was instructed to present myself at the Harvard Club for dinner at nine-thirty and, true to form, I swanned into the restaurant a few minutes before ten. The smile didn't quite reach his eyes as he rose to greet me and said, 'You're late. However, you were well worth the wait . . .' and the gaze began to work its way up from my shoes again. Idle and half-interested. Did I have him or didn't I? I just wasn't sure and the uncertainty was deliciously nerve-racking.

Halfway through the meal, he suddenly drawled, 'I hate to do this but I'm going to have to cut our dinner date short. I have to get back to the office – expecting some information from Tokyo.'

Since I'd only just tucked into my duck en croûte, this news was less than pleasant to digest and my look must have said it all.

'Try not to look too outraged,' he remarked. 'After all, if you had turned up at nine-thirty, as I suggested, there would have been time for coffee. As it is . . .' And then, just as I felt what I call my 'lethal look' slipping masklike across my stunned face, he held up his hands in an expression of surrender.

'Okay – you're mad. I guess you have a point. What do you say to *dessert*, a little later?' and his gaze was wide-eyed and innocent, the smile giving nothing away. Having already realized that we two spoke different languages, albeit in the same tongue, I now wondered if this perfectly simple word in the English dictionary had some other, more exotic implication for Americans. *Dessert* . . . What on earth did it mean? There was only one way to find out.

Twenty minutes later, I was slipping through city streets in the back of a chauffeur-driven stretch limo. Still amazed at the submissive way in which I'd allowed him to separate me from my delicious duck; still intrigued by erotic images of *dessert*.

It turned out to be a fantastic concoction of wild cherries and walnuts, flambéed in brandy and served up on delicious, wafer-thin crêpes with a mountain of cream; and I ate it at two-forty in the morning in a totally different, totally deserted restaurant. I'd been wakened from sleep by a phone call, staggering to the receiver to hear Henry's decisive, alert voice informing me that the chauffeur was waiting for me downstairs.

Of course, I could have told him to bugger off and gone back to bed. So why did I dress, make up and brave the sub-zero night all over again? I guess I was hungry, folks. Sitting opposite him, seriously impressed and lost for words, I concentrated on my food and tried to ignore Henry's amused glance. Knowing that I had anticipated something altogether more obvious, if less imaginative, he sat back in the velvet upholstered chair and pushed his plate, untouched, to one side. 'Like it?' he asked. Then he laughed, sensing that dessert wasn't the only thing which I was enjoying just then.

I could feel the blush spreading across my cheeks and admitted to myself that the son of a bitch had got me. Realized to my dismay that I was falling for Henry – hard. Falling for the fact that he wasn't falling for me. Wasn't smitten – wasn't even mildly interested, it appeared – and wouldn't play any of my games. Didn't need to, since he'd thought up such clever little mind games of his own – bringing his own ball and making up the rules as we went along.

By 4 am, I was tucked up in bed again, listening to Hannah's even breathing in the next bed and wondering about this man. This ambitious, brilliant, self-centred man who was making money hand over fist, but only as a means to an end. This man with heady political ambitions, who figured that being the first black mayor of New York was a logical first step on the road to where he wanted to go. I had never – HAVE never – met anyone like him. And long before he'd deposited me, untouched, on Amy's doorstep for a second time that night,

112

I'd decided that Henry C. Stone Jnr was the man for me. The problem was, how did I convince *him* of this fact?

By the 30th of December I was a puddle of nervous anticipation. Partly because the pagan in me laid far too much store by everything that did and didn't happen each time the last few hours of an old year seeped away. And partly because I had Henry C. Stone Jnr on the brain. He still hadn't laid a hand on me.

Foolishly, I'd thought I might give him a run for his money. Yet he was permanently one step ahead of me – a thought which was exciting, challenging and disconcerting, all at the same time.

As I dressed for dinner that night, Amy gave me a long look and a word of advice. 'Honey, you're dealing with Manhattan Man. An endangered species. There's one of him to every five available women and nobody's caught him yet.' And then: 'Enjoy him – he's as good a way as any to get to know Manhattan. But don't take it too seriously – he sure as hell won't.'

Good advice, but it had come too late. Much later that night, we sat huddled together in the back seat as the limo crept towards Greenwich Village and slid to a halt in front of Amy's brownstone. For a moment neither of us spoke and I sat there, enjoying Henry's body warmth as the snow beat against the car in soundless flurries. Then: 'Your place, Red' he stated matter-of-factly and I turned to face him, a little surprised at what sounded like a curt dismissal. 'Or would you prefer mine?' he went on. 'You can show me how you Scots make coffee.'

His place was a cavernous loft high up above the city, full of weird sculptures and thriving greenery. Stripped floorboards, large white sofas, a high tech kitchen. The bedroom was spartan – the walls bare, apart from a stylish aluminium racing bike which was suspended opposite the bed. Long after we had made love, long after Henry's massive body had relaxed against mine in sleep, I lay there and watched that bicycle frame glowing silver in the dark. Now I was even more intrigued by this man who could submit to the intimacy of sex and still give nothing of his real self away.

Early morning and I stirred in my sleep, pretending not to be aware of the fact that he had slipped quietly out of bed. Seconds later, he'd gone, closing the door silently behind him and I was left to ponder my next move. How would Manhattan Woman handle it – pick up her knickers and walk or demand coffee and the courtesy of a 'goodbye' before she hit the street? I decided to stay put until either my nerve broke or he showed me the door.

He was gone for what seemed like a very long time and I nearly wept with relief when I heard his keys rattle in the front door and he came whistling past the bedroom door. I heard the sound of rushing water and a little later, he came quietly into the room, bent across the bed and fondled my shoulders and back, while I feigned sleep.

Wordlessly, he rolled me over, then effortlessly picking me up in his arms, he strolled out of the bedroom and down the hallway. The bathroom was large and windowless, the floor strewn with rugs. It was a study in Victoriana, from the potted palms and the immense handbasin to the huge, white porcelain bath shored up on clawed feet. An impressive room – and a perfect setting for someone as high, wide and handsome as Henry. But the most amazing thing of all was the lighting.

As he gently lowered me into the foaming, sudsy water, enveloping me in the heat and steam, I gazed in quiet wonder at the three or four dozen candles he had taken the trouble to light. All around me, the tiny flames flickered in the darkness, their glow reflecting warmly on Henry's naked torso as he stepped out of his tracksuit and began to bathe me.

The sensation was *wonderful* as, squeaky clean all over, I lay back in the hot water, unable to believe my luck. Kissing me lightly on the forehead, he left the room 'To fix some breakfast' he informed me, turning back in the doorway to toss something into the water. As I searched for it in the suds, the object shot to the surface and bobbed about with a silly smile on its face. And I smiled inanely back, knowing I was lost. For who could help falling in love with a powerhouse who had everything – including his very own yellow plastic bath duck?

And so the last day of the old year slipped away, while

Henry and I curled up together on his vast sofa, playing jazz records and watching old movies. I was blind to the darkening sky and the fierce snowstorm raging outside, oblivious to everything except Henry. Illogically afraid that Henry might also be oblivious to everything, including me, I'd found what I'd only ever dreamed of – a man who excited me. Yet in just a few days, I knew I was going to lose him again. It just didn't seem fair, I kept saying, as Hannah and I rushed around Amy's apartment on our last evening in New York. We'd left our packing until the very last moment and now we were throwing clothes into bags, searching for passports and airline tickets amid the chaos which reigns when three women try to share a postage-stamp-sized flat. Soon, I was bewailing not only the loss of the lovely Henry but also the loss of my raspberry coloured mohair sweater and my lovely art deco earrings which had cost a fortune in Harrods.

Hannah was too concerned about her missing grey leather belt and a pair of white woolly ankle socks to spare me any sympathy, and as Amy bundled us out of the apartment and down to the waiting taxi, we were making so much noise that we almost didn't hear the telephone ring. I grabbed the receiver to hear Henry's voice coming lazily down the line.

'You all set, Red?' he asked. 'I'd like to come to the airport, but I'm waiting for an urgent call from Paris. . . .'

At that, my heart sank. I'd hoped for one last glimpse of him before I headed home – since yesterday and last night, the day before and all the other glorious nights had left me still hungry. Still needing more of this enigmatic man who had given me nothing – not the merest sign or smallest word – to encourage what had become my total infatuation. Yet, as I stood there wondering how to say goodbye, he gave it to me now.

'Look, Red . . . I find it difficult to convey my feelings. But these last few days have meant a lot to me. I know we'll have more just like them. This isn't the end. And, Red – I love you.' And then the line went dead.

I floated down to the street and into the yellow cab. Hardly felt Amy's warm kiss on my cheek or noticed the desperate way she hugged us both. All I knew was that Henry loved me and somehow, I would have it all again. Knowing *that*, I could get through anything.

'God, we're running late. . . .' Hannah's anxious voice broke through my thoughts, as the taxi took off and we both turned to wave goodbye out of the back window. Amy stood in the middle of the street, her face happy/sad as she waved us off wildly. 'Poor Amy, I feel rotten, leaving her behind,' she added. Then suddenly she let out a yelp. 'Shit – did you see that? She's wearing my bloody belt – and I've been looking all over for it!'

'Yep, I see it. *And* your socks!' I giggled, as the taxi picked up speed and Amy's figure receded. Then I burst into peals of laughter, knowing that the impecunious but opportunistic Amy had struck again.

'I'm glad you can see the funny side of it – especially since she's also wearing your earrings,' Hannah remarked icily. Then, seeing my incredulous expression, 'Oh, it's true. I noticed them when I kissed her goodbye . . . ' And then she burst into laughter, too.

We settled down as the taxi raced through the gathering dusk towards the airport and I silently took my leave of that magical city as we crossed the river and raced away from its unforgettable skyline. I smiled as I thought of Amy and pondered the fate of my mohair sweater . . . well, it had always looked better on her. But I was less philosophical about my other loss. Jewellery, sweaters, I could always replace. But would I ever find a substitute for Henry C. Stone Jnr?

The short answer was 'no'. Back in London, I told myself it had been one more fling – part and parcel of Christmas in Manhattan and nothing to get excited about. Might even have started believing that too, if it hadn't been for the phone calls.

Middle-of-the-night ones and pre-dawn ones. Long, hot, sticky ones; suggestive and salacious and sometimes down-right dirty as we lay in beds on opposite sides of the world and gave each other plenty to think about. That's when one or other of us was feeling horny. Other times, the calls were soft and sad. Whispered words full of missing and yearning, as his midnight loneliness interrupted my early morning solitude; or my 3 am insomnia call was slotted in between his nine o'clock Tokyo link-up and his nine-twenty check-in with LA.

February saw me flying back to Manhattan, determined to find out whether Henry C. Stone Jnr was the stuff of my future or a figment of my imagination. He turned out to be neither.

Oh, he was real enough and, in many ways, even better than I'd remembered. Just as funny, sophisticated, charming and infuriating as the man I'd met on Christmas Eve. And seemingly more crazy about me than ever. I tried to tell myself it was mere coincidence that his passion seemed to be fuelled by the news of my impending journey. But for a man who wants to evade capture, there's nothing more attractive than a woman who will shortly be taking off in the opposite direction. Nothing easier than lavishing love and attention on someone who's a temporary fixture.

Intent on escaping London, I'd begun to think that New York would be as good a place as any to begin again. This was something the Manhattan Man in Henry had quickly sensed and, as the days passed, he did his best to discourage me. Work suddenly loomed large and he hardly left the office, while I spent empty days mooning around his apartment, buying flowers he never noticed and cooking meals he was never there to eat. He would leave me each morning, long before first light; often coming home around ten or eleven each evening to find me sitting in the dark, staring moodily out at the city.

Once or twice, he invited me to join him for dinner downtown and on both occasions, we ended up back in his office, while he made his inevitable middle-of-the-night calls all over the world. I was depressed the first time I went there. Oh, the desk was big and the carpet was thick, the walls tastefully hung with limited editions of rare prints. But Henry's office was deep in the bowels of the earth, far below the pavements of Wall Street, and it made me sad to think that he went to work in the dark, headed home in the dark and hardly ever saw the light of day, although he just laughed when I remarked on it. Henry was *making money*. Henry was *going*

117

places. Henry was a man with a *mission* and, in the face of that, seeing the light was hardly a serious priority.

Strangely enough, he still talked about *our future* and all the things we would do, once I returned from my journey. Almost as if making this trip was some kind of a test I was required to pass, before Henry would take me or my emotions seriously.

I couldn't quite work him out. He insisted he was a loner and he jealously guarded his space; yet he seemed lonely. Sometimes he put up all sorts of barriers and I lost heart. Other times he held onto me as if he'd never let me go. When he wasn't refusing to talk at all, he was telling me all sorts of things about his childhood – desperate to communicate who he was and what he wanted from a relationship. Yet I could get no answer to the question – did he, or didn't he, want me?

In desperation one day, I'm ashamed to say, I conducted a little detective work in his apartment, eventually unearthing the kind of evidence – letters, cards and photographs – which proved beyond doubt that Henry *was* that mythical creature, the smiling layer and slayer of women. Lots of them, according to the pathetic clutch of letters; all would-be snarers of the eligible Mr Stone and all of them convinced that he was almost in their grasp.

And seeing *my* cards, *my* photographs, *my* letters in that sad little pile, I knew I was wasting my time. Falling for Henry had been one more mistake to add to the many I'd already made. Whatever lay ahead of me, taking Manhattan by storm wasn't part of it. Whoever I might turn out to be, I wasn't likely to become Mrs Henry C. Stone Jnr.

Of course, I told him none of that the evening I flew home. Just explained I had plans to make and things to arrange. Said how good it had been to see him; how I hoped we'd meet up again. Two people talking about how 'real' it had been and nobody mentioning love.

I'd been back in London almost a week, when the phone rang in the middle of the night and my hand hovered above the receiver, as the noise echoed through the quiet flat. It was four in the morning – eleven in the evening, New York time, and Henry was just a moment away. Calling from his neon lit office on a spring night in Manhattan – no doubt tired and melancholy at the end of a long day. Desperate to be cheered up and needing to unload.

I sensed the conversation would be a gentle one; sad and regretful, sweet and romantic. Maybe I would even find a contrite Henry at the end of the line – desperately in love with me after all. Unable to face life without me and anxious for a chance to prove it. . . .

So I lay there – idly imagining all the things I would like him to say and skipping over the things I wouldn't want to hear – while the phone rang on and on. Then it stopped, and in the stillness, my flat, and my heart, felt horribly empty.

Chapter Eight

Can't bear to go.
Don't dare to stay

February in London means Chinese New Year celebrations in Soho. It was the first night of the Year of the Rat and in and around Gerrard Street the celebrations were still in full swing, despite the torrential rain. However, the weather had beaten us and we'd fled the street party to take refuge, half-drowned, in our usual bar. Now, with Amy on my right and Hannah on my left, I sat disconsolately in the dim yellow light of the place, while Bruno served up large brandy-laced coffees and the mournful tones of Albinoni wandered between the deserted stools and tables. Saturday night – and the whole world had stayed home, cowed by the tempestuous storm. Jesus, what a long, miserable winter. I could hardly remember a day it hadn't been pissing down with rain.

'God – I can't stand much more of this,' I muttered, eyeing the drab scene.

'Well, you don't have to, da-arling, you'll soon be gone,' Amy drawled. 'Still, it rains just the same everywhere,' she admonished. 'And you won't even have *us* for company.' She fixed me with a baleful eye. I was in no doubt, yet again, that Amy was furious with what she saw as my desertion.

She'd been non-committal when I'd first broken my news but, now that she'd had time to think it over, she'd realized that my departure would mean a sudden shift in the happy balance of our three-way friendship. And that in turn could affect her relationship with Hannah – for better or worse? Who knew? And *that* might drastically change London life as Amy had known it.

She could smell the wind of change blowing through the ranks and she didn't like it much. I'd been the first to defect, but she guessed it wouldn't stop there. (She didn't know then that, just weeks after I disappeared, she herself would head back to America and the Stormtroopers would be disbanded forever.)

'Ah, yes . . . ' she sighed, sniffing the brandy aroma as she raised her cup to her lips. 'I think you're in for quite a shock, my deah!' This last uttered in her Southern Belle whine. 'I can just see you, on a night like tonight – all alone in the middle of nowhere. Wet and miserable and shivering in some doorway. Like a lost puppy dog – ' Her eyes and her smile were quite cold, as she added, 'Hmmm, I don't know about the Year of the Rat so much. This could well turn out to be the year of the puppy!'

I knew she was baiting me, but I was too disconcerted by her remarks to react. It was Hannah who intervened, saying, 'Well, Trudy, if things get too unbearable, you know we're only a phone call away.' And then, looking me straight in the eye, 'And you know you can call me any time – day or night, if you feel like talking.'

'Yes, yes! And that goes for me, too,' Amy butted in, knowing she'd taken the joke too far, as usual.

'What – even if it's reverse charge?' I'd asked witheringly, since Amy's generosity rarely stretched to her wallet.

'Yes – even then!' she laughed. 'But only if it's an emergency.'

'And how will you know it's an emergency?' I pressed on, stung by her brittleness.

'Oh – just say it's the puppy calling. And then I'll accept – promise!'

I could feel Hannah's sad eyes upon me and I thanked my lucky stars for her, yet again. She'd been upset too, when I'd announced I was leaving. But whereas Amy's reaction had been based in selfishness, Hannah was apprehensive for *my* sake. Because she was the only person who knew how scared I was about going.

Of course, word had quickly spread about my latest madcap idea and the question on everyone's lips was *why*? Since I seemed to enjoy an action-packed social life and owned a business which practically ran itself and (supposedly) had me laughing all the way to the bank, it was an obvious enough question, which was put to me lots of times, over drinks, over lunches, during chats on street corners. And my reply always differed.

To people I hardly knew, I threw out a typical Culross quip. Something along the lines of: 'I'm off in search of a rich husband!' or 'My accountant insists I've earned a year off!' as I played the game to the bitter end.

To people I knew better, I'd admit, 'I need the break – I've really had it with London.' Or even: 'I think it's time I moved on. Maybe I'll settle down someplace else.'

But Hannah was the only one who'd heard the truth, that I didn't know why I was going. Or where, or for how long. Or what I thought it would achieve. I only knew I daren't stay. And Hannah, bless her, understood. She'd sensed I was on dangerous ground long before I did. And the fact that she never once tried to persuade me to stay, showed me just how much trouble she thought I was already in.

Yet, once I left London, where the hell *was* I going to go? Mostly I didn't think about it. Then one night curled up on the sofa with Angus and a bottle of wine (I'd taken to practising Being Alone, in preparation for the real thing) I'd rooted out an atlas, just to see what I could see.

Thus it was in a slightly intoxicated, not quite serious frame of mind, that I'd planned my trip. I'd always fancied seeing Spain – haciendas and castles and vast rolling plains – and a few months on the Continent seemed sensible. It would get me used to the heat, the change of routine and my new, solitary status. And if any or all of the above proved too much for me, I was within easy striking distance of home.

Then there were the Greek Islands. And Rhodes – the place Rui had once suggested we spend our honeymoon, I remembered with a grimace, as I stabbed a finger at it viciously. Well, I'd bloody well see it now! From there, Egypt was a fingernail away. A land steeped in mystery, with its Blue and White Niles and its coal-black Nubians.

Burma . . . now *that* was a place that had always fascinated me, too. Rangoon and the road to Mandalay. Visions of swamps, tropical forests, brightly hued birds and torrential rains, filled my mind. But Burma lay to the east of India . . . Oh, well, what the hell! I'd just have to take in India, too. Then there were the exotic attractions of neighbouring Thailand. And, a mere two inches on the map from Burma lay Java. Another wonderful name to conjure with. And I hadn't realized till now it was practically tagged onto the end of Singapore. Hmmm. . . .

The more my wine-misted vision slid across the pinks, greens, blues and yellows of the map, discovering one exotic oasis after another, the more enthusiastic I began to feel. I'd take it all one step – one colour – at a time, I decided. Let loose the nomad in me and see where I ended up.

It was even beginning to sound like fun, I concluded, shutting the atlas with a determined snap and drinking to a job well done. Really, travelling was easy, once you got yourself organized.

Next morning, my newly-acquired confidence and optimism had vanished the moment I opened my eyes – although the hangover had stayed all day. Still, when anyone asked me my route after that, I was able to reel off a list of countries without hesitation.

So many places, such a long way . . . I could see the doubt in their eyes, as even my most encouraging friends wondered if I would really get that far. I could hardly blame them, since I didn't think I'd make it to Heathrow airport without throwing a complete wobbly!

Amy obviously sensed this, as she pressed home her attack.

'Don't worry, Hannah,' she reassured her with a wink. 'Our girl will be back before you know it. She'll hang around Spain just long enough to get a gorgeous tan. Then she'll be home to show it off!'

Laughing, she ordered up another brandy and, as he poured the golden liquid into her glass, Bruno gave me a long, speculative look. He missed nothing, ever. And he'd missed nothing that night.

'Trudeee . . .' he began in his sexy Parisian accent. 'When you get to Thailand, you must veeseet a place called Ko-

Samui. Eet ees very underdeveloped and quite beautiful, I understand,' and he repeated the name for me again, before sliding off with a smile and a nod.

'*When* you get to Thailand,' he'd said. Not 'if' but 'when'. Bruno at least was rooting for me, which was nice. Ko-Samui, eh? Well, I'd certainly bear that in mind.

And so, as the first night of the Year of the Rat drew to a close, I headed home, with Amy's words ringing in my ears. *Would* my jaunt really be nothing more than a quick zap to Spain and back? Or would this turn out to be the Year of the Puppy after all – complete with middle-of-the-night phone calls from God-forsaken parts of the world?

I wondered idly what would constitute an emergency in Amy's book. If I lost my make-up bag, say – would that be one? Or if I lost my Spanish-English phrasebook? What if I was near to losing my life? Would she fork out on a puppy call then?

Not such an unlikely prospect. For the more I'd thought about my coming trip, the more I'd had the strangest feeling that something very bad was going to happen to me. Something quite final. And naturally, that had coloured the way I felt about going.

I'd tried to explain this to Peter over lunch a few weeks later – how I had this premonition almost, of dying. But how I wanted to make the journey in spite of it.

'Or maybe even *because* of it?' he'd commented shrewdly, as I'd been halfway through my explanation. Peter knew better than most how, slowly but surely, my life had been coming apart at the seams. Unable to do anything to help, he'd watched the unattractive change in me. Watched me develop – as he'd neatly put it – 'a mind like a basket of worms'.

'Okay – if you really think you might end up dead, then why are you going, for chrissakes? Just answer me that,' he went on in the face of my outraged denial. '*You* can call it a premonition if you like. Seems to me, it's more of a bloody deathwish . . . ' And he sat back, his face suffused with anger and sadness and worry.

Well, maybe he's got a point . . . I conceded to myself, as

I took a sip of my wine. Although I couldn't accept that I wanted to end up dead, I had to admit that part of me was growing increasingly ambivalent about the business of living. At least, living the way *I* had been. Looking back on those twelve years with Rui, not to mention these three awful years since our break-up – well, it all seemed so bloody pointless. And, in my bleak frame of mind, death might have been preferable to more of the same miserable existence.

And as usual, Peter had worked this out ahead of me. So, in order not to fire him up even more, I refrained from telling him how my premonition had been sufficiently real for me to prepare for the event. And now, everyone who had ever mattered to me was neatly provided for in my will.

To my parents, my flat, my business interests, my bank account (if I'd known then what I discovered later, I might also have added 'my extensive debts'). To my mother, my mink coat . . . to Hannah, my sad little art collection . . . to Amy, the watercolour on silk she'd coveted for so long . . . to Colin, £4,000, provided he completed his studies (he couldn't be a fireman forever) . . . to Rui £1,000 to be spent on a party – with me as the absent guest of honour.

But no, I wouldn't trouble Peter with any of that. Instead, I told him, in great detail, about my recent trip home to Scotland. About the weather, the food, the fishing. What I didn't tell him was my real reason for heading home. My parents. And my awful sense of guilt about the way I'd treated them for the last eighteen years.

In the beginning, it had been my anger with them which had made me keep my distance. The eighteen-year-old me hadn't taken kindly to being chief cook and bottle washer, charlady and babyminder for most of my life and it was quite a few years before I could begin to view my childhood with anything other than a very jaundiced eye. And then, my parents were being kept on the fringes of my life for quite a different reason. For by the time I was Rui's wife my folks just didn't fit in with my image of who I liked to think I was. Hadn't I become this cool, worldly, sophisticated type, happily jetting between

Lisbon and London, going to and giving lavish parties, living the glamorous life?

Wasn't I the wife with the lover *and* the husband who kept mistresses? Now, just where did my practical, hard-working, down-to-earth parents fit in with all of that? The simple answer was that they didn't – wouldn't even want to. Or at least, that's what I told myself before simply excluding them from my world.

Was I ashamed of them – of my background? You know, it wasn't even as straightforward as that. It was the same old problem – they wouldn't have approved. And, God help me, I still couldn't bear the thought of their disapproval. What's more, they might have given the game away – blown the whistle on their sham of a daughter. Taken her down a much-needed peg or two, with all her smart talk and lah-di-dah ways.

There was no way I could court *that* kind of a disaster. So, apart from a fortnightly phone call and a yearly visit home, I'd pretty much kept my distance from them. Until I'd become pregnant. And then my mother had been a tower of strength. Dreading the thought that I might actually have the baby (thereby condemning myself to a life not so unlike her own), my mother nevertheless tried not to influence me, as we discussed it over the telephone. I think her sigh of relief was heard echoing across the Scottish hillsides when I finally decided on the termination. But if my decision had gone the other way, I know she would have helped me all she could.

They'd both been so understanding about the separation – apportioning no blame and taking no side in the argument. My mother had even avoided her usual gunboat diplomacy when she'd met Rui for lunch, shortly after we parted. She simply listened to his side of the story and drew her own conclusions. Even Dad tried to understand, when the unpleasant facts emerged about my lengthy affair, and he'd simply concluded that there were faults on both sides.

It was around then that I began to realize what a stalwart, caring pair they really were. Yet I'd no sooner recognized their worth and been warmed by the idea of getting to know them better, than I'd found myself turning into the kind of daughter who didn't deserve them. For by then I was operating in a sad little world that I'd grown more and more ashamed of. A world I was determined to keep from them at all costs, since they never could have understood. And so it had begun again – the careful stories, the deceits. Always keeping them at arm's length, in case they should discover the truth about me.

Until now, when – hellbent on escaping at all costs and dogged by the feeling that I wouldn't be coming back – home had begun tugging at my heartstrings. Making peace with my parents was something I knew I had to do.

Scotland's a beautiful country! The March mornings were cold, crisp and clear – hills cloaked in soft green velvet and veiled in lilac mist. Sleepy villages nestled in silent valleys, while curling blue smoke drifted up into the still air. And I gazed at it all in wonder, sad that I'd turned my back on it for so many years.

Strolling down deserted lanes with my parents, scrunching withered leaves underfoot, I watched as Angus (who'd found a new home) sniffed ecstatically in the mossy banks. They'd been thrilled to hear I was coming home – confused by my travelling plans. My poor mum wanted nothing more than for me to find a nice man and settle down. So much so that, once she'd recovered from the shock of Simon's age, she'd even been rooting for *him*, when he'd proposed! Now, the news that I was setting out, alone on a long journey, had filled them both with quiet worry.

I was full to bursting with all the things I wanted to say – all the confessions I would have liked to have made. For then, at least, they would understand why I needed to leave. But, of course, I wouldn't say any of it.

It had taken me all this time to realize my parents weren't fools. How much did they know about my life already – how much had they guessed at? Enough. I could see it in their eyes and knew that they should be spared the gory details. Wasn't it sufficient that I was here and we were comfortable together at last?

I found myself studying them more closely than I'd done for a long time – and saw with dismay that I wasn't the only one who was getting older. My father had some money worries and I realized, from the weary droop of his shoulders, that they were leaving their mark. My mother, still pretty, smiled at me as we walked through dappled sunshine. The strength still flowed from her – and that fierce determination. But when had her hair turned so completely snowy white?

We'd never talked about love, the three of us. These were the sort of soppy discussions my dad couldn't even bear to witness on television programmes. Soap opera stuff, where emotions ran high. Not like real life – our life – where a soft glance or a bit of gentle teasing were the only show of affection permitted. So I said none of the things I'd gone home to say. Not even that I loved them – which would have embarrassed them both no end and then worried them even more. Instead, we laughed and reminisced and they enthused about the coming journey because, in their quiet, intuitive way, they sensed I needed all the encouragement I could get.

Even as I made little of it, insisting I'd be home again before they knew it, I wondered if they guessed how afraid I was. Had they sensed I'd come home to say goodbye?

The little sixteen-seater mail plane bounced over the tarmac and lifted easily off the runway at Dundee airport. It swung out over the dark, brooding waters of the River Tay, hopped playfully over the bridge and pointed its nose in the direction of the rising sun, as I strained for one last glimpse of Scotland, draped in early morning shadow.

As we'd hared down the tiny runway, I'd clearly seen my folks, huddled together against the cold – my mother's heather tweed coat a flash of colour against the grey barrier, as they'd waved goodbye, in the forlorn hope that I could see them.

Then, my throat tight with tears, I'd settled back in my seat and pondered that sad, sweet little weekend. Knowing I'd made my peace with home as best I could, yet knowing that my best hadn't been nearly good enough. . . .

But I wouldn't tell Peter about that, either. Instead, we lingered on over this, our last lunch together, and our conversation meandered gently through the past and the present.

As he talked, I watched his expressive face, remembering how important he'd once been to me . . . oh, such a long time ago.

These days, I felt like that all the time I was with old friends. Sort of happy-sad at the same time. The business of maybe not coming back, the fear of dying, suddenly made lots of what I'd taken for granted so very precious.

So I was careful never to utter the words again, once I'd spoken them to Peter. Instead, like any child, I kept my eyes on the pavement of my mind – ever watchful not to tread on the cracks, as I skipped faster and faster over the stones and the weeks to my departure.

So much to do . . . so much to do. Close the business. Settle the accounts. Rent the flat. Store my clothes. Fix my visas. Get my jabs. Throw a party. Say goodbye . . . say goodbye . . . say goodbye. Yet, painstakingly tying up all the loose ends of my old life, I still steadfastly refused to make any serious plans for my new one. For this journey to God alone knew where.

March slipped into April and I changed my mind a dozen times. Found lots of good reasons for going nowhere.

I was seriously short-sighted and much weaker than I looked . . . I didn't speak any languages . . . I was terrified of spiders and I was always getting car sick . . . I had a lousy sense of direction (thank you, Bruno, for the compass!) . . . I couldn't live without my heated rollers . . . I was much too old to hump around a bloody rucksack . . . I'd miss the Peggy Lee concert – and what was that someone said about Ella Fitzgerald at the Albert Hall? I'd miss two of my favourite singers, goddammit . . . And then it would be my birthday quite soon, shouldn't I stay put for that? Shit, maybe my timing was completely out. When *was* the monsoon season in India? Wouldn't I hit it bang on, if I left now?

On and on and on it went, this pathetic dithering. Yet all the time, I knew I'd have to go. For my announcement had captured the imagination of everyone I knew. All these victims of divorce, unrequited love, thwarted ambition, failed business, advancing middle-age or just plain boredom. Imprisoned in their Porsches, defying London's rush hour; fighting hopeless rearguard actions in boardrooms; deceiving husbands and wives, only to be deceived in turn by lovers and mistresses . . . they'd all dreamed of just walking away from it all. One day.

But I'd foolishly said that I was getting out now and they sensed that I was as close as any of them would ever get to The Great Escape. Now, too many people were watching, just waiting for me to call the whole thing off. And, while they might forgive me for being a coward, I'd never be able to forgive myself.

So as April warmed and blossomed, I found I was caught up in a new kind of social whirl and I spent all my time running between pubs and wine bars, downing last drinks with people who wanted to hug and kiss me and send me on my way.

Did they suspect my nerve was failing? Perhaps. And of course it was. By now I knew how Joan of Arc must have felt before her last battle. Or Mrs Smith upstairs, the night she enrolled at Weight-watchers. Because sometimes, there's no backing out of a decision without looking like the world's worst wimp. And this was turning out to be one of those times.

But even if I'd wanted to cling to my old life, it was irrevocably turning its back on me. I just didn't fit in any more, although once or twice I had tried.

Sometimes, I would drift into one of my old haunts, hoping to lose myself for a while in the old crowd. I'd stand there, drinking in the noisy dimness or chatting up some man (old habits die hard!). But suddenly I'd take a step backwards in my mind and watch myself laughing and joking, desperately joining in the revelry. And I would know with a sinking feeling that part of me had already broken free and only the shadow of myself remained. . . .

May the twelfth . . . and down at the Medical Centre, business was brisk as usual and they were doing a roaring trade in the more exotic lines – cholera, rabies, yellow fever, typhoid. I'd experienced the heady delights of most of these cocktails already and I sat patiently in the cubicle, while the doctors checked through my list of vaccinations to date.

The last of the needles rammed home, as I stared at the world map on the wall opposite – the malaria-infested areas clearly shaded and plentiful. Such a big world. I wondered how much of it I would actually get to see.

Dressed again, I paid my final bill, stepped out into the milling Regent Street crowd and headed for my office by way of Piccadilly Circus and Leicester Square. I strolled past garish souvenir shops, glimpsed hitch-hikers sitting disconsolately on the steps of Eros. Walked by cinema houses, the gaudy flashing lights of amusement arcades, past dog-eared photographs of naked girls, flapping dejectedly in the doorways of strip joints.

London. I soaked it all up. Took it all in. This place had been my home for the last eighteen years and in a week, two at the most, it would all be just a memory. So I wandered through the crowd, trying to ignore the dull ache in my arm and the fluttering in my stomach. Thinking of the one good-bye I still had to face – wondering how it would feel, meeting Rui again.

May the nineteenth. He looked the picture of health when I finally met him for lunch. Resplendent in a dark grey double-breasted suit, the unmistakable touch of a loving and careful wife apparent in the gleaming white shirt, the crisp lawn handkerchief peeping out of the breast pocket. For Rui had married again at the end of April.

This was our third lunch in almost as many years and we had a lot to talk about. My news that I was going on a long journey killed all conversation for a few minutes. Then:

'Do you remember what we discussed, when our marriage was breaking up?' Rui asked. 'How I said I wanted to be free to go my own way – live the bachelor life, without feeling guilty about anyone else – '

'And I wanted a life of domestic bliss,' I continued softly. 'Wanted to live with someone who would get a kick out of painting the living room walls and giving cosy little dinner parties. . . .'

We fell silent again, as I considered my recent lifestyle – the young lovers, the jazz clubs, the parties. Dancing until dawn . . . No doubt he was contemplating his new wife, their new home. The redecorating, the gardening, the entertaining . . . .

'What the hell happened?' was the unspoken question as our eyes met at last. Then we'd raised our glasses. Smiled. Toasted his marriage and my journey. And moved onto other, safer topics.

Lunch over, saying our goodbyes in the street, Rui looked about him, sniffed the air and commented that spring had arrived in London. Yes, it had. Just in time to see me depart.

May the twenty-ninth . . . and, 'I guess it's all systems go!' Colin said in hearty tones which fooled no one. We were sitting at the kitchen table in Nadia's house, staring into mugs of cold, untouched coffee. And he was right, of course – I'd thrown my farewell party, moved out of my flat, kissed Hannah and Amy goodbye. And gone to ground.

Everyone thought I'd left the country, but I was staying with Nadia and Graham – and I would happily have hidden in their loft for the next twelve months. They had been like family, and they couldn't bear to see what was happening. They had got married the week before Rui and me. And the four of us had been firm friends ever since.

The three of them had tiptoed around the subject of my leaving for days. 'No need to rush off – we'd love to have you spend time with us,' Nadia had insisted. But I knew they were all afraid for me. Holding their breath in anticipation – like an audience when an actress steps on stage and seems to forget her first line. Would I do it? *Could* I?

It was almost five months to the day since I'd decided to get out of town. And now, it really was time to go.

The morning paper lay crumpled between us and I glanced through it, playing for time. And then I saw it – an ad for cheap flights. On impulse, I reached for the phone, dialled the number and a pleasant Cockney voice answered.

'I'd like a flight out of London – tomorrow,' I airily informed the voice. 'Anywhere in Europe will do – preferably Spain. I'd like a one-way ticket. That's right – I'm not coming back. Have you got anything?'

I held on while the voice checked with other voices. I

glanced down the newspaper columns, followed the pattern of the blue and white checked tablecloth, traced the fluted rim of my cup. I couldn't bring myself to look at Colin, in case he saw the frightened, cornered look which I knew was in my eyes.

'You've got something?' Even as my voice shot up, my heart dropped like a stone. 'Ibiza? Where's that?'

An island off the coast of Spain. . . .

'And I fly tomorrow – seven in the evening? Wonderful. I'll call in and collect my ticket today. Thanks. . . .'

As I slipped the receiver back on its rest, I felt Nadia's arm steal round my shoulders, knowing there was nothing left to say.

May the thirtieth . . . and my plane took off as dusk was falling, to wheel gently – the whole of London a bright illumination perched on the edge of one sharply angled wing tip.

I knew that, down there somewhere, Colin was crawling home from the airport in rush hour traffic. Down there, Hannah, Nadia and Graham were finishing a day's work – heading for the Underground, the pubs or home.

Somewhere down there, a strange Texan lady was cooking in my kitchen or soaking in my bath. And even now, some new face was sipping white wine and silently watching her drinking partners as she perched on my once favourite bar stool.

While up here, on a silent wing and a soft prayer, I was flying into the velvet night. And trying not to think about tomorrow.

PART TWO

My time to die?

Chapter One

Cordoba – the end of the line?

Even as his hand sliced through the air, I didn't believe he was going to hit me. Gazing upwards, open-mouthed in astonishment, I could clearly make out coiling blue tattoos across his knuckles, in that long second before bone connected with bone and his fist made contact with my head. Then I fairly flew across the bleached wooden bench I'd been sitting on and crashed into the dusty earth, where I lay, dazed and still – like a fly swatted casually from the breakfast table.

Stunned by the explosion in my head, my brain had gone numb and it was sheer reflex action which brought me, first to my knees, then to my feet, clutching the bench for support, while he towered above me, his fists clenched, obviously anxious to finish the job.

Only dimly conscious of the pain and a growing fear, I guessed he'd made a mistake, confused me with some other woman. Or had I done something wrong? My eyes and body asked the question, even though I was too shocked to speak.

His answer was short and sharp and there was no mistaking its meaning, as his hand shot out for a second time and slapped me hard across the face. Eyelid, bridge of nose, cheekbone – all were consumed by fire and my head whiplashed to the right with the impact, so I didn't see the punch coming. But it landed squarely below my breastbone and lifted me clear of the ground. I rose through the air in a gentle spiral and it seemed forever, before I hit the deck for the second time.

Winded and gasping for breath, my body sagged and settled onto sunbaked earth. Face down, my nose was practically buried in the warm dust, while my eyes focused on a tiny insect jauntily crossing my line of vision. Fascinated, I followed its progress. I could easily watch it forever, I felt so safe there, close to the earth. Maybe I shouldn't get up again. . . .

Cringing in the dirt, my heartbeats thumped loudly in my aching head, my lungs were on fire and I held my breath as I dared to glance around me, still dazed and confused.

I saw feet. Feet arrested in the act of walking by . . . feet shuffling and uncertain, as they ranged around me in a loose semi-circle. Embarrassed feet, belonging to people who didn't know what to do and didn't really want to know.

I could feel grit in my mouth and I spat it out, as I raised myself up on trembling arms. Then I froze as *his* shoes swam into view and stopped a few inches from my face. Mindlessly I stared at them – brown open sandals, scuffed but sturdy. I marvelled at his dirty toenails, mesmerized as he drew his left foot back to aim, then kicked out sharply at my ribcage. Even as I drew my legs up to protect myself, his shoe glanced off my knee and I was aware of another sickening pain as it sank into my stomach.

Nausea coursed through me in giddy waves and I hugged my knees and turned my face slowly into the earth. I closed my eyes tightly, determined not to look any more. Not to see any more. Instead, my mind and body would relax together – accept the pain and let it flow through me unresisted. Then maybe it wouldn't hurt so much. . . .

All time hung motionless as I lay there quietly, preparing myself for the next blow – my mind all ready to carry me beyond the pain, wherever it might strike.

I heard birdsong high above me and the neat, rhythmic clip-clop of a passing carriage pony. If I really concentrated, I could smell the rich, red earth around me and I knew it was dappled with light and shade, as sun filtered down through the leafy branches. And over and over, I asked myself *Why is this happening to me?*

Loose gravel scrunched and I sensed that he was turning away from me, uncertainly. Then, seeming to decide, he walked away without a word and I sensed that the ordeal was over – if I wanted it to be. If I stayed there on the ground, cowed and beaten. And quiet.

It occurred to me then that, during all the infinitely stretched, endless time of the nightmare – maybe no more than a couple of minutes in reality – I hadn't uttered a sound.

But suddenly, outrage forced the breath from my lungs and sent it hissing through clenched teeth. An explosion of sound, somewhere between a roar and a scream, which stabbed the still, warm air. With it came an incredible surge of power which raised me up, propelled me forward, and a banshee in my brain screamed *don't you let him get away with this*! as I ran after him, cursing and screaming at the top of my voice. I covered the ground between us in an instant, dragging on his arm and wheeling him around.

I stared hard into his face. He was in his fifties, with unkempt dirty hair – going grey and balding on top. Heavy brows met above a sharp hawk nose, while the eyes were dark and slightly slanted. An untidy greying moustache drooped over thin, dry lips and the malevolence in his face was mixed with something else. It took me a second to realize it was uncertainty, but he could see what I only dimly felt – that my whole body was quivering with fury.

Sensing the surge of violence in me, he shrugged me off and walked on a step or two and I guess I must have launched myself at his face with my nails, for suddenly my wrists were caught in his hard grip. In a rage, I tilted my head back and spat full in his face, feeling a thrill of sheer pleasure, as his eyes widened in disgust and he raised a hand to wipe the spit from his cheek.

'Yeah! How *d'you* like it, you asshole! You bastard!' I yelled, still held fast by one wrist, yet hopping around in malicious glee, screaming abuse. Until, in mid-wipe, his hand shot out again and I went sprawling in the dust for the third time.

Suddenly drained of all my fight, I gazed in frustration at his retreating back, knowing I couldn't stop him by myself. Which was when I scrambled to my feet and rounded on the bewildered onlookers. 'Well, for chrissakes DO SOMETHING! Get the bloody police. HELP ME, damn you!' I ranted. But even as I yelled, I felt my legs growing woolly and I collapsed in a flood of tears.

By this time the crowd had engulfed me and I could feel someone patting my back comfortingly while a young girl tried to brush the red dust from my clothes. Then they grew noisier, their faces filled with outrage as they discussed it all in guttural Spanish, and I sensed they'd taken charge. Sure enough, the police were called, the man was caught and we were all bundled off to the police station in a dark blue limo.

Foolish of me to expect it, I suppose, but I imagined that when a respectably dressed woman was attacked in broad daylight by a total stranger then some kind of an explanation was called for. Right?

Wrong!

Although the penny still hadn't dropped, I'd just been given a practical demonstration of Traveller's Lesson Number One: if you're foreign and you're female and you're immodest enough to travel alone, then anything that happens to you is automatically your fault. Or, to put it another way – you asked for it, lady!

Unfortunately, however, that simple fact didn't come to me in a blinding flash and it took a couple of hours of wrangling in fractured Spanish with a harassed duty sergeant before the truth began to dawn. I'd been beaten and everyone was very sympathetic. But, somehow, it was my fault.

Finally realizing that I was wasting my time, I turned on my heels and strode out of the duty room, head held high. Leather Sandals was sitting disconsolately in an outer office, doggedly denying that he'd been within a mile of me, and I could feel his gaze on me as I swept by. But I just kept on going – past lounging policemen puffing on cigarettes and eyeing me lecherously, my feet echoing along the empty corridors until I slipped through heavy wooden doors and out into late afternoon sunshine.

Ah, Trudy. Welcome to Spain!

Back in my hotel room, I wearily surveyed the damage; a large swelling on the left side of my head, bruising just above my temple and more angry colour developing across my stomach and ribcage, both of which hurt like hell. Luckily my nose, teeth and bones were all intact and it was really my self-confidence which had taken the real beating.

I stared into the bathroom mirror, tears streaming down my cheeks, and admitted what other people had probably suspected all along – that I was as naïve about travelling as I'd once been about everything else.

Oh, I'd had the jabs, fixed the visas and bought the phrasebooks. I'd packed the diarrhoea pills, the clever little gadget designed to fit every size of plughole in every sink from here to Timbuctoo, and I'd even brought along two spare diaphragms, since they'd warned me down at the family planning clinic that extreme heat played havoc with the rubber.

I'd rid myself of the high heels which were almost my trademark and now I was striding around in flat shoes for the first time in my adult life. I'd even invested in jeans, all the better to travel with (although a set of heated rollers, a silk evening dress and elbow-length black gloves were lurking in my luggage, just itching for a party).

But that had been the sum total of my preparation. As far as planning a route, booking advance accommodation or buying anything as obvious as a budget-priced round-the-world plane ticket was concerned, forget it. All that smacked of common sense and required a practical approach to the business of travelling, which was painfully lacking in me.

Really, it was a miracle I'd managed to find Spain at all, and the more I thought about it, the more I realized I'd been bloody lucky to get that far in one piece. But now I sensed my luck was running out and that thought had me checking my timetable for the next train to Madrid, determined to catch the first flight home.

I rushed around, throwing my clothes into my holdalls and stripping the bathroom shelves of soap, toothpaste and shampoo bottles – all the time trying to ignore a little voice in my head which told me I couldn't go home just yet. It was the same voice I'd heard back in London. The sound of that small, sane part of me which had talked me into giving up my old life and setting out on this crazy journey in the first place. Then I sank down on the bed, realizing it was talking sense as usual and knowing I should listen.

Angry and confused, I shrugged out of my once white jumpsuit, which was now torn and grubby, stepped into the shower and let the warm water soothe my aches.

Was it really only six weeks ago that I'd flown out of London? It felt like forever. I thought about my first stopover and how I'd tried to hide in Ibiza, pretending to be just another holidaymaker who was living it up in that Spanish version of the Wild West. Charter planes had flown in and out around the clock, providing me with an endless supply of playmates and, although the faces had kept changing, the game had always been the same, as I drank and danced my nights away in the island's cheap bars and tacky nightclubs, sleeping off my permanent hangover on beaches which were carpeted in wall-to-wall nudes. By the time I staggered onto the mainland ferry three weeks later, I was a wreck – unable to stand the smell of alcohol or the sight of sunburned flesh, while the sound of Michael Jackson singing 'Thriller' would echo round my head for weeks afterwards. Hanging over the stern of the steamer as Ibiza slipped into the distance, I'd coughed myself silly as the bronchitis which had been plaguing me for days began to tighten its grip.

I arrived in Valencia with a raging temperature and, dragging my luggage down to the taxi rank, I gave it to the oldest, kindliest–looking cabby I could find and asked him to drive me to the nearest hotel. Dusk was falling as I crawled into bed to lie shivering and shaking in the room.

By morning, I was out of my head with fever, barely able to get from the bed to the bathroom under my own steam and too ill to even think about getting dressed and going in search of a doctor. I hardly noticed the tentative knocking on my door, but the sound of a key turning in the lock made me raise my head from the pillows to find an anxious face peering down at me. It was the pretty young receptionist, flanked by a wide-eyed maid, who had unlocked my door.

It seemed that guests in the room next to mine who were checking out that morning had told the manager that someone sleeping in the room next to theirs had been coughing and moaning all night and was obviously very sick. That someone was me and, moments later, the maid was helping me to dress while the receptionist rang for a taxi. Bringing a doctor to the hotel was a waste of time, she'd decided. I was going straight to hospital.

In *'Urgencia'* a harassed young man listened with barely concealed irritation while I told him I thought I had bronchitis, but his attitude changed once he'd put his stethoscope to my gurgling chest. Suddenly there were three doctors round the examining table and I distinctly heard the word 'pneumonia', as I was bundled into a wheelchair and rushed down to the X-ray department. A false alarm, as it turned out, although the bronchitis attack was bad and they recommended a couple of days of hospitalization.

Instead, I went back to my hotel room weighed down with drugs and the days and nights melted into each other, as breakfasts, lunches and dinners were brought to my room, only to be carried off again untouched. I lost all track of time as my temperature soared, then finally the fever broke and I realized that, although I'd been all alone and sick, I'd survived. It was a scenario I'd been dreading and now it was one less thing to fear.

By the end of that week, I was back on the streets of Valencia, noticing for the first time how the world seemed to be occupied by couples. Young ones held hands and stole kisses over coffee at the pavement cafés; middle-aged ones window-shopped together or herded their children through the parks; elderly ones strolled arm in arm trailing elderly pooches behind them. All of them made me uncomfortably aware of how alone I was, as I ambled along narrow streets, getting hopelessly lost and not really caring too much.

At last, I was getting a taste of real loneliness – and I didn't have the first idea how to cope with it. Within days, I was on the move again, heading for Madrid, and I gazed from the train in wonder at the clear sunlight, the mist on the hills, the statuesque palms and shady orange groves, as we sped through the heart of Spain.

A pretty woman around my age sat next to me, her eyes alive with interest as she gazed out at the ever-changing countryside. Totally paralysed, she was held erect by metal

143

braces front and back, which propped her head up on wasted shoulders. Her wheelchair was shinily, tragically new and as I watched her out of the corner of my eye, I tried to tell myself yet again what a lucky woman I was. I had a freedom of movement and choice that she would never know – it was just too bad that I didn't know how to use it.

Madrid turned out to be a city of wide boulevards and fanciful statuary. My room was as expensive and impersonal as all the others I'd slept in, with a chilly marble bathroom which echoed eerily when I sang in the shower. Then, nails painted, make-up in place, hair fluffed out with my trusty Carmen rollers, I went in search of dinner.

To begin with, the thought of eating by myself in crowded restaurants had held real terror for me (but, then, so had the idea of slowly starving to death). So I'd made myself a promise to eat out each and every night, wherever I happened to be – and I was determined to always be dressed up and looking my best.

That night had been no exception and I'd headed for Botin's, one of the oldest and most famous family-run restaurants in Madrid. There, I'd been faced with yet another fact of life – women alone are bad for business, since they take up precious tables for two or even four and embarrass other diners with their lost and helpless air.

The waiters had scurried past me smiling sympathetically, while the *maître d'* had ushered me to a bar stool in the corner and then studiously ignored me, in the hope that I might go away. I was on the point of doing just that when a slightly built man strolled into the place with a hungry look in his eye. He was obviously alone and, on impulse, I approached him, explaining my predicament and suggesting that we'd have a much better chance of getting fed if we teamed up – and that's how I came to dine with Pierre.

A divorced Parisian who lived and worked in Barcelona, he was obviously painfully shy around women and his moustache quivered in alarm, every time I spoke. He had eyes like a timid but inquisitive bird and cocked his head to one side as he tried to follow my mindless chatter, while I talked like someone who'd been in solitary confinement for weeks.

Afterwards we strolled together through the now deserted city and it was after one in the morning, and still very warm, when he escorted me to my hotel. Outside he kissed me shyly on both cheeks before waving goodbye and walking off down the quiet street. Another ship passing in the night, I thought – unaccountably sad as I watched him go, and dimly realizing that from now on, life was likely to be one long series of 'hellos' and 'goodbyes'.

After about a week, I'd tired of Madrid and headed on south to Toledo and, once I'd toured that splendid old city, was back on the train again, speeding towards Cordoba. Arriving in the early hours of Sunday morning, I knew, the moment I stepped out of the station, that I was going to love this picturesque little town, with its gurgling fountains and singing canaries, its Moorish minarets and ivy-clad battlements. So much for first impressions!

Now it looked like Cordoba was the end of the line, I mused, as I stepped out of the shower – the last stop on my half-baked tour and a fitting end to six long weeks, during which I'd achieved nothing very much and proved beyond any reasonable doubt that, at thirty-five, I still couldn't be trusted to look after myself.

Oh, sure, life would be easier on my home turf. Back there, I knew my way around and everyone knew me. I'd be safe with the old crowd, secure in my old haunts and soon everyone would forget that I'd tried – and failed – to break away. So that maybe even *I* would be able to forget in time. But there was an alternative. . . .

Okay, so I'd had the shit beaten out of me for no earthly reason and I hadn't liked it at all – not the fear or the pain or the realization that I was on my own and at the mercy of every nutter who chanced my way. But maybe, after all, Leather Sandals had done me a favour. He'd certainly shaken me out of my apathy and put me on my guard – something no one else had managed to do for years. This travelling was turning out to be a whole new ball game – a challenge I had to square up to.

I cried some more as it became obvious I wasn't going home

just yet, because I still had something to prove to the one person who wouldn't be fooled any more. It was time to convince *myself* that I wasn't a hopeless case.

Early next morning, I was wakened by the dull thud of oranges falling on to the little balcony outside my window and I threw back the wooden shutters to let in the warm sunshine. By now, less than twenty-four hours after the beating, the bruises were standing out brightly all over my body and I ached from head to foot, so I lay down naked on the carpet just beneath the open window, enjoying the hot bars of sunlight as they played on my bare skin.

The little wrought-iron balcony overlooked a tiny secluded square and I could see a spray of sparkling water gushing from a stone lion's head set into the wall on my right. I lay there, enjoying the sweet sound of the water as it cascaded into a stone trough beneath and the gentle rustle of the breeze through the shiny green foliage of the orange tree. The peace was shattered by the sound of voices, and, a few seconds later, two men strolled into the little square.

As their heads bobbed into sight just below my balcony, my first instinct was to creep back into the shadow of my bedroom. But I was enjoying the warmth of the sun on my body and I knew that, as long as I stayed down on the floor, I couldn't be seen from below.

Both men were in their early twenties, one dark-haired and olive-skinned, the other a muscular, tanned blond. As they dumped their bulging rucksacks beneath the orange tree, they laughed and spoke softly to each other – two people who knew they really shouldn't be there and didn't want to be discovered. Well, that made three of us, I decided, as I watched them push and jostle each other like schoolboys.

They began removing their dusty T-shirts and soiled jeans. Off came the sneakers, the grubby socks, and then the two naked men strode easily over to the fountain. Playfully, they splashed one another with the cool water, laughing and yelling as it ran in sparkling rivulets down their sinewy backs and buttocks. Then the dark one plunged his head into the trough, to come up seconds later gasping for air. As he tossed back his mane of curly hair, the iridescent drops of water flew in all directions, winking like diamonds in the sunlight.

Then he stood patiently while the blond painstakingly shaved him, after which he returned the favour. Obviously they were minus a mirror, although the rucksacks yielded up soap, toothpaste and brushes and a set of fresh clothes each. Yet they seemed in no hurry to dress again as they sat companionably on the rim of the fountain smoking cigarettes – two young men, quite unaware that they were being watched, both beautiful and somehow very vulnerable in their nakedness.

I can't honestly say that spying on them was an erotic experience – the whole scene was somehow too innocent for that. Instead, I felt almost as if I'd been watching some ancient rite – the sort of thing primitive tribesmen would indulge in, safely out of sight of their womenfolk.

Later, as I was packing up to leave, I smiled as I thought of the boys playing like puppies, then grew serious as I remembered the events of the day before and considered how dangerous men can sometimes be. I'd given up trying to work out why I'd been attacked – had already come to the conclusion that it had been bad luck; the result of being in the wrong place at the wrong time. Well, no other explanation made sense.

Later, when I told people the story of how I was beaten up, they would always ask me one question: 'Did you do anything to provoke him?' Back in London, people had quietly disliked me for the woman I'd become. But out here in the wild world, my haughty, aggressive, cynical outlook was provoking a much more violent reaction that was going to happen again and again until I drastically changed my attitude – or someone changed it for me. If only I'd been able to work out then what I can see so clearly now, I might have learned some thing from the beating – or it might never have happened in the first place. Oh – let's face it, if I'd known then what I know now, I wouldn't have had to make the bloody journey at all.

As it was, I left Cordoba blissfully ignorant of the kind of trouble I was storing up for myself and with a lot of hard lessons to learn. . . .

Chapter Two

The game in Spain is pretty much the same

Thoroughly rattled and depressed by this time, I was tempted to book into a luxury hotel and wallow for a while, so I guess it was good old-fashioned masochism which had me taking a room at the sleaziest doss house I could find in Seville, my next stopover.

Hard by the railway lines in a dirty faceless street, it was run by a mammoth-sized landlady who had sweaty armpits, three mongrel dogs which appeared to be all teeth and a husband with a craving for cheap red wine who had no teeth at all. Here, I made the acquaintance of bed bugs and thanked God for letting Sony invent Walkmen, since I spent most of the time holed up in my room – my earphones clamped to my head as I played mournful dirges which suited my bleak mood. Shit, wasn't I stoic, wasn't I brave, to subject myself to this miserable existence! Full of self-congratulation, I lay on my bed, ignoring the wildlife as it gnawed away through the mattress and indulging in I'm-sorry-for-myself tears.

As for Seville, well, I'm sure it's a very nice town, with lots to commend it to discerning tourists – of which, you'll have gathered, I wasn't one.

To say that I was feeling sorry for myself would be to put it mildly as I slipped (wraithlike, I fancied) through the hot, dusty streets, hoping that I cut a tragic figure and sure that anyone who chanced to look at me could hardly miss the sadness in my eyes or fail to be moved by the air of mystery and isolation which hung about me. In reality, of course, passers-by were quite unaware of the Greek tragedy strolling in their midst and, if they noticed me at all, it was probably because I gave off a peculiar aroma – a combination of dog piss and stale cabbage, since my landlady cooked a lot of that.

Having haunted Seville for a time, I decided to honour Cadiz with my ghostly presence and, I must admit, I cheered up fractionally as the train got underway and I sat there, the only passenger in the deserted carriage, wondering about my next port of call.

Cadiz . . . the name conjured up all kinds of things. Tall-masted ships riding at anchor, the quaysides piled with rolls of silk and chests of tea all the way from the China Seas, fluffy cotton bales from India and piles of tobacco leaves from . . . well, from somewhere exotic like Malaysia or Java, I supposed. (I'd be lousy in the commodities market.) And everywhere the sailors in their blue and white striped T-shirts and the delicious smells of coffee and spices and scented oils. Was I in for a shock.

As we slid into the next station, there was a helluva racket outside the carriage and I looked up to see a rag-bag army of gypsies wrenching open the doors, arguing and laughing loudly as they tossed about colourful, untidy bundles, some of which turned out to be children.

Three women, four men and a whole brood of kids, they hung around in the corridor as the whistle blew and the train started up again, staring at me uncertainly through the carriage door and obviously afraid to come in. All except one man who fixed me for a long moment with a look that was breathtakingly haughty, before he casually slid open the door and sat down opposite me.

That part of me which had figured Leather Sandals for a gypsy trembled inside, when I remembered what a maniac he'd turned out to be – and now there were seven of them. I cursed myself for a fool, as I realized I'd chosen an empty carriage in preference to one filled with people and now my 'I just want to be alone with my crisis' attitude had landed me with another load of trouble.

Timidly, I kept my eyes down, then I stared fixedly out of the window at the flat, burning countryside – all the time watching the gypsy warily in the dusty reflection, unnerved to see that he was also watching me. No doubt considering his next move, I decided, and when he suddenly reached into the pocket of his waistcoat for his cigarettes, I all but jumped out of my skin.

All this time, the children had been watching wide-eyed and now they sidled in through the open door, followed by the grown-ups. The boy was around ten, a mixture of childish interest and adult super-cool as he chose to sit further along the compartment with the others. But the three girls had no qualms about satisfying their curiosity and I put their ages at around four, seven and twelve, as they draped themselves around the gypsy opposite, their stares bold and unblinking and impossible to ignore.

I smiled. No one smiled back. And then, since it was obvious that all four of them were staring at me, I gave up all pretence and stared just as hard back at them. Their leader was handsome, his hair very blond and curly and his eyes a brilliant blue in the golden tanned face. It was a wonderful face, the nose straight, the mouth strong, the features even and pleasant. He was tall but slightly built, his jeans were faded but clean and his shirt, though threadbare, was sparkling white. He wore a red kerchief around his neck and his waistcoat was lavender with tiny gold flecks in the material.

Watching him, I began to realize that what I had at first dismissed as cockiness and bravado was actually much more than that. He was full of a quiet confidence and an almost lordly air, which left me in no doubt that, in the world of gypsies, he was Someone.

Suddenly, the smallest girl darted towards me and made a grab for my bracelets, then sat back empty-handed, poised for a second lunge. I was amazed to see that the gypsy didn't try to stop her as she dived on me again, crawling all over me in her efforts to get even closer to my bracelets. Seconds later, the three of them were on me like a tribe of monkeys, examining my hair, my clothes, my painted fingernails, as I squirmed uncomfortably. Then the youngest one started squirrelling around in my shoulder bag and I knew she'd soon unearth the little satin purse in which I kept my gold jewellery.

All the time, the gypsy said nothing and his expression

didn't alter. We both knew that this light-fingered mob was hellbent on lifting anything which wasn't battened down and I was hardly surprised that he'd no intention of doing a sodding thing about it – hadn't I already discovered that I was fair game?

Well, in situations like that, I figure it's not what you lose but the way that you lose it that counts and I decided I'd rather give it away than have it stolen. So off came the pretty shell bangles, then the pink butterfly clip which bound up my hair and finally the pastel necklaces – cheap, pretty jewellery which was snatched up in grubby little paws, amid yelps of pleasure. At which the gypsy opposite said something to the watching women, before breaking into a sunny smile, and I knew I'd passed some kind of test.

After all that excitement, everyone settled down for a snooze and I ended up with the four-year-old sleeping peacefully in my lap, while the middle one slept by my side, her dark head rocking gently against my shoulder. Even in sleep, they scratched at themselves like puppies and I didn't doubt they were alive with fleas and lice, for they really were filthy. Yet I enjoyed the comfortable weight of the child in my lap and the feel of the warm little body tucked into my side – realizing with a slight shock that body contact was something I'd been sadly missing, as I too closed my eyes, no longer unnerved by the gypsy, who lazily watched me through half-closed lids.

We parted company in Jerez and, as the gypsy jumped down from the train, a whole tribe of people swarmed towards him down the platform. He stood there in the sunshine, acknowledging the rapturous welcome but, as the engine coughed into life again, he swung round to gaze at me through the window, before saluting me in a half-mocking bow. The little girls chased my carriage until they ran out of platform and they kept on waving – bright little figures which were soon swallowed up in the dust, as the train rattled on round a bend.

Cadiz was the pits. Dirty and mean and evil-smelling, its beaches strewn with litter and oil slicks, its streets narrow and dark, its restaurants depressing.

And as for my room! Stunningly squalid and so tiny it could only hold a wardrobe, a single bed and a sink; yet the walls were easily fifteen feet high, so that I felt like I was living in an up-ended shoebox. The mirror over the stained sink was cracked and flyblown and the small strip light above that was the only illumination in the place. Communal showers and loos were down the end of a dark corridor, but they turned out to be so stomach-heavingly filthy that I took to washing (and peeing) in the sink. It was my very own pigsty – and all for less than two quid a day.

Well, the routine started up again. Buy a map, pinpoint the guest house, trek the streets, see the sights, find somewhere to eat, someone to do the laundry, something to do with the evenings. Mostly I sat drinking coffee at street cafés at the end of each day, scribbling dozens of postcards home to people who wished they had half my chances, while I wrote nothing to disillusion them. I've since had lots of these postcards and letters returned and, reading them, even *I'm* moved to envy by the fabulous time I'm supposed to have had.

By now, I was beginning to miss things. Being able to pick up the phone and rabbit on to friends; having Angus trotting at my heels and *Hill Street Blues* on Saturday night; those far-off days when I could tumble out of bed and wander starkers into my kitchen to brew up that life-giving cuppa. Now, I had to wash, dress and hit the streets before I could get something as basic as that first cup of tea. I missed my bath – Italian, with a little built-in seat and dark green taps – and my big, bug-free double bed. I even missed my ratty upstairs neighbour, goddammit! But more than all of that, I missed simple human contact. These days, I only heard the sound of my own voice when I was asking the price of a room or buying a train ticket.

It was in this 'missing things' frame of mind that I hit the street in search of breakfast yet again. The venue that morning was a fairly posh-by-Cadiz-standards restaurant with a long chrome bar and high chrome stools, which I sat half-heartedly spinning around on, while my order of tea and toast was made up.

Staring at locals as they ambled past the glass window, I hardly noticed the grubby group of kids who came pelting down the street. But they recognized me immediately and launched themselves at me through the restaurant doors in a flood of excited Spanish which, judging by the shocked looks on the waiters' faces, was pretty raunchy stuff. Even as the manager stepped forward to throw them out, I recognized the shell bracelets and the pink hair clasp, then the coquettish smiles beneath the fresh layers of grime.

Clambering up on the bar stools, they drank and ate their way through a fortune that morning – the little ones squabbling and giggling, while the eldest girl smiled into my eyes and tried to slip her bony little hand into my jacket pocket. Slapping her fingers through the material, I tried to explain to her that friends didn't steal from each other – then stopped short with shock at the idea I should look upon these urchins as friends at all. Yet so far, they were the only ones I'd made on my travels through Spain.

The truth of it was so awful, I didn't know whether to laugh or cry and, long after the kids had gone, I sat at the chrome bar – thinking that I'd been alone for long enough. I needed company more than anything else just then; and I knew better than most women how to set about getting it.

As dusk fell, the Stormtrooper in me strolled through the streets and alleyways of old Cadiz, in search of a likely-looking bar. High heels clicking along the cobbles, I headed for a warm glow of light halfway down a dark street and felt everyone's eyes on me, as I walked into the noise and laughter. The women eyed me suspiciously, while the looks some of the men threw my way hinted at more than just passing interest. For the first time in ages, I felt in control for, although the country might be different, the game was the same. The hunt was on for a man and I was back on familiar territory.

Ignoring the long, meaningful stares from the more obvious candidates, I settled myself on a bar stool and ordered a drink, while I checked the place over with a practised eye. I was looking for someone very particular – a man who was quiet and kind of serious; maybe even a bit on the shy side. One who would take me to bed and comfort me for a few hours, as if I mattered to him, just a little. And there he was, sitting in the shadows, staring moodily into his glass. Long and lean, probably in his late twenties. Good-looking, obviously alone . . . obviously unhappy. The only man in the place who wasn't looking for a woman and hadn't even noticed my arrival – which made him the perfect choice.

Knowing that this kind of man had to think he was making all the moves, I settled down patiently to wait, every so often subjecting his bowed head to the kind of long, intense stare which had always worked so well for me in the past; until eventually he must have felt my eyes on him and the rest, as they say, was easy.

Soon we were deep in what passed for conversation. In different circumstances, his awful English and my painful Spanish might have brought the encounter to a merciful end, but loneliness made us both try harder.

He turned out to be a police lieutenant from Barcelona who'd been seconded to Cadiz and he loathed the place. Another disillusioned soul I thought, as I flirted and smiled and worked at being attractive. Then, when I was sure he was attracted, I let him talk his head off, while I sized him up – not altogether sure what I was looking for.

He seemed to be fairly straight . . . not in the habit of picking up women and a bit out of his depth . . . there didn't seem to be anything arrogant or mean about him, no sign of a vicious streak. I guess I was looking for reassurance that I'd be safe with him. Or as safe as I could ever hope to be, hitting on a complete stranger in an unknown bar in a foreign city.

Two hours later, I was sitting on the edge of a bed in a small, bare, unfriendly room, watching quietly as Paco undressed. I'd hung back as we'd walked into the shabby little hotel, painfully aware that we had no luggage and stung by the knowing look the landlord had shot me, as Paco had asked for a room. I actually think we might have been turfed out, if Paco hadn't casually placed his police identity disc on the desk, along with a small bundle of notes. The landlord's attitude had altered magically and he'd tossed a key towards Paco with a conspiratorial wink.

Turning away from him, I began to undress too, telling

154

myself this was what I needed, even though part of me had suddenly stopped wanting it. Then Paco's arms, muscular and warm, slid around my waist, and he kissed me tentatively, his eyes full of questions as they searched my face. I lay down next to him on the bed, wondering how I must look in the harsh, unflattering light and grateful when he suddenly stretched out, flicked the wall switch and plunged us both into darkness.

Burrowing into his shoulder, I tried to concentrate on his breathing, the smell of his aftershave, the smooth texture of his skin, and I was just beginning to enjoy the long-missed sensation of a man caressing me when, suddenly, he rolled away from me with a sigh and lay on his back.

Confused, but sensing I'd lost him, I pulled the sheet around my body, suddenly ashamed of my nakedness, as I cursed myself for hitting on probably the only man in Cadiz who didn't want to get laid. But then, I'd guessed that all along – loath to admit that had even been part of the challenge. I was hardly able to believe my own ears when I began apologizing to him. Really, I felt for all the world like some beefy rugger player who'd tried to seduce the virginal head girl before being overcome with remorse, so I was hardly surprised when, right on cue, this stocky police lieutenant began to cry.

Yes, you've guessed it – Paco was in love. Engaged to marry Rosanna who was pining back in Barcelona, while he fell apart in Cadiz and I got egg on my face, trying to turn him into the stuff of one-night stands. No doubt about it – I was definitely losing my touch. For maybe another hour I lay there, cradling him in my arms, and I didn't know whether to be amused, insulted or just plain envious, as he wept and chain-smoked and talked non-stop about this bloody girl. And when finally he'd talked himself out, I plied him with good advice about quitting Cadiz and heading home – advice which I wished I could take myself.

Back out on the street, I could hardly wait to escape into a passing taxi, while Paco's long lean frame loped off into the night – a man who'd decided he was heading home, thanks to meeting me.

In my room, I smiled grimly at the ghostly blue reflection of myself before turning off the strip light. Then I lay down on my bed and listened to life going on outside my little shoebox. Pots and pans clattered, children cried and a couple screamed abuse at each other, until some invisible hand turned on a radio and everyone was lulled into silence by the rich, melting voice of an opera singer.

Lying there, letting the sound wash over me, I tried to hold back the tears. All I'd wanted was company, I told myself. I'd tried to take time out with another consenting adult and where the hell was the harm in that? Okay, it had gone embarrassingly wrong, but I was suffering from more than just injured pride as I tried to stifle my sobbing. I realized I was quite hurt by Paco's rejection.

Now, of course, I can admit what I didn't even know then – that I was crying because I was afraid. Since I'd quit London, my life had been slipping steadily out of my control. I literally didn't know whether I was coming or going, as I'd wandered from town to town – I only knew that I was losing my grip.

Back home, sex had been an area in which I'd always been in complete control, and that night, I'd set out to do the one thing I thought I was good at – manipulating a man. Although I didn't much like them – and certainly didn't trust them – I only felt complete when men were around me. I wilted without a man's attention and I only fired on all cylinders when one was around. That night, I'd wanted Paco to be nice to me, to pay attention to me and make me feel good about myself – and sex was the price I'd been happy to pay.

Yet Paco had turned down the only thing I felt I had to offer. For the first time ever, my ruse hadn't worked – and that was scary. Small wonder, then, that I cried myself to sleep, for I was beginning to *need* men. I wanted their protection, their security, their strength and I sensed that, on this journey, needing men could be very, very dangerous.

After Cadiz, Granada was a pleasant surprise. So civilized, so friendly (so safe!), I couldn't help thinking when I first arrived. Mornings began with breakfast in a genteel old establishment – all gilt-mirrored walls, overstuffed chairs and doddering waiters. Afterwards I'd explore the bazaars or fritter away the afternoons at the Alhambra Palace, strolling through shady cloisters and formal gardens or tucked up in rose-covered arbours, writing still more long and misleading letters home about what a wonderful time I was having.

Yes, Granada is certainly civilized and friendly, as well as colourful and picturesque and steeped in history. But I guess that nowhere on this earth can be described as safe. At least, not when you're an accident just looking for somewhere to happen; and in Granada, I was up to my old tricks; mooching around back streets (the more dimly lit and deserted, the better), doing just what I fancied and going exactly where I pleased; dressing up and dining out and defying anyone to stop me.

Came the night I was walking home from a restaurant through silent, empty streets, when I heard footsteps behind me, hurrying to catch up. I'd heard his raucous singing moments earlier and, figuring him for a drunk, I picked up speed myself – sighing with relief when a door opened just ahead of me and a second man stepped out on to the pavement. As he started walking in the same direction as me but on the other side of the road, the drunk stumbling along in my wake probably realized that three was a crowd. As I passed an alley which ran off to my left, I hoped he'd give up and disappear along it. Sure enough, I heard his footsteps turn off just there and I glanced back to make sure he'd given up the chase.

The hands which gripped my throat cut off any cry I might have made, while the sheer weight behind the attack propelled me halfway across the bonnet of a parked car. Spread-eagled over the warm metal, my left arm trapped beneath me and my legs forced apart by his knee, it took me a second or two to work out that the man who'd appeared on the street just in time to save me, had been waiting till the coast was clear, so he could jump me!

Frenzied and muttering frantically, he was clawing at my clothes, and wild ideas of gouging his eyes out and kneeing him in the balls flitted through my head, complete with helpful diagrams. But the speed of his attack made a mockery of all those women's magazine articles on self-defence. The truth is, it's impossible to get the bastard once he's got the jump on you.

Hitting him across the head with my free hand only earned me a smart slap in the mouth and a tightening of his fingers around my throat and, even if I'd been able to scream, I guessed the front doors all around me would have stayed tightly shut.

Rape was definitely on his mind – and going along with it to save my skin was certainly on mine – when suddenly I heard coarse male laughter and girlish giggling, as a couple turned into the dark street. We both froze for an instant and he cursed long and hard. Then his fingers slipped from my throat and he ran off into the night, leaving me to throw up against the wing of the car.

Badly shaken, I went back to my hotel and tried to forget all about it. Oh, I suppose I could have gone to the police and bored them with a report of the attack, so that they could tell me I shouldn't have been walking alone in the first place and I could have said sorry for breathing, let alone going out in search of dinner. No, I'd been there and done that already and I knew it was a waste of time.

Instead, I got the hell out of Spain. I was making a beeline for the nearest thing to home and, as the border guards climbed on board my train at the frontier and I recognized snatches of their quick, surly Portuguese, I could hardly contain myself at the prospect of being in Lisbon in just six more hours.

There was no one at home when I finally rang the doorbell. So I dumped my luggage on the doorstep and headed for the local park. Sure enough, my father-in-law was giving tennis lessons, his backhand as impressive as ever, while his wife watched adoringly from the sidelines, her tiny frame swathed in blue silk. The welcome was even more rapturous than I'd hoped for, the bath bigger than I'd remembered, the bed softer, the food more delicious than anything I could have imagined.

For the best part of a week, I regaled my father-in-law with all kinds of tall stories about my travels and let my mother-in-law spoil me rotten. Yet she soon realized I was all front and when, in an unguarded moment, I admitted that I was travelling alone and that the last couple of months had been sheer hell, she tried to talk me into going home. Her advice was good – it made a lot of sense to quit while I was still ahead – so neither of us could understand why I didn't take it. But I stuck to my guns doggedly, knowing I couldn't give up just yet.

On one of my last evenings in Lisbon, old friends of Rui's invited me to a party and I must say I had a wonderful time; amazed that such a thing was possible in Lisbon, of all places – and without Rui in attendance. The taxi dropped me home just after dawn and when I reached the front door, I noticed that the little bag which the cook slipped on to the door handle last thing at night, was bulging with delicious fresh bread.

I remembered how, back in the early days of our relationship, I'd frequently lain alone in bed until the early hours, waiting for Rui to come home from his Lisbon revels, and how, more often than not, he'd come wandering in, drunk, rowdy and munching his way through the contents of the bread bag.

Slipping the bag from the handle, I tiptoed into the kitchen and left it on top of the fridge, hoping my mother-in-law would enjoy the joke. She was smiling when she came to waken me later that morning, obviously amused by the idea of me carousing until the dawn in much the same manner as her errant son.

I guess what I was really saying – and what she understood – was that I wasn't Rui's wife any more. Instead, I was living my own life, which meant having to make my own mistakes, and as we laughed about my night on the tiles, I think we both began to understand why I had to keep on travelling – I still had an awful lot to prove.

Sunday morning in Milan and I gazed down from my hotel window on to a deserted street. A week spent with my in-laws had really done more harm than good, for I'd had a taste of loving company, enjoyable conversation and laughter and it had whetted my appetite for more.

I wandered down to reception, where I stopped to pick up the obligatory street map, on which the landlady pinpointed the guest house – 'x' marked the spot, should I want to find my way home.

Out on the street, I heard the distant peal of church bells and, heading for the sound, I found myself in a crowded square, overshadowed by a mighty cathedral. People were thronging through its porticoes and, although I was a long way from being smitten by religious fervour, I joined in, happy just to be caught up in the bustle.

Once lost in the dark, cool interior, I could barely make out the vaulted roof or the dozens of arches which soared into the lofty dimness. The air was heavy with incense and I leaned against a massive stone pillar, enjoying the almost carnival atmosphere as hundreds of Italian voices swelled in harmony, little old ladies staggered by with dripping candles and children scampered unchecked along the aisles.

Fascinated by a group of sober-suited men who greeted each other in a flurry of gentle kisses and warm embraces, I shrank back against the pillar as the plump little man next to me turned and grinned broadly, his hand stretched out towards me. I looked around for help and saw that everyone else was shaking hands. So, shyly, I took his gnarled paw and he pumped my fist up and down, nodding encouragement all the while. And that was it – my daily dose of human exchange and physical contact.

Back in my hotel room, I was too pissed off with everything to be bothered dressing up and hitting the streets in search of food. Or company. Instead, I sat on my window sill, watching nothing happening in the empty street below. Then I started a letter to my mum. Then I thought: Screw this! Why make do when I can have the real thing? And then I rang her up.

She came on the phone, her voice unmistakable with its gentle Scottish lilt, and was properly amazed to hear I was calling from Italy. She was loving all my postcards . . . Dad was okay, although he had a summer cold and his car was playing up again . . . Angus had fallen in love with next door's dachshund . . . did I know it was Colin's birthday at the end of the month? He'd be celebrating it on holiday in

Corfu . . . and so on and on. I'd hung on her every word as her voice floated across the miles, but even before I put the phone down, I knew the call had been a mistake, for it had left me feeling lonelier and more isolated than ever.

I didn't want to go on feeling like this or living like this, yet I couldn't imagine a time when it would be different – when I'd happily live alone among strangers. Couldn't visualize a day when I could cope, when I could cut it – when I could finally call it quits and head on home.

So I headed for Florence instead. Which was where I met Hussein.

Chapter Three

Death of a Stormtrooper

Ten days later I found myself sitting, happy and relaxed, my body swaying with the steady rhythm as my train raced away from Florence. Sunshine and shade danced across the empty compartment and I watched as a lake glimmered blue for an instant on the horizon. Then, gazing sightlessly out at an Italy bathed in warm, golden light, I let my thoughts begin to stray.

Already Florence was becoming a memory – one I wanted to hold on to, as fragmented sounds and visions flitted through my mind. I could still hear my footsteps echoing along marble corridors once darkened by the mighty shadows of the Medicis. Could see myself slipping behind disguised doors in the palazzo to hold my breath in wonder at secret rooms, once filled with power and intrigue.

I'd gasped with pleasure at the sight of the mighty Duomo, filling the whole of my bedroom window with its iridescent green, pink and white marble gleam. Laughed with the pretty receptionist at my *pensione,* although neither of us had understood the joke. Enjoyed the large pottery jugs of fresh, steaming coffee, which appeared at my breakfast table each morning. Presented my only pink lipstick to the pert waitress who admired the colour of my mouth. Refused with a twinge of regret the invitation of a handsome young street artist who invited me to visit his studio and pose for him in the nude. Now, as my train hurtled south, I recalled all these moments. And much more besides. . . .

Sweet, haunting music was playing on my Walkman. The same music I'd played for Hussein the previous night. Or rather, that same morning, just before dawn. Face down, arms flung out, he had fallen asleep to the gentle rhythm of the music and my hands massaging his back.

Interesting man . . . Lebanese. Slightly balding, which added to, rather than detracted from, the beauty of his face. Dark, gentle eyes . . . long straight nose. Wide, sensuous mouth and a square jawline with a deeply cleft chin. Well-developed body with a fine covering of soft, dark hair. Beautiful. . . .

It could have been a purely physical encounter – God knows, I'd been trying hard enough to engineer one. But Hussein had turned out to be more than just a pretty face. He also had an enquiring mind and strong opinions on mostly everything.

After two months on the road, lively conversation had become noticeable by its absence and I'd learned to forget anything approaching a spirited argument. But with Hussein I'd had all of that – and in English, what's more! He had happened along just in time to pluck me from the midst of a group of twenty or so American violin-playing youngsters. They had been performing with more enthusiasm than talent, serenading customers in the café where I'd taken refuge from the afternoon heat. The offer of a drink had led to an invitation to dinner and, over a delicious meal in a quiet restaurant, the air had fairly crackled with our banter.

In his early thirties, he seemed to be the archetypal cosmopolitan man. More continental than Middle Eastern, with his stylish clothes, his effusive gestures and even an Italian ex-wife. But although he had lived for eight years in Florence, he still felt very isolated by his culture, his passion for the Lebanon increasing the more he tried to remove himself from his roots. Listening to him talk, it hadn't taken me long to work out that, in his own way, Hussein felt as lonely as I did.

He was a displaced person and there was a gap in his life which nothing could fill. Not his Italian friends nor his work as an architect. Nor even his latest girlfriend – an American whose 'new world' attitudes he found very hard to understand or tolerate. Their latest argument had led to her flying back to California and now that separation, too, was taking its toll.

163

While I had been gleaning all this stuff about him, he in turn had sensed my need to just talk and talk and talk. So we spent that evening and the next one discussing 'life' far into the night. I suppose both of us sensed that we would never meet again and used this anonymity to offload all kinds of personal and intimate things.

I began to feel it happening even as we talked – could feel the warmth spreading through me as I slowly responded to his attention. Finding pleasure in his face, I sat there, quietly studying him as he spoke and found myself idly wondering if maybe *he* was what I'd been searching for. I began to fantasize about how life would be, living in such a wonderful city, with a man like Hussein . . . and then despaired at myself. Give me a man – any man – and life still took on a whole new glow.

Recognizing this weakness in myself had been recent and sometimes it didn't look as if I would ever overcome it. That's what I was thinking as I settled back in the compartment, surprised when I considered how much Hussein and I had managed to cram into just a few short days. Days spent walking together, dancing together, laughing, arguing and making love.

I would always remember the little things . . . the palm tree beneath his bedroom window, shining grey blue in the early dawn light . . . gazing up at the delicately painted ceiling as I lay next to his sleeping form, comforted by his even breathing. 'My man,' I couldn't help thinking then. If only for that moment and perhaps the next.

I recalled the comfortable silence that first morning – how peacefully domestic it had felt. Watching as he carefully hung away his clothes and straightened up his wardrobe. I had sat on his bed, semi-nude in the sunshine – draped in a sheet and eating glossy wet black cherries from a cut crystal bowl. I liked the way he'd held out his hand to receive the stones, still wet from my saliva. Somehow, that act had been even more intimate and tender than making love.

I had been fascinated by his talk of Islam . . . secretly pleased by his insistence on absolute bodily cleanliness before we made love. Saddened by the middle-of-the-night phone calls from California. Because she knew, without knowing, that I was there. I could almost feel her pain as he whispered soothingly to her over the phone, insisting he was all alone. I couldn't even be offended that my existence was so glibly denied for, after all, I *was* no one. Just some woman resting for a time in his life and his bed – a stand-in for another, much more important person. It was the same role I had played with the police lieutenant in Cadiz and one I realized I would have to get used to, as long as I passed through other people's lives.

Hussein . . . a man who admired all women and seduced as many as he could. A man who loved the lofty ideals of marriage but wanted no part of the sacrifice and discipline that long-term relationships involved. He was a man who knew as well as I did that the five days we had were all that we were entitled to.

Yet, when we were saying goodbye at the station and he had hesitantly suggested I stay a little longer, I had been very, very tempted. Warmed by the thought of those weeks (maybe months?) I could spend in elegant Florence; all those mornings I might lie, feeling safe and secure, beneath the blue and white of his lovely ceiling.

So I sat on as the train sped towards Rome – telling myself I'd done the sensible thing by leaving Hussein and blissfully unaware of the danger which lay in wait for me, just around the corner. . . .

Rome, the eternal city. I strolled in the gathering dusk along the Via Veneto, showplace of the rich, the chic, the beautiful. The evening was hot and heavy with perfume and laughter, as the whole of Rome gorged itself on food and wine and good company. Or so it seemed to me, as I looked on enviously; used by this time to eating alone, yet curiously bored by the prospect of eating and drinking, now that I couldn't share it with friends.

Still, being in the noisy, colourful street was preferable to hanging around my hotel room and I covered the Via Veneto from end to end, before choosing a restaurant and settling myself at a table for two. That caused the usual momentary stir but I'd learned how to cope with the speculative stares, the suggestive comments, the proffered drinks and even the odd bit of harassment . . . get the pen and pad out and *look busy*.

Hemmed in by noisy groups, I ordered my meal, began a letter to Hannah, abandoned it and sat back to watch the world instead.

That living legend, the Italian gigolo, was hard at work to my left. Three of them, to be exact – trying to charm the panty girdles off that other living legend, the American matron. Four of those, in fact. A bizarre mixture of girlish giggles and lewd, knowing eyes; skinny bodies draped about with expensive clothes and dripping with jewellery.

Two more middle-aged American men sat in front of me. One describing the 'awesome' spectacle of Pompeii, while the bored, podgy son of the other threw up into his napkin.

On my right, a cheerful group of Italians in their teens and twenties laughed and teased each other good-naturedly as they waited for their order to arrive. And I watched it all, getting more and more depressed.

I was in beautiful, fashionable downtown Rome on a sultry summer's night – and still I wanted more. It would have been just perfect if I could share it with people I knew. We could laugh at each other's jokes, eat from each other's plates . . . and I could safely drink more than two glasses of wine, knowing I was among friends. Ah, well. . . .

Suddenly, one of the Italian girls at the next table passed a comment about me in Italian and, seeing from my expression that I understood, she smiled and began to talk to me. When she discovered I was alone, she drew me into their conversation.

It's unusual for a group, totally involved with each other, to even notice a solitary outsider. But these kids were lovely – particularly the girls. Soon they were insisting that I join their table and suddenly I wasn't on the outside looking in any more. I was part of the gaiety, the excitement of a Roman night; laughing and joking with a pleasant crowd and enjoying their hospitality, when a shadow fell across the table. I glanced up as the pool of light I sat in was suddenly blocked and watched silently, while my new friends made a fuss of this sombre stranger.

From that very first moment, I didn't like Sergio. Didn't like his face – although I suppose he was handsome, in a hard kind of way, with that cold smile, those steely eyes and that fine mouth with its harsh twist. Didn't like his world-weary attitude or his disdainful glance as he took in the table and its occupants. Most of all, I didn't like the patronizing remarks he made every time I spoke.

He was such hard work! Older, obviously successful, quick-witted and articulate – and permanently bored, apparently. But now, roused slightly from this terminal state by a new game, he baited me at every turn, while I tried desperately to placate him – all the time amazed at myself for putting up with his extraordinary rudeness. Back in London, I'd have wasted no time in telling him to bugger off. But this wasn't London, and these days, I'd learned to be grateful for any company at all. I'd been enjoying the evening until he turned up and I didn't want anything to spoil it.

So for the next hour, I tried to keep him sweet and all the time his eyes never left my face, although I was really uncomfortable, whenever I was forced to meet his unfriendly gaze. He knew, even before I did, that I was afraid of him. And that was exactly what he wanted.

Later, when I got up to leave and he insisted on driving me to my hotel, I should have refused. And when afterwards, parked in front of my hotel, he demanded to know why I wouldn't spend the next day with him, I *should* have said 'Frankly, I don't like you.' Instead, I heard myself saying, 'It's kind of you to offer, Sergio. But I've arranged to meet some friends tomorrow.'

He'd interrupted then, a pained expression on his face. He'd done his homework, asked questions at the table. Knew I was travelling alone and told me so. Still toying with me and amused at my embarrassment at being caught in a lie.

'But no matter,' he'd concluded, wearying of the game. 'Spend tomorrow with your "friends" if you must. I will collect you here on Sunday at one. For lunch.'

Even as he said it, he leaned across me and opened the car

door. Then he sat staring ahead, impatient to be gone, while, at a loss for words, I meekly climbed out of his car.

On Sunday morning, even as I dressed for our lunch date, I wasn't at all sure that I wanted to go. By now, I'd been in Rome for six days. I'd taken in the Forum and the Pantheon, I'd walked down the Spanish steps through a blaze of artists. I'd meditated before Michelangelo's Moses, admired the Vatican through its fretwork of Barbini columns. Silent and solitary, I'd gazed upon the glory that was Rome.

On Saturday afternoon, I'd taken refuge from the heat by the Trevi Fountain, hugging the shade while small Italian boys stalked pigeons and grown Italian men stalked foreign girls. Through it all, coins had twinkled and gleamed as they spiralled through the air to sink in turquoise depths – thrown by lovers who wished some day to return, together, to Rome.

All afternoon, I'd watched the world go by – more often than not in twos. That evening, I'd had dinner alone, gone to bed early and slept badly. I hadn't uttered more than a dozen words in the previous twenty-four hours.

In other words, I'd had enough of my own company. So much so, that even the prospect of lunch with the charmless Sergio seemed almost an attractive prospect.

Maybe I'd judged him too harshly over dinner, I reassured myself. He'd been rude and objectionable but perhaps that had been a reaction to my coolness. And Latins *did* have a haughty way with them, when they were around women.

But his eyes were so calculating . . . and that awful, thin smile . . . and his face, it . . . was so bitter . . . He doesn't like you . . . the little voice in my head shrilled wildly.

Oh, my instincts tried to warn me that there was danger afoot – that this was no ordinary man. All the bitterness and anger I'd sensed in him was real – as real as his contempt for me. But my sense of isolation outweighed the slight stirrings of fear.

And my arrogance won the day. The Stormtrooper in me hadn't met the man she couldn't handle. (Except for the one in Cordoba and I'd neatly drawn a veil over that.) A moody, Missoni-clad lunch companion would be no problem, since I was more than a match for anyone.

I'd met awkward men before but I'd soon had them eating out of my hand and I guess I saw Sergio as just another challenge. So, fooling myself that I was having lunch with nothing more threatening than an angry man, I strolled down the steps to his waiting car and drove off to dine with the devil himself.

It was dreadful. An uncomfortable meeting from the moment we met. To begin with, he wouldn't even talk to me. Just drove like a maniac through the city streets. And although he seemed to be in perfect control as he dodged through the traffic, he kept sweeping his hair back from his temple in a nervous gesture. Trying to ease the tension, I made polite conversation to his stony profile, while I took in his appearance.

Expensive Armani jersey, carefully worked in wool and leather. Dark grey suede trousers, impeccably cut. A gold ring with a single diamond on the little finger of his right hand. Smooth hands, with carefully manicured, slender fingers. Despite the faint scar running from his eyebrow across to the tip of his ear, his face *was* handsome. Yet even in profile, it was undeniably cruel.

At the restaurant, he ate and drank little and talked a lot. Said ugly things about his two ex-wives and ugly things about his children. He was vitriolic about women generally and contemptible of men who let women have too much control. Lunch was not a success.

In mid-sentence, apparently spent by his fury, he suddenly called for the bill and it was with real relief that I saw an end to my ordeal, little realizing that it had just begun. The row broke out as we drove back to the city and I suggested that he could drop me off anywhere that was convenient. That's when I discovered that he'd made 'plans' for us both. Cancelled appointments in order to spend time with me.

'But then, how typical of a woman to ignore a man's efforts to please. You're all the same – selfish, ungrateful – ' On and on he ranted as I sat staring at him, unnerved by this latest outburst.

He simply wasn't normal. Certainly wasn't someone to be crossed lightly, I realized as he slammed through the gears.

Which was when I decided to go along with the situation for a while longer – let him show me the city for an hour or two. He'd soon get bored with that and then I'd make my escape.

So I thanked him for the offer, he gave me a thin smile and we drove on, outwardly calm again. But my stomach was slowly clenching with nerves. Something felt strange about the whole business. Something was definitely wrong.

As I stared out at passing landmarks, I tried to bring my fear under control – reminding myself there had been a time when I could tell any man to go to hell and wondering why I couldn't bring myself to do it now. But the beating in Cordoba and the attack in Granada had left me feeling afraid in even harmless situations . . . as surely *this* one was?

'I live just down here,' Sergio suddenly broke into my thoughts. 'Do you mind if we stop by my place for just a moment? I want to pick up some books.'

'At last!' I thought. 'NOW I know what his game is.' But in this game, I knew all the tricks. Did he really think I'd fall for that line, I wondered, as I met his questioning gaze.

'I don't mind in the least. But I'll wait here – in the car,' I said evenly. And noted the twisted little smile of agreement as he drew into the kerb.

'There – you can listen to some music while I'm gone,' he said as he slid a cassette into the tape deck. Then he got out of the car and slammed the door, turning back for an instant to throw me a look which made me squirm, it was so full of scorn and disgust. As if he'd guessed my suspicions and wanted me to know that he was repulsed by the very idea of seducing me. Although I didn't know it, the game *had* begun and he was way ahead.

'Very cool,' I conceded, confused, as he sauntered off towards the large doors of an old apartment block. *Was* he harmless or wasn't he? Even as I wondered, he stopped in mid stride, as if something had just occurred to him. Then he slowly turned on his heel and walked back uncertainly to the car.

'I've just thought – ' he began. 'Do you remember that talk we had the other evening – about buying property? Well the apartment I mentioned I had bought as an investment . . .

it's also in this building. Completely empty, of course. And in a dreadful state. But I wondered . . . ' his voice by now was filled with disarming uncertainty, 'perhaps you wouldn't mind just looking at it for a moment? Tell me what you think. I would appreciate that . . . '

Alarm bells sounded in my head and my stomach was a knot. I searched his face vainly for any hint of deception. Yet his expression was one of total innocence, as he waited patiently for my answer. God, I was so suspicious! It was high time I got a grip on myself, I decided.

I climbed out of the car and walked with him, through the heavy glass door, into the ornate brass elevator. Up two, three floors and out into a green carpeted corridor. Little gilt candelabra lined the walls, the yellowing paintwork was bedecked with plaster scrolls, garlands and bunched grapes, punctuated by heavy dark doors, the faded elegance of a bygone age.

Stopping before one of the doors, Sergio slipped a key into the lock. 'This is my apartment. I'll get the books and pick up the other keys. Then we'll go upstairs,' he said, as the door was flung open. I glimpsed heavy gilt mirrors on dove grey walls, a sea of fleecy white floor covering. Then he stepped inside – and slammed the door smartly in my face!

It took me a second to realize what had happened and then I was mortified. Here I was, shaping up to a rape scene, only to find myself snubbed by the rapist. Waves of embarrassment coursed through me as I was left to cool my heels and I paced up and down the corridor, aware that he thought I was completely neurotic, feeling sorry for having suspected him and knowing it was time to stop being afraid.

By the time he reappeared, weighed down with books and ledgers, I was in a much happier frame of mind; positively chatty as we rode up two more floors and stepped out into an identical corridor. I was unconcerned as he turned the key in the lock of yet another door and it swung open to reveal – a bare hallway. Opposite, through an inner door, I could see an equally deserted room. It was an empty apartment, just as he'd said, and casually I moved ahead of him into the hall, remarking on the high ceilings, the ornate plaster cornices. . . .

The dull thud of books falling to the floor was followed by the heavy slam of the door. Somehow fierce and urgent. I swung around in surprise at the grating sound of bolts being rammed home and stared into a stranger's face.

Oh, Sergio was in there somewhere. Trapped behind the wild eyes, the wicked grin, the masklike face. And my heart leapt into my throat as he stepped towards me and sent me reeling down the corridor with a mighty push. Snarling incoherently, he continued to shove and jostle me down the empty corridor as my feet stumbled and echoed around the high ceilings. It was hard to believe it was happening but the animal strength in his hands and the shock waves of fury transmitted by his touch were real enough.

But it wasn't until I was pushed into the last room and stared around me aghast at the huge, soiled bed, over-shadowed by the massive television set, that I began to realize the danger I was in. Any lingering hope died when I saw the pictures on the walls. Starkly black and white blown-up prints, they ranged around the room at eye level, pinned up haphazardly, some curling at the corners. They were all pictures of girls. All of them were naked. And all of them had been beaten. The attacks had obviously taken place in this empty flat and the girls had been reduced to cringing, cower-ing creatures before they had been photographed on the big, soiled bed. Some of them wild-eyed and weeping. Others curiously still.

Frozen to the spot, I flinched as he brushed past me and strode across the room towards the television. Flicking on the switch he turned the volume up full, to drown the sound of my screams and cries for help, I knew.

With a growing sense of detachment, I moved towards the screen as it sprang into life and, lowering myself slowly onto the bed, I watched groups of people marching around a sta-dium. I was in such a state of shock, it took me a moment to understand that this was the opening of the Olympics – a ceremony which half the world was probably watching and somewhere out there, right that minute, people who loved me, cared for me and worried about me were glued to their screens, watching the same smiling faces, the same proud marching. My parents, my friends, my brother . . . we were all linked by this image on the screen. In a way, they felt so *near*. Yet I was all alone, locked up with a maniac. And only a miracle would save me now.

His voice began, low and tight and controlled.

Please God – don't let him lose his temper! Knowing, without knowing *how*, that it would be all over for me then.

'I don't want to have sex with you!' he sneered. 'I'm not interested in *that*. But I *am* going to beat you. Then I will take pictures. Then you can leave. How bad it gets depends on you.'

I wanted to believe him but another glance at the pictures on the walls and I knew real terror. *No – he's lying. I'm not going to get out of here. Not ever. . . .*

The frantic scrabbling and scratching grew louder in my head . . . my breathing became shallow and rapid . . . and panic rose with a taste that was sour in my mouth. I was a child again, frantic to pee. Scared out of my wits and desperate to cling to something, someone, safe.

I want . . . I want my mother. Where is she? Lightheaded and suddenly unable to focus. Uncertain of the direction of his voice, as blackness began to slide down the edge of my vision and everything, mercifully, started to shut down. No brain, no pain . . . I thought disjointedly. And then, suddenly, it happened. My head took over and I talked to myself as I would to a frightened child.

Steady on . . . calm down. Don't let him see you're scared. No panic, no shouting . . . don't do anything to unnerve him. Now – sit still. Don't take your eyes off the screen. Concentrate. That's it. The Olympics . . . see? Recognize the flags? French, German . . . concentrate on the flags. That's it. Breathe deep. Calm down. And again – that's it. Get control. Get control. Don't worry, we'll get control . . .

Obediently, I sat and I watched and I breathed. And I steadied my trembling limbs and marshalled my thoughts. And then, very slowly, I turned my head to watch the preparations.

173

He was crouched on the floor, surrounded by camera equipment. Lenses and film were being made ready and he was talking again.

'Don't waste more time. Get your clothes off!' he screamed, suddenly looking directly at me.

It's not so bad. He won't rape me. At least I knew that for certain. There had never been the light of sexual interest in his eye. Never any sexual innuendo in his conversation. That's what I'd found so strange – what didn't add up before. But I found it curiously comforting now.

He wants me to take my clothes off. Well, I've done that before. Strolled nearly nude on beaches in front of lots of people. I'll pretend this is no different. And he's going to hit me. Well, I've been beaten before and I'm still here. I tried to reassure myself, but I knew this beating would be much worse . . . and my head reeled at the prospect of the pain which was soon to come.

'Shit, just get it over with!' I whispered to myself urgently, already fumbling with the belt at my waist. But my head was still looking for a way out and some small part of me – something even beyond my instinct for survival – was making decisions now.

Leave your clothes on . . . you're not to give in to him. Not even if it means we have to jump straight through this window. He won't get the chance to hurt you – and that's a promise, the little voice in my head said.

And that's when I began to talk, the words spilling easily, glibly from my lips. Unexpected questions, outrageous suggestions, filled the air, as my feverishly working imagination threw out all the lewd and awful things my instincts told me he might want to hear. All the time, I moved around the room, calm and unhurried. Stopping for a moment to gaze dispassionately through the dusty windows, down into the busy street below.

If he touches me, I really will jump.

Pausing in front of the grotesque photographs and cocking my head to one side, in silent appraisal of their artistic merit – 'Never, by God! Not to me!' – for all the world like an art collector at an exhibition.

What kind of film did he use – what kind of camera? I

wanted to know, as I forced myself to crouch down beside him and forage through his equipment. Being so close to him struck new terror in me, but I steeled myself to stay put. Was his darkroom here? Obviously, it made sense to process the film himself. I heard my voice and couldn't believe the things I said, how normal I sounded.

Still on his guard, he rested on his heels, watching me as I got up and moved around the room again. *Don't try to run for the door. Three bolts. You'll never make it,* I reminded myself. Turning away from my only escape route to face him, confessing I'd always wanted to do something like this; wondered how it would feel to be beaten. In controlled conditions, of course. With someone who knew how far he could go.

On and on I went, telling him how much I wanted it – even offering to let him tie me up! – and all based on some half-formed theory that, if I looked like I might enjoy it too much, then beating me wouldn't give him any pleasure at all.

I wouldn't care if he hurt me, I insisted, just so long as he didn't spoil my face. Then maybe, afterwards, we could go away together for a couple of days, while I healed up. All the time I talked, I hardly dared to meet his eyes, for fear that he would read the lies in mine. Any normal person would surely see through what I'd said. But then he wasn't normal, the pictures on the wall proved that. Impossible to read his face, but if he fell for this, then he really was mad.

And then, the acid test.

'Thing is, I don't really feel like doing it right now, this minute. It's getting late – and I'm tired. And I ate a lot at lunchtime – I'm sure one good punch will have me throwing up all over the place. Anyway, they'll expect me back at the hotel tonight – and in one piece! But tomorrow morning, I could check out early. You could pick me up . . . we could come straight here and get to work. I mean, it won't take more than an hour, will it?'

His expression changed and the whole world stopped breathing with me. *Oh, God – I've overplayed my hand. He's not going to fall for this.* The seconds moved on and I tried not to watch him as he worked it through in his mind. Then he looked at me, nodded slowly. Agreed!

That part of me which had been cowering behind the whole brazen act was dazed and bewildered as he got to his feet and turned off the television. As we walked slowly out of the room and headed back down the hallway, he was talking about the next day's session and constantly shooting me side-long glances. *Careful . . . he's looking for a sign that you're lying.*

Everything he said met with enthusiastic nods, as the front door loomed into view and I clung on tightly to the last vestiges of self-control as a horrible thought began to take shape in my head. Had he really believed me or was he playing with me still – like a cat with a mouse. Had I just provided a new twist to what was an old game? And was he gloating – laughing inside at my pathetic efforts to wriggle out of it?

'Is he going to pounce, after all . . . and will it be now?' I wondered, as we stood by the front door and his hand hovered on the first bolt. *Please God, make him open it*, and I forced myself to look up into his gaze with what I hoped was a playful smile on my lips. 'You know – ' I began, 'if only you'd told me about this earlier, we could have skipped lunch altogether. . . .'

His features relaxed, the first bolt slid free. Then the second and the third. The door swung open lazily and my knees almost buckled at the sweet sight of the green expanse of corridor, the friendly elevator. I walked towards it as if in a dream, knowing that, if I broke into a run, he could still catch me and drag me back. And then we were in the lift and I stared out through the brass cage as it hummed and whirred into action and the levels fell away. Down, down we floated. He smiled. I smiled back. Ground floor. Glass doors. Street noise. Sunlight. Safety. *Thank you. Thank you, God.*

Moments later, I was back in the car and we were talking as if nothing had happened. Suddenly, we were driving through streets I recognized and then my hotel slid into view. Leaning over, he opened my door. 'Until tomorrow?' he said levelly.

Until tomorrow, I reassured him, as I stepped out of the car and gently closed the door. I even managed to wave, as he roared away from the kerb.

Less than an hour later, I sat trembling on a bench in the

station, my luggage at my feet, desperate to get the first train out of Rome. Nervously I scanned the crowd for that awful face – seeking out a man who might even then be looking for me.

Still afraid that I might not escape him, I practically ran along the platform as my train slid into the station, tumbling aboard with my bags and seeking out the safety of a crowded compartment.

It wasn't until the last of Rome's suburbs had flashed by the train window and we were safely in the open countryside, that I began to believe the nightmare had ended. But the bad dreams . . . well, I knew they were just about to begin. . . .

Chapter Four

Quietly, grudgingly, glad to be alive

By now, of course, you've probably already worked out what I still hadn't begun to realize . . . that I was a willing and eager victim. Escaping from London hadn't solved my problem, I was still programmed to self-destruct. And as I staggered from one disaster to another, something deep inside me had already accepted my fate (which was why, in the weeks before my departure, I'd been so determined to tie up the loose ends of my life). Part of me never seriously thought I'd make it back home again, never seriously expected to survive the journey.

Now it didn't matter what shape or form the danger took – man or beast, fire, flood or runaway five-ton truck – I wouldn't back away from it. And if something stopped me in my tracks permanently and finished off the job I'd started . . . well, that was okay by me.

Careless of myself and indifferent to my fate, I did things I shouldn't have done and went to places I shouldn't have gone to. Defying anyone to stop me, yet hardly surprised when someone had tried. And every humiliation, every indignity that had come my way had been accepted with the same dull resignation. Until finally in Rome, Sergio had shown me the exit door . . . and at the last moment, the survivor in me had refused to meekly step through it.

It's easy for me to understand my actions now, as I sit here at my typewriter, but the simple truth eluded me the night I fled Rome. Standing in the dimly lit corridor, my forehead pressed against the window, I'd gazed unblinking across an endless stretch of darkness, as the train ploughed steadily southwards.

Not until much later on the journey would I begin to understand the dark way my mind had been working – or discover the true value of what I had so nearly thrown away. All I knew just then was that I was still alive, when I didn't really deserve to be. And I was quietly, grudgingly, glad about that . . . I'd taken flight again, running from something I couldn't handle. But this time, I knew exactly where I was heading, as the train raced towards the port of Brindisi. Just after dawn, I boarded the first Greek-bound steamer and gratefully leaned over her stern, watching Italy's shores disappearing into morning mists. Only then would I let myself relax enough to consider my lucky escape – which is when I realized, with a numbing sense of shock, exactly what had saved me.

Sergio hadn't been fooled by my act for a minute; he knew that, in me, he'd found no willing accomplice, no slap-happy partner in crime. It wasn't what I'd *said* that saved my skin but what I'd *done.* Or rather, *didn't* do. He'd been waiting for me to panic – to lose my nerve. He'd wanted me to scream and shout; to make a run for it. Maybe even to attack him first, through sheer terror. For he couldn't lose control until I did. Couldn't hit me until I did something to 'deserve' it. Couldn't lose his sanity unless I went crazy first. Sergio had been waiting for me to press his particular button and instead, I'd *talked him* into deactivating.

Knowing all that was no consolation, when I remembered how many times I had been near to panicking. How close I had come to setting him off.

We sailed on through the day and into a moonless night. From where I stood on the top deck, the great expanse of inky sea seemed to slide unbroken into dark sky. But Corfu lay out there somewhere and I could just make out the faint glimmer of lights, as the nose of the steamer sniffed out dry land.

More than thirty hours' travelling had left me desperately weary by the time we slipped into Corfu, and the sensible thing would have been to rest up for the night and start my search in the morning. But I knew Colin was celebrating his twenty-first birthday somewhere on the island and I wanted to find him in time to be a part of it.

Hiring a cab, I headed for Kassiopi, which turned out to be on the other side of the island, and when we finally drove along the tiny village harbour front, the place seemed to be, deserted, except for one taverna. Warm yellow light spilled out from every window, laughter and music floated out on the night air. I just knew Colin was inside.

His face was a picture when he glanced up and saw me, although his language was less than picturesque. Gladly, I submitted to his bear hug and the welcoming kiss from his girlfriend, Jo. Blithely, I downed the brandies, gave myself up to the merrymaking and the horseplay. I didn't even mind when I was thrown into the filthy harbour by my playful sibling, it just felt good to be back among friends.

Just before the sun came up, we lurched drunkenly back to Colin's apartment, where I had a shower and fell into bed. And that's where I stayed for the next twenty-four hours, sleeping the sleep of the dead. For the best part of three months, I'd been unable to relax properly, even at night. Now I was under a man's protection again – someone else was in charge. I knew I was safe with Colin and I guess I just fell apart.

I finally surfaced to find the sun bouncing off the white-washed fishing cottages, puffball clouds skidding across an azure sky and seagulls hang-gliding over the harbour. And I became a holidaymaker for a couple of days – eating, drinking, swimming, sunbathing and catching up on news from home.

Although Colin was full of questions about what I'd been up to, I wouldn't be drawn on my journey, and Jo, remembering how wild my social life had been in London, was disappointed when I said little about the men she guessed I must have met along the way.

I fobbed her off with a wry smile, for the truth was that my easy, empty conquests back home had left me totally unprepared for the reality of strangers in strange lands. Now I was afraid of my own shadow and even as I laughed off her comment about how 'twitchy' I'd become, I realized that from now on, some small part of me would always be afraid of men.

Saying goodbye to Colin was even more painful than I'd expected it to be. The three of us had tried to be jolly all the way to Corfu harbour, filling the warm night air with raucous renditions of chart-toppers, as the hired jeep bounced over the pitted road. But when they dropped me off at the ferry terminal for my onward journey, it seemed foolish for me to be going in the opposite direction when they were heading home.

After they had driven off, I found a quiet corner and settled down to wait for the dawn and the steamer to Athens. Nearly twenty-four hours later, my ferry had slipped through the Corinth Canal and my mood had slipped from disheartened, to dismal, to downright depressed. Conditions on board hadn't exactly helped matters – loos blocked up, nowhere to wash, nothing to eat and every deck overflowing with the unwashed bodies of hundreds of young backpackers. A nightmare Greek ferry, it looked and smelled like a cattlemarket.

We docked in Piraeus harbour just before midnight and were herded into the waiting arms of hotel touts, who lined the dockside like Pied Pipers. They led off weary little groups with seductive talk of clean beds and cheap rates and numbly, I tagged along with one of them.

The waiting coach eventually dumped us outside a real dive – all bare light bulbs and peeling walls, where we were told there was room for sleeping bags only. And that was up on the roof. Now, Athens is a city famed for its pollution, which makes rooftop dwelling only marginally more attractive than sleeping atop a traffic island in central London. Yet all around me, the youngsters meekly lifted their packs and began to drag themselves up the stairs – which is when something inside me snapped. I'd had enough of roughing it.

I smile now, when I think how I must have appeared to the doorman guarding the posh establishment just around the corner. I was filthy – I know I smelled like a wet sheep. He probably had it in his mind to bar my way. But I was feeling venomous and the look I shot him stopped him in his tracks.

Beautifully attired guests floating around the palatial foyer turned to stare at me, as my dusty shoes mowed through the deep pile carpet, and two immaculately uniformed men behind the reception desk squirmed uncomfortably as I bore down on them.

The manager slid forward and, as I stood there beneath winking chandeliers, I could tell I'd already been classified as 'undesirable'. The next few seconds would be crucial, if I didn't want to be shown the door. With a confidence I hardly felt, I demanded a room with a very large bed and a very large bath – together with a bottle of vodka and lots of ice.

There was a moment's silence while the manager deliberated. Then, with a long look and a thin smile, he swivelled the ledger round for my signature.

The bed *was* massive, the bath the first I'd seen since leaving Lisbon. I emptied all the complimentary sachets of smelly stuff into the torrent of water and lay down gratefully in the bath with suds up to my ears and a long vodka at my elbow. This was the way a bath should be taken. It was the way I used to have them back home.

Home . . . maybe it was high time I headed back. There were dozens of flights out of Athens daily. By this time tomorrow, I could be drinking vodka in my own bath. After all, what was I proving by the journey? I hadn't even learned anything that was useful. With every passing day, I was becoming more cynical and suspicious of people – not to mention more saddened and worried about myself.

No . . . maybe that wasn't quite true, I reconsidered, as I poured out some more vodka. I'd recently discovered one encouraging thing, that the little voice in my head – the one which kept plaguing me – wasn't a sign that I was going crazy, after all. Instead, it belonged to that part of me which was determined to survive at all costs; the part which had dragged me out of London. For weeks now, it had nagged me, encouraged me, soothed me, frightened me. But the voice, above all, was what had saved me during that nightmare in Rome.

A dozen times, I'd wanted to give up and turn back, yet this persistent little voice had said *no*. I was damned if I knew why.

It was a quite unrecognizable me who stepped out of the lift into the foyer, thirty minutes later. I strolled over to the reception desk to get some flight information and was rewarded by a look of sheer disbelief on the manager's face. It's amazing what a hairdryer, heated rollers, some make-up, a little black dress and a pair of high heels will do for a woman.

After a wonderful supper, I went to bed on wings and thought fleetingly of those weary souls draped over an Athens rooftop as I fell asleep, spread-eagled beneath soft, lawn sheets.

It was a different me who sprang out of bed around seven next morning, slipped into a swimsuit and headed for the rooftop pool. Lazily, I slid through the cool water, while my breakfast was served at a poolside table. What a wonderful morning . . . perfect flying weather, if home was where I was heading.

The little voice, which had been strangely silent these last few hours, had chosen her moment well. *Home to what?* she asked me now. *Home to the same job, the same bars, the same men? Home to what's familiar and suffocating? Hell, whatever's ahead of us, it can't be as bad as what we've left behind. . . .*

After breakfast, I padded back to my room and, on impulse, put through a call to New York. It was just after midnight there. No need to wonder where the man might be.

'Hell – Red! Jesus, where are you, girl?' As Henry C. Stone's voice crackled across the miles, I called up a vision in my mind's eye. Saw him leaning back in the leather chair – jacket discarded and braces bright against a snowy white shirt. Saw the room with its massive desk, its deep pile carpet, its windowless walls.

For a few minutes, we chatted on about nothing very much – Henry complaining about the Manhattan heat, while I drew an impossibly romantic and utterly false picture of life aboard a Greek ferry. Then an embarrassed silence fell and I knew it

183

was time to hang up. Afterwards, I stood fingering the dead phone, wondering why I'd made the call.

Realizing that I had needed to contact Henry, to reassure myself that, however uncertain I was about my own situation, I sure as hell wouldn't want to swap it with his. For a moment, I had needed to *feel* the claustrophobia of that shadowy office – sense the exhaustion of a steaming Manhattan – to know that I had the best of the deal.

I was in Athens on a beautiful summer's day. The Greek islands lay just over the horizon – and it seemed a pity not to see them, when I'd come all this way. My voice was right. There was nothing to go home to. But there might well be something worth searching for, just a little way up ahead. . . .

If you ever visit Poros, stroll along the waterfront until you come to the faded sign offering rooms to let. That's where I last saw Giorgos and you'll probably find him there still, sitting on a rickety chair in the sunshine, drinking coffee and chatting to passers-by, as he waits patiently for the ferry to bring in his customers. That morning, I was the only bit of business to scramble off the boat from Athens, but he took it philosophically enough as he led me off.

In his late fifties and handsome, in that silver-haired, chisel-faced islander way, Giorgos is head of the Kifnos family and he lets spare rooms on the upper floor of his house.

Through an open courtyard, shaded by a natural awning of sweet-smelling jasmine, and up through a flight of steps, the floral roof parted to reveal a balcony painted bright turquoise. This gave on to three rooms, each one with a simple, wrought-iron grille for a door.

My room was tiny, painted duck egg blue with brilliant turquoise shutters at the window, which overlooked the back of the house. I opened them to find a little chocolate-coloured donkey resting quietly on the shady footpath below. A velvet-muzzled, liquid-eyed neighbour, who greeted me with a low whinny.

Morning and evening, I would sit in my open doorway, my feet up on the low wrought-iron balcony, and drink in the scene. Slowly, my gaze would travel across our jasmine-clad roof, down to the bay and out to the islands beyond. They seemed to change endlessly – shimmering and dancing behind blue veils at dawn, or lying languid and rose-tinted at dusk.

To my left, behind the pretty bell tower of the Greek Orthodox church, brown and pink tiled roofs trembled in the afternoon heat and shaded eyeless windows – a mellow patchwork which ran down to the harbour front, with its fringe of café tables and gaudy parasols, its clutter of dress, jewellery and souvenir shops. It was a haven for tourists, which I did my best to avoid. Instead, I rose late, dressed unhurriedly and went off to explore back streets and alleyways, as they slowly climbed up onto the hillside. Eventually I found old Poros, sleeping in the shadows, and on my third evening there, I was sitting minding my own business outside Dimitri's taverna – a nice little place in a quiet back street – when suddenly out of the evening gloom, a very tall and very athletic-looking man strode into the lights of the restaurant. This was Paul. Six foot four, with curly dark hair, flecked with grey. Tanned and muscular arms and legs suggested to me that he was the active, outdoor type. And bright, alert blue eyes lit up the kind of weatherbeaten, tanned face which gave him away as the sailor he turned out to be.

He was looking for a room. Anything going? While the waiter checked it out, he joined me for dinner. For the next couple of days we were hardly apart. He was nice. And his lifestyle sounded wonderful. A professional yacht skipper, Paul simply floated across the face of the earth, babysitting rich people's boats and delivering them from A to B at a certain time for a certain price. The Caribbean, the South Pacific, the Indian Ocean, he'd sailed them all. Now, he was on his way down to Sardinia, where he was to crew in a big yacht race. Afterwards, he was collecting a yacht which he had to deliver in three months' time to its owner in San Francisco. The weeks in between would be spent at sea, stripping and revarnishing the decks and generally making her ship shape.

And . . . he added, smiling down at me, there was a place on her for me, if I fancied the idea. Did I just!

Oh, it was tempting. And I knew why. Paul was big and

bluff and confident – completely at home in this watery element and his own master. He'd be running everything – including me. He'd tell me when to sleep, when to get up, what to do, every waking minute of the day. And life would be a lot simpler than it was right now – which was why I knew I couldn't accept his offer. It was the easy way out of my situation and I just couldn't take it.

Still, enough was enough, and a couple of mornings later saw the parting of the ways for me and him. He was still trying to talk me into going along with him as he carried my bags down to the harbour and the waiting ferry. And the last I saw of him was his impressive bulk, standing on the quayside as the steamer slipped her moorings. Climbing onto the top deck, I settled down as the boat headed for the tiny island of Sifnos – my next port of call, chosen by the unfailing pin-in-the-map method.

As it turned out, I've yet to set eyes on sunny Sifnos. For I was soon apprehended by Manolo, who'd been gazing at me intently as I sat sunning myself on deck. Even my Walkman, dark glasses and bored expression didn't keep him at bay for more than an hour. And on reflection, I'm glad about that. Twenty-nine years of age, he was off to spend a fortnight on the tiny, almost uninhabited island of Kithnos with his brother Giorgos and their boyhood friend, Stavros. And when, in the late afternoon, the ferry slid into that island's tiny natural harbour, they suggested I should join them. Three boys, two motor bikes and one tent . . . it sounded interesting. And it wasn't as if anyone was waiting for me in Sifnos.

Riding pillion on Stavros's noisy red bike was fun and the scenery was superb. There are no trees on Kithnos and it's very barren and hilly but wild and exciting, too. More donkeys than people passed us, as we rode along pointing out windmills and little white churches to each other and weaving in and out of groups of small boys, leading home their goats.

When we reached Loutros, a tiny village with one street, we were waylaid by a local who explained that, though his house was full, he could offer me a bed up on the roof. So I snuggled down into my clean sheets and gazed around me at brickwork, chimneys, other rooftops – all bathed in a ghostly blue light from the full moon. Soothed by the listlessly flapping sheets on the clothes-line to my left, I felt calm and happy and, for some reason, incredibly safe. I passed my second night indoors, sleeping among rusty motor bikes and old car spares in a garage. Even here the sheets were clean and I had three kittens to keep me company through the night.

Next day, all four of us travelled on until we reached a tiny sheltered bay lying at the foot of a steep hillside. A gentle curve of pebbled beach edged with young trees – deserted, still, and a real sun trap. This was where we pitched the tent and that night I slept inside next to the two brothers, while Stavros's lanky frame lay outside, snoring gently in his sleeping bag.

It was my first ever night under canvas – and I got up in the morning, determined it would be my last! It had been very windy with some rain and, although I was fully dressed, I'd been cold and miserable all night. It took a dip in the warm sea to waken me up. And then, as I was splashing around bad-temperedly, the delicious aroma of coffee wafted out across the water from our camp fire, to restore my good humour.

Life became a gentle, easy routine and we passed the days fishing and swimming while the evenings were spent round a glowing fire, roasting slivers of meat, swigging from a large bottle of Metaxa and telling each other stories.

The boys reminded me a lot of my brothers and though they didn't have much money, they shared everything with me and their concern for me and their pleasure in my company was genuine. They were good-natured, playful and rowdy and really, it was like being part of a family again – although sometimes their attitude towards me was less than fraternal! Of course, I enjoyed being the centre of attention and couldn't resist playing them off, one against the other. Anyway, the flirting was gentle and harmless enough and no one seemed to mind.

As the days slipped by, I became quite a seasoned beachcomber and came to know every inch of our little world. With no washing facilities to speak of, I would wander off to stand waist-deep in the bay each morning, working up a lather with my Greek soap, shampooing my hair and brushing my teeth – all the while staring out at distant islands in the morning sun. Nice!

I was beginning to get that unmistakable look of women who spend their time out of doors. My hair was becoming bleached out and wild-looking, my skin was slowly tanning. The face that stared back at me from the cracked mirror I hung from a tree didn't look like my own. But it did look relaxed.

Then came the morning I woke with that old, restless feeling inside. Creeping out of the tent, I strolled aimlessly along the beach, slipped out of my clothes and plunged into the water. I knew, as I broke the surface, that it was time to move on.

The boys were angry and upset when I told them my decision over breakfast. Manolo took his fishing gear and went off to sulk, while Giorgos made out he couldn't care less. Stavros said he'd take me to the ferry. Silently he helped me gather up my belongings and we took off on his little red bike, racing up the zigzagging track to the main road, which ran high above our bay. As we reached the brow of the hill, I gazed down one last time on the tiny curved beach which had been my home.

We two bade a sad farewell and Stavros wrote all sorts of nice little things in my address book. Later, hanging out over the steamer's rails, I waved as he took off on his bike – and kept on waving until he was nothing more than a cloud of dust and a flash of chrome on the distant hillside.

Soon, I was sitting on the top deck of the ferry in my swimsuit, shoes kicked off, sunspecs perched on the end of my nose, Walkman up full blast and a smile on my face. A school of dolphins performed aerobatics for me in the warm slipstream, while all around little boats churned up the blue seas. I was travelling again, heading for Rhodes. And I didn't have a care in the world.

Sitting in my usual corner, a large orange juice at my elbow, I scribbled away in my diary, while Alexis the waiter – and, incidentally, my new landlord – yelled my breakfast order through to the steamy kitchen.

I'd arrived in Rhodes nearly three weeks before and had come straight to the sleepy village of Lindos – an enchanting muddle of old houses with intricately cobbled courtyards and painstakingly carved doors. Business is conducted in the early morning, then everything magically stops around midday and the whole village falls into a deep slumber only to come alive again at night – like a fairytale town waking up from a spell.

Lindos is a holidaymaker's stamping ground and there was no room at any of the inns when I first arrived. So it was back to rooftop living for a few days. Still, when I sat up on my mattress to greet each new day, the view was breathtaking – a mêlée of pastel-painted houses, with gleaming roofs, which tumbled down to the pretty bay, while yachts, which had sneaked in under cover of darkness, rode gently at anchor.

One morning, I happened to mention my accommodation problem to Alexis and he immediately offered to rent me a room in his house. High up on the hill behind town, it turned out to be a lovely old place, with all the rooms giving out on to a central courtyard – again with its canopy of leafy vines, heavy with bunches of ripe, green grapes.

My room had two shuttered windows, a big old wardrobe and a large bed which stood about four feet off the ground and had little steps built into its base, so that I could climb up on to the mattress. I felt at home here, from the moment I walked in and actually unpacked my belongings for the first time since leaving London, filling the shelves with my baubles and beads.

I soon had a little routine going and rose late each morning to shower and wash some clothes, before strolling down to the village through a riot of bougainvillea and tumbling ger-aniums, carefully side-stepping past tortoiseshell kittens and droopy donkeys. In the late afternoon, once the crowd had thinned out, I'd wander down to the beach, and sit chatting to my new friends. There was Hafez, a pleasant Egyptian who often took me sailing in one of the speedy little Lasers. We discovered we had quite a lot in common, he and I. Things like disillusion and confusion and a deep mistrust of the opposite sex, even though we spent a lot of time and energy trying to pretend otherwise.

Although he was charming, witty and worldly, I wasn't entirely relaxed in Hafez's company. Probably because *it takes one to know one* as they say. If I knew that Hafez was playing out a role, had he also worked out the truth about me? It was disconcerting to think that we might be two of a kind.

I spent a lot of time on the beach and every day, I swam for the best part of an hour. I'm a rotten swimmer and actually very afraid of water. But each day, I swam a little farther and felt a little more confident. Often, I sat by the water's edge chatting to Ingrid, who ran the windsurfing school. She'd been a mixture of envy and fascination, when I'd told her about my journey so far. And, by the time she'd finished telling me how incredibly lucky I was, I'd begun to realize that it was true. I'd actually been given the opportunity of a lifetime – only I'd been too blind to see it.

Four months earlier, when I'd left London, my spirits had been at an all-time low. Trying to escape from something I couldn't describe, but which frightened me just the same, I'd gone looking for something I couldn't put a name to and probably wouldn't recognize, even if I found it. That's how confused I'd been. Now, I had to admit that I never wanted to go home. Instead, part of me would be happy to relinquish my freedom in exchange for the love and protection of a caring male. Would that be so terrible – to settle down in a quiet backwater to live the simple life with a safe, reliable man? Maybe, after all, that *had* been the object of my search. But I'd had no luck so far.

Now, summer was almost over in this part of the world. The beaches were less crowded, the bars quieter. One or two restaurants had already put up their shutters, as business began to tail off. Europe was settling down for the winter and the tourists were heading home. But Cairo was only an hour or so away – the Nile, the Pyramids, the Valley of the Kings were easily within my reach.

Nothing ventured, nothing gained, I mused, as I ate my breakfast. And decided, as I headed for the post office, that it wouldn't do any harm to ask about flights to Egypt.

My eyes lit up as a big fat envelope was handed over at the post office and jubilantly, I carried it off down to my usual spot on the beach. Sitting by the water's edge, I tore open the package impatiently and several letters fell out on to my beach towel. Most of the handwriting I recognized – letters from my mum, my girlfriends, my brother. But I had a sudden, sinking feeling in my stomach, as I stared down at the slim, buff-coloured envelope – somehow official-looking, with my name formally typed out. Addressed care of American Express – posted in London in June, it had chased me all over Europe for the best part of four months. Only bad news could be so tenacious.

The letter was from Jeffrey, my accountant – and it contained the worst possible news. Long and complicated though the letter was and hung about with confusing columns of figures, the bottom line was simple enough to understand. I was broke. Jeffrey tried to soften the blow by suggesting that, once everything was sorted out, maybe I could resume my journey. But his instructions were clear – I had to stop spending money and return home straight away.

Dropping the letter in the sand, I gazed out across the bay in disbelief. How the hell had it happened? Already I knew that, whatever had gone wrong, it was my responsibility. My business, like the rest of my life, had been going steadily downhill by the time I cut out, with bookkeeping ignored, correspondence unanswered and everything neglected. Jeff had been wading through the mess of paperwork when I left but, although I had a lot of outstanding bills, the bank balance had seemed healthy enough and he'd figured that, at the end of the day, I'd have a few thousand pounds to call my own. Once upon a time, I would have hoarded it. But I'd decided to blow the lot on this trip.

Why, oh *why* hadn't I contacted Jeff before now? He'd written the letter in June – I'd been spending steadily since then and God alone knew how much the debts had mounted. Why wasn't there any money? Where had we miscalculated? How soon could I get home? Just how much of a mess was I in?

Part of me was afraid, for the very idea of being in debt had always terrified me. Part of me was angry for ever allowing it to happen. But even as I panicked, part of me was wryly amused. Well, it *was* a joke! For months, I'd been desperate to go home and I'd have given anything for a face-saving excuse to turn back. Now, here it was. I'd been summoned home – by my accountant, no less – and my ordeal was finally over.

Yet instead of being thrilled to bits, I felt sad. Even cheated. With a shock, I realized my longed-for excuse had come too late. For now, the *last* thing I wanted to do was give up. When had I stopped gazing longingly over my shoulder? It was impossible to say. But now I'd actually begun to enjoy myself. Without realizing it, I'd had a change of heart. At last I was ready for the real adventure and now, suddenly, it was all over.

Or was it? I'd been doing the smart thing all my life and it hadn't got me very far. Going home was the smart thing to do, but was it the best thing for me? Maybe it was time to stop being ruled by the past. Instead, I should be making the most of today and tomorrow. And as for the future – well, that would probably take care of itself.

If Jeff's letter hadn't caught up with me, I'd never have known I was in trouble. So I'd just pretend I'd never read it and I'd keep on going, until someone, somewhere, relieved me of my credit cards and forced me to call it a day. Hell, it was only money after all.

A heady, reckless sensation engulfed me, as I thought it through. Maybe I was about to make the biggest mistake of my life. Or maybe it was the most sane decision I'd ever made. In twenty-four hours, I could be in Egypt, if I got my skates on. Cramming all my things into my bag, I glanced down at Jeff's forlorn letter, sticking out of the sand at my feet. Then, turning on my heel, I walked calmly away from it and shook off the last reminder of my old life as lightly as I dusted the sand from my toes.

Chapter Five

Last seen heading for the Sahara

Cairo from the air . . . well, it just wasn't there. Late afternoon sun was flooding the earth, its golden rays slipping over the endlessly undulating desert as I peered down at where this city should have been, straining to see any sign of movement or life. And all the time, Cairo was gazing up at me. Her buildings and roads cleverly camouflaged in the same dusty tones as the encroaching desert, the city was indistinguishable until we were deep into our descent. And even when it deigned to show itself – bereft of foliage or anything else resembling colour – it was a dreadful disappointment.

By the time I found my luggage and a grossly overweight and toothless policeman had freed me from the clutches of a dozen or so 'taxi drivers', I was as nervous as a cat at Cruft's. The taxi ride into the heart of the city didn't help much since my driver seemed intent on killing both of us and, each time he was forced to slow down or – God forbid – stop, the cars around us seemed to be crammed with ogling Egyptians. So that, by the time I was deposited in teeming T'alathaarb Square, I was practically hugging the floor of the cab.

The Black Tulip Hotel was on the third floor of a singularly ugly building and I'd only ever seen anything like it in old war movies. You know the sort of thing – bombed out shell of once beautiful palace; the stairs broken and crumbling, strewn with falling masonry; the once beautiful elevator now a twisted metal wreck. The whole place a death trap of exposed electrical wiring. And, for budget travellers, this was one of the better venues.

Personally, I'd far rather have gone to ground in the Hyatt

Regency, but, all those long months ago in London, I'd foolishly made a date with a man – today was the day and this
was the rendezvous.

I'd been introduced to Phil by an old friend in the White
Swan pub in Covent Garden. A successful advertising man
with the regulation expense account, spreading waistline and
black BMW, he had finally come around to asking himself the
sixty-four thousand dollar question: What the hell is it all
about? The kind of question to which no disillusioned media
man is ever likely to find an acceptable answer. So Phil had
decided to cut and run and our mutual friend thought it was
a smart move to bring two of life's deserters together for a
drink.

I sympathized when Phil admitted that he didn't have the
slightest idea where he was going, but confessed that he had
a hankering to see Egypt. By now, we'd polished off a couple
of bottles of wine, we were enjoying each other's company
and it seemed sensible (the way most crazy things do, when
you're half-pissed) to meet up again and 'do' the banks of the
Nile together.

Back in Rhodes, I'd had an update. Phil was somewhere
nearby and heading for Cairo. Was our date still on? our
mutual friend and go-between wanted to know. Recklessly
I'd said yes and had been given instructions to be at the
Black Tulip on the evening of this particular day. Yet when I
enquired at the grubby little reception desk, the name 'Phil'
caused much perplexed raising of eyebrows and scratching of
fezzes. His name wasn't in the guest book and there were no
rooms available. But I had no intention of leaving. My first
taste of Cairo – with its teeming masses, its disgusting smells
and choking fumes, its furious traffic and its lecherous locals
on every corner – had scared the hell out of me.

So I settled myself down in a torn, greasy armchair, determined to sit it out until Phil arrived. Five hours later – midnight, to be precise – and neither Phil, nor a vacant room,
had materialized. All that time, I'd sat bolt upright – so afraid
of having everything I possessed stolen that I wouldn't even
leave my luggage to go to the loo. I had toyed with the idea
of going out to eat, but one glance through the window at

the bustling humanity in the streets below and I decided I'd rather endure the hunger.

2 am . . . and a hand laid tentatively on my shoulder brought me out of a fitful sleep. The reception was in darkness and the young boy who had wakened me beckoned for me to follow him down the shabby corridor. He turned a large key in the lock of one of the bedroom doors and motioned for me to go inside. Grateful to think that someone had either moved out or simply not turned up to claim their room, I dragged my bags along the floor and dumped them at the foot of one of the twin beds.

It hardly mattered that the room was filthy and smelled of shit and, in the dark, I was spared the sight of the stained grey sheets which covered the bed. Taking the key from the boy, I locked the door from the inside. Then, exhausted and hungry, I lay down fully-clothed and was soon in a deep sleep. . . .

I felt Rui's warm breath on my cheek and realized that he'd moved over to my side of the bed, as I impatiently rolled away from him. . . . Yet a second later, there he was again, his breath tickling my cheek, pungent and unpleasant as it assailed my nostrils. . . .

Then I realized that Rui was a dream but the breath was real – the shock of it jarring me wide awake. Instinct warned me not to move a muscle, as I sensed that the face of a total stranger was hovering just an inch above my own. Quietly I gazed up at him, my night-accustomed eyes able to discern his nose, lips, moustache, although he obviously couldn't see me in what was, for him, total darkness. I would make no sudden moves but I'd scream the place down the instant he touched me, I'd already decided. And then he spoke.

He was the manager of the hotel, he assured me in low, whispering tones. This was his room. And I was his 'guest'. If I hadn't been so dog-tired – and if I hadn't been so appalled at the thought of heading out into Cairo in the dead of night – I think I would have been out of there quicker than I could have said 'Nice asp, Cleo'. But I *was* tired. And I was much more scared of what lay in wait for me out *there*. Far better to take my chances with my oily little host, I decided, thanking

195

my lucky stars that I'd been too tired to undress and reassured by the fact that I was tightly zipped into a rather fierce jumpsuit. With its elasticated wrists and ankles, it had been chosen with mosquitoes in mind and, with any luck, it would deter this attacker, too.

So I thanked him politely for his hospitality, waved him away to the other bed and listened as he threw himself down on its groaning springs, whining miserably in the manner of spurned lovers everywhere. And then – although it amazes me now to think of it – I turned on my side, all the better to watch his every move. And promptly fell asleep again.

The next day I woke to find I was alone in the room – that's if I didn't count the massive cockroaches which were parading across the floor – and my door had been thoughtfully locked again. Washed and dressed, I went back to reception and asked to see the manager, who duly appeared. I'd never laid eyes on him before. Did they have a night manager, I asked. Yes – and he was it, he informed me. In fact, he was just about to go off duty. So who was the man who had let himself into my room during the night? Eyebrows were raised. Shoulders were shrugged. Fezzes and crotches were scratched, as the assembled staff took on a puzzled air. The conclusion was that I had imagined the man – and I might almost have gone along with that. Except I hadn't imagined the jumble of bedclothes or the still-warm mattress on the bed opposite my own.

All morning, I waited for Phil. And most of the afternoon. By four o'clock, I was starving and decided to brave the streets alone. That night, I piled all my luggage up against the door and fell asleep sitting up. Next morning, I lost all hope of ever seeing Phil and, taking my courage in both hands, I decided to go out and see Egypt instead. And for me, as for everyone, Egypt began with the Pyramids.

I was sitting in the back seat of a rattling taxi when I caught my first sight of them. Filling the car's windscreen like some huge stage backdrop, they reared up behind the city's buildings, although they were still a long way off. Even from that distance, they were awe-inspiring and, by the time the taxi set me down at the little town of Giza which sprawled at their base, I was a bundle of excitement.

I'd timed my arrival well. The last tour coaches had already moved out and, with business over for another day, the landscape was slowly emptying. Plodding camels, wild-eyed Arab steeds, money-changers, beggars and thieves came past me in a tired stream and headed on down the hill towards Giza which lay sprawled out below us.

Ignoring them I hurried on, for with each moment that I climbed the slope the sun dipped lower in the bronze sky, her last rays piercing the swirl and billow of dust to light on sweating flanks and polished harness.

In this part of the world, the day doesn't end in a rosy blush. Instead, a fiery glow lights up the desert as far as the eye can see, while the empty sky, strangely devoid of any colour I could describe, seems to deepen and grow a darker shade of pale.

I'd hardly dared hope that I might find myself completely alone at the burial place of the Pharaohs. So I stood motionless in the empty silence, aware of the sense of mystery, power and timelessness which seeped from the stones – hardly daring to breathe, in case I broke the spell.

I don't know how long I'd been standing there, deep in thought, when the song came floating lightly down the wind, at once wild and sad, a rich, deep voice soaring high on certain notes and filling the evening stillness with its melancholy.

Suddenly apprehensive as I saw a silhouette clearly etched against the darkening sky I thought of hiding, but I knew I'd probably be safer out in the open. Nervously, I stood my ground as a camel swayed towards me out of the gathering gloom and lurched to a halt at my side, a quivering mass of fur, decked about with pink, green and yellow tassels.

The song died on the air and the singer gazed down at me from what suddenly seemed to be a great height. He was heavily robed, his face almost completely hidden by the folds of his headdress.

Leaning down towards me, he spoke a few words in German, then French. I answered that I was Scottish, hoping to confuse him. But he just laughed good-naturedly as he swung down from the saddle and stood before me. The head-dress flowed free to reveal dark, laughing eyes in a face which was young and smooth, the colour of a walnut. His moustache was luxuriant beneath a strong Egyptian nose and white, even teeth gleamed in a friendly smile.

'*Marhabah*, Scottish!' he murmured softly, touching his forehead in a salute.

And that's how I met Amer el Habib.

Thinking I was a stranded tourist who'd missed her coach party, his eyes widened in surprise when he discovered I was travelling by myself and that I'd chosen to be out here, alone at sunset.

Leading his camel, he strolled with me down towards the little town where I hoped to get a bus back into Cairo, and we talked of this and that. Although he wasn't sure where Scotland was, he knew we had some good football teams and, although his English was basic and halting, it soon became obvious that I was talking to a shrewd and clever man who made a healthy living out of foreigners like myself.

As we reached the bottom of the hill, he slowly turned to me and invited me to his home for dinner – never thinking, I'm sure, that I would accept. And I don't suppose I would have done, a few months, or even a few weeks, before. But more and more, I'd realized that putting myself to the test would involve some risk taking. Anyway, trouble seemed to find me, no matter how I played things. I was due for some good experiences – and I'd begun to trust myself enough to take a few calculated risks.

Now, I was curious to see something of the life this man led and the village he lived in – which, if I followed the direction of his outstretched arm, lay somewhere out in the desert. It was the mention of his wife which decided me and before I knew it, I was saying yes to dinner at their home.

His complaining camel was brought to its knees and I clambered aboard, aware of the rough saddle blanket against my legs and the creature's body warmth where my ankles rubbed against its coat. Then Amer climbed up in front and we slid off in that peculiar, rolling gait my body would eventually learn to move with, but which, on that first occasion, jarred me from neck to tail.

Amer kept up a dialogue of bruised English, then fell silent as he realized my attention had wandered. He'd already lost me to the gentle hiss of the sand as it blew around us and the dark sweep of sky, dusted with stars. Behind me, the Pyramids became small, black triangles against the horizon. Inside me, the sense of excitement and anticipation grew as we padded into the Sahara.

I lost all sense of time and distance and it wasn't until I heard the far-off barking of dogs that I noticed the dark outline of buildings looming up ahead of us. The camel, sensing it was almost home, picked up its pace and we trotted jerkily into the village. Gazing down from the lofty camel, I peered effortlessly through the windows. The bedouin houses were low and squat – mostly two storeys high and made of mud bricks. Oil lamps flickered everywhere, casting giant shadows on walls, as people moved around their homes or leaned out of their windows chatting to neighbours.

Traders chased light-fingered children away from their baskets of exotic looking fruit and vegetables and some of the braver ones leapt barefoot across our path, yelling shrilly and scattering the long-haired goats which rummaged through the rotting debris piled up against the walls.

Everywhere there was hubbub . . . which slowly died away, as Amer's camel strode by with a light-skinned, red-headed woman on board. Amer acknowledged the cries of greeting with a slight nod of his head. I could tell he was enjoying the stir we caused as we passed and, by the time we turned into a courtyard, festooned with a gay banner of billowing laundry, it was obvious the grapevine had carried the news to Amer's wife.

She waited expectantly in the dark, a small chubby woman, swathed in black. As I climbed stiffly off the camel and placed my hands together in greeting, I tried to peer through the veil, searching her gaze for any sign of displeasure. But her eyes, black as jet, danced with mischief – unmistakably friendly and warm.

That evening, all three of us tried to dodge around the

barriers of language, tradition and culture and I'm still left with many memories.

I remember Amer solemnly kneeling on his prayer mat, hurrying to complete his devotions before dinner – and checking my hands to make sure that they were clean! . . . I remember his wife, Samira, throwing back her veil to reveal a pert, pretty face and giggling behind her hands whenever I spoke . . . Amer sitting cross-legged at the low wooden table, pressing me to eat the 'best' bits of camel meat, which consisted almost entirely of fat . . . and me steeling myself to force them down, all the while trying to remember whether it was the right or left hand which must never be allowed to touch food! As it turned out, I could happily have sat on both of them, since Amer popped most of the food directly into my mouth . . . I remember lots of chat and happy laughter about nothing at all, while the camel looked on haughtily from the open doorway and the donkey proceeded to chew the shoes I'd carefully discarded at the entrance. It was such an incredible night, that I could only say yes, when Amer suggested I return straight away to Cairo to collect some clothes and then move in with them for a few days.

Out in the desert, the temperature had dropped sharply and I huddled behind Amer's bulky frame, glad of the burnous which Samira had draped over my shoulders as we left. I was dog-tired by the time the camel strode into Giza and clung wearily to the saddle, while Amer arranged for a taxi to take me back to Cairo.

Back in my room in the Tulip Hotel, I flicked on the light switch and gazed around me thoughtfully. I'd left this place just a few hours before – but it seemed a lifetime ago, so much had happened since. I'd had a glimpse of a totally different way of life, in an unknown world. And I could hardly wait to get back to it. . . .

The rhythmic beat of drums, the shrill sound of reed pipes and the odd blood-curdling cry reached us in wave after wave of sound. An engagement was in the offing and excitement was in the air.

I walked along in what I hoped was a modest fashion,

aware of the fierce sun beating on my head, the sweat trickling through my hair and down my back, as I tried to ignore the open stares of the women surrounding me. Shapeless black forms, they'd been creeping out of doorways and appearing out of side alleys all along our route. And now they seemed to glide through the dust to the right and left of me, swelling the steady stream of partygoers.

I moved along a respectful two paces behind Samira, who was immensely pleased with herself that day. She, too, was swathed from head to toe in voluminous matt black. But we both knew that underneath it all was a riot of colour, heavily gilded and adorned – a real feast for the eye. She couldn't wait to show herself off, any more than she could wait to unveil the rich gift for the young couple which was even now being carried on her head in a heavy copper urn. Rare spices and herbs, perfumed teas and all manner of costly delicacies were borne proudly through the dust of the afternoon atop her sturdy little neck. And as if all that wasn't enough to cause a stir and proper envy amongst her neighbours, she had another treat in store. Me.

Although I'd been sharing her home for nearly a week now, Samira's flair for the dramatic and her innate sense of theatre had made her keep me under wraps for the right moment and a proper audience. Now, she was about to upstage the prospective bride.

God knows, we'd spent all morning preparing ourselves for the big event. Samira had carefully examined the few clothes I'd brought, before choosing a white blouse with long sleeves and a high neck, together with a full ankle-length purple skirt. I'd cinched my waist in with a white leather belt, slipped white leather pumps on my feet and offered to cover my hair. But Samira wouldn't hear of that – she seemed to like my sun-bleached, shoulder-length mop.

She'd watched eagerly as I'd put on my make-up, clapping her hands in glee as I'd slicked on the bright pink lipstick which immediately transformed my pale face. And she'd been most particular about the nail varnish – it had to be a fresh coat with no cracks or chipped bits.

When I was ready for inspection, her one disappointment

had been my earrings and the four or five bracelets which jangled at my wrist. They were only silver, after all – a metal much despised by self-respecting bedouin women, who receive much-coveted gold as a dowry. And pity the social standing of the wife who appears in public without at least half a hundredweight of it draped about her person.

Samira herself was a vision in the traditional dress, which is round-necked, with a buttoned yoke, from which yards of material billow out in a full, floor-length skirt. But this particular dress was made up in rich burgundy and blue velvet, the pattern picked out in gold and silver wire, while the bodice was worked in a rainbow of silk threads. I knew that underneath it hung a whole wardrobe of undergarments – from pantaloons and a bodice to leggings and underskirts.

Her black hair was bound up in two plaits which fell almost to her waist, while heavy gold earrings dangled from her lobes and an armour of complicated goldwork protected her ample chest. Even her headdress for this day was of finest linen, the veil delicately worked with embroidery. I have a photograph of her, posing long-faced in her bedroom and trying her best to look stern and matronly – although she appears to be nothing more than a naughty child, dressed up in her mother's finery.

We'd giggled like a couple of schoolgirls as we'd dressed, chatting away in our different tongues, yet understanding the gist of everything that was said, as if some invisible de-coder was at work. I know she understood me when I told her she looked terrific and she was thrilled when I said she reminded me of her mother-in-law (a woman who looked like the rear end of a camel, but whose standing in the community Samira aspired to).

Meanwhile, I understood perfectly when she admired my pale skin, bewailed the fact that my ankles were showing and cheekily suggested that I might even meet an eligible man at the party.

One final look in her much prized mirror and we were off, Samira's tiny five-foot frame held erect as befitted the wife of the dashing, handsome, much sought-after Amer el Habib.

Our impact on the celebration must have surpassed

Samira's wildest dreams. From the moment we entered the front entrance of the fiancée's parents' home, I was set upon by a horde of women and children and I felt my feet lift clear of the ground as they jostled and manhandled me across the courtyard.

Ahead of me, up on a dais, a life-sized doll sat on a makeshift throne for two. Her face was heavily made up, the eyes a concoction of green and gold, while the lips were starkly red. Her hair was a tortured weave of beads and plastic flowers, her dress an uncomfortable-looking froth of pink and silver nylon frills.

She sat erect in her chair, seemingly oblivious to the crowd around her, while at her back, palm leaves were artistically arranged with bunting to convey some kind of a throne. The whole effect was bizarre to say the least and, when I was deposited at her feet – presumably to pay my respects – I didn't know what to say or do.

I quailed to think that every eye was upon me expectantly and that whatever I did, it would probably reflect badly on Samira . . . when suddenly a fanfare of drums and pipes announced the timely arrival of the fiancé, who'd spent the last couple of hours parading through the streets, escorted by the men of the village.

Smiling shyly at me, he took his place next to his betrothed and I was surprised to see that he was wearing an ill-fitting European suit, complete with a tie the like of which I'd only ever seen in old gangster movies.

A roar went up, as his mother stepped forward bearing the gold jewellery which he would present to his betrothed, and I thought this would be the perfect time to slip back into the crowd.

But suddenly a stool appeared on the dais and the bride's mother motioned for me to join the blushing couple. I'd have been happy for the ground to open up and swallow me at that moment. But the bride-to-be, whose face was inscrutable beneath the cosmetics, raised her hand and gestured towards the stool.

So we all three sat there, high above the noisy crowd. Among the sea of faces, I recognized Samira, laughing heartily. By now, she was divested of her robe and she sparkled in the sunlight for all to see. They'd even asked her to play one of the drums – a real honour, we both knew. And as she tapped out a complicated rhythm, her face was a triumph of smiles.

Just then, Amer appeared in the doorway, glanced across the courtyard towards me and raised a hand in salute – smiling to see how the house of el Habib had stolen the show.

Later, flushed with success, we strolled companionably back through the village in the blue of the evening. Once or twice, Amer glanced across at me and smiled – gratefully, I fancied, for I'd been the feather in Samira's cap and we both knew it. Now, it pleased him to listen as, over and over, she related the afternoon's events like a tired and excited child.

As the days had passed and I'd come to know her better, I'd begun to understand how precarious was her standing in the community and how important each small victory was. For Samira, married since her fourteenth year, was twenty-two now. And still she had borne no children. This might be seen as a sad state of affairs for any European woman, but it was a source of real private misery and public shame for a bedouin like Samira.

Next morning, a gentle powdering of dust on my upturned face tickled me from sleep. It drifted lazily down between the cracks in the ceiling boards, a sign that the livestock on the floor above were awake and looking for breakfast. Feeding them was one of my chores.

I got up from the sofa, fully dressed as always, and opened the door into the central room of the house – which was really a large, square entrance with double metal doors in one wall leading to the street.

On the other side of this area lay the only bedroom, together with the bathroom and kitchen. Their home was the most modern in the village.

Muffled noises told me that Amer was performing his ablutions and Samira was fixing the first meal of the day. I could never think of it as breakfast, since it consisted of strong-smelling camel meat and various vegetables with strange-sounding names.

Knowing what was expected of me, I went through the house to the storeroom, swept the hens from the circular wooden table and rolled it indoors. I dusted it down with a palm leaf, brought out the pitcher of water and collected the bread and meat from the kitchen, nodding to a silent, bleary-eyed Samira on the way.

Then I went back to my room, which was actually the living and receiving area. The brick walls had been faced with a coating of plaster and painted a violent blue, while the sofas, ranged around the room, were upholstered in a singularly unattractive material, printed with a harsh blue and orange floral pattern.

The windows along one wall were worked in wrought iron, also painted in vile orange, while the shutters were hung on the outside of the building. Sticking my hands through the ironwork, I knocked the shutters back against the wall to let in the day. Even though it wasn't yet six in the morning, beams of sharp light scythed through the room like knives, while the sudden blast of heat all but melted the paint on the ironwork which in ten minutes or so would be burning to the touch.

The floor of the room was of packed earth, covered with palm matting, while a monstrous sideboard affair in dark wood held all the Habibs' prized possessions – a vase with dusty plastic roses (had Samira ever seen or smelled a real rose?), a china cup and a massive old wireless set, bristling with knobs and dials, which I suspected hadn't worked for years.

Dominating the room, a large sepia photograph of Amer's worthy Mama gazed shrewishly down. I searched the eyes, the mouth, for a hint of softness. But she was stern in every line and wrinkle. And to think Samira wanted nothing more than to one day be like that!

That morning, the young mistress of the house was depressed and refused to smile for either of us. I could under-stand why. So could any woman who'd gone to a party, been the centre of attention and floated on cloud nine all evening . . . only to come down to earth with a bump, the next day. I guess anti-climax is anti-climax, whether you experience it in the glamour of London or the silent sweep of the Sahara.

Despairing of women, Amer ate his food moodily, while we dragged a spitting Rameses out of his stable, scattering large dung beetles and squealing mice beneath our feet. The camel always looked obscenely stripped and naked when we roused him each morning – like a flabby, whiskered old Dickensian gent who'd somehow managed to wriggle out of his nightcap and nightshirt while he slept.

Samira didn't like him at all – I was amazed to learn she hadn't ridden on a camel in years. To tell the truth, I wasn't too keen on him myself – something which I'm sure he sensed.

Close to, he really was like some smelly incontinent old man, with his rotting breath and his chiselled, yellow teeth. Always farting and belching – usually when I was standing at the end which mattered. Then he'd look down his nose at me, as if *I* were the source of the unpleasant smell. Still, I had to hand it to him – he came into his own in the desert.

I well remember the day Amer took me off to make the acquaintance of the Sahara. We'd left while the village was still asleep, the air still full of night sounds. The camel, Amer and myself had swayed along as one, while dawn stole softly through the palm fronds which shadowed the start of our route and startled hens, with legs like Olympian athletes, dived shrieking across our path.

Rameses never once checked his stride as we were swallowed up by the desert. And as the sun rose high in the sky – the better to gaze with its burning eye down on us poor mortals – I developed a whole new respect for the camel.

He ploughed steadily through the golden sea, indifferent to the sizzling heat which gently fried my brains, blind to the searing light which seemed to coat the very sockets of my eyes. I was wearing a headdress like Amer's to deflect the worst of the heat, yet I found myself shrinking back into the folds of my clothes, as fingers, toes, chin and nose tingled in the hot breath of the sun.

Lulled by the steady movement, hypnotized by the wriggling, shifting landscape, I felt the very rhythm of my body beginning to falter as the internal machinery started to seize up. My heart and lungs seemed to take up residence in my skull, somewhere next to my ears. I could distinctly hear them working away in a cacophony of gentle thumping and hissing, as they tried to save my slowly baking frame.

Yet still Rameses pressed on stoically through a smooth, featureless vista of hills and valleys – the sand untouched ahead of us and swept clean behind us by a tidy wind.

No, I never liked Rameses and he never liked me. But ever since that day I'd felt grudging admiration for him. Maybe he felt the same way?

Anyway, Samira and I led him bellowing into the yard, where we coaxed him to kneel and silently piled on his embroidered saddle rug, then his tasselled saddle bags, which we filled with hay and tender green shoots. Then came the saddle with its shit-covered under-the-tail harness and the bridle with its beaded headband and dancing pom-poms.

When we'd finished, he was an impressive sight. As was Amer, when he strolled out into the sunlight. It has to be said that, charming though the villagers were, they weren't, generally speaking, the most attractive looking people. Their clothes were, more often than not, torn, faded, grubby and stained. While their seamed and lined faces, rotten or missing teeth, eye cataracts and various other battle-scars were proof of their hard way of life.

Not so Amer el Habib. Today, as every morning, he was closely shaven and fresh smelling. His *galabayah* of coarse linen was blindingly white, the slate blue vest atop it had every button accounted for. The dark grey robe which flowed over all had been carefully edged in darker braid, while his close cropped head was swathed in the finest white linen headdress.

Hours of work had gone into his appearance, of course. I had good cause to know, since I'd almost sweated blood trying to wash the dust of the desert out of those exact same clothes a couple of days before. While Samira, sitting along-side me, had carefully sewed and darned a whole pile of his things.

Now, pleased with our handiwork, we stood together and

207

waved him off. He'd spend yet another busy day fleecing the tourists up at the Pyramids, while we two would get on with much more back-breaking work.

Used to the routine by now, I climbed the uneven stairs to the first floor of the house with a basin of grain and a load of over-ripe vegetables and was greeted by the stamping of dainty feet as the goats met me – four of them with two velvet soft kids. I kept well clear of the half-dozen or so hissing geese, stepped over the ducks and collected the eggs from the chickens which ran free among the debris of the unfinished building work.

The floor above that one was even less developed – the outer walls had been raised but the partition walls were still nothing more than wishful thinking and a pile of bricks and the whole level was open to the sky. Amer had hoped to have the house finished months earlier, but he'd used the money to send his mother to Mecca instead.

As I leaned out of what would one day be a window, I saw Samira pumping more water from the well down below and guessed we were in for another day of laundry. She suddenly looked up, sensing my presence, and scolded me for wasting time. I smiled as I went downstairs to help her. In this world, every single woman had her place and her allotted task – and even house guests had to pull their weight.

A couple of hours of solid pounding later, fresh clothes billowed on the line – although my bras and panties, which had thrown Samira into a fit of uncontrollable laughter, were drying out discreetly indoors.

Now it was time to clean the house all through, lift the matting and beat it in the yard, sweep the floors out with palm leaf fronds, then sprinkle them with water to damp down the dust.

The heavy pottery pitchers had to be cleaned out and refilled with fresh water and the four or five stoves topped up with paraffin, in readiness for another mammoth cooking session.

For Samira, the kitchen was still something of a novelty and she preferred cooking in the more traditional way – sitting cross-legged on the ground, watching over her little primus stoves – even though they had an unfortunate habit of blowing up in our faces and leaving every pot and utensil burned black. Which meant another long session, scouring them with sand and scrubbing with latherless soap, until they sparkled like new again.

She was most particular about food and preparing it took for ever. I sat there, carefully topping and tailing vegetables which looked like okra, shelling and pounding endless cloves of garlic, kneading dough for the flat bread and finally – the worst chore of all – sifting painstakingly through the rice for all the debris it contained. Cleaning it could easily take up an hour of my day – and I never did it well enough for Samira.

And as if all this wasn't enough to contend with, we were plagued by squadrons of flies, every minute of the day. Huge, oily blobs of bad temper, they bombarded us continually and, at first, I'd tried to fend them off, swiping here and there, wherever they landed. But in that kind of heat, energy has to be conserved and movements limited. So gradually I'd learned to let them be and grown to tolerate the way they tickled and sucked at my skin. It got so that if I suddenly stirred after being motionless for a few minutes, a whole cloud of them would rise up from where they'd nestled in my hair or dozed on my clothes and they would buzz around me angrily, until I consented to be still again.

By the time the chores were finished, the sun had fallen low in the sky and I went off to the bathroom for my shower. This room had a proper sink with a cold water tap and there was even a shower head with cold water. But a carefully scooped out hole in the ground replaced the usual lavatory, with slightly raised stones on either side for one's feet and a little pitcher of water at the ready. By now, of course, I knew exactly what my left hand was for. . . .

Washed and dressed, awaiting the imminent arrival of the master, I took time out and retired to my favourite spot, up on the roof. In the centre of the unfinished second floor, Amer had built a simple lookout tower. A flight of rickety stairs rose twelve or fifteen feet into the air, leading to a tiny balcony with a waist-high wall all round and space enough for a couple of chairs.

This was where I liked to sit and write letters home, catch up on my diary or simply gaze around me at village life going on below and the great expanse of shimmering desert all around.

Samira never understood what I found to do up there and complained that I'd get too much sun. But that hour or so each day before sunset was a peaceful and much cherished time. My life was so full and busy – so physically tiring – that this was the only time I got a chance to think.

By evening, Samira was her old self again and ready for all sorts of mischief. She teased and flirted with Amer from the moment he walked in the door and plagued the poor man to death, while he stood on his little mat, trying to pray. Sitting in front of him, she made silly faces and fluttered her lashes grotesquely. Even though he closed his eyes to shut out the sight, my stifled laughter told him the pantomime was still going on. And a tolerant smile played about the corners of his mouth as he chanted the age-old words.

Over dinner, she entertained him some more – and, as usual, my antics that day proved a good source of amusement. I remember the night she had regaled him with the tale of how she'd come upon me taking out my contact lenses and how she'd squealed with shock – as if she'd caught me out in some dark, satanic rite.

Judging by her elaborate mime, I guessed that this evening's story centred round my pathetic attempts to wash my clothes. While I'd carefully rubbed and kneaded them, Samira had pounded them to within an inch of their useful life – laughing and shaking her head at me in despair.

Amer liked that story. And he was still laughing when he bit on something hard in the handful of rice he'd just shovelled into his mouth. Samira moaned ruefully as he spat out a small stone and immediately laid the blame at my door. I could feel myself withering beneath Amer's disappointed gaze and they both fell silent for a moment, to give me a long, considering look. I knew exactly what they were thinking . . . who is this woman, who can't wash clothes, doesn't know how to clean rice?

I was a stranger from nowhere, heading somewhere

unknown, with no man, no children – not even gold jewellery. They obviously thought I was a sad, sorry figure. And, more and more, I was inclined to agree.

Most evenings, while Samira finished off the day's chores, Amer liked me to keep him company. Sometimes we would sit up in his tower, gazing out at the blue desert and the star-studded sky, while I tried to describe my life back home and he told me stories about his grandfather – one of the true bedouins who had roamed the desert.

At other times we'd sit in the front doorway, where I would give Amer lessons in 'long writing', which he liked to watch flowing from my pen, or he'd teach me how to count in Arabic.

Some evenings, we would play his favourite game, the rules of which were very simple. Amer would make a whole series of requests, which I had to fulfil. He always asked for the same things and in the same order and, if I was in the mood to play and humour him, he sometimes got a long way down the list.

Water would be poured into his glass, his bubble pipe would be brought to him, then carefully cleaned and lit. He would have a stole for his shoulders, his precious photo album, perhaps even a cushion for his back, and, once in a while, if I was feeling really tolerant, I would sit prettily at his feet, next to a dutiful Samira – a couple of female bookends.

At other times, his very first request would meet with firm refusal, a toss of the head and the suggestion that he should fetch it for himself. No matter how many points he scored, the best bit of the game for Amer was when I finally rebelled. Then he would laugh uproariously, rolling his eyes when I flounced off disobediently – all the time insisting through his mirth that I was 'a bad woman' for his wife.

He was closer than he knew. For although Samira pretended to be shocked and scolded me, when she witnessed this temporary breakdown in service, I could tell from the thoughtful gleam in her eye that she was warming to this idea of a woman being able to say 'no' . . . and a man not altogether minding.

I only ever teased Amer this way in the privacy of his own home. When we were in public together, I always conducted myself properly – even taking care to walk a few paces behind him, as was expected of a woman.

It has to be said that he never asked me to conform in this way. Although once, when we came in from the desert on Rameses, Amer stopped on the outskirts of the village and asked me if I would mind getting down to walk alongside the camel.

'I think Rameses is tired – ' he began apologetically, but we both understood the real reason for the request. Silently, I walked along at Rameses's flank, my hand resting lightly on the stirrup, while Amer – grateful, I'm sure, for my sudden co-operation – beamed and salaamed at his neighbours, as we moved slowly through the streets. Nodding their approval, they smiled at us and waved back.

Well – what the hell! Ten minutes spent walking in the dust cost me nothing, while letting me ride would have meant a severe loss of face for Amer. And I liked him too much to bring that about.

Samira was certainly mistress in her house and wouldn't put up with any shoddy work on my part. But she was very affectionate towards me – always happy when Amer paid me compliments and pleased when he brought home little gifts for both of us. And, even when we were hard at work, she could always be persuaded to play.

I know she trusted me and I remember one day, when she'd been unusually quiet, she suddenly began to cry as we crouched together, washing pots. I listened carefully as, through her sobs, she told me how much she loved Amer, what a wonderful husband he was. How she was desperate to give him children and had taken all sorts of potions and pills to help, although nothing did.

I guessed that her period had arrived that morning, dashing her hopes yet again. So, giving her a hug, I told her that Amer adored her, with or without children, that she was a perfect wife and he was lucky to have her.

At this, she wiped her tears away and smiled at me grate-

212

fully. We'd both spoken in a language the other could never hope to understand. But we were women together and one knew exactly what the other was trying so hard to say.

Yes, I liked Samira – loved her sense of fun, her girlishness and her busy little ways. She was a terrific companion and I knew I would miss her. But I knew, too, that it was nearly time for me to go.

A few evenings later, I dropped my bombshell and, when Amer explained that I intended to travel south through Egypt, Samira stared at me in disbelief. This village was the only world she knew. She rarely travelled into the neighbouring town of Giza – had only been to Cairo once in her life. I doubt if she'd ever heard of Karnak or Luxor or Khartoum. And as for travelling alone! She thought I was quite mad and begged me to stay, while Amer was moody with me all evening. But my mind was made up.

My last day in the Habib household was frantic. Samira had insisted on personally washing every item of my clothing for the journey and prepared a real feast for our last meal together. Amer arrived home earlier than usual and took me shopping – a rare treat for a mere woman – so that I could choose some provisions for the long journey south.

I slept little that night. In fact, the household seemed to be restless. I could hear Amer and Samira muttering together in their bedroom, while, above me, the goats pawed the floor nervously. I was up long before dawn and already dressed when Samira came to me and led me to their room.

Laid out on the high bed was a bright pink *galabayah*, trimmed with braided ribbon, together with a fine white Egyptian cotton headdress and a headband of purple, blue and red knotted silk.

'You travel like a good Egyptian woman,' Amer insisted, while his wife smiled at me encouragingly. I realized they'd bought the clothes for me in the hope strangers would respect me more in this traditional garb. Their kindness was so overwhelming that I couldn't trust myself to speak.

Amer went off to saddle up the camel and, wordlessly, Samira helped me dress, arranging the headdress over my bright hair and putting it low over my forehead, before anchoring it with the headband, which sat like a halo about my brow. I looked in the mirror and was surprised at the transformation. In the long, straight robe and the flowing turban, I was certainly unrecognizable – although I could never be mistaken for an Egyptian.

Later, we three stood in the dark of the courtyard, uncertain what to say, while Rameses sniffed the cool air, impatient to be gone. Suddenly Samira hugged me and smiled one last time, before covering her face with her veil.

I placed my hands together in the familiar gesture of greeting or goodbye – just as I done all those weeks ago, when we first met. Now, as then, her eyes through the veil shone black as jet. Except now, they were very, very sad.

All the way into Giza, Amer coached me on 'things-to-say-to-keep-the-men-at-bay'. A litany of Arabic which I think I could recite to this day, so often did he make me repeat it. Finally, he made me promise to return to them, whenever my trip south was over. And I didn't have the heart to refuse.

So Amer el Habib left me as he'd found me, standing in the shadow of the Pyramids. And I felt curiously desolate as I headed towards the sleepy little town of Giza, sprawled at the foot of the hill. Aware of his dark gaze upon me, every step of the way.

Chapter Six

Going home to the bedouins

Streamlined, elegant, the *Nubian Queen* tugged languidly at her mooring ropes as the Nile rocked her gently to and fro. Draped between her funnels, a necklace of fairy lights winked out at the night, casting pink, green and gold gems into the dark reflection of the water.

On this brilliantly lit stage strutted a stylish cast, providing entertainment on a lavish scale – and I had a ringside seat from the river bank. I remember, as a little girl, getting endless pleasure from an Advent calendar which had lots of little windows on its front – one to be opened each day until Christmas. Every morning, I'd pull back yet another paper shutter to gaze in wonder at the tiny festive scene beneath. Now, here was the grown-up version, with each illuminated port-hole giving a different view of the revelry, and I took in every detail of the sumptuous dining room, the shiny chrome of the cocktail lounge and the cosiness of the little bar, as my gaze wandered idly from the dim bowels of this floating palace, up to the splendour of the first-class cabins.

Flurries of chiffon, satin and silk waltzed and foxtrotted smoothly across the polished wood of the upper deck or draped themselves seductively over the ship's rails, the better to converse with evening suits and bow ties.

There was even accompanying music, as a playful breeze skipped through the ship from stem to stern, dodging between diners and dancers to snatch a peal of merry laughter here, the clinking of glasses there – even a line or two from some romantic melody. Then, as if bored with her loot, the breeze tossed the whole lot overboard and the sounds floated gently to the shore, where I sat, enjoying the scene.

I'd heard the music and laughter as I'd strolled back towards my hotel after dinner and I couldn't resist climbing over the low parapet and slithering a little way down the bank, to see at close quarters how the rich toured Egypt.

As my eyes grew accustomed to the darkness, I realized I wasn't alone. Around me, lots of small, still forms crouched among the stones, equally fascinated by the colourful show. Now they turned curious eyes upon me – little Nubian boys who wondered why I was slumming with them, instead of dancing down below. But I had no desire to join the revels. In fact, I wouldn't have swapped places with these people for the world, I thought, as I strolled back to my hotel. They were paying a fortune for a real tourists' version of Egypt. I'd noticed some of them the previous day – an obedient crocodile of couples casting furtive glances to left and right as they scuttled along behind their beaming courier.

And then later, when I'd glided past the *Nubian Queen* in my little *felucca*, several of them had gazed down at me – craning out over the ship's rails like penned sheep, as they wistfully followed my progress. They might not have been quite so envious of my freedom, though, if they'd known about the war of nerves which was being waged on board my little vessel!

It had all started that morning, when I stepped out on to the balcony to see what Aswan looked like in daylight – and was thrilled to discover that my hotel was a stone's throw from the Nile. I'd arrived in the middle of the night, exhausted after my sixteen-hour train journey from Cairo. Tumbling into a pony and trap, I'd asked the driver to take me to a hotel – any one would do, as long as it was around a certain price. But I hadn't realized that he'd set me down in such a perfect spot.

Gazing out across the expanse of river, I was surprised to see that it wasn't a muddy brown as I'd expected, nor yet green or blue. In the blazing sunlight, it flashed a million points of silver and dazzled the eyes in the same way polished metal will, when it captures the light. On the tiny islet in the middle of the river was a riot of green foliage – the botanical garden – while the opposite bank was an unbroken line of shimmering sand, brushstroked in every shade of gold, beige and silver, as it basked in sunlight.

To my right, the river disappeared in a lazy curve and I could see the *Nubian Queen*'s sister ships riding at anchor in the distance. Meanwhile, a whole fleet of tiny open *feluccas*, their elegant, tall sails billowing in the stiff breeze, seemed almost to fly between the shores – like large white dragonflies skimming the water. They looked like lots of fun and I could hardly wait to try one out for myself. But first, I had to find my *felucca*. . . .

Today, I can haggle with the best of them – summoning the cool nerve, the infinite patience necessary for the game. In an instant, my poker face can register a look of scorn or disbelief, while disinterest – or even 'deal's off!' – can be conveyed with the slightest shrug of my shoulder.

That morning, however, I was a rank amateur completely outclassed by the wily boatmen who figured they'd have a bit of sport with me, before they picked me clean. Like five schoolboys preying on the class swot, they crowded around, shrouding me in evil-smelling clouds of tobacco smoke, while demanding sums of money for an hour's hire which could buy a *felucca* outright. That's the trouble with rich tourists, they spoil it for the rest of us.

Really, I didn't stand a chance of getting a fair deal and I guess it was beginner's luck that I wound up with Faisal. Although it didn't seem lucky at the time.

Of the five men gathered round me, he was the one I hoped I *wouldn't* get. He was the tallest and he looked the meanest. His dark, leathery skin was tightly stretched over cheekbones and eye sockets, giving his face a skull-like appearance. No trace of humour in the cold, speculative gaze, nothing friendly about the mouth. Torn and tattered, from his slit earlobes to the frayed hem of his olive-green robe, he hovered above me, a gaunt, beaked figure, and stated his price in a dull, flat voice.

I knew it was fair – the hotel receptionist had told me what I could expect to pay – yet I hesitated. Something about him made me very uncomfortable and I sensed I couldn't trust him an inch. What would happen once we were stuck in the middle of the Nile and he was calling all the shots? True, I wasn't much of a catch. My jewellery was cheap fun and I never carried more than the equivalent of ten pounds on me. I had nothing worth stealing. But that would be small consolation, if I ended up floating down the Nile with my throat cut.

As he stood there quietly, waiting for my decision, thirty years fell away and I was six again, running down the street ahead of my dad. I had skipped round the corner – and run straight into the biggest dog I'd ever seen. Its pink tongue lolled wetly from jaws crammed with teeth and it cocked its head, the better to fix me with a malevolent stare, while it debated whether to devour me in one gulp or eat me a little at a time.

Finding me rooted to the spot an inch from its dripping muzzle, Dad had calmly talked me though the crisis. 'He won't bite you – not unless you give him cause. Now, raise your hand, very gently . . . show him you want to be friends. . . .'

I trusted my father, so, following his instructions, I wiggled my fingers in front of the dog's nose while he sniffed me, then placed my hand carefully on his head, rubbed his ears. His tail wagged, and he sat down while I patted him some more. He could easily have bitten me, but he'd decided against it.

Thirty years on, nothing had changed. I'd run slap-bang into another mastiff who was already licking his chops. The question was – would he bite . . . or would Dad's maxim hold true?

If Faisal was surprised when I agreed, he didn't show it. But then, impulsively, I put my hand out, to seal the bargain – and that's when his expression altered.

He seemed confused, almost afraid, as he looked at me and I noticed an uncertain fluttering inside the long, full sleeve of his robe. Hoping my smile was encouraging, I stuck my hand out still further and didn't even glance down, when his stole into it. So it wasn't until my fingers closed tightly around a smooth, polished stump with little knobs protruding from it, that I realized my boatman was a leper and his hand had been practically eaten away.

Shaken, I jumped down into his little skiff and he followed, agile as any Nubian cat, as he paced the tiny area, casting off, raising the sail and steering us into the fast flow.

A narrow bench ran all round the inside of the boat and, once I'd perched where he pointed, I opened my bag and drew out my lunch – two very gooey pastries, which clung damply to their newspaper wrapping. He pretended not to watch me, as I laid the paper between us and motioned for him to take a piece. He refused with a hard, unfriendly glare and made a production of examining the sail, instead.

Undaunted, I ate my piece and placed the other one next to him, where he stood at the stern – the toes of one foot grasping the rudder, as he wound in some rope. No doubt about it – he could have his hands free any time he chose, which didn't bode well for me, I thought, as we glided past the *Nubian Queen*, under the watchful gaze of the tourists assembled on her decks.

Then the wind caught the gleaming white sail and Faisal barked a sharp command which had me on my feet and diving across the boat in an instant, as the *felucca* suddenly swung into the wind and turned about smartly. The place where I'd been sitting was drenched, as the boat all but tipped into the water, so sharp was its angle. The boatman gave a mirthless laugh at the expression on my face and I joined in – watching in fascination as teeth and toes were employed to do the work of the deformed hand, which he kept concealed as much as possible.

So we tacked our way across the Nile, catching the wind and racing ahead of it, only to falter as the sail went limp and Faisal turned us about in search of a fresh gust. Slowly, we headed towards the island and I guessed my first stop was the botanical gardens – whether I liked it or not.

Expertly, he brought the *felucca* alongside the little quay and I hopped ashore. Nodding towards a flight of steps, he turned away to secure the boat and I strolled up them into lush gardens, where I spent the next ten minutes examining a bewildering array of palms and trying to find a loo. I finally located it next to a small restaurant. Tables, complete with linen, were carefully laid out beneath delicate palm fronds and flowering bushes and I was ushered to one by a beaming waiter, the buttons of his white jacket bursting across his ample middle. I sat at a table next to a low wall and when I glanced over it, I could make out Faisal's lone figure patiently staring into space, as he awaited my return.

The smiling waiter grew sombre when I explained what I wanted and pretended not to understand my elaborate mime. But it was simple enough – I wanted him to ask the boatman to join me for tea. He was so outraged, he called the manager over to change my mind and they shook their heads hopelessly when I insisted.

Only the battle wasn't quite over – and I watched, amused, as waiter and boatman argued below me. Obviously, Faisal was equally outraged by the invitation.

He was rigid with ceremony when he joined me at the table – still not sure whether to be pleased or not. But he quickly took charge and ordered tea from the discomfited staff. Once he got used to the idea, he really enjoyed lording it over them and, when the bill arrived and he checked it, his anger was something to see. After all, there was to be no fleecing this particular tourist and as they gesticulated and yelled over the price, I sensed that Faisal had finally decided not to bite me.

He was quite transformed as we strolled back to his boat and as we weaved our way to the next port of call, he took it upon himself to give me Arabic lessons – pointing to sun, sea, the boat, his eyes, nose and ears and yelling out the appropriate words in a way which made me wonder if he was slightly deaf. Just in case, I yelled back the English equivalent – breaking off every few minutes to dive across the deck as the skiff swung this way and that. Then, with some rapport finally established, I settled back relaxed at last and watched how the Nile unfolded and other *feluccas* skimmed across the surface like flocks of nervous white birds. Each time I glanced at Faisal, he responded with a nod and a screwing up of his eyes – which was the nearest he ever came to a smile.

What should have been an hour's trip turned into an afternoon's outing and at each stop, we took on board Faisal's friends – all of whom seemed happy to be sailing nowhere in particular and were openly curious about his passenger.

We must have looked like a gang of pirates when we finally returned to our departure point, shortly before five. As Faisal escorted me up the steps to the road, I pulled out some notes, uncertain of how much more than the original price he would expect. But he refused anything more than what we'd agreed upon. Then he stopped a passing pony and trap and gave the driver the name of my hotel. While I climbed inside, they haggled over the price . . . and then Faisal handed over money for my fare. Before I fully realized what he'd done, the driver cracked his whip, the horse set off with a jolt and I could only shout my thanks at Faisal's bony back.

Around seven, I was showered, dressed and debating where to have dinner, when a hotel porter arrived to inform me, in a voice heavy with disapproval, that a man was waiting for me downstairs. A ragged Faisal lolled by the reception desk, indifferent to the displeasure his presence was causing among the staff.

In long-suffering tones, the manager translated Faisal's excited jabber. It seemed he'd come to escort me to a tailor. For a moment, I was confused. Then I remembered complimenting Faisal on his robe which, though worn and faded, was cut on long, flowing lines which I thought were very attractive. I'd actually fancied one of them myself and now, Faisal had come to arrange it.

The manager, who was about to send my boatman off with a flea in his ear, was amazed when I nodded happily and we stepped through the hotel entrance together. We must have looked a most unlikely couple, as we padded through a labyrinth of streets until finally, we were in the middle of the market – a place I wouldn't have ventured into alone after dark. I'd felt uncomfortable enough there in daylight. But now, with Faisal by my side, it all felt quite different. People waved and smiled as we made our way to a tiny booth, wherein resided one of the best tailors in Aswan.

He sat imprisoned behind an ancient treadle sewing machine, hemmed in by rolls of the finest Egyptian cotton, and I stood patiently through the inevitable bargaining, during which Faisal exploded and walked away twice (a trick I successfully employed on future haggling expeditions) before we reached a rock-bottom price for two *galabayahs*.

The delicate business of measuring took place next, under the suspicious eye of my protector, after which he further infuriated the tailor by insisting that both garments should be ready by the following evening.

Well pleased with his efforts, Faisal then led me off to a dilapidated eating house which stank of old blood and even older meat. It seemed I was to be his guest for dinner. Giving full attention to our conversation, I tried to switch off that part of my brain which registered disgust at the very sight of the stewed innards and telegraphed urgent warnings of imminent nausea with every mouthful I ate.

Later, on the steps of my hotel, my champion nodded, *salaamed*, and screwed his eyes up one last time, before disappearing into the night.

I never saw him again but I think of him often as the man who taught me the value of the friendly overture and the importance of treating everyone – from Nubian lepers to Indian Maharajahs – with the same respect.

On my journey, this knowledge proved more valuable currency than any amount of dollars or American Express traveller's cheques. For many times since that encounter with Faisal, I've sensed the warring good and bad influences in strangers I've met, who've considered taking advantage of me. Every time, I've tried to give them the benefit of the doubt – tried to be open and friendly – and it has always brought out the best in people. So I guess my dad was right, after all.

Dawn next day found me at Aswan's military airport, heading for Abu Simbel on a plane bristling with bare knees, baggy shorts and baseball caps. All around me, American senior citizens proudly sported name pins proclaiming 'Ethel' or 'Walt' or 'Marvin'.

Once grounded, I hung back as this noisy, excited crew disappeared in the direction of the ancient temple of Rameses II, so recently saved from a watery grave. I waited until I judged they were all safely inside it, then I strolled down the hill alone and rounded the cliff face to stare in awe at this splendid and seemingly deserted place – the dark entrance flanked by four towering statues of the Pharaoh, gazing blindly for ever across the shimmering expanse of Lake Nasser.

Then I turned north to Luxor, with the majestic and mystical temple of Karnak. Here, the brooding figures of Pharaohs and their consorts mount endless guard over an enchanted forest of columns. Tall and slender, they created a weave of light and shade which sent shivers up my spine, as I tiptoed through them by moonlight. The place was no less chilling when I retraced my footsteps in the heat and friendly light of day.

Then there was the silent wilderness of the Nubian desert, its endlessly shifting sands creeping over the worn stones of tombs and palaces in the Valley of the Kings, anxious to reclaim once more those ancient chambers it had hidden from prying eyes for centuries.

Here, Mohammud translated for me the violent story that was Egypt. A young and serious student of Egyptology I'd met through my hotel manager in Luxor, he brought to life the faded ochre paintings on the walls – all the imagery of war, treason and death, of slavery and riches and religion. As I trailed along in his wake all the cruelty and brilliance of that age was clear to see as I began to recognize the symbols and the signs – could name the gods of war and death and the underworld, came to know Queen Nefertiti's profile, Queen Hatshepsut's triple crown, at a glance. And Mohammud's pleasure matched mine as I began to understand a little of what the friezes were trying to say.

It was such a powerful experience that I lapsed into silence and padded thoughtfully after him as he led me to yet another tomb, which was closed to visitors.

The caretaker, resting in the cool shade of the outer chamber, smiled in greeting as he recognized Mohammud and we stood quietly at what was the edge of a steep tunnel, its carefully hewn walls and floor angling down sharply into the bowels of the tomb. This was the passage down which the sarcophagus had made its final journey, once the many false entrances and passageways had been sealed.

I peered down into the shadowy depths – anxious to explore, yet somehow strangely afraid. And when Mohammud gestured that I should go down alone, I glanced at the caretaker, almost hoping he would refuse permission. Smiling and nodding encouragement, he held out his hand as I stepped hesitantly past him and dropped two ripe, brown dates into my outstretched palm. And that's how I came to be all alone in the cool, airless burial chamber of an Egyptian king. Perched on a dais where once had nestled a fortune in golden ornaments, precious stones, rare oils and essences, I ate my dates slowly and stared for a long time at the giant sarcophagus, its granite lid smashed by the grave robbers of a thousand years ago.

Only recently excavated, the tomb smelled somehow dry and sweet, the slightest movement I made echoing in the stillness. More paintings told a story to anyone who could understand – their colours, so long protected from the air, seeming to vibrate on the walls.

Mohammud had known what he was doing when he left me to discover that room alone – the experience was devastating. And I still have the dry datestones to remind me of that amazing trip back in time.

So I travelled on through an Egypt filled with unforgettable images, experiences and encounters until eventually, I found myself heading back towards Cairo.

Like a child afraid to stray far from its mother's skirts, the train never quite loses sight of the Nile, as it heads steadily northwards. All of Egypt hugs the banks of this life-giving river and I watched from the dusty train windows as women came to beat their laundry and scour their pots at the water's edge, small boys came to wash their oxen or splash naked with their friends in its shallows, heedless of dead sheep and goats which drifted by, bloated and stiff-legged.

Here I saw a class of children studying in the open air, there an ox harnessed to a crude mill, walking in endless patient circles while the stones rubbed together on corn and wet washing flapped from its massive horns.

In village after village, ox carts, donkeys and camel trains crowded hard against the barriers at the level crossings and I would catch a tantalizing glimpse of bright turbans, flashing metal, grimy faces and naked children as our train flashed past.

But always, always, there was the Nile, with its gleaming mud banks, its bright *feluccas*, its fluttering canopy of date-heavy palms. While behind this green and fertile ribbon, the silent desert rose up shimmering in the distance.

The sun was low in the sky as my taxi rattled up towards the Pyramids and we were engulfed by the usual escort of wild-eyed horses, groaning camels and chanting boys, who banged on the roof and bonnet of the car, trying to attract my attention. But I knew who I was looking for and, as the taxi drew to a halt, I shouted the name 'Amer' from the open window. Immediately the cry was taken up and I sat back patiently to wait.

A few moments later, the crowd began to fall back, as a camel picked its way through – a bemused Amer urging it on, as he tried to peer down into the cab.

It's hard to describe how I felt as I stood there before him and saw the mingled amazement and pleasure written on his dark face. But it was a feeling which grew as he climbed down from the beast and walked towards me, his eyes approving my turban and my flowing green *galabayah*, even as he shook his head in mock despair.

As he touched his forehead in the formal greeting and *salaamed*, I distinctly heard him whisper, 'You are a crazy woman.' Then he broke into laughter, as he led me from the circle of interested onlookers.

I knew he was thrilled to see me and the knowledge left me feeling warm inside, as I settled myself behind him on Rameses and the animal struggled to its feet. Off to one side, the last tourist coaches of the day were spluttering into life and, as I glanced across at them, I realized that the windows were crammed with people taking snapshots of me. I smiled to think that I'd become an oddity to my own kind. But in that moment, it did seem that we were worlds apart. And now I could describe how it felt to stand before Amer. It felt a little like coming home.

As we headed out into the desert, his questions about my trip met with monosyllabic answers, for suddenly I felt weary in every limb. And soon I was sleeping soundly against his broad back, oblivious to the gathering dusk or the first of the evening's stars. . . .

The late afternoon sun cast swathes of blinding light and swirls of dark shadow across the empty acres of sand beyond the village. The air was heavy and still, the laughter of children and bleating of livestock drifting up to where I sat in Amer's lookout tower, my favourite place, at my favourite time of the day.

Sighing contentedly, I smiled as an image of my ex-husband suddenly popped into my mind. He'd been in my thoughts for most of that day – ever since I'd noticed the date on my watch and realized it held some special significance. A relative's birthday . . . some family event? I'd wondered, as I'd gone about my chores. And then it had dawned on me . . . another lifetime ago on this very day, I'd married Rui. Now I wondered what quirk of fate it was that had forced me to realize Rui's fantasy – the freedom to travel – while, living the domestic life in London, he was fulfilling mine. And what on earth would he say if he could see me now?

I turned at a slight sound and saw Samira climbing the uneven stairs to the roof. Wordlessly, she handed me a cup of cool water and we sat together companionably enough, although every so often she threw me a glance which I found impossible to translate. In fact, she'd been strange ever since my return to the village a few days earlier – outwardly pleased to see me and affectionate, yet somehow withdrawn and, in odd unguarded moments, almost . . . unfriendly.

Taking my empty cup, she left as silently as she had come and, as I sat on, it occurred to me that the change wasn't only in Samira. It was a fanciful notion . . . but I had the weird sensation that the whole village had subtly altered its attitude towards me.

It had started on the first morning of my return, as one visitor after another had called at the Habib household to pay their respects and take tea. Patiently, Samira had sat cross-legged at her primus stove, brewing up endless kettles of the strong, sticky potion. And at the end of forty-eight hours, she'd played hostess to more than half the village. Usually gregarious and hospitable, she had endured it stoically, but without much evident pleasure.

And the evening before, when we'd cleared away after the meal and Samira had laid out the utensils for the tea-making ceremony, Amer had casually suggested that I should try my hand at it. Samira's little face had been impassive enough as she moved over to let me carry out the ritual, but her eyes had been cold as she watched me.

No doubt about it – something was going on, I decided, as I went downstairs to await Amer's return.

He seemed edgy over dinner and was almost awkward, as he suggested I should go with him to a 'homecoming'. One of the village elders had returned from his pilgrimage to Mecca and that meant a celebration.

I put on my green *galabayah* for the party but left my head uncovered and was surprised when Samira made no move to get ready. I was even more confused when Amer explained that she would be staying behind. We walked quietly through the village, guided by the haunting sound of drums and reed pipes, which showed the party was already in full swing. But I stopped short just before the entrance of the elder's home, when I spied sixty or so men sitting on rugs in the courtyard and realized I was the only woman there.

Amer urged me on as the chatter died about us and, with eyes properly downcast, I sat cross-legged next to him in the dust, staring hard into my lap until conversations were resumed and the noise began to swell around me once more.

Then, surreptitiously, I took in the amazing scene, as the men around me, dressed in their finery and puffing on ornate bubble pipes, laughed and argued good-naturedly. Many of them had recently visited Amer's home and one or two of them nodded in greeting, when I inadvertently made eye contact.

227

Tuning into the conversation Amer was having with two men close by, I realized he was talking about me – recounting my journey through Egypt. They listened politely but seemed unimpressed by my travels. Then Amer made a remark which had their bushy silver eyebrows almost disappearing into their turbans, they were so surprised.

Later I asked him: 'What did you say to shock them so?' And proudly, he replied, 'I said you were so clever, you could do the shopping, if I allowed it!' Praise indeed – and no wonder his neighbours were shocked. Who'd ever heard of a woman shopping?

As the night wore on, the music grew wilder and, one by one, the men rose to dance. Raising the fine dust as their feet pounded out the rhythm they twisted and turned their bodies and lunged at one another with their wooden staffs in a display which was at once warlike and sensuous. A powerful sight. But why had I been allowed to see it? I wondered, as we wandered home afterwards.

Then Amer turned to me in the dark and spoke the words which suddenly made sense of it all. The endless stream of visitors . . . Samira's reserve . . . his awkwardness . . . my invitation to the party . . . even my overseeing of the tea ritual . . . I understood everything, now that I knew Amer wanted me for his second wife.

Stunned into silence, I walked by his side as he described how my life would be. I was to have the rooms on the first floor – the livestock would be moved to the level above. I could choose all the furniture and it would be my private domain.

I wasn't expected to do household chores – Amer had already divined that I had a business head on my shoulders and he was willing to fly in the face of convention and set me up with my own perfume stall or a papyrus stall, if I preferred. Or maybe I could have my own camel and work the tourists with him up at the Pyramids – a revolutionary idea, which certainly placed him as a man ahead of his time.

Whenever I wanted, I could go home for visits – even bring my parents out there to live. There was nothing he wasn't prepared to consider. And all I had to do in exchange was bear him lots and lots of children. Even as I wanted to laugh out loud at the absurdity of it, I knew he was paying me a great honour as he saw it and tact was everything.

'But – what about Samira?' I hedged. 'And the villagers would never accept me – ' I faltered, trying to find an escape route.

Amer had foreseen all the difficulties. Samira had already accepted his decision, as had her parents, who were embarrassed by her failure to have children. His parents, meanwhile, thought a new wife made sound sense and the village elders, after coming to look me over, had given their consent. In fact, the whole village was aware of the coming nuptials and had given its blessing. Now, happy that I was accepted into the community, Amer had finally let me in on the secret. He'd even anticipated my initial refusal and assured me with a tolerant smile that I would change my mind in a few days. What he *didn't* say was that, no matter how long it took, I would be confined to the village until I finally agreed. . . .

After that, the days took on a strange quality. Samira and I still worked together but the old camaraderie was gone. Now that her status as mistress of the house was threatened, she was understandably defensive. Yet she had enough sense to know that, sooner or later, Amer would be forced to take another wife, if she remained childless. And living with me, a foreigner, was a far less humiliating prospect than sharing her house and husband with some young chit from the village. So, even as she resented my presence, she knew me to be the lesser evil.

Now, I couldn't walk anywhere without being invited into houses to conduct impossibly stilted conversations over endless cups of tea, while children ran after me in the street or hung around the courtyard, calling my name. Through it all, Amer's smile was benign, his look knowing, as he waited for common sense to overcome my coy hesitation. In the end, my acceptance would be a formality.

But more amazing than all of that was the effect Amer's proposal had on me. As I methodically washed, cooked and cleaned, the idea grew and blossomed in my mind. Until I actually found myself thinking: 'Why can't I stay?'

For months now, I'd been travelling aimlessly and I was tired of wandering – tired of always being the stranger, the outsider. Here at last was somewhere I could settle down. People were kind and neighbourly, they had accepted me without question. Already I'd adapted well to their ways, watching the role women played and realizing that, although they were expected to be obedient to their menfolk, they were a long way from being second-class citizens. They had an important and well-respected place in this society. There was no crisis of identity, no confusion about their function. They seemed secure and happy, unlike lots of women I'd left behind in London.

Physically, it was a hard life, but it would be comforting to be under the protection of a man who took upon himself all the worries and problems. My days of being alone and self-sufficient would be over at last. True, this disciplined existence was unlike anything I'd ever known but that wasn't to say I wouldn't be happy with it. If my old life had had anything to commend it, I wouldn't have turned my back on it. So perhaps, after all, my coming to this village had been no coincidence. Maybe it was somehow predestined?

Oh, I was tempted – for practically the whole of one afternoon and for a good part of that evening, as well. And who could blame me, as Amer hoisted me up on the back of his camel and together we rode companionably into the desert, as the day drew to a close.

Dismounting on a high dune, Amer sat a little way apart from me, as I gazed out at a full moon hanging low over the distant Pyramids, as it outstared a dying sun. Sky and sand, Pyramids, sun and moon – everything was one colour, as if seen through a golden lens. And all shot through with the same bronze glow. I turned to see that Amer had taken on the same golden colours, as had the haughty Rameses parked a little way off. It was a spectacular sight and I found myself wondering again, 'Why can't I stay?' The answer came the next day. . . .

I suppose the morning got off to a bad start, thanks to a

herd of goats which wandered in through the open door and proceeded to eat the palm matting which I'd just finished laying in the central room. Alerted by the faint sound of chomping, I managed to chase them out eventually – but not before one of them had dumped its steaming calling card on the floor which I'd so carefully swept, just moments before.

Samira stood in the doorway of the kitchen, watching me clean up the mess with a superior air – although she was the one who had left the door open in the first place.

Back at my chores, I was dusting the fine sand from the blue and orange sofas and chasing flies with the switch, only dimly aware of a mournful dirge emanating from the shiny new radio Amer had sweet-talked from some tourist. Suddenly the music faded and the familiar sound of a striking clock reverberated round the room.

There was only one clock in all the world which sounded like that – and, like Cinderella at midnight, I stood transfixed as the room seemed to recede with each stroke.

. . . *I was strolling along the Embankment, hands deep in pockets and collar turned up against the fine rain, as Big Ben's comforting chimes rang out in the dusk and echoed across the Thames*. . . .

For an instant, London was all around me – more real than the buzzing flies, the stinging heat, the scratching of the hens as they foraged in the room above my head. And when it faded and I found myself again in Samira's receiving room, the pain of homesickness was overwhelming.

I looked about me in confusion – shocked into awareness of how alien my surroundings were. What had seemed normal just a moment before was now unfamiliar and other-worldly. *What the hell did I think I was doing there?*

I was subdued all day and wandered into the village later, carefully picking my way through narrow alleys filled with rank-smelling debris and camel dung. I heard the angry noise just as I turned a corner and walked straight into it – a living wall of filthy black flies, which rose up in a heaving mass from a carcass. I steeled myself to walk through them with my eyes tightly closed and was battered from head to toe by thousands of angry winged bodies which stung like hail stones. It was a horrible sensation.

In the next street, I stopped to talk to Samira's sister, who sat in the doorway of her home, her sleeping son spreadeagled across her lap. Even as she chatted, I stared at the army of flies which marched across the child's face – crawling into his tiny open mouth, his runny nose, his ears. He was a pitiful sight as he jerked and twitched uncomfortably in sleep. But then, there were so many pitiful sights, now that the scales had fallen from my eyes.

Amer arrived home later than usual, very disgruntled and leading an equally disgruntled Rameses, who'd been difficult all day and was off his food. Amer explained all this, as he unsaddled the camel and brought armfuls of fresh greens from the stable – delicious, tender shoots which Rameses dismissed with a jaundiced eye. Which meant force-feeding.

There was the small matter of who was going to stuff it down his throat and Samira flatly refused the chore. So it was left to me to deal with the mangy beast. Sitting there in the dirt, forcing the shoots – *and* my hand *and* most of my forearm – deep into his filthy maw and trying all the while to avoid his excruciating breath and his wicked teeth, I finally admitted it. There was no way I could accept this kind of life for my own.

That night, as I lay on my bed, plagued by hungry mosquitoes, I listened to that other side of me – the voice of reason and common sense I'd stifled since coming here. Free at last to state her case, the voice in my head rebuked me soundly and confronted me with more unpalatable truths.

I'd been playing at bedouins – taking childish pleasure in being even more obedient, submissive and hard-working than the bedouin women themselves. But in the end, it was nothing more than a game to me – a charade I could carry on for weeks, or even months, but which made me a fraud, nonetheless.

Oh, I hadn't done it maliciously. I'd escaped my old life and shaken off my old identity, only to realize that I needed to replace them with a different lifestyle and a fresh purpose. I knew the kind of woman I didn't want to be any more, but I'd no clear idea of the kind of woman I might become. And, lost without a role, becoming a bedouin woman had seemed to be a solution.

But beneath the robe, the turban, the meek expression and downcast eyes, I would always be essentially a woman of my time and place – a product of European culture. No matter how much I might want to deny it, I'd spent almost twenty years as a businesswoman. I was strong-willed, determined – my own person. I liked to exercise choice, make my own decisions. Even if that meant paying for my own mistakes. And, although I might have tired of it recently, I'd always assumed responsibility for my welfare. Now, I knew I could never be happy if I relinquished that.

And, what's more, I was used to so many other things . . . material comforts, good medical care, a balanced diet. I'd always enjoyed a sense of freedom, the companionship of like-minded people, the pleasure of speaking my native tongue. There were countless things I'd taken for granted, which would all be lost forever, if I stayed here.

It was one thing to know I had to leave – quite another to convince Amer. He flatly refused to discuss it with me and blocked every attempt I made to leave.

Reading this, you might think it would be simple enough to pack up and move out. But there *was* no way out of the village without transport. And no one would provide that without Amer's say-so. Now, I don't know whether it was real or imagined but as the days passed, I felt that the whole village was conspiring to keep me there. And, not for the first time on this bizarre journey, I found myself out of my depth and more than a little afraid.

Then came the evening my nerve broke and I had a stand-up, toe-to-toe row with Amer. The diminutive Samira, upset by the yelling, crept to my side and, slipping her tiny hand into mine, gave me the only support she dared. Eyes wide in dismay, she stood between us, like a child between parents, searching our angry faces and finding nothing to allay her fears.

That night, she didn't share Amer's bed, but slept on the blue and orange sofa opposite mine instead. And even though her still form was almost invisible in the darkness, I knew she was watching me and wondering what would happen next.

Amer ignored me all through the morning meal and I didn't feel too friendly, either. But Samira and I were back on our old, friendly footing and she smiled at me sympathetically as we saddled up the camel. Just before six o'clock, Amer swayed out of the courtyard – the hurt and anger obvious in the stiff line of his back, as he disappeared without so much as a glance. Shrugging my shoulders in resignation, I went inside to plan.

Slipping out of my *galabayah*, I chose my white, long-sleeved blouse, my ankle-length skirt, my flat white shoes. Round my waist, I hung a belted leather pouch, large enough to hold my passport, credit cards, address book and sunspecs. Slipping my camera over my shoulder, I wrapped my turban around my head like a shawl. My clothes, my precious tapes, my Sony Walkman – they were too much to carry. But I hated to leave them behind.

Samira glanced up in surprise when I walked into her bedroom and a look of panic crossed her face when she took in my appearance. I didn't say goodbye in so many words. Neither did she. But we walked arm in arm into the bright courtyard. And she kept on walking beside me – granting me uninterrupted passage through a village which had become my prison.

On the outskirts of the village, she hung back silently and I strode on, my feet sinking into the already hot sand, my sunspecs only marginally shielding my eyes from the glare.

I knew roughly the direction I had to head in to reach the Pyramids, and somewhere between them and me was a rough road which I'd passed over on the camel once or twice. I knew, once I reached that, I'd get a lift into the little town of Giza. From there, Cairo was within easy reach.

So, head bowed, I walked out of the bedouin village – and out of Amer el Habib's life. I wonder if he ever thinks of me. And if he does, if he has ever forgiven me?

Chapter Seven

Sanctuary – at a price

After the almost pastoral calm of the village, Cairo came as a bit of a shock when I rode back into it at the end of a long, burning hot day. I'd made it to the half hidden, sand swept track which connected up all the tiny encampments littered on the edge of the desert and before too long, as I had hoped, I'd managed to get a lift into Giza on one of the little rusty dormobiles which were the local form of public transport. From Giza I'd treated myself to a taxi ride into the city, arrived as daylight was fading and made my way back to the Black Tulip Hotel in T'alathaarb Square, where I'd left most of my clothes and, I'd begun to suspect, my sanity.

There was lots of excitement at the reception desk when I wandered in and I finally understood that Phil had come and gone in my absence. The manager showed me his signature in the dog-eared 'aliens'' book and as I headed down the grubby corridor with my room key firmly clutched to me I wondered how Phil's Egyptian adventure was progressing. Surely his experiences couldn't be as bizarre as my own?

Different room, same grubby bed and flooded loo, same ragged curtains over filthy window – home sweet home. At least in Samira's place, everything had been spotlessly clean, I thought, as I lay down fully clothed, just as if I was still under Amer's roof. Then I fell into a deep sleep, despite my empty, growling stomach.

Next morning, after a breakfast of fruit and yogurt in a seedy little restaurant around the corner, I mooched about in a half-hearted way. I visited the museum, then realizing I couldn't be bothered going in, I headed off to the Embassy, with some half-formed idea that I might find a few other travellers or ex-pats hanging around, but the place was deserted. So I sat there alone, reading week-old English papers in the dusty gloom of the reception area, before mooching out into the streets again. Yes, you've guessed it. I was looking for company. Didn't care about the age or the gender – or even the quality of the conversation – just so long as it was in a language I could understand.

Back in my hotel room that afternoon, it was inevitable that my mind would get around to Hafez. After all, other than Phil, who could well be forging through Africa by now, Hafez was the only contact I had in Egypt. True, the link between us was tenuous. I hadn't spent enough time in his company to get to know him really well. And the little I *did* know made me wonder if we were too *alike* to be friends. But, all alone in Egypt and knowing no one, I figured anything was worth a try.

I'd last seen Hafez moving into his new rooms high on the hills behind the little town of Lindos and we'd arranged to have a drink together that evening but I hadn't turned up and a couple of days later, I'd flown the coop. Still, he'd known I was heading for Cairo. And he *had* insisted on giving me his address. Yes, there was always Hafez. . . .

But he'd made it fairly obvious that he had designs on my body and though I'd quite enjoyed his company, I'd not done anything about it. Still, that was then and this was now and surely there was no harm in calling on an old acquaintance? It didn't take long for me to convince myself that this particular Egyptian would be thrilled to hear from me and, when I rushed down into the street to ring him, I wasn't disappointed.

'Trudy . . . ? Good God – still here in Cairo! Where the hell have you been, lady – I'd almost given up on you!' Standing in the phone box, surrounded by a crowd of yelling, clutching kids and overwhelmed by the traffic noise, I could barely hear Hafez's voice on the other end of the telephone but he certainly didn't have to repeat the invitation to drinks at his place. Minutes later, I was rattling across town in a rust bucket of a taxi, heading for Zamalek, Hafez al-Hakim and, I hoped, a taste of civilization.

Zamalek is the posh part of Cairo, although you'd never know it at first glance, surrounded as you are by the same horse shit, the same swirling, choking dust. But as we drove through the crowded streets I noticed the vegetables displayed by the roadside were fresher and more varied, parked cars, half-buried in sand were obviously foreign – even the beggars looked less lean and hungry and my spirits lifted with each passing mile.

The caretaker eyed me suspiciously when I reached Hafez's apartment block and I could hardly blame him. Although my image of myself had been restricted to what I could see in my make-up mirror, I had a nasty feeling that these weeks in the desert had taken their toll and that, compared to the stylish, perfumed women who wafted past this little Egyptian on their way to the Hakim lair, I was probably something of a disappointment.

That feeling was confirmed when a grinning Hafez threw open the door moments later, his lecherous mind already racing but the lascivious smile fading from his face, as he beheld the object of his desire. For there I stood – the result of twelve daily cups of sweet tea, endless meals of rice, garlic, stuffed bread, goatmeat and chicken. Or, to put it another way, I was fat. I was also dried up, worn out and all-in, something I began to realize as I squirmed uncomfortably beneath Hafez's incredulous gaze. He recovered his composure sufficiently to usher me into his home and I stepped into what was, for me at least, unaccustomed luxury.

Four large windows ran along the length of one wall, their blinds drawn against the sun's glare. Richly woven rugs were scattered about the wood block floors and hung against the painted walls.

There was a long brown leather sofa against one wall, two soft leather director's chairs, a low table strewn with photographic catalogues and fashion magazines. A whole library of books lined the opposite wall, tucked beneath a flight of open wooden stairs which connected this room with the upper floor. Examples of Hafez's camerawork were everywhere;

stunningly beautiful women in states of undress smiled up at me from sheets of positives and curves and undulations, exquisitely shaded and highlighted, goaded me from their framed vantage points on the walls.

Everywhere I glanced, thighs, bellies and buttocks reminded me of what women could look like – what I used to look like, all those long weeks ago in Rhodes. I'd known Hafez was a photographer but I hadn't realized he was such an artist – his eye and his camera all-seeing and all-revealing. And now he trained his eagle eye on me.

'What the hell have you being doing to yourself?' was all he said as he poured me a large vodka and I watched in quiet fascination as the liquid splashed over the ice – more unashamed luxury. Keith Jarrett's unmistakable piano-playing streamed out from the tape deck as I took my first sip of alcohol in an age and suddenly, it was all too normal, too commonplace, too much to cope with.

As Hafez's arm stole consolingly about my shoulders (no hint of lechery now), the tears slid down my sunburnt face and I blurted out my sorry tale, while his long-lashed eyes grew wider and amusement, disbelief and disapproval appeared turn and turn about on his face. By the time I was halfway through it, of course, I was milking my story for all it was worth and long before I'd finished it, we were rolling around the sofa, helpless with laughter at the very idea of me trying my hand as a bedouin.

Already that period was like a dream, although, just hours before, I'd fallen exhausted across my bed in the grubby little hotel, still unable to believe my luck at getting out of Amer's village – not to mention the desert – unscathed except for a burned face and a splitting headache.

By this time, the sun was sliding down the Cairo sky and I was badly in need of some sleep.

'Why not stay here?' Hafez put the question casually enough when I mentioned getting back to my hotel. 'I'm going out for the evening, so you can have the place to yourself. And you look as if you could do with a bath,' he added, his tone mocking. 'Come on – I'll show you mine.'

I followed him up the stairs to the second level, which

consisted of a bedroom totally dominated by the bed and a bathroom leading off it. He was right about the bath. It was long and deep with big chrome taps and a massive shower head. Towels, lots of them, were piled up on the shelves, together with bottles of this and jars of that. It was the way a bathroom should be, I thought with a sigh, as a fleeting image of Amer's ablutions room with its length of green rubber hose, its hole in the floor, its ever-ready pot of water and its scratching chickens, filled my head.

'Have you got hot water?' I asked, trying to keep the childish excitement out of my voice, and was lost when he answered, 'As much as you like'.

That's how I was sold to the Egyptian gentleman with the beard and the black eyes. His for the price of clean sheets and a tub of hot water. Some might say I was cheap at the price but, given my sorry appearance that day, I think I got the best of the bargain.

By the time he arrived home much later that night, I was safely tucked up, naked, in Hafez's bed. Oh, I had thought about playing coy – dragging blankets down to his sofa and insisting I was perfectly comfortable, thank you. And I'd considered climbing into his bed wearing at least my knickers, since in bedroom parlance that usually signals one's intention to share space without sex. 'But what the hell,' I thought. 'It's been a long time.' Anyway, after our gentle flirting in Greece, I figured Hafez and I might have some unfinished business to attend to.

To tell the truth, I think I needed the reassurance of having Hafez make love to me – an ego boost, if you like. Because a self-critical, unflinching ten minutes of appraisal in his very large and revealing bathroom mirror had confirmed what I'd all along suspected. Physically, I was a most unappetizing sight. My body was pale and pasty where the sun hadn't touched it, yet my face, neck and hands were dark and leathery. My skin was spotty, thanks to my very unhealthy diet, and a whole network of lines had appeared around my eyes. My lips were dry and cracked, my hair bleached to a manic orange, my nails split and torn.

Frankly, any man who volunteered to make love to me, considering my miserable appearance, would definitely be doing me a favour, I decided, and congratulated myself on reaching the safety of Hafez and Zamalek not a moment too soon.

All that mattered that night was that I felt clean, relaxed and safe, tucked up with a man who made love to me in a way that made me feel as beautiful as the women on his walls and reassured me, as he stroked me to sleep, that in a week – two at the most – I'd look and feel just as good as new.

He was right, too; a fortnight of pampering later, the woman who had flown out of Rhodes had again taken up residence and my body showed no sign of the punishment it had received out in the desert. I'd had my hair permed at an expensive salon and after a couple of weeks of serious dieting, I was able to get into some of the more expensive and stylish clothes I'd packed all those months ago in London. I needed them, too, for Hafez's life was one long round of socializing with a smart and very upper-crust set.

Although many in his circle were the posing, pontificating type you'll meet in every smart and showy city crowd, a few of them were wonderful people. Martina was an Egyptian beauty – a woman some years older than Hafez who was a very loyal friend, caring for him in spite of his less attractive personality traits. (I was shortly to discover those for myself.) Nips was a wonderfully Bohemian antiques dealer with a taste for fine and lovely things. His attitude towards Hafez was tolerant and amused, his fondness for him beyond question. Mohammed was an old school friend whose continued love of learning was only outstripped by his love of good old whisky. And painting. He loved to paint and was as sensitive with this as he seemed to be with everything and everyone he encountered.

The fact that they all cared for Hafez proved that he was a person worth caring for and the easy way they accepted me into their circle was something I really appreciated – even though they welcomed me for Hafez's sake rather than my own.

And it was lovely to live a life of unmitigated ease again, with Hafez's daily maid to clean up after me in the bedroom, the bathroom, the kitchen. It certainly made a change from running everywhere at Samira's beck and call and cleaning up after Amer and his bloody camels.

Although Hafez worked some days, he was his own boss and pretty much pleased himself. So we spent lots of time together – lunching out, visiting his friends, going for boating trips on the Nile or just lazing around indoors, playing music, talking and getting to know each other.

I was quite happy on the occasions he left me alone; more than content to roam around Cairo by myself or explore the food shops and vegetable markets in Zamalek, where the local shopkeepers soon got to know me. Other times, I would spend hours in the bathroom lavishing attention on my skin, painting my toe nails or playing around with my hair – as lazy as the day was long.

None of this went down too well with his daily help, who regarded both me and my laundry (which she insisted upon doing) with the same mild distaste. The wisps of knickers and slips of dresses I'd begun to wear again obviously branded me as yet another of these loose European women – so many of whom, by Hafez's own admission, had flitted in and out of his bed and his life.

Was I shocked, hurt – disappointed, even? How could I be, for hadn't I spent endless years with a man who almost made womanizing a virtue? And, with my own rather colourful track record, I was hardly in a position to cast the first stone. Anyway, I liked the idea that Hafez felt comfortable enough with me to tell me about his past which was, in places, fairly racy. He admitted to at least two ex-wives, endless mistresses and certainly one child – let's say he'd lived life to the full. Knowing that gave me courage and, little by little, I gave him details of what I regarded as a pretty lurid and sorry track record of my own.

I wasn't proud of myself by any means, but I wanted him to understand who I had been (maybe still was) and to accept me, warts and all. Cosmopolitan, jet-setting Egyptian meets sophisticated, world-weary Brit, was how I saw it. Cards on the table; don't try to kid a kidder and all that crap. I thought he understood that I was trying to break down barriers but I still had an awful lot to learn about men in general . . . and Hafez in particular.

Simplistically, I concluded that Lisbon life had come to the Nile and I was back in a world I understood – a world of night clubs, parties, successful men and beautiful women. And money. And sex.

Hafez seemed to have an endless supply of the former and an insatiable appetite for the latter, which was fine by me, though I did pay my way. I've never fancied myself as a kept woman and in no time at all I'd crammed his cupboards and fridge with food I'd bought on my shopping expeditions. I'd put fresh flowers in the rooms and I was full of ideas for face-lifting the whole place with a coat or two of paint – all of which seemed to meet with his approval. Still, it was nice to have him wine and dine me; comforting to know, when he picked up the tab in a restaurant or club, that it was 'coming off a broad back' as my grandmother was fond of saying.

As to the sex . . . well, that was comforting, too. If a little manic. Hafez, while not 'knock-em-dead' handsome, was certainly physically pleasing. Five foot ten at the most, he was slightly but powerfully built with unusually fine but surprisingly strong hands. His dark curly hair was thinning slightly at the crown and he wore it cropped close to his head. Thick, bushy eyebrows met and mingled across the bridge of his nose, while an attack of desert blindness years before had given his dark eyes a strange transparent quality when the light caught them at a certain angle. His nose was incredible. Beautiful, really, with its beaked shape giving his face an intense, hawklike appearance.

But under the laughter and behind that deep, rich, playful voice, there was nothing jaunty about Hafez. I suppose I'd known it from the first – realized as far back as Rhodes that, like me, he was searching for something. Restless, uncertain about the decisions he'd made in the past and almost afraid to make any decisions about his future, he suffered from black moods and severe depressions.

He worried all the time about every conceivable thing. Did he have any talent at all? Would he ever take another decent picture? Should he stay in Cairo or head for Europe? Was there anywhere in the world where he would feel really, truly content? And while he looked for answers to all of these quality-of-life-threatening questions, he submerged himself in sex and women. Lots of sex with lots of women. Tireless sex that went on all day and all through the night. Sex during which he had to give, give, give, so that women thought he was a wonderful, intuitive, selfless, generous lover. The perfect, caring partner for anyone looking for a real relationship – which was precisely how he wanted to see himself.

But this wasn't true, although it took me a long time to tumble to this fact. I mean, I swallowed the bait, too. Went weak-kneed when he stroked my hair, gazed into my eyes, said, 'Listen, lady, I'm crazy about you,' and then made love to me as if he'd really meant it. Admittedly, I was a pushover. All through these endless miles and lonely months, I'd been looking for a place to settle down, desperate for the opportunity to be a 'nice' person around some man again. I'd exhausted my old brittle, ball-busting 'seek and destroy' tactics and now I was ready to start acting like the female I'd always known I was. And it was no chore to be gentle, supportive, responsive around this man, since all the things Rui's ex-wife had excelled at were the very qualities Hafez seemed to need.

I clucked over his constant migraines, pandered to his hypochondria (his medicine cabinet stored enough drugs to refloat the NHS). I indulged his habit of playing emotional mind games and his theatrical outbursts. Even took it in my stride when he lost control of his tongue and became that saddest of things in men – a lacerating, wounding, mean-mouthed bitch.

Submissive, compliant, loving (and, hopefully, lovable), I went on buying the flowers, restyling the rooms, dusting down the bookshelves and the framed images of women's boobs and bottoms, in a haze of self-deluding domesticity – trying not to mind when the women themselves descended upon us unannounced.

Eyeing me warily, they would nonetheless contrive to ignore me completely, as they launched themselves upon a Hafez who was never slow to bury his head in hair, cleavage or any other areas of exposed flesh – such warm welcomes being the order of the day in the Hakim household. While I, no stranger to jealousy but (I liked to think) always its master, would slip off to the bedroom or the bathroom to pluck my eyebrows and contemplate my precarious position. I wanted to stay with Hafez; wanted to share his pleasant life and his lovely friends. Wanted to encourage him with his work and help him over this period of self-doubt. Wanted to be wanted, I suppose. Wanted to be indispensable. Wanted to be involved in the restructuring of his life, so that I could be sure of building a niche in it for myself.

I didn't love him, but that wasn't an obstacle. Right then, I could have loved anyone who loved me – out of sheer gratitude, if nothing else. And there was always the sex. I remember one day, he walked in on me in the bedroom, when I'd just finished dressing to go out. I was minus my clothes in no time and the sex was great, as usual. Twenty minutes later, I was dressed again and just stepping into my shoes, when he strolled out of the bathroom, fixed me with that look I'd come to recognize . . . and I was minus my clothes again. The sex was still good. The third time, I was halfway down the stairs and he was lolling around on the sofa in the living room. I saw him looking up at my legs and felt my dress practically removing itself. I suppose the sex was still okay but I was preoccupied all through it, knowing the shops would all close at midday. That scene was repeated seven times, believe it or not, by the end of which episode, my dress was a crumpled, unwearable heap on the bedroom floor and I wasn't much better.

I'd be a liar if I said I wasn't pleased about it. After all, wasn't this the proof I needed that I was getting to him? But part of me probably knew that, although the seduction was real enough, the sentiment was false. Hafez insisted that he loved and adored, even worshipped, women. The truth is that he disliked them a lot of the time and distrusted them completely.

Looking back, I suspect the pattern was the same with every woman he met – he'd come on strong with the sex, the sentimentality, the compliments, the caring. Then he'd sit back and wait for her to fuck up. Knowing that, sooner or later, women always do. And I was to be no exception.

All to do with his mother, of course, and the fact that she left the marital home when he was no more than a young 'un – going off to live with and eventually marry another man. She'd left baby Hakim with a legacy of rejection and desertion and the unshakable knowledge that all women are whores, destined to disappoint you, no matter how much of a good little boy you try to be. Now, from deep inside this thirty-eight-year-old scuba-diving, desert-wandering, artistic, articulate, wealthy, urbane, sophisticated man, baby Hakim watched me with a jaundiced eye. And waited.

Meeting his mother turned out to be bizarre for lots of reasons, the main one being the venue – her home. As Hafez's monstrous custom-built jeep drove out of Cairo and headed for the Pyramids, the mere thought of yet another encounter with his mama brought on one of his black and nasty moods. That started another migraine, which made any conversation impossible, so I amused myself instead with the passing view.

Little by little, I got the uncomfortable feeling that I'd travelled that particular route before. For sure, I recognized some of the landmarks. As we turned off the main highway and headed off down a secondary road bounded by high walls on one side and a stream flowing sluggishly on the other, I realized I'd swayed along this very road weeks before, on the back of Amer's camel.

We had been making one of our rare trips into Giza and from my elevated vantage point, I'd gazed in envy at some of the palaces which lay behind these high walls. One in particular had been a magical place of minarets and arches, fountains and flowers – and half a dozen fierce mastiffs.

At Amer's bidding, Rameses had stepped up to the wall to give me a better view and it was as I'd 'oohed' and 'aahed' my appreciation that some son of a bitch had released the dogs. They'd raced across the lawns and hurled themselves against the walls in a frenzy, much to the delight of the gardeners who had watched from the safety of an outhouse. Terrified, Rameses had shied away abruptly, almost unseating

245

me as he'd roared and farted his terror, before lurching off along the track in a most undignified way.

Even as I recalled the beauty of that residence (you could hardly call it a 'house') and remembered the handsome iron gates which rose a good fifteen feet into the air, Hafez wrenched hard on the steering wheel and in a cloud of red dust, the jeep screeched to a halt . . . outside the very same gates.

I was too surprised to comment as a couple of workers – presumably the same ones who had enjoyed my discomfort all those weeks before – rushed over the lawns and pulled the gates back, while Hafez casually lit a cigarette before driving slowly through. His manner was nonchalant but I wasn't fooled for a minute. He hated his mother every bit as much as he loved her and it showed. I could hear the baying of the dogs as I jumped down from the passenger seat and before I had time to really consider the irony of the situation, I was being ushered along corridors, up steps and through little courtyards until finally I was deposited before The Presence herself.

She was lounging on a sofa draped with silk, borne up on a sea of cushions. The room was very large and roofed over, although it seemed to be open along one side. There was an ornamental pool in the centre, with a fountain playing in it and rose petals floating hither and thither in the water. The furniture was mostly French, very old and quite, quite beautiful – the combination of things European and Eastern creating an atmosphere at once stylish and exotic. It was certainly palatial but hardly warm and welcoming. In fact, I could have been taking tea in a museum with an icily beautiful curator.

Hafez's mother was a stunningly lovely woman, very much in control of everything, it seemed. Except her emotions, regarding her son. While I sipped tea and simpered, they went at each other like dogs in a pit although it was all done in the best possible taste.

The trouble was that Hafez's mother, a patron of the arts, gave all manner of support and encouragement to whichever artist struck her as being flavour of the month. Even as we sat there, some moderately talented dauber was humming happily into his paintbox on one of the upper floors, secure in the knowledge that he had a comfortable meal ticket. And, whenever he felt ready to face his public, his patron would arrange an exhibition of his works in her wonderful gallery. Meanwhile her son was racked with self-doubt and plagued by a sense of failure and, if she knew, she seemed not to care.

Growing bored with their thinly concealed antagonism towards each other, I slipped off to explore and realized as I moved quietly through it that the house had been designed to ensure an uninterrupted view of the Pyramids from every single room. There they were, their colours changing from blue to purple to gold as the evening 'Son et Lumière' show lit up their ancient stones. And beyond them, somewhere in the desert, sat Amer and Samira – the former perhaps contemplating my fate, the latter considering her own.

After that, it was home to bed and another surfeit of sex – although this time, Hafez went at his task like a man possessed, as he surely was that night. Long after he fell asleep and all the way into the dawn, I lay by his side, listening to the sounds of Cairo waking – to the wailing of the Mullahs as they called the faithful to prayer. High up in that twelfth floor apartment above a forest of minarets, I lay thinking, while the light changed from darkest sapphire to silver grey to brilliant white, stealing through the blinds to disturb Hafez with its persistent brightness.

He blinked and gazed at me vacantly for an instant. Then his smile was sweet, his voice tender, as he drew me to him. But I hadn't forgotten the wild anger of his lovemaking the previous night and, as I put my arms around the man, I wondered if I'd ever learn to cope with the unhappy child.

As it turned out, I didn't get time to try. A couple of days later, as we were washing together in the bathroom, he checked his equipment for what must have been the tenth time that morning and then announced that he had 'a problem'. All concern, I listened sympathetically as he described the symptoms – discharge, itching, slight sensation of pain – and reeled back in disbelief when he added, 'Which means, my lady, that the problem lies with you. After all, I haven't slept with anyone in several weeks – apart from you, that is.

You, on the other hand, would seem to have had rather a busy time of it.'

I knew that was a reference to all the men in my past. Although I probably deserved the remark, I felt ir.credibly hurt. I guess it's one thing to be honest with a man and quite another to expect him not to use your confession as a weapon against you. His look was hard to interpret, as was his tone. Tolerant and philosophical was the attitude he tried to convey. But there was hurt and betrayal there, too. A 'how could you do this to me, when I've treated you so well' quirk to the mouth. Baby Hakim had come into his own.

Although I'd had lots of lovers, I'd never had a venereal infection and it had never occurred to me that I might. That sort of thing only happened to other people, I began to tell myself. Only this time, Hafez's weeping and sorry-looking appendage seemed to prove it had finally happened to me. But where and when – and who had infected me? Not once did it occur to me to question Hafez's evidence, his findings or even his verdict. I was unclean – Hafez had said so and not even my own perfect health would make me query the fact.

Having dealt me a death blow, Hafez proceeded to assure me that 'We're both sophisticated adults and we know this sort of thing is an almost inevitable result of sleeping around.'

I was sick with gratitude.

'It could just as easily have been my problem as yours. Now it's our problem and we'll sort it out straight away.'

What did I do to deserve such a wonderful man?

I was still thinking that half an hour later, when Hafez looked up at me sternly from the pages of the medical tome he was reading (like all hypochondriacs, he had several of these to hand). Shutting it with a decisive snap, he said in a controlled voice, 'Well, I've checked out all your symptoms (*my* symptoms!) and I'd say you've got syphilis.' He might just as well have said I had a week to live, the shock was so profound. How long had I had this dreadful thing? Who else might I have infected? I was nothing more than an animal, to have brought this plague to his door.

Hafez, I concluded, was a saint to have taken it so much in his stride.

The saint soon had me fixed up with a doctor and I tottered off to bed that night, terrified of what the next day's appointment might bring. Hafez's attempts to make love to me were my final humiliation. What a forgiving man. Imagine even wanting to touch me, after what I had done.

I wept buckets with remorse. Baby Hakim must have had a field day.

The following afternoon, I walked alone into what Cairo laughingly called its venereal diseases centre. And may I say now that, until you have sampled the delights of a clap clinic in Cairo, you don't know what humiliation is.

The place was in a particularly sleazy part of town and the front entrance was hardly visible for a knot of gruesome-looking men who hung around the door. I marched past them purposefully enough, the way I fancied the Salvation Army girls back home do, when they stroll into working men's clubs and pubs in search of donations. But no one was fooled by my innocent air. I could tell by the way they laughed at me that the men knew exactly why I was there.

Climbing the filth-littered stairs, I found myself in an outer office where everyone, from the receptionist on, was male. Then into the waiting room with four or five male patients, who watched me stare so hard at some imaginary object outside the window that one of them finally poked his head out there to see what I was looking at. I sat nervously plucking at the buttons on my white blouse, fingering the embroidery on my white skirt, imagining scuff marks on my white pumps. Feeling so dirty. Knowing that all this vestal virgin white was fooling no one and wishing I could die. I very nearly did just that, when the 'nurse' came to collect me. He was small and fat and incredibly filthy. Forget the uniform, this guy was just barely dressed at all, in a collection of rags which should have been burned on the spot. I'd already decided that I'd die of syphilis and all its attendant horrors before I'd let this fiend touch me, when he opened the door to a tiny room and I found myself sitting opposite an immaculately dressed and reassuringly distinguished-looking gentleman. Almost faint with embarrassment by now, I told him my story, such as it was, and looked blank when he asked about my symptoms. He looked equally blank when I said I didn't have any.

'So why are you here?' he asked patiently.

'Because my boyfriend thinks I need treatment.'

'But surely, if he is the one displaying symptoms, he is the one who should be examined?' he said tentatively. It made sense.

'No matter,' he went on pleasantly. 'Looking at you, I would say you have nothing to worry about (I was grateful for the comforting lie), but we shall check you out thoroughly, just to put your mind at rest. We will do every test possible.'

And so it began – the indignity of the internal. But this was a million miles from the Marie Stopes Clinic for Ladies; there was no sweet woman to understand my fears; no pleasant pictures on the walls to take my mind off things; no welcoming brew in the waiting room afterwards to calm troubled nerves. There was just this grubby little room with its brown walls, its brown floor, its bare light bulb and the slovenly shuffling of the 'nurse' as he came and went with the swabs. I tried to comfort myself with thoughts of Hafez, sitting patiently outside in the darkened jeep – and realized, with a sinking stomach, that *that* was cold comfort.

The next evening, I went back for my results. They were clear, which meant, so was I. Whatever ailed Hafez's equipment, I wasn't the culprit and that news came as such a blessed relief that it was a while before I began to wonder just what, in fact, the culprit was. By that time, the doctor had insisted on seeing Hafez. 'Nurse' had been sent to fetch him from the jeep downstairs and he was already de-bagged in an ante-room, receiving a similar experience to my own. I'd glimpsed his face for an instant as he'd walked by me – apprehensive and pale with worry. Or was it anger?

Twenty minutes later, we were back on the street – me with a light heart and Hafez with a much lighter wallet. The diagnosis? No syphilis, no gonorrhoea, no clap of any shape or distinction. Nothing. I was as fit as a flea and so was Hafez.

'Put it down to an overactive imagination,' he laughed as he hugged me tightly in bed that night; and I tried, I really tried. But the dreadful episode had brought me back to earth with a jolt.

After all, the dreaded syphilis – that tangible result of my destructive and debauched way of life – had never existed. But now I wondered how often Hafez had looked at me and seen – not the calm and happy companion I'd tried so hard to be – but some careless, irresponsible slut. How long had he been waiting for the mask to slip, for the real me to give herself away? And when that hadn't happened, how easy had it been for him to convince himself that I must be diseased?

From then on, Hafez was full of plans. We were going to take the jeep out into the Sinai – he was sure I'd fall in love with the desert. Then, later, we'd head down to the Red Sea. Stay there for a few weeks, while he taught me to scuba dive. And he'd teach me about photography, so that I could help him work towards his next exhibition. Suddenly, he was full of ideas and they all included me. His acceptance of me should have made me happy. But it had come too late.

Hafez had discovered his 'infection' on the day that there had been one other world-shattering event. Indira Gandhi had been assassinated, but I'd been so caught up in my own crisis that I'd hardly noticed. More than once I'd mentioned to Hafez that I would eventually be travelling on to India – partly to alleviate any fears we both might have had that I'd become a permanent fixture and partly to remind myself that I still had something (God alone knows what) to achieve.

It's hard to say whether I'd ever seriously intended to see that continent but a couple of days after I was diagnosed plague-free, I took myself off to the British Embassy and asked them about the situation in India. The official line was that making a trip to that part of the world just then was ill advised and that was enough for me.

The Air India office was closed, but I found a travel agent who thought she could get me on a flight within forty-eight hours. I left her and went wandering off around Cairo to think about it.

The situation was straightforward enough. If I stayed, a future with Hafez was unlikely. Partly because I doubted if he could trust any woman enough to give her a chance but mostly because I'd underestimated myself. I had thought I needed a man in my life at all costs but it was slowly beginning to dawn on me that Hafez's price was much too high. If I stayed with him, he'd be forever calling me to account over imagined infidelities and God alone knew what else. I'd always be the scapegoat for whatever went wrong in his life – and although I'd subjected myself to some fairly cavalier treatment during these last months, I'd begun to realize I didn't have to be anyone's whipping boy.

If I went home, I'd get there just in time to celebrate Christmas with my family, but what would life in London be like, once the novelty of going home had worn off? A reunion with The Stormtroopers and my usual seat in my usual bar; a fight to the death with the Inland Revenue and not even a place to lay my head, since I'd rented out my flat.

Nope, it still wasn't my time to go home.

'So far, so what?' seemed to sum up my mindless wandering till now. If this trip really was a learning experience, I still had a long way to go. So . . . that left moving on. But which way? Not Africa. Too much famine, too much border war, too expensive. The more I thought about it, the more I knew that India was the only way ahead.

The smiling travel agent handed over the ticket which would take me all the way to Singapore. At the thought of the stopovers – Bombay, Delhi, Calcutta, Rangoon and Bangkok – my heart gave a little lift. Then it sank again at the thought of Hafez. Resolutely, I stuffed the ticket into my shoulder bag and walked all the way home to Zamalek, wondering how best to break the news.

The wave of bonhomie preceded Hafez through the door. The flowers were beautiful, the apologies effusive, the twinkle in the eye as devilish as ever. Dinner, he promised, would be a particularly romantic affair, in a glitzy restaurant overlooking the Nile. Hafez was his old self again.

The usual 'And what have you been doing today, my lady?' was uttered as he poured me a long drink and brought it out on to the balcony. This was where I could be found most evenings, gazing down at the city turning blood red in the dusk. Marvelling at the ribbon of molten metal which was the Nile, as Cairo's noise floated up from this place of a thousand mosques. For a time, I'd really felt safe up here, set apart from humanity.

'Oh . . . nothing much,' I murmured, gazing up into the golden, sand-laden sky. 'I wrote a letter to my mother, checked in at the Embassy, had lunch with Martina. And I bought my plane ticket to India,' marvelling, as I uttered the words, how easy they had been to say.

It turned into a long evening. A longer night. Hafez begged, cajoled, accused – threw moods and tantrums in turn. He even cried and so, finally, did I. Because somewhere in this crazy affair, there had been elements which pleased both of us.

He refused to speak to me for the next two days, maintained the silence even when I slipped out of bed on that last morning and only relented when I went into the bathroom to prepare for leaving and he realized that nothing – least of all his refusal to speak – would persuade me to stay. He made tea and we had it in the bathroom together – perched on the edge of the bath and neither of us with the faintest idea of what to say or how we could painlessly bring this encounter to an end.

Baby Hakim contrived to look pathetic in his bathrobe with his hair standing up and his eyes full of sleep but I was beyond being moved. In the living room, he held on to me as if he would never let me go. Then, when I disentangled myself, he petulantly refused to help me downstairs with my luggage. So the last image I had of Hafez was through the grille of the elevator – his dark eyes with their strange transparent gleam fixing me with a look of need and anger.

Twelve floors down, a taxi waited in the dust. The air was still full of that early morning desert chill and I shivered as I threw my bags into the boot. High up above in his eyrie, I knew Hafez was leaning out over the balcony, willing me to look up. I could feel his eyes on my back as I climbed into the taxi and drove off without a backward glance, knowing that I'd probably never see him, or Cairo, ever again.

'Still,' I reminded myself, 'it's time to look ahead. Cheer up – you're off on another adventure, sweetheart!' As we rattled over the stony road in a cloud of ochre dust, I began to wonder where exactly on India's coastline, the city of Bombay lay. And were the Egyptian TV reports accurate about all that carnage and bloodshed, riots in the streets and wholesale slaughter? See Bombay and get your throat cut . . . well, it was better than being bored. I'm ashamed to admit it but, even as my taxi bounced erratically off the other end of the Zamalek bridge, Hafez had begun to be yet another memory to be logged with all the others.

India was just six hours away and suddenly, I had more urgent things to think about.

PART THREE

My time to fly

Chapter One

The courage to be *me* again

Bombay airport was as quiet as a graveyard. It was three in the morning and, jet-lagged and uncertain, a small knot of travellers huddled together at the currency exchange desks, swapping Swiss, German and French traveller's cheques for bundles of grubby rupee notes. All around me in the queue were faces, drawn and pale beneath the strip lights, and I wondered if I looked as worried as they did. The Air India flight had been two-thirds empty; the bulk of the passengers made up of Indians who hung around in the aisles outdoing each other with gruesome tales of communal violence, of street riots and wholesale bloodletting, while the few Europeans on board grew more and more apprehensive.

Too late, I began to wonder if flying to India had been such a smart move and my conversation with one of the stewards – an Anglo-Indian who advised me to stay out of the city – didn't cheer me up a whole lot.

We'd landed to be informed that we couldn't leave the airport till dawn, because of the curfew. So we sat on our luggage waiting for first light, while groups of policemen hung around the exits, gazing nervously out at the dark.

Jan was the first to move out. A young, shy, painfully skinny Swede, he'd literally bumped into me a couple of weeks earlier in one of the Cairo streets. Then he'd just had his passport and wallet stolen and he was wandering around, looking for the Swedish Embassy, so we'd tracked it down together. I'd been impressed when he'd told me he was cycling around the world and meeting up with him again on the flight out of Egypt had been an unexpected surprise.

Now, he gave me a last tight little smile as he slung his knapsack over his shoulders and wheeled his bike to the main exit. I watched him through the window. He looked incredibly vulnerable in his T-shirt and shorts as his pale legs pumped at the pedals, and I knew, as he was swallowed up by the shadows, that it was time I moved out, too. But for once, I took notice of someone's advice and headed for the outskirts of the city as the steward had suggested.

The taxi ride to Juhu beach seemed to take forever and I couldn't get any information from the sullen driver, who rattled along at top speed through what looked like the largest rubbish tip in the world. We drove through street after street of what I dismissed as piled up refuse, not realizing that literally thousands of people were sleeping beneath the corrugated iron, the cardboard sheets, the tarpaulin strips. Whole families were living a miserable existence just feet away from the wheels of my taxi – and they were the lucky ones.

I drove on past the Holiday Inns, the Sea & Sand, the Majestics, the Royals and Imperials, knowing that Bombay hotel prices were astronomical by any standards and feeling loath to part with my precious rupees unnecessarily.

The hotel I chose looked okay from the outside, in that all four walls were standing, the glass was intact in most of the windows and there was actually a doorman, who stepped forward as my taxi drove up to the entrance. I was surprised to see that he was a Sikh (according to the wilder reports I'd heard, there was hardly one of those left alive in India since the Troubles). But this one stood at least six feet four in his turban and was very much in the land of the living.

Two pretty Indian girls in grey silk sarees welcomed me at the reception desk, divested me of my passport, my luggage and suggested I leave any valuables in their safe. I followed a threadbare porter of around fourteen into the tiny, rickety lift and stood in the middle of a garishly illuminated room while he dumped my luggage and plied me with personal questions on everything from my age to how many children I had.

By now, grubby depressing bedrooms were commonplace to me, so this one, with its vomit coloured carpets and vile blue walls, came as no surprise. I turfed a large tortoiseshell-coloured cockroach out of the sink and rinsed my face. Then I turned down the bedcover to see whether the sheets had been washed recently and was cheered by the grease-free pillow case and the complete absence of tell-tale creases in the sheets. Satisfied that the linen hadn't had a previous occupant, I tore a wad of loo paper from the roll in the bathroom and stuffed it into holes in the door to thwart any Peeping Toms. Then, groggily, I stripped off, bedded down and slowly lost consciousness while, on the other side of the dusty brown brocade drapes, Bombay city struggled into life.

I woke around ten in the morning and opened the curtains for my first real look at India. Four or five floors below I could see the shacks and lean-tos clustered around the hotels, Indian women queued up at a well on the corner of the street to collect water, naked brown children played in the dust and threw stones at a pack of twenty or so wild dogs which were setting about each other in a wild-toothed frenzy.

A row of yellow and black cabs snaked along the street, some of their drivers touting half-heartedly for custom while others, playing a game of cricket in the road, risked being mown down by a fleet of motorized rickshaws which dodged through the heavier traffic like demented lawn-mowers.

As the scene shimmered outside my window in a heat haze I realized that even the poverty and filth of Egypt compared favourably with what lay outside the walls of my hotel . . . but I hadn't seen anything yet.

Showered and dressed, my contact lenses inserted, I was studying my face in the bathroom mirror, while my fingers rummaged around in my make-up bag for mascara. I yelped in fright when they closed around something which wriggled out of my grasp and cosmetics were scattered all over the floor as the lizard and I took off in opposite directions. It was to be the first of many encounters with India's wildlife, as I gradually reconciled myself to sharing cramped living space with snakes and spiders, roaches and rats of a size and scale unknown in Europe – and with a sense of aggression to match.

I do believe I began the day with quite an appetite, until I happened to poke my head out of the bathroom window to see what the rear view afforded. Beneath me, the hotel 'kitchen' was a camp site – a bewildering hotch-potch of open fires and primus stoves set up at the back of the hotel and completely open to the elements. Raw meat was piled up next to dirty crockery, baskets of bread stood alongside dustbins heaped with refuse. Everything – including the beleaguered cook – was under attack from mangy dogs which slunk around the perimeters of his kitchen, all bared teeth and bones. Even as he chased one off, another slid up just outside his field of vision to lick the empty plates, while large shiny black crows and dull brown-feathered hawks dive-bombed him from above, making off with bread rolls, eggs and anything else they could steal. I decided I'd survive without breakfast.

Down in the street, it's hard to say what hit me first. Was it the wall of sound – hundreds of car horns and bicycle bells vying for attention, yet drowned by the din of Indian pop music and the wail of voices? Was it the heat, which forced its way into my lungs or the dust which filled my eyes and mouth? No, I think it was the smell which made the first and most lasting impression; a lethal pot-pourri of stagnant water, rotting vegetation, putrefying animal corpses, urine and human excrement, with a subtle top note of unwashed bodies and the merest trace of curries and spices. Odour of India . . . one whiff of it could bring a dray-horse to its knees.

With a heaving stomach, I made for the nearest taxi but not before the cry had gone up that there was a fare on the loose. Cab drivers came at me from all directions, like Saturday fans streaming towards the local football ground. Even as I wrenched open the rear door, a fight broke out over who should get the business and a couple of punches were thrown as my driver scrambled into the front seat and took off in a squeal of worn tyres. Once we were safely under way, he turned and fixed me with a grateful, gummy smile which grew wide when I said I wanted the American Express offices. Obviously, he'd landed a good fare, while I (although I didn't know it yet) had embarked on the most awesome car journey of my life.

For the first ten minutes or so, I didn't know which way to

look next, there was so much to see and all about us was mayhem. Massive bullocks, their horns painted scarlet and magenta and jade green, lumbered by pulling open carts piled high with sugar cane, vegetables and all manner of food. Ramshackle lorries and buses, vintage cars and ancient motor bikes coughed and spluttered their way over the holed and pitted road surface, while the drivers screamed abuse at each other.

Forget traffic lanes or rights of way. Instead, it was every man for himself as my driver – thin shoulders hunched over the wheel and nose an inch from the fly-splattered windscreen – launched himself into the mêlée with a chuckle of childish delight. Barefoot, his long horny-nailed toes slammed up and down on the brake as he dodged between taxi and rickshaw or gently nudged the mud-baked rear end of yet another wandering holy cow. Beneath his ragged khaki shorts, I could see the muscles on his skinny shanks standing out with the effort (likewise the veins on his scrawny neck). What a way to earn a living.

Beyond the car windows, Bombay was a feast of colour. Shop fronts, temples, street signs, ad hoardings – everywhere was painted in garish shades of orange, lime green, pink, yellow and purple. While everything, from cow horns to car windscreens, bicycle wheels to religious deities, was hung about with gold and silver tinsel, metallic streamers of every hue, or garlanded in necklaces of jasmine, rose petals and marigolds. Through it all flitted a host of brightly garbed women. So many of them that the roar of the traffic and the wail of Indian music was all but drowned out by the clinking of a million bracelets on arms and ankles, the ringing of a million tiny bells on ears, noses, fingers and toes.

Anxious not to miss any of it, I guess I must have leaned too far out of the car window – making my presence obvious to everyone as we slid up to the traffic lights. Amid the sea of faces, my gaze fastened on one – a boy of around eight or nine who had climbed up the pole of the traffic lights and seemed to be intently scanning the traffic as it drew to a halt. His face was, quite simply, horrible. It didn't look human at all, instead, it resembled nothing so much as the muzzle of a dog. His jaw jutted out grotesquely while his mouth was opened in a grimace, the lips stretched tight. Even as I recoiled in disgust, he caught sight of me and slid down the pole in a flash. He darted towards us through the traffic, reached my open window in an instant and pushed his awful face at me, his lips and jaws working frantically as he tried to beg for money. He had *two* pairs of jaws, one set slightly behind the other and somehow fused together – the parted mouth sporting four rows of strong, white teeth. I know I panicked as his face drew close to my own but I think – I'm sure – that's what I saw. Just at that moment, though, the lights changed, the driver took off and the appalling image slid away from the window.

I was so busy gazing back over my shoulder in horror that I didn't realize the lights up ahead were also changing to red, but as the car's motion slowed down at the next traffic island, the huddle of humanity marooned upon it had also noted my arrival. Another small boy on crutches had already taken off at the sight of me, his legs – one minus the foot and the other cut off just below the knee – swinging uselessly between his wooden limbs, as he moved with incredible speed.

Frantically, I tried to wind up the window but the handle had set solid with rust and, as I wrestled with it, the boy leaned his torso against the taxi and effortlessly swung his sawn-off stump over the rim of the glass. There it swung, the shiny kneecap and the three or four inches of calf ending in a smooth stump and looking for all the world like a large crooked finger.

I couldn't even speak, I was so frozen with shock, and it was my driver who screamed abuse at the boy as the lights changed and we roared off again. This time, my gaze was riveted to the third set of lights up ahead and even as I threw myself from one side of the seat to the other in an effort to force the windows closed, the rusty handle came away in my grasp and the lights changed again to red.

By now, I knew what was happening. I was obviously travelling a main route into the city centre – one which lots of tourists from Juhu beach probably used – and the beggars congregated at the lights just waiting for the rich pickings.

Sure enough, here was a third lot – mostly women this time and all fairly young. In spite of myself, I found I was scanning them for yet more physical deformity but, apart from looking pitifully thin, they seemed quite normal. A girl of about fourteen with a bundle of rags clutched underneath her arm walked up to the driver's window, put her bunched fingers to her lips in a pantomime of eating and then shoved her bony hand through the window demanding money.

Refusing to look at her, he spoke roughly as he pushed her hand away and released the car brake in readiness to move off. She stepped back a pace as we freewheeled past her and looked hard at me. Then without any warning, she threw the ragged bundle through the window and it landed heavily in my lap. I cried out in surprise and the driver, thoroughly rattled by now, slammed on the brakes, twisted around in his seat and yanked at the filthy cloth. The ragged bundle was a baby.

Completely out of my depth and utterly unable to think, let alone act, I just sat there with my mouth hanging open, while the driver shot out of his seat, yanked open my door, picked up the baby and ran back to the lights with it – where, presumably, he dumped it with one of the other women. I'll never know for sure because I didn't watch him. Instead, I sat shaking in the car, staring down at my empty lap – at the damp patch where the baby had been. A tiny baby with dark eyes and a large red sore on its mouth. A hungry, half-starved baby someone had been ready to throw away, it had lain for a moment on a silk dress which had cost more than most Indian labourers will earn in a year. I'd been travelling on Indian roads for less than half an hour and already I'd discovered the real meaning of the words 'immoral' and 'obscene'.

Nothing could have prepared me for the poverty that was a way of life for this country but now, in this crumbling and rotting city, I passed mile upon mile of it – an endlessly unfolding panorama of life on the edge. Saw beggars, too many to count; street dwellers who lived, slept, gave birth and died by the side of the road. People who suffered the blistering heat of summer and the torrential monsoon rains without so much as a corrugated iron sheet, or a few yards of polythene to protect them – nothing even resembling a roof over their heads.

Now, when we drove past an upturned cardboard box, I understood why the man peering out of it looked pleased with himself. 'Philips . . . electrical goods . . . handle with care' had been printed on its side but who cared that it had once housed a refrigeration unit? Certainly not its present happy occupant, enjoying this refuge from the burning sun. Compared to this, the thousands of Bombay citizens who lived in the sprawling shanty towns were fortunate indeed.

That turned out to be the first of many trips into the heart of Bombay and on every single expedition I saw incredible things. In the shadow of all that Victorian architecture, thousands of families lived on the city's sun baked streets, unperturbed by the endless throng milling past them. Many times, walking along the pavement, I realized I'd entered what was for some woman, her kitchen or bedroom. Once, I was so busy sidestepping a sleeping husband, that I didn't see the discarded newspaper lying in my path and my foot was only an inch from the newsprint when his wife screamed and threw herself in front of me, stooping to lift the infant which lay hidden beneath it.

Another time, quite by accident, I came across a Bombay prison and watched as dozens of men crowded at the barred windows on floor after floor of the building, their arms pushed through the grilles as they tried to catch the attention of their womenfolk, gathered down below. The women had brought food and baskets of bread, potatoes and carrots which were winched up the prison walls on makeshift ropes.

For some, life was desperate on a scale I couldn't have imagined, yet many survived, even thrived, in these conditions. I was left in no doubt of that when I dropped in at the Taj Hotel for afternoon tea. It was like a stage set from a glittering Indian movie, in fact it wouldn't have surprised me at all to learn that many of the beautifully dressed Indian women sitting at tables all about me were princesses and starlets. In India, the rich are very, very rich indeed – totally oblivious to the poverty camped, quite literally, on their doorsteps.

In between rich and destitute are the millions of inhabitants who keep the wheels of India turning and, in this nation where the written word is everything – especially when it's in quadruplicate – thousands of pen pushers stream into Bombay. Commuters in the best British tradition, in neat, if threadbare, shirts and trousers, and every one proudly sporting that symbol of officialdom – the briefcase.

Floating on an ocean of paperwork, the whole country is quite literally falling apart; with buildings crumbling at their foundations, the streets cracking up and criss-crossed by open sewers. Moving ahead on a wing and a prayer, held together by nothing more than endless red tape and an intricate network of corruption, India courts disaster and, sometimes, it happens. Although not always on the scale of Bhopal.

For instance, there was the Bombay train crash.

It had taken me several days to work up the courage to travel to Juhu from central Bombay on the train. The city's transport system had a dreadful reputation for everything from pickpocketing on a massive scale to robbery with violence and even murder. Finally, I convinced myself that it couldn't be any worse than London's Underground, and one evening at dusk, I joined the tens of thousands streaming into the station and squeezed into the 'ladies only' carriage of a train heading my way. There must have been nearly two hundred of us in there – women and children literally sitting on top of each other as the ancient machine heaved and gasped its way along the tracks. Large, kohl-lined eyes gazed into mine from every side and gentle smiles lit up pretty faces wherever I looked. I noticed that all around the compartment were graphically illustrated advertisements offering free abortions and vasectomies, compliments of the government – some even holding out the promise of money to any woman willing to be sterilized. And, in that unbearably hot, jammed compartment, I could begin to see why – the sheer weight of India's ever growing numbers is grinding her into the dust.

Safely back in my hotel, I congratulated myself on yet another first, reflecting that, apart from being unbearably crowded, the train hadn't been such a nightmare. Next morning, when I was driven into the city centre, the newspaper hoardings were full of the story; in the early hours, a train travelling out to Juhu from the centre had jumped the tracks, ploughing into the station platform and killing hundreds outright.

With no metal-cutting equipment to speak of, hardly any stocks of blood or plasma and few available hospital beds, the emergency services were still running around like headless chickens, trying to help the injured. But even more awful was the news that it was the 'ladies only' carriage which had suffered the worst damage. It had turned turtle, the metal becoming so twisted and distorted that it had proved impossible to open the doors.

My mind went back to the previous evening – to the carriage with its patient, good-natured occupants, the walls covered with family planning advice, the windows with their iron-barred grilles instead of glass. I was appalled to think of the hundreds of women and children trapped in that metal prison right now; many of them injured and dying, packed together like terrified cattle while the temperature soared and their rescuers grew more frantic.

And then I had another thought. That train had been running along these very same tracks, ever since the British had built the system nearly a hundred years before. For the best part of a century, it had been allowed to fall into disrepair and, if the sleepers had collapsed just a few hours earlier, when I'd been in the carriage, that might have been the end of me. The fact that I was safe and sound was incredibly comforting as I recalled that, ever since I'd left London, I'd been waiting for disaster to strike. Now, I had the oddest feeling that it had struck at last – that my number had indeed been up, if you like – and for some reason, I'd been spared. It sounds crazy, I know, but that evening, when I read the newspapers and saw the final massive death toll, it somehow turned my thinking around and left me with the absolute certainty that nothing on my journey could harm me now.

So this was India . . . my eyes, you could say, had been opened and I had survived the kind of culture shock which sends many visitors to Third World countries scurrying back to the airport and the first available flight out. Consumed by guilt and disgusted by the poverty, they completely miss the irrepressible life of the place – its colour, its noise, its bustle, its sheer, raw energy. Just as they fail to pick up on the tremendous optimism, childlike curiosity, unfailing good nature and pure, unquenchable spirit of its inhabitants.

I'd never expected to enjoy this continent. I'd regarded it as a place I had to go through to get to Burma. But everything changed during these few days in Bombay and, by the time I was ready to move south I knew that I was completely and permanently under the spell of India, with its awful splendour, its heartbreaking sadness and its heartstopping, breathtaking beauty.

After years of being unmoved by anything or anyone, I'd fallen in love with a country and I arrived in Goa feeling excited, exhilarated – incredibly happy. In that frame of mind I guess it was inevitable that I would also fall in love with a man. Completely, madly and head-over-heels.

The first time I saw Martin, he was stoned; slumped over a beer-sodden table in the shack which served as the local bar. It was the most popular hang-out in the dusty little village of Calangute, not that there was much boozing done here. The thirty or so patrons had gathered – much as they did all day and every night – to pass around a few *chillums,* smoke some brown, buy and sell and roll resin and grass. There were a few Goans, but mostly the clientele was European and almost part of the scenery. You could tell at a glance which were the out-of-towners. The French and Italian contingent – fresh out of Rome and Paris in search of an alternative holiday – worked hard all day on their tans and slid out after dark on a slick of after-sun lotion.

Contriving to blend in with the Sixties hippy look which was much in evidence here, women would carefully muss their hair and deck themselves out with Indian jewellery, ankle bracelets, nose rings and caste marks – these accessories looking incongruous teamed with leather and silk designer rags. Their men tended to sport bare chests and worn denims;

sometimes with waistcoats and neckerchiefs to complete the 'Woodstock' look. It was laughable, really, the way these well-off kids aspired to the unwholesome, emaciated image of drug addiction, assuming the lifestyle of a druggie for a month or so, before heading back to continue their law studies in Paris or run a chic boutique in Florence. Sometimes they pushed their luck, of course – there were lots of stories of tourists who had come to Goa to play the addict, only to turn into that very thing.

Some of them were probably there that night. Men and women whose ragged clothes and runny noses were the real thing; pale, skinny limbs and blackened teeth indicating that, whatever kept them in Goa, it wasn't the sun and the healthy diet.

All in all, The Shack, with its primitive furnishings, its fag strewn sand floor and its tarpaulin roof, was home to a motley crew of foreigners. Not my kind of place and certainly not my kind of people, I'd decided the first evening I'd strolled in there, but I'd grown adept at making the best of any situation.

So, ignoring the unfriendly atmosphere, I'd sat down at a table, ordered a vodka with tonic and proceeded to outstare my table companions, with a gaze every bit as bored and cold as theirs. Which is when my eyes slid over Martin's sleeping features and my stomach gently flipped over.

I've seen plain but pleasant-looking men. I've studied faces I would describe as ordinary but nice. I've known men who were attractive and others I might label 'good looking'. Now and again I have met handsome men who merited the description and I think that, once or twice in my life, I have gazed upon men I could only describe as beautiful. This was one of these times and Martin was one of these men.

He was completely out of his box, it must be said. His head tilted slightly back, his eyes closed, his lips slightly parted. His face was long and angular – the cheekbones standing out sharply, the jaw narrow, the chin finely chiselled with a large dimple in its centre. His hair was shiny black and cut short into the sides and back of his head, although curls fell forward across his temples. His nose was very long and straight, his mouth wide and full. I figured he was in his mid-twenties and, as he snoozed off the effects of the resin he'd been smoking, totally unaware of my existence. I just sat there and drank him in. Thinking that he was the kind of man women like myself never seem to get, I didn't even consider the idea of trying to engage his interest. That's how beautiful he was. And, after gazing at him quietly for the best part of an hour, I left.

Calangute is a small place and I saw him often during the next few days – drinking in bars or just walking through the village. He was incredibly tall – six feet four inches – and very thin. Yet he carried himself well; you might almost say elegantly. I'd heard him talk. He was German and his voice was every bit as beautiful as the rest of him. Much as I tried to put him out of my mind, I thought about him constantly – amazed at myself for being lovesick over a man I hadn't so much as spoken to and who wasn't even aware of my existence. The merest glimpse of him in the morning was enough to set me up for the whole day, while the simple act of him smiling at or chatting to another woman was enough to cast me into bleak despair.

Then came the evening I was walking alone, as usual, along the endless stretch of beach. I'd taken to wearing wide skirts with petticoats and I'd hitched some of the material up into my waistband, so that I could stroll barefoot along the water's edge. That evening, like every other, there was a breathtaking sunset; the whole width of the sky streaked with pinks, reds and purples, while the sun – massively round and somehow incredibly close – slowly dipped into waters which rolled in endless waves of gold and scarlet and black. Behind me, the stretch of sand was edged with swaying palms, giving way to denser undergrowth, while nearby families of piglets rooted and squealed and local fishermen mending their nets nodded a greeting as I passed.

I'd been in Goa for four days and I couldn't believe how lovely it was. Green and lush, relaxed and friendly – an exotic mix of Asian and Portuguese, Hindu and Christian. Rui had often talked to me of this far-off place which he, as a Portuguese, wasn't allowed to visit.

'Ah Rui . . . here I am in the paradise we dreamed about.

And where are you tonight?' Deep in thoughts of my old life, I walked on with my head bowed, marvelling at the designs each wave left in the sand and the way the water smoothed over my footprints even as I made them.

The voice, deep and pleasant, almost made me jump out of my skin as Martin, sitting cross-legged in the still warm sand, motioned for me to sit down beside him. We talked until the sky grew dark, watching for the first star to come out. Then we strolled companionably back to the village, ankle-deep in the foaming waves, as a warm caressing wind blew in from the ocean, billowing my skirts and ruffling Martin's dark hair. Martin's voice, an endearing mixture of English and German, floated across the darkness and as I watched the moon bob up above the palms, I felt I would burst with sheer happiness.

That's how it began, this love affair so sweet and filled with tender moments; reawakening a girlish love of life in an unhappy, weary woman. This is how I met the man who gave me back my sense of dignity and the courage to be me again.

The next day, as we'd arranged, I met Martin in the village square just after dawn and we hired a motor bike from one of the locals. Soon we were speeding through the Goan countryside, flying between jade green rice paddies fringed with palms, rattling across makeshift bridges over fast flowing streams. Swinging around bends, we would come across decorative white stuccoed churches, like large wedding cakes nestling in the palm forests, or we would bump across the brow of a hill and gasp at the scene below – sometimes a deserted palm-fringed beach pounded by gleaming surf, at others a tiny village nestling by the roadside, its schoolchildren, its barber and its tailor all going about their business in the open air. Weaving in and out of cows and bullocks, swerving to avoid dogs and chickens, we raced on for mile after mile, while my arms wound themselves happily about Martin's waist and our peals of laughter echoed in the hills all around.

By mid morning, we had reached Martin's secret destination – a place he had refused to describe to me but insisted I would love. We parked the bike in an overgrown track and walked along the footpath towards the sound of crashing surf. At the end of the path, the track opened out to a wide curve of beach, shimmering white and totally deserted. To the right, a rocky headland decked with palm trees rose up sheer out of the water. I could just make out a path running between the beach and the rock face, which twisted and turned back on itself before disappearing into the swaying, rustling palm grove.

Together we crossed the sizzling curve of sand and followed the leafy path. To my left, the ocean slid in and out of tiny secluded coves while on my right, the rocks rose up to the sky, thick with palms and dotted with a dozen or so tiny whitewashed cottages which seemed to be deserted. After a few minutes, the meandering path widened, then I stepped out from the canopy of palms to find I was walking on yet another broad swathe of sandy beach which stretched beyond me in a gentle curve. On my left, waves pounded up from the water's edge and the ocean stretched as far as the eye could see. What I saw on my right, took my breath away.

The beach ran up sharply, then dipped, and on the other side of this small hillock lay a freshwater lake. Edged with large shining boulders and flowering bushes, it sparkled a welcome in the sunlight, its waters gently lapping the edges of the beach while, just twenty feet away on the other side of the hillock, the Arabian Sea roared. In the centre of the lake a large flat rock rose up out of the water, while totally untouched jungle tumbled down the hillsides all around, the vegetation a riot of colour as it fringed the opposite side of the lake. Through the lacework of trees, I could just make out sparkling movement as a hill stream emptied itself into the still, blue waters.

'A paradise, no?' Martin murmured at my side.

'A paradise, yes!' I answered with my eyes, too overwhelmed to speak.

Completely alone, completely naked, we played there for most of that unforgettable day; body surfing in the sea, then bounding across the sands to plunge beneath the sweet-tasting waters of the lake. For hours we frolicked like children, lolling in the shallows, while shoals of small striped fish darted around our limbs and nibbled our fingers and toes, then swimming out to the rocky island in the lake's centre, where we lay basking in the hot sun, the stone burning beneath our flesh.

Naked, Martin was a joy to look at. A bout of shellfish poisoning had resulted in a serious weight loss but in spite of that, he was physically impressive. Broad-shouldered, slim-hipped, his belly flat and his limbs long and slender. His hands and his feet mesmerized me, the toes and fingers narrow and tapered and delicately shaped. And then there were his eyes – blue as cornflowers in his deeply tanned face, his teeth brightly white against his two-day growth of beard.

I can't tell you how relieved I was that he seemed to enjoy looking at me, too, although I'd been uncharacteristically shy when it came to taking my clothes off. From that first day, I felt girlish and gauche around Martin. 'Modest', I suppose is the word I'm searching for and, as we lazed by that lakeside, 'innocent' is the only way I could describe the events. For, although I wanted him so much I could hardly bear the sense of longing and the body language between us made me light-headed with anticipation, we both totally avoided even the slightest physical contact. Except for one moment when, as we were swimming together, he suddenly twisted like a seal and I felt his stomach and hips slip across the small of my back, the fleeting touch of flesh on flesh leaving me embarrassed and giddy with pleasure.

And so we teased each other all day – both of us sensing that, when it finally happened, it would be perfect but neither of us wanting to bring the delicious waiting and wondering to an end.

Well, it happened that night back in Calangute, after dinner and a last easy stroll along the beach. It happened slowly and ever so gently on Martin's narrow metal bed in a tiny, dark room bathed in moonlight. It happened quietly, because the walls were paper thin and all around us, other travellers slumbered. It happened while time stood still – minutes and hours slipping by unnoticed as we moved and breathed as one. It happened again and again – both of us surprised by our hunger for each other. And it was perfect.

I moved into the guest house with Martin next day and settled down to enjoy what turned out to be the most idyllic six weeks of my life. We slept and ate as and when we pleased. Made love wherever and however we felt like it – on the beach, in the sea, in the bedroom, in the shower stalls – sometimes even in bed. We explored the beaches at low tide; roamed the highways and byways of lovely old Goa; went to beach parties; had days filled with pleasure.

Strangely enough, although I never seemed to tire of Martin's company and the mere sight of him in the distance or the sound of his voice outside the bedroom door was enough to give me a funny sensation in my stomach, there were times when, for no good reason, I would feel the need to slip away and spend a little time by myself. On these occasions I would walk the deserted beach, slipping into the water every so often to just roll over on my back and float idly, staring up at the blue sky. At other times I would sit motionless in the sand, staring out across the water at imaginary foreign shores, knowing that beyond the distant horizon lay Africa. These times were, for me, incredibly peaceful as my mind flew free to think of my family, my friends and those remnants of my past which mattered more the further I moved away from them. Sometimes, my thoughts were of the present and Martin; of how happy he made me and how much I would miss him when we parted, as we inevitably would. That thought made me immensely sad but it's one I grew to accept, as I sat alone.

Now I know that these solitary times served a useful purpose, as I gradually learned to enjoy being by myself.

Still, of all the hours in our days, it was the evenings I enjoyed most. Sitting on the front verandah, our chairs tilted back precariously and our feet propped up on the balustrade, we would chatter away to the other residents – all of them travellers – swapping stories with them as we shared a bottle of beer. All the time exchanging secret glances or teasing each other with smiles, our bodies signalling promises of yet more lovemaking far into the tropical night.

Ours was lovemaking with a difference; it was lovemaking I could never get enough of – something I was enjoying for the first time in years. I would often watch Martin when he wasn't aware of it – when he was deep in conversation or when he lay asleep in our bed. And at these times, I would love him so much it almost hurt.

How was this man different? I've often wondered since. What was it about loving him that made me different, too? I've tried to rationalize it, telling myself the setting was idyllic and perfect for romance; I was happier than I'd been for a very long time, totally relaxed and receptive to everything. I remind myself that there were other men before him and there have been men since and perhaps, after all, he was just another in a long line of lovers. Or maybe time and memory have embroidered what was just another encounter . . . but I know this isn't true.

Not since I'd been twenty and crazy over Rui had I known anything like this. The way he smelled, the way he tasted, the way he laughed . . . everything about Martin tugged at my heart and, of all the things he made me feel, the thing I felt most around him was protective. That came as a bit of a surprise, for hadn't I been the one who was always looking for someone to take care of me – do all my thinking and make all my decisions? But now I was worried and apprehensive; and for someone other than myself.

Because Martin wasn't worldly; Martin wasn't even very smart. He had a lazy streak and an indolent attitude towards life. Raised on his father's farm, he'd been totally disinterested in helping to run the place and had gone to work at a local sawmill instead, where he'd continued to be bone idle. Then, on a trip down to Spain, he'd seen a way of making some easy money and he'd stashed a load of cannabis in his car. Arrested at the border, he'd found himself in a Spanish jail and was soon shipped back home and handed over to the German police.

There was a court case and he was sentenced to four years' imprisonment. The authorities had instructed him to present himself for incarceration on a particular day and, rather than do time, Martin had simply flown the coop. Now he was heading for Australia, in the hope of losing himself permanently in its vastness. And this with very little money and only three months until his passport expired. Obviously, he couldn't go to the German Embassy for a new one and buying a forged one, even in India, would cost a fortune.

Martin was, first and foremost, a country boy. He wasn't used to big city life and he completely lacked the instincts necessary for survival in this tough old world. The chances of him getting all the way to Australia were slim and as to how he would survive if he ever got there . . . well, I just couldn't begin to imagine.

Yet he was incredibly kind and gentle, always tuned into people and wonderful company. Slow and quiet, he worked hard at the things which interested him and was very artistic.

I remember one afternoon, I'd been sleeping in our bedroom and woke to find him gone. The guest house consisted of a long central corridor with the kitchen at one end of the house, the verandah at the other and sixteen small bedrooms opening out onto the central corridor. At that time of the day, the house was deserted, yet I could hear some gentle, haunting flute music and I walked barefoot down the corridor towards it. Martin was sitting in a wicker chair, the house dogs at his feet and a group of black piglets milling on the verandah steps, and he was playing the flute, the notes sweet and mellow in the hot stillness of the afternoon. This was more than just the odd snatch of music; it was a sad and lilting piece, intricate and, I would have thought, almost impossible to play on the cheap wooden whistle he'd bought from a passing Indian. He was nothing if not full of surprises and the biggest surprise of all was the way he saw me.

The night he described me to myself, I was dumbfounded. I lay in bed next to him, listening to words like 'brave', 'honest', 'generous', 'capable', 'loving', 'feminine', and argued that I wasn't any of these things. I became quite upset when he insisted it was so, as I began to think that perhaps I'd been up to my old tricks without realizing it – leading this man to think I had qualities which simply didn't exist. I'd fooled him into believing I was special, just as I'd tried to fool Hafez and Amer and God alone knows how many others. Since the last thing I'd wanted to do was manipulate Martin, this was a scary thought.

In the middle of what was fast developing into our first real argument, he turned to stare at me as we lay together on the bed, took me in his arms and said, 'You are my idea of a complete woman – do you understand or is it my bad English?'

I didn't argue any more. Just buried my head against him and lay quietly, marvelling at what he had said. Instinctively I knew that he had spoken the truth, had described me as I appeared to him, and the woman he saw was every bit as real as the woman I thought I was.

I'd never told Martin about my murky past or about how bitter and afraid I had become. Or how hard I had been running, in an effort to escape from myself. Now he saw me in a completely different light . . . so might that mean that the thing I'd most hoped for had happened – that somehow, I had changed? I hardly dared to believe it but I looked into Martin's lovely face, saw the expression in his eyes and knew that it was true. I was a different woman from the one who had left home.

'I watch you many times, so do other people,' he went on. 'You are very – calm. Is that the word? Strong. And, I think, out of reach. Beyond being touched. I admire you because you know who you are. And because you do not need anyone's help. Perhaps that is why I love you so much . . . '

He said them so naturally, so easily; the words which, without realizing it, I had waited so long to hear a man say. And the night that Martin said he loved me was the night I finally began to care about and value myself.

Learning to love yourself . . . they write popular songs about that, don't they? And psychiatrists write books about it; agony aunts fill column inches with it and everyone, but everyone, concludes it's someone else's hang-up. 'Self-esteem? I've got plenty of that!' they scoff. 'Poor self-image – me? You're full of crap!' they'll insist. But the world is full of people who love themselves too little and, until I met Martin, I was one of them.

I'd been out of love with myself all my life, I realize now.

And that in turn must have made me difficult for anyone else to love. Now I can admit it's because I always saw myself as a fraud and, although I might have managed to fool a lot of the people most of the time, I always felt I was letting myself down, by never admitting who I really was and what I needed to make me happy. I think the pattern had been formed early – probably when I was that little girl who repressed her anger and resentment over all these brothers and sisters. Furious with her parents, yet pretending to be the perfect little help-mate, the ultra-responsible child. Convinced that being loved was beyond me, I'd settled for currying favour.

The young woman in me had gone on to pose as a capable, creative journalist, earning everyone's grudging respect, yet swanning around London with a massive chip on her shoulder and a real confidence crisis. Later, the role of sophis-ticated wife had been challenging, as I'd convinced Rui I was tolerant, worldly, understanding and undemanding. He'd taken me at face value, unaware of my rage, my jealousy and my constant, woeful sense of inadequacy.

And then had come my starring role – that of the wronged wife. The bitter divorcee in me had masqueraded as a woman who didn't care about anything or anyone. I'd styled myself into something every man tried to lay and no man cared to love. Which was exactly what I wanted, because it was no more than I thought I deserved.

I had spent the best part of thirty-five years trying to be the child/wife/lover who would most readily find acceptance; forget love – that was setting my sights much too high. My God . . . how pathetic.

No self-esteem. That had been my problem all along, only I'd refused to acknowledge it. Yet it was a legacy I'd carried with me everywhere and it had coloured every relationship I had tried to form. Until I had set foot in India. I'd given myself up to this country, for once expecting nothing in return; yet somehow, it had given me confidence in my ability to look after myself. Instilled in me a sense of peace and the feeling that I was beyond the reach of old hurts and disappointments, so that, at last, the wounds had begun to heal.

This, then, was the woman Martin had met, had admired,

had begun to love. And the unconditional love of another human being now gave me the courage to go on being just *me.* Average and ordinary. Normal for probably the first time in my life.

Of course, this self-analysis is something I've embarked on only recently and, back there in India, I was incapable of being quite so objective about my state of mind. All I knew was that I didn't feel like a fraud any more – and that felt wonderful.

Chapter Two

Marvellous people, magical places

A couple of days before Christmas, we were sitting quietly on the verandah when the telephone rang in the office of the guest house. The odd job man picked the phone up and we distinctly heard him repeat Martin's name. Someone was trying to trace him and we knew, even before the odd job man came to warn us, that the police must be on Martin's tail. We didn't hang around to find out exactly why. Instead, we threw a few things into a knapsack and headed for the market place where we soon hired a motor bike. While Martin haggled over the price, I picked up some bread and vegetables from a food stall, then we got out of Calangute – fast.

We headed for the only place we knew where no one would think to look for us and a couple of hours later we were back on 'our' beach with its rolling ocean on one side and its freshwater lake on the other. One of the locals, who owned the coconut grove, also owned the tiny whitewashed cottages up on the hillside and that night we moved into one of them. It was pretty spartan. Just one room about eight feet square, alive with cockroaches and bugs of all kinds. We spent the rest of the afternoon sweeping it out with palm fronds and damping down the dusty floor with water I raised by hand from the big stone well nearby. There's definitely a technique to raising water this way and I was amused to think how the skills I'd learned with Samira had finally begun to come in handy. We had no electricity, of course, no running water, no loo or shower and no cooking facilities.

Instead, as the day drew to a close, Martin started a fire with the dried coconut husks and driftwood he had collected and, with the loan of a couple of pots and forks from our new landlord, we got down to cooking our first meal. The scrambled eggs and tomatoes went down a treat, as we sat on our little front porch and watched the sun go down on our tiny domain. Then, feeling suddenly tired out with the tension of the day, we decided to call it a night.

We were calling it a whole lot of other things next morning, when we staggered out into the sunlight. It was around four-thirty and the early sun was casting long shadows as we whined and complained about the dreadful night we'd spent on the rope mattress bed. It was the only piece of furniture in the room and it was crawling with bed bugs. The rats had been gnawing away at the roof all night, while every so often, one of the coconuts fell on the roof, just inches above our heads, and scared us both out of fitful sleep.

Martin went off for a swim in a very grumpy mood, while I went down to the well, drew up some water and proceeded to pour it over my head – an al fresco shower, which was all the more memorable for being in such a beautiful setting. By the time he came back – looking a bit sheepish, I might say – I had a pot of water boiling away merrily and was just about to make some tea. Suddenly, all was right with the world again.

That day we went exploring deep into the jungle, wading into the stream which ran into the lake and following it up into the forest. The smells and the sounds of that place were rich and heady, as large butterflies swept past our noses and monkeys swung high above us through the trees. I could feel the heat beating down on us as the sun rose in the sky but down here, bathed in dappled sunlight, I felt very comfortable, even though my limbs were soon shiny with perspiration. Then, in what was quite literally the middle of nowhere, we heard the far-off sound of a flute being played. For about fifteen minutes we followed the sound and soon came across the most enormous banyan tree I have ever seen. It must have towered eighty or ninety feet above us, with two mighty arms stretched out – the span being as wide as the tree was high. It was colossal. I stood there gazing at it, my eyes following the outstretched limbs, from which massive tubers hung vertically, seeking a foothold on the jungle floor, and was reminded of nothing so much as the inside of a cathedral. And there was a silence here too – almost as if the birds and wild animals living in the area also sensed how mighty the tree was, how impressive this jungle clearing. And then the music began again, floating down out of the tree.

The musician turned out to be a young French Algerian and we found him when we walked round the back of the tree and climbed up inside the trunk. He lived the equivalent of three or four floors up, very much at home living on a natural platform of the tree which was easily the size of the average living room back home. He did admit to being troubled by his neighbours – the monkeys, who were in the habit of stealing anything left unattended, the snakes, who turned up unexpectedly, and of course the large bats, who also used the tree as their living quarters. He and Martin settled down to roll some joints while I sat appreciating this superb natural habitat.

I'm very glad that on the way back to our lake Martin was in the lead, because he suddenly let out a yelp of terror and jumped back, knocking me off balance and falling in a heap on top of me. Once we'd picked ourselves up, we moved forward gingerly to see what had scared him so – what it was that he had felt against his bare chest. Then we realized that Martin had walked into the largest spider's web I ever want to see. Now Martin is pretty tall, and his face was on a level with the centre of the web, so you can imagine how large its span was. When I eventually found one of its anchor threads, attached to a rock, I pulled at it and, when I let go, it sprung back, as strong and as taut as cat gut on a violin. It really was a work of art – a shimmering lace of spun steel and, precisely at its heart, sat an incredible spider.

She was certainly larger than my hand span and every single hair on her legs was visible from about four feet away. I could see, quite clearly across her furry back, a sharp white outline which resembled a skull. Horrible she was and fascinating, too.

By now, the sun was beginning to slip down the wall of the sky and, knowing that we still had a few chores to do before light faded, we headed back to our cottage. We soon had the fire crackling merrily and Martin was peeling sweet potatoes while I went to fetch water, my mouth watering at the prospect of fried potatoes and green peppers. But the peppers were off that night, thanks to the unexpected arrival of our only near neighbour – a young, golden brown calf whose soft muzzle had discovered the newspaper-wrapped peppers. She ate our supper, newspaper and all, while I hung on her neck, yelling like a banshee.

We sat quietly together on the porch and watched as the sun slowly sank beneath the waves. Sat on, arms about each other, as the skies turned from pink, to purple to midnight blue and the first star appeared (by now, we had adopted it for our own). There had been a storm out at sea and now the rollers came in bearing some strange substance from the ocean's depths. It turned the foam a brilliant green and, in the light of the rising moon, the breakers glowed bright neon.

Martin lit our precious candles and their gleam shone fitfully in the impenetrable darkness, while some forty feet below us, the neon winked ever greener between the trees and, light years above us, shooting stars burst silently across the inky sky. I lay back, watching the moon shine silver-blue on the palm fronds above my head, as Martin began to make love to me. And as I gave myself up to those sweet sensations – my stomach empty but every other part of me filled with happiness – I felt sorry for all those millions of people who couldn't ever know this much contentment. Wherever my friends were right now, whatever they were doing . . . no one, but no one, in the whole wide world, could feel as ecstatic as I did.

It was Christmas Eve.

We were up with the dawn next day, simply because we had slept out of doors all night. We'd decided the cottage was much too hot and stuffy to sleep in, so we'd moved out on to a small grassy platform which jutted out of the rock face and bedded down there. I'd put some dreamlike music in my Walkman and we'd lain closely together on our backs, each of us plugged into a set of headphones and lost to everything but the music, the warm night wind and the Southern Cross, as it made its slow arc across the Indian sky.

It was the sound of a fresh breeze in the palm trees and the crashing of the surf which woke me and I sat quietly, gazing down at the beach below me, looking so fresh and clean in this early sunlight.

We spent Christmas Day, naked, as usual, swimming and messing about until the sun was high in the sky. Then we tried to act like responsible adults for the rest of the afternoon. Martin had some idea that we could catch fish – with a length of line, a hook he carried with him and some bits of our precious carrots. Well, it was a magical few hours, as we sat together on a large rock, patiently casting our carrots while the crabs below the water line helped themselves to our bait and the ones above the water line continually crept out of the rocks to nip our backsides.

Needless to say, Martin fell into the water twice, pushed me in once and we didn't catch anything at all. Still, I remember gazing around me at the golden beach just a few yards from our fishing rock and tilting my head back to admire our little house, nestling some forty or fifty feet above us. A small herd of goats suddenly appeared on the sand, the little blond kids jumping skittishly when waves slid too close. Then I glanced down at myself – my body tanned golden and my ribcage and hip bones in evidence for the first time in years – and I laughed to think how all my friends were right now dressing up for parties, drinking too much champagne and eating far too much. Exchanging expensive presents and tucking into massive pricy meals, had they given me a thought, at all? And would they believe their eyes if they could see me now – skinny, brown, naked, sober, hungry – and happy as a sandboy?

Christmas dinner . . . and the main course was bubble and squeak. Martin was dessert. I don't think I've ever had such a feast.

At the end of it all, Martin wished me Merry Christmas and as we waited for our star to come out, he began to talk about the future – and about the fact that he had to head out for Australia. I'd known this was coming, but I wasn't too impressed with his sense of timing. Yet here he was, talking about leaving our little white house in a couple of days, heading back to Calangute for his gear and then going south.

'Trudy . . . come with me?' he suddenly said. 'I know – I know you want to travel alone,' he interrupted when I opened my mouth to speak, 'but Australia is an exciting place. My friends tell me it is a wonderful place for a clever woman like you. We could have a good life there. Think about it.'

And I did. Thought about it as the year drew to a close and we left our little paradise behind. Thought about it back in Calangute village – which, after the peace of our hideaway, seemed as frantic as any city. Thought about it, while Martin did the rounds of his new friends, saying goodbye; and realized that, much as going with Martin was foolish, I couldn't bear to be left behind in Goa without him.

Two days later, we headed into Panjim, Goa's capital, with all our worldly goods and caught a rickety old bus heading out of Goa and south to Mangalore. As we moved slowly out of Panjim, past the wonderful old Portuguese houses, the iced cake churches, the gardens ablaze with hibiscus and palms heavy with fruit, I knew that a wonderful period in my life was coming to an end. I'd lived a dream time, I'd had a glimpse of paradise and saying goodbye to Goa was very, very hard.

The journey south took twenty-six bone-rattling hours, with lots of tea shops and pee stops along the way. Martin had a contact in Mangalore, an Iranian he'd met earlier on his journey, who would probably be able to get him a forged passport and, armed with a new identity, he hoped to get a boat from Madras across to Thailand. He chatted away happily about his plans – our plans – as the bus ate up mile after dusty mile but although I tried to be enthusiastic, somewhere deep inside me, it just didn't feel right.

Martin fell asleep eventually and I stared out of the window, trying to make sense of what was happening to me. I loved Martin and I was worried about him. I knew he had to reach the safety of Australia as quickly as possible but . . . I didn't want to go to that country. It had never been part of my grand plan. There was still so much of India to see – and what about Burma?

And say I did make it with Martin all the way to Australia, what then? He was almost ten years younger than me; a beautiful-looking man without an ounce of ambition and a considerable distaste for anything approaching work. How long would we survive together, once we were exposed to the real world? I knew I could turn my hand to anything; knew I would survive whatever the cost. But could I say the same for this man who slept beside me? And then I had to admit what I'd known all along – I loved Martin but not enough to go on the run with him. He wanted to lose himself in Australia, so be it. Yet I sensed I was on the edge of some discovery about myself and I'd come too far to give up now.

To think that a year ago . . . or three months ago . . . even just a few weeks earlier . . . I'd been desperate for some man somewhere to make just this offer and now here I was – about to turn it down. The irony wasn't lost on me.

We were exhausted by the time we arrived at his friend's house. The man assured Martin he could fix him up with a new passport and offered us a room in his apartment where we could stay for a few days until the deal was completed.

That night, we made love with an urgency we'd never felt before. It was as if Martin already knew the decision I still couldn't bring myself to tell him I'd made. Yet as we lay talking in the dark, I finally whispered, 'Martin . . . I'm sorry, but I can't go with you to Australia. So I'm leaving at first light tomorrow. I'm sorry – '

Anything else I'd wanted to say was lost as he pulled me to him and held on tight but as we caressed each other, we both knew this was the only way it could be.

I woke as the very first fingers of light crept into the bedroom and opened my eyes to find Martin gazing down at me. Without a word, the touching, the kissing, began again, although part of me wished it wouldn't. Saying goodbye with your body must be the saddest thing a human being has to do. I know it made me cry and I think Martin wept, too.

When it was over and he ran his hands slowly over my body, his fingers traced the calf of my leg and played with the bracelet he'd given me, what seemed like a lifetime ago. 'So that I will always know where you are!' he had joked, as he'd slipped it on to my ankle, and there it had stayed, its little silvery bells jingling with every step I took, so that he had always known where to find me. Now, I slipped it off my skin and held the silver chain up in the shadows, the bells tinkling gently. I knew that sound would always remind me of our lovemaking, for how many times had my bracelet jingled happily – almost with a life of its own – while our bodies had mingled in the night? Mournfully, I dropped it into Martin's outstretched palm. 'Please – don't ever forget me,' I whispered. 'Because I know I will never forget you.'

'How can I let you leave here – how do I know you will be safe?' Martin asked pitifully. 'I will worry about you.'

I kissed him then and his sad gaze followed me as I left the room and crept along to the loo, to wash and dress. I was back in ten minutes, hoping, I suppose, for one last hug, another kiss. But Martin had fallen asleep, as he lay there waiting for me in bed. It was the sort of light, contented sleep which follows lovemaking and, although part of me wanted to wake him, I thought better of it.

Instead, I crouched down by the mattress and studied him. Gazed upon that beautiful, still face just inches from my own – the eyelids almost transparent, the lashes long and dark. Tried to memorize the contour of the cheekbone, the generous outline of the lips.

I remembered another time and another place – the first time when I had sat quietly admiring this same face. And then, just as I had done all those long weeks ago . . . I got up and crept away from the sleeping German.

Quietly, I closed the front door behind me and headed off along the deserted street. Up on the main road, I hailed a passing rickshaw and moments later we were rumbling towards the railway station, my eyes full of unshed tears and my head empty of any ideas about where I was actually going.

Even at such an early hour, the station was a hive of activity; the porters bow-legged beneath bales of this and boxes of that, while crates of screeching chickens and even a couple of goats stood ready to be shipped aboard the next train. Mysore, I finally discovered, was the destination of the first train out that day. Comforted to see that most of these eager

286

passengers had even less idea about their destinations than I had about my own, I bought a ticket to Mysore and then headed for the *chai* stall and breakfast. The chipped cup filled with dark, steaming tea and the *chappati* went down a treat, as I read up on Mysore in my trusty *Lonely Planet Guide*.

Sandalwood City . . . Indo-Saracenic palace . . . shady trees, clean streets and you can walk from one end of the place to the other in twenty minutes. They'd called it 'the traveller's Mecca'. I figured it was as good a place in which to be heartbroken as any other.

I'd been sitting on my luggage for the best part of half an hour, when I noticed another European woman arrive. She had the air of a traveller who had been there and seen it all many times before, as she muscled her way through the ticket queues, bad mouthing a couple of young Indians who tried to chat her up. By the time she'd braved the booking office queue, the seat purchasing queue and moved along the line for second-class train tickets (like I said, they do everything in triplicate in India), she obviously needed a drink and she made a beeline for the *chai* stall.

A minute later, we'd broken the ice and she was chatting away to me in her soft Irish brogue as if she'd known me forever. Her name was Siobhan and she was originally from Dublin although, for years now, home had been wherever she hung her hat, she explained. Later, I was to discover that 'hanging her hat' was the least of it; she'd made a career out of removing far more interesting items of her apparel. For Siobhan was, by her own account, a very talented dancer, an adept and artistic stripper and, when the occasion demanded, a most accomplished whore.

Needless to say, I didn't learn this during our first chat over tea. A girl in Siobhan's line of work has to be a little circumspect, after all. But the chat continued on the long train journey to Mysore and, by the time we reached that historic city, the last battle stand of the dreadful Tipu Sultan, it made sense to go in search of a hotel together.

We settled for a tiny, windowless room in what my latest landlord was pleased to call 'the annexe'. It was in fact a hastily constructed lean-to at the back of his ramshackle building, very like the shed my grandfather once built at the bottom of his garden to breed budgies in. Siobhan, even more used than me to being on the road, had that wonderful gift which is granted to women – the ability to turn any dump into a home in ten minutes flat.

Out came her tiny cassette player and on went the music. The iron bedstead was covered with a couple of the sarongs she carried everywhere – the bright turquoises and pinks covering the grey, moth-eaten sheets. Her yellow towel was flung over the edge of the bed to air, the rickety table was soon hidden beneath a jumble of shampoo bottles, make-up and beads and the air was filled with the scent of jasmine incense sticks. By the time I'd followed her example and my most colourful bits and bobs were strewn around the place, the grubby little room looked like a real home from home.

Then we strolled out in the mellow afternoon light in search of something to eat. And, Siobhan added with an unmistakable twinkle in her eye – a little action. The bad news is that the last 'action' Mysore saw was back in 1799, when poor old Tipu got his; but the good news is that Mysore has a wealth of eating places. We were soon tucking into huge plates of vegetable curry and Siobhan's appetite turned out to be as healthy as everything else about her.

After dinner, we explored until the light faded. Then it was back to our room and more good news – the annexe had electricity. True, it was only one bare little light bulb but it meant we could still function after dark and that was unaccustomed luxury for me. I'd no sooner settled down on my bed with a book than the light went out. All over Mysore, it transpired, as that bane of Indian life – the power cut – struck yet again. Still, that didn't stop Siobhan's battery-run cassette player from sending out a stream of music and I drifted off to sleep, trying not to think about Martin and oddly comforted by Siobhan's voice in the darkness, as she hummed along to Peter Gabriel.

The sensation of something moving past my bed woke me out of a sound sleep and I lay very still, trying to remember where I was and aware of someone padding about the room. 'Oh, so you're awake at last, you lazy cow . . . ' were Siobhan's first words, as she flicked on and off the dead light switch half-heartedly. 'Thank God for small mercies, I'm tired of trying to keep quiet.'

'Whassatime?' I mumbled, still confused.

'Well may you ask, you dozy bitch. It's nearly four. So I've ordered a pail of water for your shower, I've already had mine. Well – come on!' and she gave my bed a sharp kick with her outstretched foot. 'Get a bloody move on. There's only one shower stall and half a million sodding natives will be queuing for it soon.'

Bemused to have made the acquaintance of a woman who was even more of a morning person than me, I staggered off in search of the shower stall, which I located at the end of the lean-to. I recognized it by the queue of five or six men waiting patiently outside – hardly worth calling a queue by Indian standards. I got talking to the men, who were all very short and slender and painfully shy, baffled to find me in their midst. Obviously I wasn't the kind of guest they often saw in this dosshouse and I learned they were itinerant labourers, more than glad for this chance to work in the city, even though it meant sleeping in dorms of twenty or thirty and sending most of their earnings home to their family villages. For them, as for every Indian, the day was beginning with all-over body washing and prayer. India may be sinking in a sea of filth but her people are among the cleanest on this planet.

When I got back to our room, I made yet another discovery about Siobhan – she was every bit as concerned with keeping up appearances as I was. When she'd strolled up to me at the *chai* stall, I'd noticed her make-up – her blue eyes dusted with grey shadow and carefully edged with kohl, the arcs of her eyebrows carefully plucked, her tanned complexion skimmed with blusher and her lips painted in a rose pink. While her shoulder-length black curls were clean and shiny.

Her clothes had been the height of fashion, too. Ridiculous tight pink cotton leggings were tucked into white ankle socks and flat leather, lace-up ankle boots. While her heavy cotton top had been pulled in by a large black belt which skimmed her hips. Now she was wearing similar clothes, this time in shades of peach and turquoise; she'd piled her hair up on top of her head and tied an azure silk scarf, turban-like, about the curls. She could have been on her way to a Saturday lunchtime drinking session back in Covent Garden, she looked so trendy. And out here in Mysore, she turned heads everywhere we went.

That suited me. For months now, I'd stuck out from other travellers like a sore thumb with my painted finger and toe nails, my eye make-up, my colourfully stained lips. My clothes and jewellery had been colourful to say the least – unlike the usual travellers' uniform of dusty jeans and T-shirt, dirty feet in Jesus sandals, cumbersome money belt, greasy, unwashed hair and a three-day growth (and that's just the women). Now I'd met a kindred spirit – a woman who cared about the way she looked to the rest of the world and the impression she made.

Siobhan wasn't only good-humoured and lots of fun. She was also clever, classy and incredibly moral about everything, including sex outside working hours – something else I discovered, as I got to know her better.

For a couple of days, we roamed around Mysore, taking in 'the Indo-Saracenic palace, clean streets and shady trees' of Sandalwood City, as per my trusty guide. But the best moment of all was when we came across their glorious covered market – the best kept secret of Mysore. Unable to believe our luck, we rummaged through stall after stall of healthy, happy vegetables and fruit, marvelling over the plump pineapples, sweet mandarins, delicious bananas and sackfuls of peanuts. Like kids in a treasure trove, we wandered from bead stalls to saree stalls, perfume and spice and dye stalls – the latter piled high with baskets of powdered dyes, in jade and deep purple, canary yellow, cobalt blue and shocking pink, a kaleidoscope of colour.

Shoppers to the last, we two rattled around this place for hours, chatting to the traders and yelping with delight at each new find. That evening, we had an impromptu fashion show back in our room as we swirled around in our new finery, our baubles and beads, while Mysore's electricity supply surged and faltered, throwing our fitful, dancing shadows against the dingy walls.

The next morning we woke up of the same mind – it was time to travel on, the prospect of being on the road again firing me so much that I made it to the shower stall before Siobhan had so much as shaken a leg. Bags packed, room vacated, we breakfasted at the rail station, while we waited for the first train to Ootacamund – a hill station once popular with the British and situated about 7,500 feet up the Nilgiri mountains. Unbelievably picturesque. And sodding freezing, we were soon to discover.

So glad were we to escape the heat and humidity of Mysore that we were quite pleased to find the temperature dropping as the steam engine chugged determinedly up the endless incline from the plains. We didn't even mind when we had to rummage in our bags for an extra sweater. But it got so that we were sitting closer and closer together for body warmth and rushing off the train in search of a warming *chai* stall, whenever it slid into a station.

Things didn't improve in Ooty, and we outdid each other on the whinge scale as we dragged around the various guest-houses, looking for somewhere to sleep. This time, warmth was the criterion and we thought the YMCA met it. Built high up above the little town by some Victorian Brit who had delusions of grandeur, it's a large, sprawling building on two floors. Spacious and very welcoming, with its large reception area dotted about with bright rugs and large brass urns full of flowering plants. I took in the wide, burnished wood staircase, the freshly painted walls, the magazine racks and the linen-covered tables in the dining room at a glance and heard the sound of a piano being played in another room – this place certainly was civilized. But what sold me was the large fireplace just at my back. True, it wasn't lit but surely it was a sign that the management kept the place warm?

Warm-ish was the answer. And then only until the sun went down. Shivering and shaking, we went in search of supper and although we found a reasonable inn and the food was middling to good, we were chilled to the bone each time the restaurant door swung open and a blast of icy wind rolled in.

Then followed a long, long night. We slept in separate beds in our little room and I swear that both of them had moved several inches away from the wall next morning, so much shivering and trembling went on inside them. Time and time again either Siobhan or myself had got up to put on yet another layer of clothing. By morning, literally everything I possessed was on my back and I still couldn't get warm.

'B'Jesus, I wouldn't want to go through this again,' Siobhan's soft Irish lilt drifted out from beneath a wardrobe of clothes. Then the mound moved and her face peered out at me, followed by legs encased in three sets of leggings, while scarves, skirts and God knows what else were draped about her.

A knock on the door and the water wallah announced the availability of the wet stuff. 'Cold water or hot, pliz?' the wily old gent asked, when I opened the door. 'Cold very nice – two rupees only. Hot much nicer, only twelve rupees.'

Now, when you consider that we were living in rooms for fifteen rupees a night, that we ate a meal for around ten and breakfasted like kings on five, you can see that hot water was an expensive luxury. But I do believe we'd have paid the little man anything that morning, in exchange for a circulation-restoring hot shower. The shower room was a few doors along from our bedroom and I dived in there, my teeth chattering like castanets in my head. The shower room was about the size of an average bathroom and sub-zero. It had a drain in the centre of the cement floor, a large barrel of freezing cold water, a second barrel which was piping hot, and a pitcher.

Stripping off was a lengthy process, by the end of which I'd almost lost the ability to control my limbs; and then I remembered that rule about creating pain in one area to counteract the pain you experience in another. Mad bitch that I am, I suddenly leaned over and completely submerged my head in the cold water and as I surfaced, yelping with shock, it is certainly accurate to say that the rest of my body suddenly felt a damn sight warmer than my exploding skull.

Siobhan also turned the morning ablutions into a full-scale

drama, after which we filled up on all the available carbo-hydrates and tried to get enthusiastic about the idea of exploring Ooty. It is an amazing place, scattered about with terribly English houses, sporting the kind of fenced-off front gardens you see all over the Kent countryside. We had our fortune told by some soothsayer, strolled down to the lakeside and hired a couple of mares, intending a quick canter around the area but managing instead only a lethargic walk and the odd half-hearted trot. These mares knew who was boss – and it wasn't us.

Then it was back to another jaw-clenching night, during which sleep was all but impossible. I had half a mind to suggest that we doubled up in one bed, but already I'd noticed that Siobhan was very defensive of her personal space and awkward about physical contact (although I still didn't know *why*). So I kept my suggestion to myself and shook, rattled and rolled in my bed, while she mumbled and grumbled in hers.

Next morning, I started to pack the moment I'd cleared the bedclothes and Siobhan did likewise. We were out of Ooty in under an hour, desperately trying to jump the bus queue. Dozens of pilgrims – their luggage wrapped in white cloth, balanced on their heads, their bodies naked apart from white and orange lungis and garlands of marigolds about their necks – seemed just as desperate to quit town as we were. So all hell broke out when the ancient bus rattled to a halt and we pushed and shoved with the best of them – pilgrims' ribcages and unshod feet being as susceptible to attack as anyone else's.

Of course, the bus was like a fridge on wheels, its barred windows devoid of glass and its metal bench seats freeze-burning exposed flesh. And sitting in the back seat over the rear axle, our spines took the brunt of every single hole and mound the vehicle passed over. Still, we hardly noticed the discomfort as we twisted and turned for hour after facinating hour down the Nilgiri mountains. Just beyond the wheels, we could see the edge, falling away into space. At each bend I would glance back to see the stretch of road we had just traversed and my stomach would tighten at the sheer drop, sometimes hundreds of feet, while far below, the road ahead snaked on like a silvery serpent. On the neighbouring mountains, I could make out flashes of movement as waterfalls tumbled from the undergrowth and spewed into the abyss although every so often, thin veils of cloud would slip past, obscuring the view below.

Down, down, down we went, as monkeys landed screaming on the bus roof, to stick their greedy paws through the windows, and sandalwood forests gave way to tea plantations, which in turn gave way to palm groves and finally tropical forest. Slowly, the temperature rose from bloody cold to cool; from cool to pleasantly fresh; from fresh to warm (clothes coming off, here); from warm to exceedingly hot (overpowering aroma of baking bodies). Three hours later, we were creeping across the plains towards Coimbatore in a heap of sizzling metal and I was heading for meltdown.

By the time we growled into the bus station I had completely lost my cool. So that when we limped into a *chai* shop for a resuscitating cuppa, I was in no mood for the audience of a dozen or so men of all ages who trooped in after us and ranged themselves along the wall, the better to gaze at these foreign women. So I screamed at them, marched up and down in front of their terrified faces and yelled all kinds of abuse, knowing they didn't understand a word but feeling much better for the outburst. Realizing I had finally OD'd on India, as every traveller does sooner or later, Siobhan drank her tea and let me get on with it.

An hour later, we were on the road again, moving in a south-easterly direction towards Madurai, and, although I was calmer now, I was still in a rotten mood – something Siobhan was determined to put right.

I glanced down as she bent over and fumbled inside her ankle sock, where she kept a lot of her 'gear'. 'Here – suck this,' she ordered, as she shoved a wad of brown stuff into my mouth. It was as large as my thumb, from tip to knuckle, and it tasted *foul*. I stared at her in disgust, whereupon she laughed wickedly and said, 'Don't you *dare* spit it out, you cow. It's worth a bloody fortune.'

So I sat there, sucking obediently, while mile after mile fell

294

behind us. Slowly, my eyes glazed over, my brain disengaged, my body moved away from its centre, my hands and feet felt as if they were attached to limbs which were yards long. Utterly stoned, completely zapped, totally out of my box, I stared unblinking out at a bizarre and beautiful India – a colourful and weird hallucination.

Much later, rattling on through the darkness, the laughter started bubbling up from nowhere and spilling over about nothing in particular – certainly nothing which the normal me would have laughed at. Siobhan, who'd been sucking on yet another dollop of the resin, was in the same high spirits. So we screamed hysterically at each other's rotten jokes and sang along at the tops of our voices to the Walkman we were both plugged into.

Overcome by the intimacy of the occasion as we bowled along together in the dead of night – surrounded by dozens of slumbering Indians but feeling curiously apart from them all – we began to tell each other our best kept, most closely guarded, most personal secrets. And that's when I learned that my travelling companion was a woman of many parts.

I dare any woman to deny that she's ever wondered what it would be like to receive payment for services rendered; to wield the power of her sexuality. It's a fantasy most women have had at some time – the idea of being part of a harem or of being forced into a sexual encounter (by a dashingly handsome man, of course). It's the stuff of Mills & Boon romantic novels, the backbone of Barbara Cartland epics; but that evening, I was given a vivid description of what life was really like 'on the game'. It isn't a fate I would wish on my worst enemy.

Well, I felt quite touched that she'd decided to confide in me – and decided the least I could do was return the compliment. And so I began to tell her bits about my own past. I felt almost apologetic that I couldn't top her stories in a sexual sense. But I sure as hell made her laugh at some of the sexual situations I'd got myself into. Screaming and choking with drug induced laughter, we entertained each other all the way across Tamil Nadu, completely forgetting that we were still plugged into the Walkman and its endless music and blissfully unaware that our bawdy, raunchy exchanges were actually being bellowed at the tops of our voices.

I don't remember reaching Madurai in the middle of that night. When Siobhan shook me awake next morning, I was lying like a stone across a bed in a room I didn't recognize (she'd practically had to carry me up the three flights of stairs to get to it) and dying seemed infinitely preferable to her suggestion that I should get up, shower and go with her in search of food. It took more than twenty-four hours for the cannabis to clear my body – the first time I'd ever tried it and, I promised myself, absolutely the last.

Madurai is a sun-soaked, over-populated, colour-washed city of pilgrims and beggars, traders and tailors. The famous Shree Meenakshi temple lies at its heart – a Disneyland spectacular of multi-coloured walls and towers, the whole edifice covered with lifesize carvings of gods, goddesses, animals and creatures of myth and legend. It's home for hundreds of monkeys, which will happily swing from a statue of Ganesh or sit with their tails drooping over a figure of Lakshmi, displaying wild irreverence in the presence of these and other gods.

Between the inner and outer walls of the temple lies one of the liveliest markets in southern India, selling everything from bangles to brassware, silks to snakes, while on a raised platform above the traders, fifty or sixty tailors sit at their ancient Singer treadle machines turning out made-to-measure clothes at a fantastic rate.

Even more than in the northern cities like Bombay, Madurai and its sister towns bubble over with irrepressible good humour. The place isn't so much colourful as gaudy, not just noisy but frantic with decibels. Its people are more than just friendly – they display all the innocent curiosity and tireless energy of hyperactive children. The water was undrinkable, the food dreadful and the accommodation worse. Yet Madurai's carnival atmosphere persuaded us to linger much longer than we'd intended.

On the road again, we headed ever south until we reached Trivandrum, at the southernmost tip of India, then turned north and made our way to Quilon. As usual, we arrived in the middle of the night and took a rickshaw to the edge of town, where the one-time British residency – now a guest house – stood at the river's edge. Unfortunately, it wasn't until the rickshaw had dumped us and disappeared that we discovered the place was locked and bolted for the night and the area nearby was deserted, with no buildings or any sign of life.

Siobhan wandered off in search of a friendly doorway in which to settle down. But by now, I knew that I was safer in India than I had been anywhere in the world to date. So, quite unperturbed, I dumped my bag over the garden wall, which was about four feet high, lay on my back along the coping stones and fell sound asleep.

The sound of bicycle bells being rung in greeting woke me, as workmen rode past on their way to work. The hotel came to life just before dawn and before the sun had quite risen, we had taken possession of a wonderful new home. The dining room seated fourteen, the bedroom had two four-poster beds. The bathroom had a shower and a bath, with an outer dressing room, and the loo – a real one with a seat and everything – was a quivering mass of the largest black ants I'd ever seen. Hundreds of them and all easily an inch long. The outer walls of the rooms were made up of a series of louvred doors, which flattened against the corners of the rooms, leaving them completely open to the wide verandah which ran all round our stylish new home. It really was a palace – and all for two pounds a day.

The management seemed a little nervous at the prospect of two women living alone in this wing of the residence and suggested we might prefer living in the main part of the house. Of course, we poo-pooed the idea, but a couple of hours later, we understood their apprehension.

Siobhan had been sitting on the wide verandah steps, admiring the parrots as they flitted through the trees and enjoying the cool sight of the river flowing by just yards from our front door. The Indian had walked by once or twice, his long skinny legs sticking out of his grubby lungi and his thin torso hidden beneath a garishly checked shirt. Once he was sure he'd caught Siobhan's attention, he began to coyly part the material covering his shanks and treated Siobhan to what must surely be the first wanton exposure of genitals in India. (I've always regarded flashing as a peculiarly European habit.)

How was he to know he'd picked on the wrong girl? But Miss Ireland, who had surely seen more exposed genitals than he'd had hot dinners, or even square meals, was distinctly unimpressed. When it came to the art of the striptease, this girl knew all the moves. Even so, she called me out to witness this exhibition and it was as I stood there, trying not to laugh at this person's antics, let alone his rather dejected equipment, that I noticed a large brown object, crouched in the lower branches of a nearby tree. It was a man. And as I trained my eyes on the trees fringing the residence, I could make out another, and another. Obviously Quilon was the natural habitat of a strange species of male, fond of exhibiting his private parts and preferring the higher branches of trees, to the usual *chai* shops or bars.

We weren't unduly bothered until night fell and we pulled the wall of louvred doors together. We'd just settled into our respective four-posters, when I heard the louvres rattling in the far corner of the room. Moments later, a set of louvres much closer to me began to rattle and I could distinctly hear the scratching of fingernails on the wooden shutters just behind my head. I couldn't quite make out Siobhan's face in the dark, but she said nothing and seemed to be asleep. I figured she'd be nervous if I woke her. The scratching and the rattling went on and I could hear the soft padding of bare feet as shadowy forms slithered round and round our apartment. While I didn't necessarily feel under threat, sleep was certainly beyond me until dawn began to break and our guests disappeared. That day, we thought it was wiser to move into the main part of the residence.

From Quilon, we travelled north to Alleppey and made the beautiful lazy journey along the backwaters to Ernakulam. Our little boat took the best part of eight hours to complete the trip, gliding through shallow waters filled with fishermen and heron; brightly sareed women washing both laundry and infants on the banks. Every now and again, a large barge would bear silently down upon us, its sails billowing in the slightest breeze, and once in a while, we would see the water up ahead churning, as water buffalo submerged themselves along with their dusty shepherd boy.

Around every bend there was something new to see – a working elephant or a religious procession marching along the river bank – while the stops for *chai* were a marvellous insight into rural village life.

For most of the afternoon, Siobhan and I lazed on the roof of the boat or sat up on the prow with our legs dangling just above the surface of the water and I found out much more about her. Her parents were quite well-off and she herself had been very well educated at a convent. Although she had intended going on to university, she had taken a year off to travel and been bitten by the bug. Inevitably she'd found herself in some out-of-the-way, arse-end of the world places and had more than once been an unwilling overnight guest in a less than salubrious prison. I guess, if you live on the edge like that, you've got to make a decision about how you finance it, sooner or later.

And, surprisingly soon in her life, Siobhan had decided to make the most of her natural assets. However, she wasn't into perversion and she'd have nothing to do with s & m. She assured me that these days, she had top drawer clients, some of them super men she'd come to know quite well over the years. Her network of pimps stretched from Amsterdam to Java and any one of them was more than happy to line up this freelancer's regular clients, whenever she breezed into town. She impressed me with her businesslike attitude to it all, but I knew it was one I'd never want to adopt. However, it became obvious that she was, if anything, fairly prudish about men and sex in her private life and was totally faithful and loyal to her present long-term lover, who was English, lived in Birmingham and had no idea about his girlfriend's real profession. And – surprise surprise – she was fairly disapproving of me and my free-and-easy attitude to sex.

After we parted, I thought about our conversation a lot and wondered whether, of the two of us, she might have had the stricter moral code. Certainly, during my relationship with Martin, lovemaking had been an expression of love and caring. But until I met him, I had indulged in sex less for pleasure and more as a way of manipulating men. As recently as Hafez, I had tried to barter my sexuality in exchange for protection and acceptance and now I had to give serious consideration to what Siobhan had said; that many women – wives among them – regarded their sexual role as one they had to fulfil in exchange for their food, their clothes, their children's welfare and even the roof over their heads.

Viewed in that light, weren't we all whores to a greater or lesser degree? And did the fact that Siobhan saw sex as being a fair exchange for money make her, if anything, *more* honest and *more* moral than the rest of us? It was something to think about.

Ernakulam gave way to Cochin, then Calicut and further north still, to Mangalore. For me, Goa beckoned again, while Siobhan intended journeying east to Bangalore and a rendezvous with a girlfriend who was travelling in from the Philippines.

I remember standing with her in Mangalore bus station, as the sun slipped low in the sky and the air was filled with that golden light which is so unique to India. She looked as pretty as ever as she suddenly leaned forward and gave me a self-conscious hug. Just then, my filthy old bone shaker of a bus rolled into the station and she gave me a last long, wry look.

'Well – go on. Fuck off . . . ' she said in a conversational tone, as she turned on her heel. And I did, realizing, as I climbed on the bus and searched in vain for a last sight of her, that this was what travelling was all about. It wasn't about places you saw – although some were unforgettable. It was about the people you met along the way. It was knowing, even as you said hello, that sooner or later, you would have to say goodbye. And at the end of the day, travel was about nothing so much as being alone.

I've often thought of her since. Such a super girl, with so much energy and a genuine love of life. The stuff of good friends . . . and the best travelling companion I could have hoped for.

Chapter Three

Journey to the land that time forgot

The Bombay Hotel was just as I had left it – the walls still standing, the turbaned Sikh still guarding the door. I, however, had obviously changed beyond recognition as I walked up to the reception desk.

' . . . Miss Culross?' the pretty receptionist queried when I asked for a room and my luggage which they had been storing for the best part of three months.

I could understand her confusion. At least eight pounds lighter, with my skin deeply tanned and my shoulder-length hair bleached red-gold, I bore little resemblance to the pale-skinned, nervous woman who had arrived here from Cairo all these weeks ago.

Gracefully recovering her composure, she smiled knowingly and said, 'Well, that *was* a long weekend. Did you enjoy Goa?'

Had I enjoyed Goa? That had to be the understatement of the year, I mused, as the porter showed me into yet another grubby room and I waited around for my luggage. Although the Goa I'd just flown out of that morning had lost a lot of its magic. I'd arrived there from Mangalore a couple of days before and realized, as I walked through the streets of Calangute, that I couldn't bear to go back to our little guest house on the beach – it brought back too many memories. Instead I'd moved in with Jill, a vivacious green eyed blonde from Nottingham who had a little cottage about a mile down the beach from where I used to stay. She was a bundle of raw energy forever running along the beach before breakfast and swimming like a fish. And she was game for anything, whether it was a heavy drinking session, a boogie at the local disco or a long, philosophical middle-of-the-night chat. But Goa for me had been Martin and, without him, I simply couldn't stay.

The luggage arrived and it came as a shock to find that I owned so many clothes. As I unpacked skirts and suits, trousers and evening clothes, I kept glancing at my little hold all crouched in the corner. It was true, I'd only intended to visit Goa for four or five days and I'd packed just a couple of skirts, petticoats and tops to see me through. They'd done it, too, and, with my little bit of hand luggage, I'd travelled free as a bird.

'Whatever made me think I'd need all this gear?' I wondered now, deciding that my first chore was to send some of it back home, pronto. I separated everything into two piles, although I must confess the evening dress wasn't thrown on the 'going home' heap. Neither were the long black evening gloves or the black silk stilettos. Never again would I apologize for the fact that I enjoyed dressing up (something Siobhan had taught me) and I had a feeling that, before this trip was through, I'd wear that dress.

For the same reason, I hung on to all my make-up, most of my jewellery, a couple of pairs of high heels *and* my wonderful, image-altering heated rollers. Still, I did dispense with lots of gear; and one or two other things I'd never thought I could bear to part with. For instance, I had a bag full of the weirdest objects – a match box, a silk handkerchief, a compass, a tiny book of world maps and a whole other collection of things. Every single one was the property of someone who mattered back home – a tangible link with the past which I'd often looked at and touched in an effort to maintain contact.

And there were my letters. Loads of them. Collected hungrily from every *poste restante*, every Amex office I'd passed en route. Most of them from my dear old ma, who'd faithfully written to me at least twice a week and never complained when I didn't reply. My talismans, my good luck charms, could all go home now. I didn't need them any more.

I soon had everything bundled up and stitched into the regulation white cotton wrapping. I practically had a fit at the post office, when I discovered that sending it the cheapest way (on a six-month-long, slow boat trip) was going to cost the equivalent of fifteen pounds. I'd been long enough in India to appreciate the value of every single rupee and this was daylight robbery. But I paid it anyway.

From the post office, I made a beeline for Amex to pick up more traveller's cheques and, hopefully, the mail. Mum hadn't let me down; Hannah had written me a whole script; Nadia and Graham sent some happy snaps; there was a letter from Hafez. I decided not to open it until I was somewhere very quiet.

From the Amex office, I hit the Air India office and booked my flight north to Delhi for the next day. Then I hotfooted it out of the Bombay heat back to Juhu beach and my hotel.

In the late afternoon, when the sun became less fierce, I went strolling along the beach, which was alive with Bombayites (none of whom would dream of taking off an item of clothing and *sunbathing*). The place was full of ice cream stalls and ponies pulling go-carts up and down the beach – rides for two rupees each. Juhu beach did not compare favourably with the Goan equivalent, but I hardly noticed or cared much – I was too busy thinking about the contents of Hafez's letter. It had been very short and to the point:

Lady, where are you?
You have left a big, black hole in my life.
Come back.
Even if it IS the long way round.
HAFEZ.

Poor man . . . I'd blamed him for everything that had gone wrong in Cairo – and even now, if I was honest, I felt a bit raw and hurt about the way he had chosen to deal with me. Yet I'd learned enough these last weeks about the way I'd been functioning to know I wasn't exactly an innocent, injured party. I had tried to muscle in on his life, thinking I could adopt it for my own, and he'd always – quite rightly – suspected my motives. For I had never loved Hafez and our relationship had been based on all the wrong things. He hadn't yet worked that out, obviously. If he had, he certainly wouldn't want me back in his life. The 'Dear John' letter wasn't pleasant to write but, wherever my future lay, it wasn't in Cairo with Hafez – and the sooner he knew that, the better.

I wasn't sorry to leave Bombay, for I'd seen enough of India now to know that this major city was as unrepresentative of its country and its peoples as every other in the world. I didn't suppose Delhi would be much different but you know how it is: have plane ticket with stopover, must fly. And from Delhi, surely there were lots of marvellous places I could reach?

Saturday night in the heart of Delhi found me supping with High Society. Twelve of us at a circular table, celebrating someone's birthday – and all the very best Brahmins were there. The table groaned beneath the weight of silver salvers piled high with lamb, chicken and vegetables, all delicately flavoured with cream and nuts and spices. We were circled by attentive waiters – a tide of navy and gold uniforms which surged forward and then fell back at the slightest raising of a hand or the merest nod.

The women around me wore a rainbow of hand-painted, jewel-studded silks in deepest purple, brightest jade, richest saffron; while the formal attire of the men was relieved by the warm glow of old gold and diamonds winking cheekily from rings, cufflinks and shirt studs.

A cabinet minister on my right held his audience spellbound with intimate details of the Gandhi household, while the ever-silent Prakash, sitting to my left, turned to me and complimented me on my appearance. I smiled wryly as I glanced down at my full-length evening gown, made of black and rose pink silk and draped across one hip in a massive bow. The long black gloves hid my bare arms, my feet were shod in the black silk stilettos and my hair, wouldn't you know, was elegantly coiffed, thanks to the ubiquitous heated rollers.

That part of me which had always expected to find the odd, sophisticated oasis had been well prepared for it and, although I'd dragged this bloody frock more than halfway round the world, my forward planning had finally paid off.

I was strutting my stuff in the Ashoka Palace hotel, in the smart suburbs of Delhi. A one-time royal residence, it was now one of *the* places to be seen in and my first visit had been a couple of days earlier, when I had been desperately searching for a hairdresser to control my wayward mop.

The hotel's salon had been uncomfortably smart – full of rich Indian women with pukka accents and a whole gaggle of American matrons whose husbands had been shipped over for some conference – and I'd felt suddenly very aware of the fact that my 'wild woman of Borneo' look was somewhat out of place. Personally, I don't think I'd ever looked better (and I have the photographs to prove it) but it was time to tone down the island girl image and I decided to start with the hair. Off it came – a good six inches of it. And as I watched it swirl on to my lap in red-gold strands, I felt as if I was severing still one more link with Martin. Two hours later, shorn and permed – the new growth looking much darker, now that the blonde bits had gone – I stared at my smart reflection in the mirror and was very glad that my German would never see me like this.

That evening, back in my tiny hotel room (a luxurious place with a dressing table, a *bath* and room service!), I decided it was time to get back into the old routine – and that meant dressing up for dinner. Recklessly, I decided to wear a saree, since I'd bought several on my trip south, and a whole pains-taking hour later, I'd transformed myself with five yards of brown and peach silk. I really couldn't believe my reflection in the mirror. Although my hair was far shorter, it was much healthier, I was wearing more make-up than usual and the fact that I'd lost weight meant that the bits of my body which showed looked tanned and supple, instead of unappetizingly fleshy.

Not to put too fine a point on it, I thought I was a show-stopper – and I didn't doubt the rest of Delhi would think so too, once it got an eyeful. As it turned out, I was uncannily prophetic.

My hotel was actually on the first floor of the building – the ground floor being given over to a very smart restaurant, the main entrance of which was used by diners and hotel resi-dents alike. A narrow stairway connected the two floors, after which it was necessary to walk the length of the restaurant in order to reach the main exit on to the street. Thrilled to bits with myself, I minced out of my room and strolled past reception, then I swept imperiously down the staircase, uncomfortably aware of a slight loosening sensation of the silk which had been tucked into my waistband.

Haughtily ignoring the admiring glances which came from all sides, I made the lengthy walk down the centre aisle of the restaurant and glided out the front door. I'd made it across the road and was just about to step into a taxi, when the 'loosening' sensation grew into a distinct 'slackening' of my garment and I realized my saree was beginning to unwind. Now, if my bra comes undone, I know how to fix it. If my knicker elastic gives, I know what to grab to save my blushes. But this was a totally alien garment and I didn't know which bits to clutch.

In a blind panic, I dived out of the taxi and headed for the safety of my room. Needless to say, I never made it. I was halfway down the restaurant – my face taut with fear and my heart hammering – when whole swathes of silk began to flop around my knees. Unable to run or hide, I began to climb the stairs as the silk slid from my right shoulder. I'd almost reached the safety of the top step when the silk unwound itself from my hips and the saree – all five yards of it – slid silently back down the steps. High above the diners I stood rigid with embarrassment, naked but for my little silk bodice and (the final humiliation) a pair of shocking pink, sheer lace french knickers. You could have heard a pin drop. In fact, a pin had dropped. Unfortunately it was mine – and it was all that had held my silk creation in place.

The receptionist's mouth had dropped open when I rushed back upstairs in my underwear and moments later, she knocked tentatively on the door – my saree in a rustling pile in her arms, compliments of the head waiter. I gradually overcame my first instinct, which was to hole up in the room until I starved to death. Eventually I saw the funny side of it and set to work again, winding on that bloody saree – this time anchoring it with a whole network of safety pins.

Leaving my room, I only just managed to brave the receptionist but there was no way I could steel myself to face the packed restaurant. So I nipped out of a landing window and climbed down the fire escape. I chortled all the way to the Ashoka Palace hotel, where I was determined to treat myself to a cocktail and then a slap-up dinner. And it was as I sat sipping a Bloody Mary in the Garden Bar (quite unaware that it was for members and hotel guests only) that Prakash introduced himself to me.

Later, he confessed that he had approached me because he had never before seen a European woman wear a saree so well. It was just as well he hadn't been eating in the Host Inn restaurant an hour earlier. However, on that first evening, we talked for half-an-hour or so, after which I insisted I wanted to eat alone, although I did agree to meet him for lunch next day.

Prakash – more than a little wealthy and more than a little lost – became my escort for the few days I was in Delhi, although I am pleased to be able to report he was never more than that. I had turned over a new leaf, the Stormtrooper had finally snuffed it and so had my interest in casual sex.

Now here I was – Prakash's guest at a handsome party and the object of some curiosity. How long had I been travelling . . . where had I visited . . . what did I think of India? The questions came thick and fast and I was happy to answer them all.

'And where are you travelling next, my dear lady?' the cabinet minister at my elbow suddenly enquired.

'Jaisalmere,' I chirped, which caused a moment's stunned silence before the table erupted into laughter.

'But . . . my dear girl, why on earth would you want to journey all that way? It's the end of the earth,' he finally spluttered in an old Etonian accent. 'My goodness – Prakash, tell her. Why, you'll see nothing but desert for hundreds of miles in any direction. It's – well, it's positively primitive!'

It took a few more minutes of this gentle ribbing before I began to realize that, although no one at the table had anything good to say about the little town of Jaisalmere, none of them had actually seen it. And why should they? It was the last stop on the endless railway line which ploughs through the Rajasthan desert – a place none of these sophisticated

Indians would dream of visiting, which was precisely why it would be worth seeing.

The talk passed on to other things until the dancing caught everyone's interest and I took the floor with a succession of charming Indian gentlemen, whirling beneath the chandeliers to a medley of popular ballads. Danced and laughed and tried to imagine this tiny, forgotten town in the middle of nowhere, which now – more than ever – I was determined to see.

As the hour grew late, the talk turned to business; and their business was politics, as was Prakash's. Assuring him I didn't need an escort home, I left him downing brandies with his friends in the Garden Bar and discussing the state of the nation.

I walked down the sweep of marble steps flanked by richly uniformed attendants and slipped into a waiting taxi, heading for Connaught Place and bed. But as we were driving past the railway station, I asked the driver to pull over. Carefully stepping over sleeping bodies in my high heels, I asked at the ticket office about a train to Jaisalmere and learned there was no such thing. The journey from Delhi involved three trains at least and I couldn't possibly get there in less than twenty-four hours.

Still there was a train leaving at 4.12 a.m. heading west to Jaipur. At least it was going in the right direction, I thought, once back in the taxi and, by the time I reached my hotel, I had a plan of action. Out of the glad rags . . . into some travelling gear . . . pack a few clothes . . . store the rest of the luggage . . . settle the bill and hotfoot it back to the station. It was already three o'clock.

Elated at the prospect of being on the road again, I rushed round my room whipping damp washing from the shower rail and odd shoes from beneath the bed. Forty-five minutes later, my luggage was locked away, the bill was settled and I'd scribbled a note for Prakash.

Down in the silent street, searching for a cab, I was waylaid as usual by the little beggar who lived under the arches hard by the hotel. Hearing my footsteps, he rumbled out in his push-cart – the little wooden wheels echoing eerily as he manoeuvred himself alongside me. A tiny torso on wheels, completely without legs, he smiled up at me hopefully – still rubbing the sleep from his eyes with one hand, while the other was stretched out, palm upwards. No more than eight or nine years old, he had become part of the routine of my days – impossible to ignore and able to move like lightning if anyone tried to outdistance him. He rumbled back into the dimness of the arches, my five rupees clutched in his hand, just as a taxi pulled up.

The Pink Express was fretting on Platform 3, blowing out great plumes of steam and anxious to be gone. Workmen nimbly scurried over the great hulk of the locomotive, testing pressures and gauges – their teeth flashing white in their coal-smeared faces, as their torches flung beams of light out into the darkness. I looked down at the ticket clutched in my hand and gazed back along the platform at the snake of sugar-pink carriages.

I'd made it, with time to spare, and, as the engine bellowed out news of its departure with a blare like fifty saxophones and its deep brass bell clanged out frantically, I gleefully hopped aboard.

Inside, I settled down in a bright pink plastic seat and stared across a bright pink plastic table at my Indian neighbour, while tea was served in doll-sized pink plastic thermos flasks. So we charged out of Delhi on a surge of incredible power – a metal monster hissing smoke and steam, while a pale pink plastic dawn broke across the land. I was on the move again, which meant I was happy.

The pretty blonde next to me was casually dressed. As casually, that is, as an Italian fashion journalist *can* be, when she's photographing next season's ranges against a backdrop of India – which is what she told me later. Her travelling attire consisted of white gaberdine trousers and a white silk shirt, while the palest blue angora sweater was tied about her neck. I guessed she wouldn't stay white for long. She didn't.

Suddenly aware I'd dined and danced all night and hadn't slept a wink, I sleepily removed my shoes, tucked my legs beneath me on the seat and snuggled down beneath my Kashmir shawl. The last thing I remember was watching Miss Italy brushing large sooty smuts from her white and blue ensemble, only to find them settling on her face and hair like fat, exhausted flies. Then I slept contentedly, lulled by the rhythm of the train.

Just before eleven o'clock, the Pink Express slid into Jaipur. I felt refreshed and ready for anything as I jumped down on to the platform – which was just as well, since I had to battle with what seemed like half the Indian army cluttering up the station. The business of buying another ticket took over an hour (and why four queues?). So it was just as well that the train to Jodhpur – which should by then have come and gone – was two and a half hours late or I would have missed it.

I was safely ensconced in my second train by two-thirty; although, with its uncomfortable wooden slatted seats, it wasn't a patch on the Pink Express. I chatted away to my new neighbours – four policemen on their way to a shooting competition. They looked doubtful when I said I hoped to reach Jaisalmere by nine the following morning. But that was when the desert festival began – the festival of the full moon. Having raced across half of India to see it, I was confident I'd get there in time.

A few hours later, darkness fell and it was becoming obvious that they were right; I'd never get to the next town in time to connect with the last train to Jaisalmere. It pissed me off to think I'd miss the opening, when I'd come so close. Then, as we drew into a small station, one of the policemen quizzed a passing guard, who confirmed that the train we could see dimly outlined in a siding a few yards away was actually going to Jaisalmere.

The problem was, our train didn't stop here – although it had slowed down to pass through. But quick as a wink, the men had opened the carriage door and dropped me and my holdall down on to the track, just as our train began to pick up speed. The ground was an ankle-jarring five feet below me and I landed in an ungainly heap. I straightened up to see my policemen friends anxiously leaning out of the carriage as their train disappeared down the track.

At that moment, the second train coughed into life and I hobbled quickly along the track in the darkness towards it.

Panicking, I swung myself aboard just as the whistle blew and with a lurch and a rattle of metal, I was off again.

The harassed conductor was surprised to find me wandering around with no ticket and no reservation. We soon sorted that problem out, but it was standing room only for the six-hour ride to Jaisalmere. I soon discovered that – yes, it *is* possible to sleep standing up.

Tucked into a corner of the corridor, trying to avoid the icy draughts, my dreamless slumber was interrupted by a man who wanted to use the loo – I'd fallen asleep against the door. By this time, the temperature had really dipped and I was half-frozen so, when he reappeared and invited me into his first class compartment, I was tempted but suspicious – until he held open the door.

A compartment designed for eight was bursting at the seams with sixteen or so adults and children. Such was the overcrowding that one more hardly mattered – and there was a lot to be said for the body heat that was being generated. So I lay down carefully across some of the still forms, only to have other snoring bodies spread themselves out across my arms and legs. In this way we headed for Jaisalmere – a heaving tangle of humanity, gently powdered by a fine mist of red sand, as the Rajasthan desert worked its way in through every nook and cranny of the train.

Shortly before dawn, I was in so much discomfort I had to take out my contact lenses. Thus it was in a completely exhausted, half-blind state that I tumbled from the train at our destination, five hundred and seventy-five miles and twenty-five hours out of Delhi.

Although I could barely make out his features, I trusted the voice of the boy who offered me a room at his hotel and, bouncing around in the back of his Land-Rover, I gave up trying to distinguish buildings from sky – it was all a blue-grey blur. And I knew better than to be annoyed when I discovered there were no rooms at the inn after all. I could hardly blame him for sticking to the Indian's first rule of business – first, catch your tourist. *Then* worry about what you're going to sell her.

Still, he promised there would be a vacant room in a couple

of hours and he had no objections to me sleeping up on the flat roof until then. I followed him up half-finished steps to a flat earth-baked roof, lay down wrapped in my shawl and fell asleep within minutes, only barely conscious of the heavy rug which he brought upstairs and laid over my dusty clothes.

A couple of hours later, his gentle voice woke me and I opened my eyes to blinding sunlight which was gently steaming the dampness out of my clothes. He led me down to a little room where he'd thoughtfully left a bucket of cold water and, stripping off, I emptied it over my head (shades of Ooty here!). Fifteen minutes later, lenses in, fresh clothes on, eye make-up applied, I stuck my head out of my room window and yelled my breakfast order down to the smiling cook, then I climbed back up on to the roof . . . and got the shock of my life.

It was as if I'd slipped through a time warp and wakened up a thousand years ago to find myself in the land that time forgot. Below me, the town of Jaisalmere offered up her narrow streets, her minarets, her carved porticos, her latticed windows, to a brand new day. And a multitude of sounds, myriad colours, presented themselves to my astounded eyes and ears.

Fat grey donkeys sidled round corners, goats picked carefully through abandoned rubbish. Camels stood patiently cross-legged outside shop fronts, as provisions were unloaded.

I spun round in disbelief and behind me a hill soared skywards, crowned with a castle which seemed woven from golden light and air. A fretwork of towers, spires and casement windows, it was like every castle I'd ever imagined in the *Arabian Nights*. And in every direction, the red desert of Rajasthan rolled off into infinity, like a magic carpet.

After breakfast, my young hotelier offered to take me down to the plains outside the village, where the festival was to begin. Perched up behind him on a groaning camel, we padded softly through the oddly deserted village but the crowds grew thick as we headed down to the foot of the hill.

I'd seen literally thousands of Indians on my journey through the south and they'd been warm, friendly, innocent

312

people. Small and slight, thin and black – and not particularly attractive. But this was a whole different world. Here the men frequently topped six feet, were muscular and fit, with skin the colour of bronze. Their eyes carefully made up with kohl, their ears festooned with gold crescent moons, while heavy bracelets and anklets tinkled merrily . . . they really were the most amazing-looking men. Sporting luxuriant, drooping moustaches, their eyes flashing wickedly from beneath their amazing, multi-coloured turbans – they were dressed in their finery for this special day. Dhotis were spotless, feet were encased in richly embroidered slippers, which curled up at the toes, while more embroidery decorated their waistcoats and cummerbunds.

We turned the corner of the last building to find perhaps twenty women perched on a low wall. Laughing and twittering, a blaze of iridescent colour, they were like a flock of exotic birds poised for flight. And they very nearly took off when they caught sight of my camera. Screeching and flapping wildly, they waved me away – hiding their faces behind their veils.

We lumbered down on to the plain to find that an area the size of a football pitch had been cordoned off, while the crowd was large enough to grace any Wembley final. As the sea of humanity waited patiently on all four sides of the square, I sat restlessly on Rajan's camel and wondered what we were waiting for.

When I first heard the sound, I thought it was a distant roll of thunder. It seemed to rumble somewhere out of the plain . . . then it died on the wind . . . then grumbled anew. When I craned my head to the right, I could make out a dustcloud moving in the distance. The sound grew so deafening that I couldn't hear Rajan when he spoke and when the ground began to shake, I could feel the tremor rise up through our camel, as he sidestepped nervously.

And then they came, wave after wave of them. Hundreds of camels galloping at full stretch – thundering down on us in a storm of sand. During my wanderings in Egypt, I'd seen many of these creatures plodding by; sometimes even seen them trotting bravely across the shimmering Sahara; but never before had I seen them moving as fast as this, or with so much grace and power. But the race, which had begun far out in the desert, was now almost over – and everyone's blood was up.

Wild-eyed and urged on with yells and lashes, the animals flashed past me, a sea of white, beige, brown and even black. By now, the crowd had erupted noisily – and even I whooped and yelled with sheer excitement. The thunder of hooves in the baked earth, the frantic jangle of harness, the vivid flashes of colour, as pompoms danced madly about the richly woven saddle blankets . . . it was impossible to watch the spectacle and not be moved.

There were lots of events that first day, but I drifted away from the show and wandered among the people instead. And when, finally, I got closer to the women, I began to see what the attraction had been for the ancient Persians who had invaded and plundered this land for so many centuries leaving their mark indelibly on future generations of tall, light-skinned, almond-eyed Indians. These women were delicious.

They looked as if they had been poured into dark corset-like bodices, which were fastened at the back with just one string. To this was added two or three wide, full skirts, brilliantly dyed with traditional patterns in colourways of green with navy and orange, or pink with purple and gold. The skirts were edged with silver and gold ribbon and festooned with paste stones. Beneath their skirts, the women wore leggings, fastened tight at the ankles with six or seven copper and silver anklets, weighed down with bells. Sleek black heads of hair were veiled in yards of shimmering cotton, anchored with heavy jewellery and splashed with sequins. Bare arms proudly displayed ivory bracelets (their wealth), which frequently stretched from wrist to shoulder if the woman was quite well off.

As darkness fell I was back on the plain again to watch the dancers. They whirled like dervishes to the mournful beat of drums and the thin wail of reed pipes, while children sang and old folk told stories and legends. This went on for three days and nights.

When I wasn't enjoying the festival, I went exploring and

enjoyed some new experience each time I ventured out. One day, I came across what the locals called their 'sacred lake'. Still and mysterious, with no hint of a ripple to mar its glassy surface, its mirrored temples, tiny palaces, crumbling summer houses – all mellow, golden sandstone – seemed to soak up the Indian sunlight, only to release it, strangely altered and magical, back into the warm air.

I sat there for hours, lulled by the silence – watching as a flock of ebony crows rose lazily up into the air. They had been disturbed by a grandmother who came to the water's edge to fill her pitcher. Sheathed in magenta and silver, her old body was ramrod straight, as she placed the heavy copper on her head and walked off delicately, spilling not a drop.

Another time, I sat in the village square, staring up at the solid old castle walls towering above me and writing endless postcards to people who couldn't begin to visualize what I was trying to describe. Then came the day I visited the castle . . . and found my special room.

Walking past the massive wooden doors, I toiled up the steep winding road – over ancient flagstones and under massive arches – while crows circled in their hundreds high above the ramparts. There was a whole community living inside the walls and, wandering along the narrow alleyways, I came upon a fat, jolly Indian sitting on the front steps of his house. He turned out to be the local schoolteacher, his English was faultless and we were chatting away in no time.

He invited me inside and I salaamed when I met his wife, his mother, his father and two sisters. Then followed a tour of the house and I followed him up and around a flight of worn steps, passing richly carved doors, all of which were chained and padlocked.

Suddenly he stopped outside one of the doors, unlocked it and ushered me inside. The room was like nothing I'd ever seen before but as I stepped across the threshold and he threw open the shutters, I got the strangest feeling – almost as if I'd been in the room before. The shock I experienced at the recognition of it must have shown in my face, but the schoolteacher just stood smiling and watching me – as if he understood.

When I asked if I could rent the room, he smiled apologetically. 'We are not having guests . . . ' he started to explain softly, with a gentle sideways motion of his head, but he tailed off when he saw my pleading expression. He had a few words with his pretty, childlike wife and I was installed that same afternoon.

What can I tell you about the room? It was about twelve feet square with two beautiful windows set into one wall. Tiny, balconied, Romeo-and-Juliet affairs, they had slender columns and narrow arches. The front view was of the castle rooftops and the Jain temple opposite, with its stone gargoyles silhouetted against the sky; while, to my left, the castle walls were just a few feet away. Beyond them, I could see the desert shimmering in a heat haze which danced to the horizon.

In the centre of the room, the stone floor dipped into a shallow pool, about three feet by five, while the ceiling had a corresponding hole, which formed a well up through the next two floors of the house and was open to the sky. The pool was surrounded by more slender columns and the only piece of furniture in the room was a simple, rope-strung bed, which stood on a low dais in an alcove. I loved that room and stayed there for days, supremely happy and taking endless photographs of this place, which I often gaze at now, in quiet wonder.

That first night, I lay down on my back in the pool and waited patiently for the swollen moon to ride over my few feet of sky. Later, too excited to sleep, I sat up in bed and watched the stars slowly travel across the night – the way I'd watched them with Martin on Christmas Eve.

Dawn came and I was wakened by the gentle cooing of pigeons, as they fluttered down into the well in pairs and eyed me beadily, before gliding around my bedroom and escaping through the window in a flurry of feathers.

The last night of the festival . . . and I sat in the dust, lost in the dancing and singing. The night was cool and clear, everything bathed in blue shadow from the light of the moon, which hung low in the sky. I had watched it grow and fade in many different places since I had left home. And I had been in many different moods when the full moon had made

316

its appearance. But I would always remember seeing it here, at the desert festival of Rajasthan.

And even now, when I gaze up at it in a wintry London sky, beset by scudding storm clouds . . . it never fails to remind me of these dreamlike, Indian desert nights.

Chapter Four

Some royal, some wretched but all of them kind

The train from Jaisalmere screeched into Jodhpur station in the dead of night, as usual – I seemed to be forever travelling through India under cover of darkness. Now I was on the edge of the Thar desert in what was once known as 'The Land of Death'. Yet as my rickshaw trundled past silent houses and the odd group of Indians huddled round a street fire, I was in no mood to dwell on this city's history. All I wanted was somewhere to lay my head.

I barely took in my surroundings as my driver careered off the dusty highway, rattled through a set of wrought-iron gates and sped along a driveway edged with flowering bushes, and I only dimly took in the outline of the building he stopped in front of. But a slight, pretty girl appeared from out of the shadows, her eyes mischievous in her dark face and her skirts swishing as she lifted my luggage out of the ricky. This was my first encounter with Hapi, one of the Ajit Bawan Palace's most trusted servants and a woman who certainly lived up to her name.

Her anklets jingling cheekily as her bare feet padded along flower-fringed paths, she finally led me up a narrow winding flight of steps and opened a wooden door. Barely awake, I followed her into a circular room which was probably the most beautifully decorated place I was to stay in on the whole of my journey, although I didn't properly appreciate that until the early hours of the morning, when I woke up in my comfortable bed and gazed about me.

My bed was large, made up with expensive, clean linen and topped with a richly coloured, handwoven quilt. The bed-

318

head was high and made of ornate, carved wood encased in a sheath of tiny, mirrored squares. The ceiling was painted white, the walls red as rubies, while little carved chairs boasted plump satin cushions and the wooden floor was covered with bright woven rugs. There was a small window and what seemed to be a patio door in the wall, both of them gleaming with assorted panes of jewel-coloured glass, while the filmy white curtains were suspended from delicately carved wooden rails. These in turn were attached to the wall by wooden brackets carved in the shape of peacocks, their feathers painted in aquamarine and pink. Everything was gilded with tiny mirrors; they were sewn into the curtains, the bedspread and sunk into the wood of the chairs. Mirrors, mirrors everywhere, so that the whole room winked and sparkled in the sunlight.

The entrance to my room was a heavy wooden door, ornately studded with brass rosettes on the outside and with delicately painted scenes of lovers in gardens decorating the inside. More slant-eyed Moghul princes and bejewelled princesses decorated the black wooden door leading to my gleaming white, tiled bathroom, its loo and washbasin shiny clean and fluffy white towels piled up next to the shower stall.

My living quarters, which consisted of a bedroom and adjoining bathroom, were actually a little cottage or pavilion – one of twenty which were dotted around the grounds and gardens of this old palace and all of which were individually designed and exquisitely furnished. My pavilion was built in the form of a circular stone tower, which stood about twenty feet above the gardens and was reached by the little flight of winding stone steps. The steps themselves formed a natural bridge across a bubbling stream, which wound through the whole pavilion complex. Shaded by orange trees, edged with rustling reeds and filled with pink and white water-lilies, the water tumbled over rocks and into little pools, racing alongside landscaped paths and emerald lawns. I'd stumbled on another corner of paradise – a magical oasis in the middle of the desert.

Unable to believe my eyes – or my luck – I strolled along the pathways, disturbing stripe-backed squirrels and bright green parakeets. Every pavilion looked empty and the place seemed to be utterly deserted when suddenly an early morning jogger came sprinting round a corner. Dressed in a navy tracksuit with a white towel tucked into its neck, this strikingly handsome Indian gentleman motored to a halt in front of me. Tall and athletically built, his black hair greying at the temples, he sported a luxuriant moustache – and dark almond-shaped eyes studied me from beneath bushy eyebrows as he bid me 'Good morning' with a generous, white-toothed smile.

'You have just arrived . . . you came in the night?' he enquired pleasantly.

'Yes – from Jaisalmere,' I replied. 'And I can't believe how lovely this place is. Or how peaceful,' I added, realizing we were probably the only two guests in the place.

'Hmmm, it *is* very quiet just now. But I understand some other people are arriving later today.' Then: 'Have you had breakfast yet?' he asked. 'No? Then shall we have it together – on the lawn?'

We had no sooner sat on a swinging garden seat on the apparently deserted lawn than three turbaned men seemed to – quite literally – roll out from beneath the bushes flanking the pathways. They must have been sleeping peacefully beneath the canopy of leaves, coming to life at the sound of our voices. Even before they'd untangled themselves, they began to play – one on a flute, another on a fiddle and the third on a little drum.

The youngest musician, wearing what looked like a tweed jacket over cream dhoti, kept up a mournful dirge throughout a breakfast consisting of fried eggs, toast, marmalade and strong tea. This had all arrived on a little four-legged table – complete with white linen and a single flower – carried effortlessly on the head of the irrepressible Hapi. I couldn't quite believe my eyes as the table bobbed along above the bushes, its bearer hidden from sight. Even the service at the Savoy couldn't compare to this.

Breakfast over, my entertaining fellow guest asked if I had visited Jodhpur before. 'No? Ah, then you are in for a pleasant surprise. The countryside is very beautiful – as is the town itself, of course. Would you care to see some of it this morning?'

Mr Singh, as he had introduced himself to me, was obviously a man with a few hours to kill and a reasonable knowledge of the area, I thought, as he left me in the garden and went off to change his clothes. I really was on a winning streak, with a lovely room in a civilized setting and a charming escort to show me around.

He returned moments later and led me off to a battered green jeep which was parked at the rear of the palace. So he had his own wheels – this was getting better all the time. We drove out of the palace and turned into the highway, bowling merrily along it away from town. Then we passed a little group of people who glanced up at the passing jeep – only to bow slightly and touch their foreheads fleetingly with their fingertips. I didn't think much of it the first time, but it happened again and again – people we passed genuflecting courteously at the sight of the jeep and its occupant. Sitting in the passenger seat, I shot him a sneaky, sidelong glance, but the proud forehead, steady eyes and strong curved nose gave nothing away.

The morning passed too quickly, as we drove up into the hills and went walking through the wild, scrubby woodland. Here, until recently, tiger and wild boar had roamed and Mr Singh pointed out the crumbling stone buildings which had once served as hides for the princely Rajhputs and their hunt guests – the upper-crust envoys of Queen Victoria.

We climbed on up through hills and into low valleys, until we came across a long, low cave in the rock face where a holy man once lived. Mr Singh pointed out strange markings on the cave floor – a circle which was about two feet in diameter, slightly risen from the surrounding area and clearly decorated with an ochre-coloured footprint. Seeing the puzzled look in my eyes he explained this was the spot where the Sadu had chosen to die. A hole had been dug for him and he had been placed in it. Alive. And upside down, hence the footmark.

Soon, we were heading back to the palace and the same thing happened on the return journey, as camel riders and rickshaw drivers acknowledged our appearance. Again, my escort seemed not to notice – either gazing ahead intently as he drove or turning to me to chat pleasantly. It bothered me though – something didn't quite add up about this Mr Singh. It wasn't until I had strolled into the palace for dinner that evening – made up to the nines and dressed in high gold slippers and another of my sarees – that I solved the mystery.

Mr Singh stood before a large metal brazier, his imposing figure outlined against the dancing flames as they crackled into the desert night sky. He was sumptuously attired in a thigh-length gold brocade tunic over gleaming white jodhpurs, gold and red brocade slippers and a wonderful long coat of rough wool dyed in glowing shades of russet, gold and black. Then, smiling wickedly at my embarrassment, Mr Singh – or should I say, the Maharaj Swaroop Singh, a member of the royal family and a relative of the ruling monarch – stepped forward to greet me.

That evening I dined in the central courtyard of the palace. Open to the sky, it was hedged in on the ground floor by a colonnaded walkway which connected all the chambers, while the first floor – once the women's quarters – was hidden from prying eyes by delicately latticed windows. In the four corners of the courtyard, large gargoyle-like stone statues clutched shields and gazed down haughtily on the nightly gathering. While the guests mingling below served themselves to delicious foods and ate it at long tables beautifully decorated with crisp linen, silver cutlery and flowers.

Uniformed waiters dashed to and fro under the watchful eyes of the energetic Hapi, while musicians played and boys tended the flickering lanterns or stoked the four large braziers, sending flickering shadows dancing along the old walls.

For two weeks I relaxed here – spent my days exploring the lovely old market of Jodhpur, with its tooth-puller and its snake charmer. I bought some lovely turned-up slippers from the shoemaker and found a wonderful little white-haired tailor in the labyrinth of covered walkways. He took charge of the endless yards of glazed cotton I'd bought – a concoction of peppermint green, shocking pink, flame and peacock blue and all for thirty pence a yard – and turned them into wide, billowing skirts. He even made me some new petticoats – pink and lilac and black, with deep frills on the hems.

Wearing them, I was transformed again and when, one evening, a sweet German lady remarked on how wonderfully colourful I looked, I smiled to remember how the Storm-trooper I used to be had worn black from head to toe. I recalled the depressing wardrobe of suede, leather and silk – a sea of dark clothes with maybe just the slightest hint of green or red. Bleak and tailored, tight and serious, these clothes belonging to the old me had been making all sorts of downbeat statements about their wearer. Now this froth of colour I walked around in was saying something much more optimistic.

During my stay, I got to know the Rani just a little. 'Mr Singh's' breathtakingly beautiful wife, she was always very kind and gracious – and quite a businesswoman. She it was who finally initiated me properly into the secrets of saree wearing – getting down on her hands and knees one day to readjust a fold here and a tuck there, while I stood in an agony of embarrassment. I understood only too well the shock on his face when a servant, passing my open door, had stopped in horror at the sight of his beloved Rani on her hands and knees before me. It was absolutely *not done,* as both the lovely Rani and myself knew, although she refused to stand up until she had my saree exactly right.

Afterwards, we stood together, studying my reflection in the mirror. Me asking if black and pink silk was quite the right colour combination to wear to a wedding celebration, while the Rani – resplendent in the traditional Rajasthani costume of bodice, full skirts and veil, wonderfully scarlet and heavy with gold embroidery – assured me in her soft, gentle voice that I looked perfect.

She had invited me to a wedding – a sumptuous affair which had already been going on for two days. Climbing into the Rani's wonderful old chauffeur-driven car, I felt so excited, anyone would think it was my first ever party, and when we arrived, women fell back, eyes downcast as the Rani swept through them. Then the Maharani of Jodhpur arrived – the only woman in the place, as far as I could see, to whom the lovely Rani herself had to defer.

It was a night of sweetmeats and cymbals, incense and laughter. A night of wonderfully dressed men in white trousers, gold-buttoned tunics and outrageously colourful turbans. A night when each woman looked lovelier than her neighbour in sarees which were hand-painted, strewn with flowers or edged with blocks of gold leaf. It was a night of twinkling jewels and sparkling eyes; of questions and compliments; of warmth and music and bright company. Oh, what a night!

Eventually, of course, I had to move on again and, learning that I intended to travel to Jaipur the next day, the Rani, who had planned a car trip up to Delhi, invited me to join her on the journey. We left early in the morning before the sun had risen, so that at least the first part of our journey might be cool. 'Mr Singh' waited to say goodbye on the wide sweeping steps of the palace – obviously loath to part with his gorgeous wife even for a few days. But soon we were purring through the palace gates, the car's engine disturbing hundreds of parakeets which had been sleeping in the bushes lining the drive and which now rose up in the air, a noisy curtain of ruffled feathers.

To pass the time, I told the Rani a little of my life in Britain and she gave me an insight into the world of an Indian princess. Originally from the beautiful, cool, mountainous region of Kashmir, she had been the daughter of modern parents; a princess who experienced an unusual amount of personal freedom and whose quick intellect and lively curiosity had resulted in her going to university, during her late teens and early twenties. This clever, carefree, pretty girl had been introduced to the Maharaj, her chosen husband, several years before, when she was no more than sixteen. Although she had found this dashing older man with the dangerous eyes very attractive, she had been quite determined to finish her studies. He, mildly amused, had acquiesced.

Leaving Kashmir, her own kingdom of snow-topped mountains, green pastures, lakes and flowers, the bride had eventually travelled south to the inhospitable, barren, desert wastes of Rajasthan – to this land of warrior kings with its battle-steeped history. And she had almost gone into a decline when she had set eyes on her new home. But still worse was to come. After her marriage, the Rani discovered that she was expected to retire permanently to the women's quarters – a lonely enough way of life for a woman raised to the idea of purdah, but a shocking proposition for an alert, modern-minded, well-educated girl, used to a certain amount of independence.

Despite her pleas, the rooms on the first floor of the palace – the ones with the secret latticed windows which had looked down over the central courtyard – became her home for the next seven years. Here she ate and slept, entertained her husband, chatted to her women servants and bore her sons. Here, years later, she waited for news of the Maharaj's father, as he lay seriously ill. Then came the day when, for some reason, no nurse was available to watch over the old man.

The Rani was requested to attend his bedside and, in a flurry of panic, she found herself sitting by the side of her father-in-law, in whose presence she must always avert her eyes, veil her face and maintain total silence.

Her face hidden, her eyes downcast, her silence absolute, she sat on while he whispered to her, painfully and breathlessly – asking her questions and then giving her permission to reply. After that meeting he requested her presence again and in the following days, the Rani became accustomed to visiting her father-in-law's bedside and even talking to him, as long as no one was around to hear and spread the scandal of this outrageous behaviour.

When it became obvious that the old gentleman was near death, the Rani asked to see him once more. By now, the old man had become fond of her and enjoyed her intelligent conversation and when she asked for his permission to leave purdah, he consented. So the Rani slipped back into the real world and now, she stood at her husband's side – a loyal wife and a capable business associate.

She was a lovely woman – warm and friendly and endlessly curious. She giggled with shock when I told her I was a divorcee; was fascinated to hear about my ex-husband and how we had met. What fascinated her more than anything were the peculiar habits we Europeans insisted upon displaying – such as handshaking, which she found particularly distasteful. When I explained one of the things I'd found uncomfortable about Portuguese society had been their habit of greeting with kisses, her eyes widened in disbelief. *How* did I kiss them, she wanted to know; where, when and how many times? When I told her I frequently had to kiss complete strangers anything up to three times on the cheeks, she collapsed against the seat in a heap of girlish laughter. Obviously shocked, she insisted she could never be so intimate with anyone, then insisted I explain the technique. Did my lips actually touch flesh? Did I do it with my eyes open or closed? And – the sixty-four thousand dollar question – didn't noses get in the way? How could you tell whether the person you intended to kiss would move her head to the right or left? I explained there was no hard-and-fast rule and that, once or twice, strange, unfriendly noses and chins had collided with my own. By which time, we'd both been overtaken by helpless laughter and the chauffeur looked very disapproving.

On the outskirts of Jaipur, the Rani told me she had been invited to the palace for lunch and asked me to join her. So we swept regally into the Pink City, dodging children and camels as we cruised along its crowded streets. Lunch was a fairly formal affair in a large room, the walls of which seemed to have been entirely painted by hand.

Afterwards, the Rani and I strolled together along dusty palace corridors and finally stepped out into afternoon sunshine. Several servants stood at attention as we walked down the wide sweep of steps and stood together by the side of the car, while one of them removed my luggage from the boot.

'Have you *no* idea where you are going to stay?' the Rani asked, concerned – this much freedom of spirit and personal independence being too rich even for her blood.

'Oh, I'll soon find somewhere. I always do,' I assured her, knowing it was time to take my formal leave of the Maharaj's wife, yet uncertain about the protocol. I placed my palms together, fingers upwards, and held them in front of my heart – a gesture of welcome or farewell I had seen her make so many times – intending to bow my head to complete the movement.

Smiling mischievously she stopped me and said, 'I think, this one time, we shall say farewell as you Europeans do.' Adding in a whisper, 'And I am going to the right . . . ' Then suddenly she darted forward and, to the outrage of the servants all about us, she kissed me lightly – first on my right cheek and then on my left.

More than a little amused by my blank look, she stepped back from me, wished me a safe journey, then slipped into the back seat of the car while her chauffeur, stiff with disapproval, closed the door behind her. A moment later they were off – kicking up a cloud of pink dust as they headed through the palace gates. Aware of the servants' cold gaze upon my back, I picked up my luggage and walked out into the heat of Jaipur.

A couple of hours later, I was settled in my new home – an old palace with faded, hand-painted walls, high ceilings and uncomfortable, stuffy Victorian furniture (the bed turned out to be one of the hardest I'd ever had the misfortune to sleep on), and I set off for my daily dose of exploration. I mooched around the Palace of the Winds, which is, quite literally, two-dimensional. Its incredible façade is backed by nothing but steep flights of steps and a 'floor plan', if you like, of the rooms which used to exist. Walking around it, I could have sworn I was backstage on a Hollywood lot and what seemed from the street to be an honest-to-goodness, four-square building was actually all front.

After that, I did what I like doing best – I wandered for hours along the endless maze of back streets, moving further and further away from the teeming heart of the city and into the areas where the Jaipurans lived. I strolled with the flow of traffic, dodging open sewers and the dogs and cows which sprawled on the warm, baked earth, while gradually a little crowd began to collect just behind me. At first, my escorts were a few children who sang the usual litany – 'I have no mother, no father, give me money pleez' – and so, to break the monotony, I sang along with them, the idea that I had no mother and no father and wanted money too, pleez, reducing them to wild laughter.

Soon, the little crowd following me had swelled to quite a size and now it included men who, while appearing to be genuinely curious and friendly, worried me just a little. Friendly overtures are usually the safest bet in a situation like that – a variation on the 'if you can't beat 'em, join 'em' theme. So I allowed myself to be persuaded to stop for tea here or come and meet someone's mother sitting in a doorway over there, until my progress along one particular street came almost to a complete halt. Tired by now, I finally hailed a passing rickshaw and headed back to the peace of my hotel, chatting to my thin, frail, white-haired driver as we went.

Sanjay, who looked every second of fifty, turned out to be thirty-two. Although I suppose he was already in the autumn of his life, when you consider that the average life expectancy of a labouring man in Bombay is thirty-seven. He was very sweet and friendly and arranged to pick me up early next morning for a tour of the outskirts of Jaipur. Sure enough, he was standing in the palace grounds next morning when I came down for breakfast – flapping his arms energetically across his thin chest to dispel the morning chill, his gaunt face and silver head wrapped in a large woolly muffler.

Then followed a magical day as we put-put-putted from one landmark to another. I strolled round the well-kept gardens of a legendary concubine, visited the stunningly ornate marble edifice which was the last resting place of another. Then we drove on past yet another palace marooned in the centre of a shallow lake – its endless green carpet of water-lilies being gently hoovered by an army of buffalo wading, shoulder-deep, in search of a lily lunch.

Up and up we climbed, out of the hazy plain and into the surrounding hills, the only other traffic on the road consisting of huge lumbering elephants with brightly painted foreheads and trunks. Elephants are the only transport to and from the Amber Fort, which nestles high up in the rock cliffs. Mighty and impressive, its massive towers surveying the land for endless miles, it boasts beautiful gardens with tiny shaded pavilions, the walls of which are heavily decorated with semi-precious stones. The rooms themselves are encrusted from floor to ceiling with millions of tiny mirrored squares forming elaborate patterns. Wherever you walk, whichever direction you look, the mountains rise up, while at their feet, the desert plains seem to shimmer on forever.

By the time the sun was beginning to sink and we were rumbling back down on to the plain, I had spent an entertaining few hours with Sanjay, and I'd insisted on paying for his lunch. So when he invited me to his home for dinner, I accepted. He drove through the maze of narrow, overcrowded alleyways I'd glimpsed as I'd gone walkabout the previous afternoon. Heavy with flies and the stink of rotting vegetation, the area was alive with scrawny chickens and lean, mean-eyed dogs; while the neighbourhood was so alert to every single event that word of my arrival reached them well in advance. Sanjay parked his rickshaw at the mouth of one of the alleys and we walked into a mean little courtyard. It was hemmed in by lean-tos built higgledy-piggledy on top of each other and packed with neighbours who'd turned out to welcome us.

No such thing as privacy here. Even when Sanjay had pulled back the scrap of cloth which served as a door to his house, we were followed in by the local turban-maker, who insisted on showing me his latest creation – a gaudy sequinned and bejewelled wedding turban destined for the head of some trembling groom.

'Home' turned out to be a dark little windowless room about nine feet square, which Sanjay shared with his huge Burmese wife (literally twice his size) and his three young children. There was, of course, no loo, no running water, no electricity and no kitchen. The furniture consisted of a rope strung across the room on which were hung their few clothes and a raised dais about three feet high and around five feet square, on which everyone sat, ate and slept.

'Dinner' was cooked on a small primus stove which was pulled out from under the bed area, which also served as the larder. A grotty cardboard box was fished out and from it she hauled some okra, a couple of potatoes, a couple of root vegetables I didn't recognize and a few very limp-looking

329

green leaves. None of that worried me too much – but the scrawny bits of raw chicken did. Even in the dim light they were an ominous colour and, as she began to cook them over the stove, I sat there, trying to ignore the unpleasant aroma of garlic mixed with paraffin and steeled myself to eat a meal which I knew would have me throwing up for the next twenty-four hours.

Wedged in between the bed and the wall, she sat on her ample haunches, cutting the vegetables up into minuscule pieces and frying them in ghee. All the time, she gabbled on happily, while Sanjay tried to translate – although by now on his fifth or sixth swig of a rum bottle, he was fast becoming as incoherent as his wife. Throughout it all, I sat on the bed with his three children and soon, all four of us were scratching like puppies.

Much, much later, a rather inebriated Sanjay drove me home – still singing snatches of the song which he and his drinking cronies (they'd visited us immediately after dinner) had insisted upon serenading me with, over and over again. Sitting in the back of his rickshaw, shivering in the chill night air, I realized we were driving past the royal palace. I gazed out at it, ablaze with light in the darkness, and reflected on that old adage. Breakfast like a king, lunch like a prince and dine like a pauper . . . wasn't that how it went?

Well, yesterday, I'd breakfasted with a Maharaj, back there at the palace I'd lunched with the Rani. And now, tonight, I'd dined with paupers. A traveller's lot is nothing if not a strange one, I reflected, as the palace slid out of sight.

I left Jaipur on the night train to Delhi a few evenings later. After weeks of travelling second- and third-class rail (and spending at least one overnight journey asleep in the string hammock which served as a luggage rack) I decided to treat myself to first-class accommodation *and* a bed. I suspect that the booking clerk made a mistake with my name and assumed I was male. Whatever went wrong, I stepped into this tiny, cramped compartment to find I was sharing it with three Indian men. I think they were even more disconcerted than I was yet, when I double-checked my name on the list pasted to the carriage window, I realized I'd have to stay put.

While that didn't exactly thrill me, it didn't worry me unduly. Until I began to realize that it was exciting them half to death. They were all strangers to each other, which was, on reflection, probably just as well. If they'd been in a position to gang up on me, things might have got a bit out of hand. As it was, no one spoke a word throughout the journey – the consolation being that as long as there was silence, I knew they weren't saying anything rude, crude or lascivious about me.

Still, even the silence was oppressive. Especially since I was on one of the two bottom bunks and every time I moved or made a sound, three pairs of eyes were riveted upon me. Actually, they stared at me throughout most of the journey. How do I know? Because I refused to turn my light off (I'm not entirely daft), and I lay there in its weak glow, trying not to watch them watching me. No doubt they still tell their friends about the night they slept with a European woman – omitting to mention, of course, that absolutely nothing happened. Ironically, although it was the most expensive – and probably the most comfortable – train journey I made in India, it was the only one on which I didn't get a single wink of sleep.

Back in Delhi, it was time to hit the Amex office for more traveller's cheques and the latest post. Then it was on to the travel agent for confirmation of my flight across to Calcutta and my connecting flight for Rangoon a few hours later. On my last night, I had dinner with Prakash, who swore undying love; much later, I managed to finally outmanoeuvre my little four-wheeled beggar, who just swore. I know it sounds gruesome – outrunning a legless child. But you really do have to experience these cunning little beggars at close quarters, to understand how they can wear you down. And anyway, I gave him a generous handful of rupees when I left next day.

My flight to Calcutta was uneventful, as was my middle-of-the-night ride to a hotel. The drive back to the airport in the early hours of the morning was another matter. Now, if I had to name one place which I thought was the armpit of the world – I would say Calcutta. If I had to describe my idea of what living a nightmare entails – I'd say it means being a street-dweller in that same city. I won't try to describe the scenes I passed because, even if I could find the words, I know I could never convey the horror I felt without sounding melodramatic. If you want the details, buy *The City Of Joy* by E. Lapierre. I dare you to read it and not weep.

My flight to Rangoon was scheduled to leave just before seven that morning and I'd been warned to arrive at least two hours before. There is only one flight a week and Burma Air are notorious for all kinds of things – not the least of which is just cancelling the flight. So I guess I half-expected it, when I arrived to find that they had no record of my name and it didn't look as if I would be flying anywhere. I tried reasoning my case – showing my validated ticket, complete with date and time of departure, and backing it up with a passport which showed that my Indian visa *and* its extension was due to expire in twenty-four hours. They were totally unmoved by the news that I would shortly be an illegal alien.

So I tried a new tack – mixed a little begging with a little cajoling and a great big dollop of charm and a sprinkling of female helplessness. They wouldn't wear it. What did it take to move these people? I wondered. Knowing instinctively that raising my voice and throwing my weight around was *out* and not for a moment considering that age-old remedy which turns all firm refusals into mere misunderstandings . . . yes, you've got it, THE BRIBE.

However, the art of bribing requires as much talent as any other and it is something which most British are peculiarly inept at. My own attitude about bribing is the same as my attitude towards stealing; I'm sure the only reason I have never attempted either is my fear of doing it badly, thereby getting caught. I'd come across bribing on a grand scale in Cairo. Nothing but nothing ever gets done, unless you're prepared to grease a whole line of sweaty palms and I often gasped with admiration at how deftly Hafez kept the wheels of his life turning with a smile, a wink and a ready supply of the readies. Something I knew I could never do. But then, you never know what you can do till you try. . . .

For a few frustrating moments, I stood with the little group of German businessmen who had also been booked to travel on this flight and had met with the same refusal. Middle-aged, successful and obviously with friends in high places, they were shell-shocked to discover that invoking the names of various Burmese government big-shots did nothing to improve their case. As the time for take-off grew close, I finally grew philosophical and decided that, since I was staying on Indian soil and I was down to my last few rupees, it made sense to change some money.

Standing at the currency exchange desk, I'd just received my passport with fifty quid's worth of rupees tucked inside, when my name was called over the tannoy and I went rushing back to the ticket desk, where the little man asked if he could check my passport yet again. Innocently, I handed it over – my heart almost stopping with shock as he turned the page then glanced up, giving me a long, level look. Too late, I realized I'd left the money inside. 'Now he thinks I'm trying to bribe him,' I remember thinking in a panic, wondering what the penalty would be for trying to corrupt an official and wishing I had the courage to grab the little book back.

Both man and passport disappeared into the back office to emerge a moment later. 'Miss . . . ah, Culross? A mistake. Your ticket is in order. Now hurry please – plane is leaving in a few moments.' And he handed over my passport and tickets with a wide smile – happy that Miss Culross, at least, knew the way to brighten up his day.

Without even meaning to, I'd discovered the secret of the bribe . . . let them suck it and see; and my man had swallowed the bait. Racing back down the airport lounge, I saw the Germans gazing after me, their expressions puzzled and envious. So I doubled back and whispered breathlessly, 'It's money he wants! Stick some deutschmarks in your passports!' and buzzed off before my ticket tout changed his mind.

It wasn't until we were safely airborne – my new German friends a few rows behind and wreathed in grateful smiles – that I dared to open my passport. If it had cost me every penny of the fifty quid to make the flight, I wouldn't really have minded too much. As it was, I was rather touched to discover that he'd helped himself to a tenner's worth of rupees and the rest was still safely tucked between the pages. Who says there isn't any honour among thieves?

Settling back in my seat, I watched as the browns and reds of India fell away and were swallowed up by sunlight and soaring clouds. India . . . I'd had every intention of crossing it in a week; had never had the slightest desire to see the country or harboured the mildest curiosity about its people. Now I sat there, bereft at the thought of leaving it and already nostalgic for its colour, its sounds, its plains and forests.

A lot had happened to me in these unforgettable four months and although I couldn't quite understand how or why – I sensed that the experience had changed me. There were so many sights and sensations I hoped never to forget; so many lovely people and times I was desperate not to lose. . . .

Long before we'd cleared the coastline and slipped out across the blue expanse that was the Bay of Bengal, I'd made myself a promise.

That no matter what the future held for me or where I finally settled down, one day – somehow – I would wander through India again.

Chapter Five

My road to Mandalay

I'd been in Burma for forty-eight hours before I realized what was missing. Noise. The wailing of temple music, the chattering of womenfolk, the cries of the hawkers, the racket in the street bazaars . . . the high-pitched clatter of India which had jangled in my head for months was gone. And now, everywhere I went, the sound of silence was deafening, as the Burmese went quietly about their business.

That first morning, in Rangoon, I'd breakfasted in the deserted dining room of the Inya Lake hotel – an empty cavernous place which was Russian-designed and financed. Although you'd get no prizes for guessing as much, since its soulless proportions and massive pillars have more than a touch of 'Moscow mausoleum' about them. Built on the edge of a lake about four-and-a-half miles out of town, it's highly overpriced and overrated and the only reason I ended up there was because I'd shared a taxi with the three German businessmen and their destination had seemed as good as any other to me. What I hadn't realized was that they were in fact VIP government guests and as such had no say in what they would see, where they might go and where they would stay. Each hour of every day they were to spend in Burma was already scheduled, while they themselves were escorted everywhere – including, I suspect, the loo.

While I, on the other hand, being the guest of no one and a person of no importance whatsoever (my passport carefully omitting to mention that I was a journalist), was free to wander as I pleased – at least officially. Unofficially, getting around Burma is as easy as walking the length of Oxford

Street on all fours on the last shopping day before Christmas. A practically impossible feat, even for anyone who's daft enough to want to do it.

The problem is that, although the Burmese authorities want our dollars, deutschmarks and pounds sterling, they'd happily do without us, the foreign visitors. And since they can hardly separate us from our lolly and then send us packing, they do the next best thing. They make us wish we'd never bothered to set foot in the place.

The aversion therapy begins at the immigration desk, where an army of officials meticulously check immunization certificates, passports and visas, and insist upon the completion of endless forms. By the time I'd been processed, they knew everything about me, from my age to the fact that my granny had red hair.

How many credit cards did I carry? How much credit was on each card? How much cash did I hold? It all went down on a sheet of paper which I would be forced to carry around with me, filling in the cost of every single transaction and purchase I made. Then, when I was on the way out, woe betide me if the money I started with and the money I finished with didn't tally with the amounts I'd spent in between.

They'd listed all my worldly electrical goods – the hairdryer, the heated rollers – together with my jewellery and my camera. They'd also listed the market value of everything, explaining that I would have to cough up for any items which were no longer in my possession when I left the country. Then, warning me about all the places I couldn't visit and the dire consequences of changing money on the black market or, worse still, smuggling in any foreign currency, they escorted me to the currency exchange desk. There, they robbed me blind with an official rate of exchange which meant that every cup of coffee I drank would cost me just over a pound, while a night in a half-decent bed wouldn't leave much change from an arm and a leg.

As if all that isn't enough aggravation, they then give you exactly seven days to get through Burma and back to base. Knowing as they usher you out of the airport that you've already wasted three precious hours of that time answering insane questions, writing your name a hundred bloody times and trying to find your luggage. Once outside, you run into the black marketeers who immediately offer you so many more kyats (the local currency) for your pound that you want to weep, and attempt to divest you of your duty-free booze, fags, and perfume for what sounds like vast sums of money.

Having survived the induction, you're left to wing it through a country, most of which is officially out of bounds and practically devoid of any form of communication, with only the most unreliable road or rail links and a laughable internal flight service. Armed with a completely illegible map and surrounded by equally illegible signs on everything from streets and buses to menus and railway stations (Burmese not being a language you can learn at home with teach-yourself tapes), you're left to sink or swim – and that goes double for lone travellers who aren't part of an organized tour group. Not so much a holiday, more a character-building experience, Burma's no place for the faint-hearted.

All this I now know from personal experience. But that first morning, I was blissfully ignorant of what lay ahead as I waved goodbye to my besuited and beleaguered German friends and headed for the centre of Rangoon. Up on the highway, I hung around for ages with a group of twenty or so locals who watched me watching them as we waited for transport, and the first thing that struck me was the lack of colour.

The men were dressed in loose shirts over sarongs woven in dark stripes and checks, while the women wore close-fitting tops and sarongs decorated with flowers and birds – tiny feet shod in rubber thongs and hair pinned into tight little buns. There was little sign of any jewellery or cosmetics – not even the odd flower which even the poorest Indian woman would tuck into her hair.

Faces were broad and flat, eyes tip-tilted and teeth white in smiles which were guileless and shy. From the first, these people struck me as neat, healthy and very much conformists in dress and manner. Every bit as curious, friendly and helpful as their Asiatic neighbours but much more reserved and without the zest and energy, the natural sense of expression and the spirit of the Indians I'd grown so fond of.

When the bus arrived, it turned out to be a little covered mini van, with three bench seats running along its length – two fixed to the walls and the third sliding unchecked in between. The tail had been dropped and hung suspended from two chains and, as the bus filled up inside, it was soon standing room only on this little platform. The scramble to get on was rather more orderly than I'd been used to but I was still reduced to riding the tail, with just the tips of my toes making any purchase on the metal and my fingers clutching for a handhold on the chains.

As we took off in a belch of smoke, the women giggled behind their hands at the sight of me hanging on for dear life, my hair streaming and my skirts billowing out in the wind; while the men shyly tried to make room for me in the crush.

That first precious day was spent wandering around Rangoon, trying to locate the official tourist office, without whose authority and blessing nothing but nothing can be achieved by a foreigner. My *Lonely Planet* guide to Burma was nothing less than a battle plan of how to get in, get out and shake it all about for the least possible expense and with the smallest amount of hassle. The carefully researched action plans and detailed instructions on how to save a precious hour here, a precious few kyats, there would have done credit to any military headquarters embarking on war games. Already, I was beginning to view the trip with a jaundiced eye – not quite sure that I *wanted* to blitz Burma at any cost.

I recognized one or two other tourists who had arrived on the same flight – already fairly wild-eyed and panicky as the clock ticked steadily on. The morning dragged by and we grew confused, then frustrated, then irritated, as we realized that the Burmese authorities weren't just disorganized, they were downright disruptive in all matters relating to travel.

Firstly, I was told that I could only travel north by rail or plane; forget the road to Mandalay. Secondly, I discovered that there was no chance of a seat on the flight due out that day – or even any information on the likely flight departure time. Could they guarantee me a seat on next day's flight? I thought it a reasonable enough question, but it provoked what could almost have been a smile on the stern face of the little man who was 'helping' me. It seemed organized government tour groups got priority on flights – as they got priority on everything else. And, no matter how much I jumped around, I couldn't fool him I was more than one person.

He would, of course, put me on standby. But by the time I knew whether I was confirmed to fly or not, my only other way out of Rangoon – the train – would already have headed north. I'd heard the rail journey was miserably uncomfortable but I figured it was safer to cut my losses, so I bought a rail ticket.

That afternoon, I decided to invest in a pair of shoes and picked up a pair on a stall for what I thought was a good price. Then I decided to head back to the hotel but, since all the bus signs were indecipherable to me, I asked a passing Buddhist monk if he knew where the Inya Lake hotel was. He nodded vigorously that he did and beckoned me to follow him and soon we were rattling along in yet another little bus. This time I'd managed to get a seat inside but, bent almost double under the low roof, with the seat bucking and sliding beneath me each time the driver took a bend, I began to wish I was outside on the tail.

The Buddhist was curious about the contents of my paper bag and, when I pulled out one of my new shoes to show him, he held out a yard or so of the orange robe which was draped about his body. Not only are monks not allowed to make any sort of physical contact with women, they aren't allowed to accept anything directly from them. So my shoe had to be dropped into the little hammock he'd fashioned. He held the shoe up and asked how much it had cost, my answer making him grin widely in that international expression which tells you you've been ripped off.

He wasn't the only one who thought so, either. As the shoes were passed around the dozen or so passengers, the consensus of opinion seemed to be that the trader had seen me coming and everyone really enjoyed the joke at my expense.

After we'd been bouncing around for about fifteen minutes, the bus drew to a halt at a place which seemed to be a popular destination. Surely not my hotel . . . I thought, as my new guide ushered me into the road but, having come this far, I decided to follow him a little further. We walked along a narrow alley through a market, covered over above, so that I couldn't see where we were heading, as we began to climb steadily up wide flights of wooden stairs.

Up and up we went, past wonderful stalls filled with all sorts of offerings. Beautiful flowers worked into delicate garlands and posies, the colours so delicate that it was impossible to tell which were real and which were false; tiny thrones covered with gold paint; paper ceremonial umbrellas; sweet-smelling incense sticks, combs and bracelets; richly dressed puppets; intricate papier-mâché lions and dragons. I was so taken by the display that I hardly noticed we'd reached the end of the climb until we stepped out into glorious light.

Misunderstanding me, the monk had brought me to the most famous landmark in all Rangoon, the Shwedagon Pagoda, and now he took enormous pleasure from watching the expression on my face. To gaze at the Shwedagon is to experience visual overload, as the eye attempts to process the light, the colour, the shape, which overwhelms at first sight. Built on top of a hill, this cluster of pagodas covers more than twelve acres and, whichever way you view it, that's a lot of paint and marble, a treasure trove of precious and semi-precious stones. And a fortune in gold.

Statues tower up on all sides – some of them twenty and thirty feet into the air. Fanciful images of dragons and lions painted blindingly white, wickedly scarlet, green and blue are lavishly decorated with gilt. Silently they stand sentinel over a whole circular city of shrines, pagodas and temples dressed up in a wild riot of colour while behind them rises up the most mighty pagoda of all. Standing on a twenty foot high platform and shaped like a bell, it towers up more than a hundred feet into the clear blue sky, girded about with nearly fifteen thousand foot-square solid gold plates. Hung about with gold and silver bells, the topmost level is gold plated and studded with more than a thousand diamonds. The top of the pagoda is a golden sphere studded with more diamonds weighing 1800 carats and tipped with a single diamond weighing eighty carats.

One of the bonuses of flying into and out of Rangoon is that you can actually see that diamond winking from an aeroplane.

I spent the rest of that magical afternoon just walking round and round the pagoda, my bare feet enjoying the sensation of the black and white marbled walkway as I OD'd on the imagery of the place.

That evening, I dressed for dinner in one of my prettiest sarees – leaf green chiffon tinged with gold, embroidered with gold flowers and studded with dark green and russet paste stones. My taxi was yet another ancient American Chevy, my young driver a bit of a wide boy, who was thrilled to hear that he was to escort 'The Italian Actress', which is what the staff of the hotel had decided I must be. I went to a lot of trouble to convince my man that not only wasn't I an actress, I wasn't even Italian. But the truth wasn't nearly so glamorous as the gossip so, for the rest of my stay, I became The Italian Actress to please them – playing my part to the hilt, need I add.

Much later, after dinner, I had him drive me back to the pagoda, just for the pleasure of sitting outside it in the dark and admiring its bright gold gleam. But my luck was in – even at ten o'clock, the pagoda was still open to the public, although, when I climbed the steps to the marble walkway and carefully removed my high gold shoes, I was surprised to find the place deserted. All alone, I walked silently between the dark shadows of the temples, loving the peace and the sense of isolation. The night was warm and a breeze played gently with the tail of my saree, blowing the chiffon around my hair. Then it raced on ahead of me, making the thousands of candle offerings flutter and blaze; casting the sweet, heavy smell of burning incense into the air; causing the hundreds of tiny gold and silver bells to dance wildly, so that the night was filled with their high, tinkling music.

Long before dawn next morning, I was pacing up and down the station platform, making the most of the opportunity to stretch my limbs. My holdall, with a couple of changes of clothes, was already in my seat – and my neighbours for the journey were watching me curiously as I strolled around. When finally I took my place next to them, I saw that both women were sitting in the lotus position on their seats. They were asleep minutes after we slid out of the station and they slept on without moving or changing their positions at all for pretty much the next twelve hours.

To begin with, I could see nothing out of the dusty window, except the odd cluster of shacks – their thin beams of lamplight shining out into the night, signalling that the family within was stirring itself. A heavy mist hung about the countryside, creeping along the paddy fields, rolling into gullies and rising above the streams. As dawn broke, a cold grey light filtered through the mist, silhouetting banana palms, coolies bent low beneath baskets balanced on bamboo poles, water buffalo meandering along ancient tracks.

Then the sun broke through, transforming the creepy, unfriendly landscape into a wonderland of rich dark forest and bright jade paddy fields, criss-crossed by a shimmering network of liquid silver streams. While on the horizon, pink and purple shaded hills basked beneath the cobalt blue sky.

Lunch for me consisted of a hard, tasteless cheese in a cardboard bread sandwich, a small pastry and an apple – supplied at great expense by the hotel kitchen. Still, it sure as hell beat lunch for my neighbour, who leaned out of the train window in one station and bought a long skewer of what I took to be grilled meat. Which I suppose it was; although the meat in question turned out to be giant grasshoppers, with legs and mandibles intact.

Meanwhile, the woman next to me slept on. Twelve hours without stirring, while the dust slowly settled in her hair and on her shoulders. By the time we arrived in Mandalay, she looked like a little white Buddha and when at last she rose from her seat, the dusty outline of her figure was left behind, clearly marked on the upholstery.

Darkness was falling by the time I left the station and headed across to the parking lot of trishaws – bicycles with side carriages attached. I paused as a small hand gently grasped my arm and I looked down into the gentle enquiring face of a young boy. I'd just been adopted by Mimo. Around twelve years old, slight but wiry, he was the eldest of three sons, the sole breadwinner and the apple of his mother's eye.

Although, in time, I met his lovely family, the whereabouts – or even the existence – of his father remained a mystery.

That first evening, Mimo took me to a hotel which was not on the Tourist Burma official list, which meant that it was cleaner and more comfortable than anything I would have found if I'd gone through the usual channels. Then, making it quite plain that I was his responsibility for the rest of my stay, Mimo cycled off home happily, his income assured for at least the next twenty-four hours.

I should point out that the conversation was conducted in two languages because, although many of the old Burmese can understand English, the younger generations have no knowledge of it. Still, unlikely as it may sound, conversations, the exchange of information and even jokes, can be made without the use of words – something I discovered as far back as Egypt. In fact I'm now of the opinion that, once people have dispensed with the spoken word and rely on signs and body language to transmit their thoughts and needs, the communication – while not necessarily easier – is a lot more honest. While even the most passing friendships become that much more intimate. And, since words have ever been my stock in trade, you can imagine what a discovery this was for me.

Next morning, young Mimo was hanging around the guest house – hair slicked down and wearing what appeared to be his best shorts and shirt. Something I wouldn't have picked up on, if the other trishaw drivers hadn't been teasing him something rotten about dressing up for me. Ignoring their laughter for his sake, I climbed into the wobbly carriage and Mimo took off with his nose in the air.

The town of Mandalay lies on a dusty plain and the streets run to a neat grid plan – all straight lines and crossroads. And no hills, which must be a blessing for the hundreds of cyclists who swarm the streets. There are few cars and ox carts are the main mode of transport. We headed out towards Mandalay hill, which rises up about eight hundred feet – and that's an awful lot of steps.

Still, it was worth the trek for the view from the summit and I gazed down at the forest of gold-tipped spires which had lined my route and which now carried my eye all the way down to the plains. There in the distance, I could see the royal palace, the town of Mandalay with its network of tree-lined streets and, every so often, a flash of brilliance, as the sun struck gold on some far-off pagoda or shrine.

On my way back down, I passed a tiny monk sitting cross-legged by a bell. He couldn't have been more than eight and by his side sat a little girl of two or three, dressed in a tiny sarong. She stood up when she saw me and took a few paces forward, at which point her sarong began to come undone. Even as she clutched at it ineffectually, her bottom lip began to tremble and I realized that the natural reserve and modesty of these people was already fairly well developed in this baby. Kneeling down beside her, I spent the next ten minutes wrestling with this sarong, which had been actually quite intricately wound and bound and wasn't at all easy to re-tie. She submitted silently to all the pushing and pulling, her eyes wide and serious in her pretty little face and big fat tears quivering on her lashes. Remembering the loss of my own saree, I knew exactly how this young lady felt and was very glad to be able to save her blushes.

Back down at the entrance, flanked by massive white and gold lions – jaws wide, eyes slanted, as they growled thirty feet up in the still, clear air – I came across Mimo sound asleep in the trishaw. And we were off again, pedalling furiously to this pagoda and that temple. Stopping here to admire a palace built entirely of carved teak. Taking time out there to watch ivory carvers, or an army of young girls spinning silk. Eyes downcast, smiles tentative, they were more unnerved by Mimo's presence than my own. Their smooth bronze faces were curiously decorated – as if a fine coating of paste had been applied to their cheeks and a leaf had been pressed into it, the fine tracery of veins and the outline of the leaf itself leaving a delicate impression on the skin.

Giggling and spinning, they contrived to ignore Mimo who strutted around importantly explaining things to me in a big voice – no doubt thrilled that he'd taken the trouble to look his very best.

Next morning, I was at Zegyo market bright and early,

looking for a jeep ride up into the hills. I was heading for Maymyo, a one-time British hill station, where I'd heard they actually grew strawberries. It had been a year since I'd tasted one of these and the prospect of strawberries and cream at the end of it, made the trip seem well worthwhile.

The journey is made by jeep – ancient and dilapidated survivors of the Second World War, which cough and splutter in the market place, waiting for the regulation eight passengers, who cling on precariously to a vehicle built for four. My jeep was almost full when a couple of American boys turned up with a pretty teenage Burmese girl in tow. They were students, heading for Maymyo in the hope of pushing on to Lashio, which was strictly out of bounds to foreigners. The Burmese girl was a distant relative of one of them and I was envious of their guide, who might just manage to sneak them into parts the rest of us could never hope to reach. But although they suggested I move back along the transport queue and join them, something in me decided against it.

They waved goodbye as I moved off, my teeth practically working loose in my head, as we bumped and rattled along. I was sitting next to a charming old gentleman of around seventy – one who remembered the last war as if it had happened yesterday and had a wonderful command of English. We started up a conversation which continued all through the journey – thoroughly enjoying each other's company and quite oblivious to the weeping baby which screamed incessantly in its mother's arms and the outraged chickens which poked their scrawny necks between the bars of their crate, clucking furiously at the passing countryside.

The trip took the best part of three hours as the jeep wheezed and spluttered up tortuous gradients, catching its breath each time we stopped to fill up the radiator with water, the tank with petrol and ourselves with tea. The country we passed through was wild and inhospitable, the land dry and dusty, so that we seemed to travel in a perpetual cloud of the stuff. While I wouldn't say the journey was dangerous, the drops – just feet from the edge of the road – were the sort that you wouldn't get up and walk away from, should you be careless enough to step off the edge.

Next day, I learned that my new American friends had done just that. The word was out all over Maymyo – a jeep had gone over the edge, jettisoning its occupants into space. There had been two foreigners on board. Americans. One had bad head injuries, the other suspected internal injuries and a badly broken leg. Unusually, they had been travelling with a Burmese girl. She had died instantly of a broken neck. The stories were many and contradictory; I couldn't find out where the boys had been taken. When I got back to Mandalay, I heard they'd been air ambulanced to Singapore. Lashio, after all, had kept her secrets safe from prying eyes.

I was set down in Maymyo, although the rest of my jeep were travelling on, into the forbidden territories. My elderly companion insisted upon taking my address in London. And now, he never forgets to send me a Christmas card, of all things.

I put up at the Candacraig guest house – a famous pitstop for travellers and once the bachelor quarters for employees of the Burma Bombay Trading Company. There were already some Europeans in residence and as we gathered round the roaring fire before dinner, we decided it would be a good idea to ask the cook to prepare a meal for the six of us. Two hours later, we sat in a lovely old room in this English-style mansion – all of us wearing our best clothes for the occasion and the conversation every bit as spruced up and tidy. It could easily have been mistaken for a yuppie Maida Vale dinner party, instead of a rag-tag gathering of weary travellers en route for India, China, Malaysia and God knows where else.

Come morning, I did what I always do in a new town – I headed for the market, knowing that's where the action always is. It turned out to be a luscious place, with wonderfully arranged stalls of fruit and flowers; the vegetables plump and wholesome, the smells of spices and fresh herbs absolutely delicious. And, even in the good-natured bustle of the market, there it was again – that uncanny, unnerving sound of silence. The Burmese must be the only race on this earth who conduct everything – even trading – in a well-mannered murmur.

When I reached the covered sector, I found myself in a

treasure trove of objects and artefacts. Wonderful old pieces of jewellery, detailed brass and copper work, carved wooden dragons and amazing, fierce-faced puppets – they were all here. Intricately carved opium pipes, tidy little sets of opium scales in carved boxes, families of brass opium weights in the style of chickens, lions and dragons; temple bells and tiny Buddhas; parasols and fans – the display was immense. Some of it quite new but much of it certainly very old and certainly genuine.

And I – the lifetime jumbler, second-hand stall merchant and haunter of Oxfam shops – couldn't buy any of it. With no dollars or sterling tucked into my knicker elastic, my rupees regarded as worthless and my officially bought kyats making a mockery of wise buying, I simply had no money with which to snap up what were surely the bargains of a lifetime. But one trader and his teenage son seemed unperturbed. What did I have with me? he wanted to know. A camera, perhaps? Or some Johnnie Walker whisky? Anything at all, I might like to exchange? But I was, for once on my journey, travelling really light and I pointed to the overnight bag at my feet to prove the point.

Still, he wasn't to be put off and, in next to no time, all my worldly possessions were spread out for inspection. Ten minutes later, my bag was a whole lot lighter. My make-up was already used? No matter, he'd have it. And my deodorant and hair shampoo. He went nutty about my jewellery – a string of cheap turquoise beads I'd bought back in Greece and some shell earrings. He liked the cotton lungi I'd got in southern India – its shocking pink dye making his eyes light up. A battered pair of sneakers went, too – together with a smooth-rolling ball point pen, which I'd managed not to lose during all these months of travel. But it was the perfume which made his eyes glaze over. It was two thirds used but it was more than just foreign; it was French. It said so on the bottle and that was good enough for him.

In return, I picked up some opium scales, a couple of sets of weights, some carved wooden pictures of lions (designed to be hung up inside the front door, to ward off bad luck) and a wonderful old temple bell, its handle moulded in the likeness of a dragon. Both of us were thrilled with the transactions – probably because we both thought we'd got rid of a load of old rubbish in exchange for some really good stuff. And as I left the market accompanied by the wily old trader's son, I was smiling from ear to ear.

The boy was about sixteen and his English was surprisingly good. Walking through the market we met his friend Roger (yes, I was puzzled, too), who, at around six feet, was incredibly tall and stood head and shoulders above everyone else. They invited me to a tea house and for the next two hours we sat over pots of the awful, tasteless stuff while they plagued me with questions. What was England like; how tall were the buildings; what did snow look like; had I ever seen the sea (wide eyes, when I said I'd actually swum in it); had I ever been to the cinema; how did it feel to fly; what did the Queen look like; did I have any children/husband/father; how old was I anyway (stunned faces, as they tried to comprehend how a woman as ancient as thirty-six could look like me).

On and on it went, the boys hungry for information and me anxious to paint for them a picture of the outside world – conscious, even as I did it, that this was precisely why the Burmese authorities tried to keep foreigners at bay. One way and another, we made the natives restless. These lads, unable to get a passport (it cost too much), unable even to travel internally (it cost too much), would likely never get the opportunity to see what lay just over their horizon. As it was, the news that I had actually walked around their beloved Shwedagon Pagoda – not once but twice – was nearly the last straw.

As they walked me to the jeep which would take me back to Mandalay, they were pictures of dejection at the thought of all the experiences ahead of me which they could never hope to share. And, not for the first time, I marvelled at my ability to just take off at a moment's notice for this town or that country; my freedom to hop on this train or that plane, with nothing and no one to hold me back. Impulsively, I raked around in the bright pink leather pouch I always wore at my waist and which contained those few things I could never afford to lose. My credit cards were in a little leather holder and, removing them from their plastic sleeves, I handed the holder to the trader's son. He took one look at the stamp inside 'Real calfskin. Made in England' and whooped with pleasure.

Roger stood silently, too polite to ask if I had something for him. But there was nothing else. Except . . . In my pouch, I kept several copies of my passport photograph (you need dozens of 'em to stick on endless forms). Taking one out, I wrote my address on the back and gave the photo to Roger, knowing from past experience it would thrill him to death. I wasn't wrong. He went wild. Or as wild as a well-behaved Burmese will ever permit himself to go.

'Believe me, Roger – some day, you *will* travel. I know it. And when you get to London, look me up,' I said. Both of us knowing it was unlikely, yet both of us wanting to believe it might be so.

The jeep coughed into life then and I waved as the boys walked off – Roger clutching his precious photograph and his friend eagerly offering the little leather holder in exchange.

I spent that night in Mandalay and just after three o'clock in the morning, the faithful Mimo was there to pedal me to the bus for Pagan. According to my *Lonely Planet* guide, Pagan is the most amazing sight in Burma, if not south-east Asia. And I think I second that. For Pagan is a deserted city which begins on the shores of the Irrawaddy and stretches back – mile upon mile of glorious, ruined temples.

The bus journey turned out to be an absolute pig – we left late in a nightmare of red tape (thanks again, Tourist Burma), the trip was hot, sweaty and indescribably uncomfortable and by the end of it, I was unbelievably pissed off with the whole of Burma. We finally rattled into the outskirts of Pagan around three that afternoon and I transferred to a little horse-drawn wagon, feeling dangerously ratty and with a splitting headache. Still, the gentle clip-clop of the pony and the relatively comfortable swaying of the trap did a little to improve my mood. So that, by the time I'd reached a guest house, booked in, dumped my luggage and grabbed a life-saving drink, I was feeling almost human again.

Obviously, the driver had seen it all before – roaring foreign lion gets off Mandalay bus, has refreshing drink and turns into foreign person again – and he'd wisely waited outside for what he knew would be another fare. He didn't even ask the equivalent of 'Where to?' when I climbed back aboard. In Pagan, there's only one place to go.

The sun was beginning to slip down the sky and the temperature, while not exactly cool, was pleasantly warm. Sitting on the tailboard of the covered trap, gazing back along the way we had come, I missed the initial impact of the scene – only realizing we were trotting through the deserted city when two massive buildings slid into view on the right and left. Squealing with excitement, I climbed up into the driver's seat – and there it was, spread out before me. Pagan.

Utterly silent. Completely deserted. Temple after ruined golden temple soaring into the empty sky – prayed in by no one and watched over by none. Eerie, other-worldly and awesome.

My driver made for one of the largest temples, which towered over all its near-neighbours and was the best place from which to watch the sun set, he indicated – pointing at the glowing orb which was now very low in the strange, gold-coloured sky. And so I climbed the Gawdawpalin Temple – all one hundred and fifty feet of it. Scrambled up the tiny stairwells in the dark, popping out every so often into daylight as I covered terrace after terrace. Completely out of breath and certainly red in the face with exertion, I finally made the top and leapt out of the final carved doorway, searching for the setting sun. I was facing the wrong way. So I chased the sun around the terrace, strangely excited at the prospect of watching the sunset all by myself in such a high-up, magical place.

There she was – huge and burning red. Setting the land all about dancing in a dusty golden glow and seeming to touch the distant Irrawaddy with bright fire. It was . . . it was . . . *superb* I decided, choked with emotion and yearning to be poetic, yet unable to find the words.

'Nice up here, i'n'tit?' a disembodied voice suddenly piped up and I whirled around, amazed to discover there was another human being on the planet, let alone my beautiful temple. And even more deflated, as I detected his Nottingham accent.

There I was – on top of the known world, I like to think – in a mind-blowing setting, getting an eagle's eye view of a spectacular sunset. It was a once-in-a-lifetime experience. And I was sharing it with – with a retired policeman from the Nottingham force, as it turned out. A nice enough chap in his khaki shirt, his policeman's knees peeking self-consciously out from beneath his khaki shorts.

And certainly friendly; chattering on about how his wife had died and nothing had seemed worthwhile any more and he'd hated the idea of retiring – so lonely, you know? And so he'd thought, 'Sod it – take the retirement money and blow the lot.' On a trip. A long one. Just keep going and see where I end up. And the lads had been very good about it, once they'd stopped laughing. Gave him these expensive binoculars – terrific, aren't they? – and threw in a couple of maps and a packet of sandwiches, just in case he got peckish along the way. Ah, good lads right enough – and he did miss them. But not on evenings like this. Not when you got an eyeful of that view. And would you just look at that sun, bloody marvellous, eh?

And of course I looked. And of course it was. But the magical moment had come and gone. The fact is, the world is a small place, getting smaller all the time and, wherever you go, you can't get away from home.

As it turned out, Fred even lived at the same guest house. So, having seen the sun on its way to India or Egypt or wherever, we trotted home and ate a matey supper. Next morning, we met up for a matey breakfast and I decided I really liked Fred, whose high good-humour was masking a whole lot of loneliness and sorrow. Still, I turned down his offer of company back in the deserted city. Decided, for some strange reason, that I had no desire to see the place again. So I spent my last free morning half a mile from the place thousands of travellers brave mediocre food, mean accommodation, lousy trains and blind bureacracy just to be able to see. I turned my back on Pagan, the jewel of Burma, and

351

wrote a long letter home to my folks instead. I'd had enough – I just didn't want to play any more.

That afternoon, I flew south to Rangoon. That evening, I had dinner with my German businessmen at the Inya Lake hotel. I was an Italian Actress – again – this time in a saree of shimmering gold silk, edged with a pink gold and hand-blocked with a delicate pattern of bronze gold flowers. The Germans were as full of questions as the boys in Maymyo had been – the Burma they'd experienced not being a patch on the little glimpse of it I'd seen for myself.

That night I took a taxi back to the Shwedagon Pagoda. Strolled around its empty marble moonlit walkways under the watchful eye of its grinning lions, its mean-eyed dragons, its gods and goddesses and golden Buddhas. And as I listened one last time to its thousand pealing bells and gaily tinkling wind chimes, I hoped that Roger would one day see this wonder for himself.

Back in my hotel room, I gave up trying to sleep in the sticky heat of the night. Instead, I lay naked on my back atop the bedclothes, listened to the drone of the fan above me and wondered about tomorrow. And Bangkok.

Chapter Six

On a Balinese beach . . . the moment of truth

Bangkok turned out to be Culture Shock City – swarming with fashionable teenagers in the kind of clothes I hadn't seen since I'd left Italy. The smell of money was everywhere – from the towering office blocks to the shop window displays – and I was blasted with pop music, tempted by bright, shiny consumer goods everywhere I went. One part of me was thrilled to be treading well-paved streets and eating clean food again, while another part was disgusted by this city of shoppers, with its American hamburger restaurants, its escalators, its acres of shiny glass and gleaming chrome.

Still, I succumbed eventually to that long-repressed shopping instinct of my own, buying a couple of dresses and some new high-heeled shoes, so that I blended in with the crowd – all of us in a subtly 'orientalized' version of whatever Western fashion had decreed was 'in' that year.

I was living in a colourful if slightly seedy area of Bangkok which was popular with budget travellers. My unerring eye for the cheap and cheerless led me straight to a guest house which specialized in windowless rooms – devoid of furniture, apart from the lumpy bed. The walls were painted puke green, the ancient lino on the floor was muddy brown, the bed was covered in a rough cotton spread decorated with orange, blue and brown flowers. Gross. The bathroom was tiled from floor to ceiling, with a cracked loo and basin and a grating in the floor to take the water from the large old showerhead. It was a surprisingly large bathroom – and a very densely populated one. That much I discovered a split second after I undressed and walked into the room to shower.

Years ago, when I'd been a naïve young flat-sharer in Scotland, Mary, one of my social worker flatmates, had arrived home one evening, really upset. She had walked into an empty tenement flat shortly after its very elderly and very dead occupant had been removed and even as she had stepped across the threshold, she'd been set upon and practically devoured by a mass of fleas. They'd been hanging around for days, waiting for a fresh blood supply, and poor Mary had been it. Even as I'd listened to her harrowing tale of defumigation back at headquarters and her boss's kindly warning that 'this sort of thing is all part of the job, lass', I couldn't help thinking she'd exaggerated just a bit.

She hadn't. Minus my contact lenses, it took me a moment to realize that the hundreds of tiny black dots all over my body weren't the accumulated smut and dust of travel and a moment longer to understand that I, too, was being eaten alive by thousands of fleas. Shuddering with revulsion, I dived under the shower head and turned the water full on in an effort to wash them off. Then, hugging my towel to me, I ran barefoot down to the 'office' and demanded to see the 'manageress'. Horribly fat, with a fag hanging out of the corner of her mouth, she swept greasy tendrils of black hair out of her squinty little eyes as I mouthed off about my roommates. Not that she could have heard much over the sound of the television *and* the radio *and* the chugging of the ancient fridge.

Shrugging her shoulders, she had one of the boys move my stuff to another room which, while it was equally depressing to the eye, at least harboured the kind of livestock which kept itself to itself.

While all this was going on, a Belgian woman struck up a conversation with me. Small and squat, wearing grubby, ill-fitting jeans and her ample boobs flattened out beneath a jaundiced yellow T-shirt, she whined incessantly. Told me how long she'd been on the road; what a drag it was all getting to be; how sick she was of being ripped off by the bloody locals; what a dump Bangkok was. I took in her greasy brown hair bunched into an elastic band, her spotty complexion, cellotaped specs and grubby bitten nails and decided

354

– not only wasn't she my kind of traveller, she wasn't my kind of a woman.

Which is why later, when she yelled through my door that she was going out soon and did I want to tag along, I pleaded a headache. That led to an embarrassing moment when, around eight o'clock, I was locking my room door on my way out.

'Good God . . . where are you going, dressed like that?' her voice suddenly whined behind me. And then: 'I thought you had a headache?' There she stood in the corridor, still grubby, greasy and unwashed. While I shifted uncomfortably, aware of her eyes on my washed and curled hair, my make-up, nail varnish, my brown and peach silk saree.

'Shit! I've never seen anything like it,' she laughed, leaning back against the wall with her arms folded across her chest. 'Well . . . ' she went on accusingly, 'where *are* you going?' And then, when I mentioned the Oriental hotel: 'Hey that's on my list of places to see, I'll get my bag and come with you – '

Which is when I did something I'd never before done with even the poorest, most ragged person I'd met on the road – I flatly refused her company. 'Sorry but I've made plans of my own and I'd rather go alone,' I said as I walked past her, trying to ignore the surprise and disappointment on her face. Later, heading off to the Oriental in a rickshaw, I wondered at my reaction. But there was no getting away from the fact that she had no excuses for her sorry appearance or her negative attitude. She was a mess – the sort of traveller I never wanted to become or even befriend.

The Oriental is the most expensive and the most famous of all Bangkok's hotel's and after walking through its gardens in the warm evening, I went into the piano bar for a pre-dinner cocktail. The bar was small and intimate, with one or two groups already gathered. As the pianist played softly in the corner, I ordered a Bloody Mary and asked to see the menu from one of the hotel restaurants.

A few moments later, the waiter reappeared with one Bloody Mary, one menu . . . and one message. The pianist would be happy to play any of my requests. I asked for

'Falling Leaves', a Nat King Cole song I'd loved since I was a little girl. He played it. I nodded my thanks. A little while later, the pianist rose and walked over to me. 'I have a few moments before my next session. May I sit with you – or are you expecting company?'

Major San Nu, as he introduced himself, was perfectly charming. He rejoined me after his second session and invited me to have supper with him. 'Here in the hotel, if you prefer,' he added, doubtless noting the suspicious glint in my eye. 'However, if you have not eaten Thai food until now, I would like to take you to what is, in my opinion, one of the very best traditional Thai restaurants in my city. . . .'

I had a quick consultation with my instincts, which said that, while his title might be rather fanciful (he looked much too young to be a Major), the pianist himself was kosher. Twenty minutes later, I was sitting in his rather grand car and twenty minutes after that, I was being fêted by a host of pretty Thai girls in a chic, stylish restaurant, with the 'Major' ordering up all kinds of delicacies which my 'I've-been-to-Burma' appetite more than did justice to.

During the meal, my companion regaled me with all kinds of stories about his army days, topping them with the most unlikely tale of all.

'I love playing the piano – particularly at the Oriental,' he mused. 'And it makes such a change from my real job . . . '

'Which is . . .?'

'I am the vice-president of the such-and-such bank,' he replied airily. 'A position which I quite enjoy, although I would much rather play piano.' And then he went on to discuss something quite different, while I tried to hide my total disbelief. A pianist who fancied himself as a retired war hero and the vice-president of a bank . . . Walter Mitty was alive and well and living in Bangkok. And trust me to find him.

After what was a very pleasant evening, the Major (by now, I couldn't think of him as anything else) insisted on driving me home – although his face registered dismay when I gave him my address. Parking the car outside the hotel, he was frankly horrified when he saw where I was living and bemused by my complete indifference to my squalid surroundings. The 'manageress', ever-watchful from the dim interior of her 'office', eyed me knowingly when the Major bid me goodnight and walked away. Then he paused, turned and said, 'Would you care to join me for lunch tomorrow?' reaching into his wallet and scribbling an address on a scrap of paper, when I accepted his invitation.

Next day – after my morning's shopping – I turned up at the address I'd been given and found myself walking into the reception area of a glittering, high-tech world. A hum of activity – high-pressured, high-powered – it really was impressive; banking, Bangkok style. While high up above me, standing in a futuristic, glass-walled office, Major San Nu (retired major, decorated war hero and vice-president of the bank) waited to greet me.

He smiled as his secretary ushered me in and I got the distinct impression he'd known all along that I'd doubted his story. 'Oh, there is just one thing . . . ' he murmured, as he led me through the bank. 'Should we bump into any of my associates during lunch, would you mind not telling them how we met?' And then, apologetically, 'Their vice-president, a pianist at the Oriental . . .? Really, I would prefer it to remain our secret.'

Well, I'm sure your penchant for piano-playing has been discovered by now, Major, and at last, it's safe for me to spill the beans.

For a week or more, I wandered around Bangkok. Took endless photographs of the Grand Palace, rode the water taxis up and down the busy river, explored the markets, ate delicious snacks at the street food stalls. Then I travelled north and spent a day boating around a colourful floating market. Travelled north still further and saw for myself the scene of so much misery and suffering – the bridge over the River Kwai. Stood gazing out across the lush, green tranquil banks of that river and wondered how it could look so peaceful, when by rights, it should still have carried the smells, the echoes, the stain of so much death.

Back in Bangkok, I was greeted at my old hotel like a long-lost family member, the 'welcome back' card from the Major making me feel quite cherished. But by now, after what had been several weeks of hard travelling, the lure of sun and sea was becoming irresistible. To the south, just off the Isthmus of Kra (and an overnight journey by bus), lay Ko Samui.

Ko Samui . . . lying on my bed in my room, I gazed at the tiny island on my map and thought back to the evening I'd first heard its name. Remembered the empty little wine bar with its dim yellow light, Albinoni's 'Adagio' playing softly, as the rain fell in torrents outside. Remembered Amy's prophecy – that I'd never make it further than Spain; Hannah's sad eyes; Bruno the bartender's knowing smile, as he suggested I visit Ko Samui, when (not *if*) I reached Thailand. That night – it had been the first night of the Year of the Rat. Yet in a way, Hannah had been right; for me at least, it *had* turned out to be the year of the puppy.

Ko Samui turned out to be everything Bruno had promised. Lush, hidden, undeveloped. A taste of the quiet, simple life, as I slept in a tiny thatch-roofed shack built on the beach – the palms rustling gently overhead and the sea rolling in silently just feet from my front porch. Good food and constantly changing company as travellers came and went. Lots of time to walk nowhere in particular; lots of time to sleep undisturbed. Lots of time to sit alone and endless time to think. About how much I enjoyed this freewheeling life and how I never wanted it to stop. London was another time and, for me, another life. My friends, my family . . . I missed them. But not so much that I couldn't bear it.

Although I didn't realize it on that beach in Ko Samui, I was reaching an interesting stage in my journey – the point at which those travellers who still can, find the discipline to give up and head home to friends and lovers, jobs and responsibilities. While the others seem to relinquish everything, severing all the old ties to make travelling a way of life. I'd already met people like that – wanderers who owned nothing, built nothing, needed nothing. More and more, I couldn't think of a better way to live. And if I arranged to sell my flat – used the money carefully – I realized I could wander unhindered like this for years.

My dear old mama must have sensed something in my

letters for, when I flew out of Bangkok and landed in Singapore, my usual first stop (the American Express office letters desk) yielded up yet another instantly recognizable letter. The blue air mail envelope, its modest green stamp overprinted with an outline of the Tay Road Bridge, proclaimed this a Missive from Mother. And Mother thought it was high time I headed home.

Realizing that a year had come and gone and she probably had a point, I went down to the telephone exchange and hung about for a couple of hours until my call went through.

'Singapore!' Mum breathed, faint with excitement. 'Oooh, I've always wanted to see Singapore – but I guess I'll have to make do with the phone call,' she laughed and, listening to her chatter on, I was glad to see that nothing had changed. She was just about to make a nice cup of tea – no cakes, though, she was on a diet. Again. Dad was walking Angus and Dundee looked miserable from where she stood by the window, gazing out at the fine, icy rain.

Then, suddenly mindful of the cost: 'And when *are* you coming home, young lady? Dad and I can't wait to see you.'

'Well not for a while yet, Mum. I was thinking I might go to the Philippines. Or maybe New Zealand. I'm not ready to come home,' I added, stressing each word, as her voice went all of a witter. 'Yes . . . I know it's been ages. Yes . . . I know it's costing money . . . yes, Mum. I miss you too.'

And then, the brainwave. 'Look, if you want to see me that much, why don't you come here? No, I'm not kidding. Why don't you? Dad could do with a holiday, he hasn't had a rest in years. Come on, Mum – don't you fancy a couple of weeks – in Bali, say?' That did it and, by the time I'd hung up the telephone, Mum had agreed to go to work on poor old Dad.

I wandered back to Chinatown, where I'd found a lovely old hotel called the Majestic, with its own cheap restaurant and a wonderful Chinese laundry next door. Up in my room, I got dressed for dinner, smiling all the while to think of my old mum – a veteran of coach trips to Edinburgh, shopping trips to Glasgow but little else – considering for a moment the idea of flying halfway round the world. Even her rare trips to London had assumed the proportions and forward planning of Arctic expeditions. She'd hated the rush on the Underground, the funny accents of the Londoners, decided the meat was stringy and expensive compared to its Scottish equivalent and had been cut to the quick when a shop assistant had refused to take her 'funny money', the good old Scottish fiver.

'No . . . it was daft of me even to suggest it,' I decided, as I flicked off the room switch, locked the door and headed out into the Singapore night. 'She'd never in a million years fly all the way out here.'

Which just goes to show how little I knew my mum.

Four weeks later, in the heat of a Balinese night, I strolled restlessly beneath the still palms. Beyond me, the airport arrival lounge was a blaze of light, a hive of activity, as the flower of Japanese youth milled around inside. One hundred honeymoon couples – two hundred starry-eyed romantics – they savoured the last precious moments of their package tour weddings, before heading back to Osaka, Yokohama and points north. While I gazed up at the starry night, straining for a first glimpse of the plane which would bring my family in from Java.

The last time I'd seen them had been at another airport – two slight little figures buffeted by wild winds as they'd watched my plane take off from the little Scottish airstrip, all those months and miles ago. I'd thought then that I might never get to see them again – thought maybe that was just as well, the way my life had been falling apart. At least if I just disappeared, they'd be spared a lot of disappointment. But now here I was – large as life and twice as troublesome – waiting to receive their verdict.

For endless months, I had lived among strangers and been influenced by them. Been obliged to reconsider my views and opinions, alter old habits and adopt new attitudes in the face of my constantly changing circumstances. I'd been taken apart – sometimes subtly and, at others, dramatically – and, little by little, I'd been put together again. Rebuilt. Yet of all the hundreds of people I'd encountered, none could comment on the restyled me, since none of them had met the prototype. Until now. And as the original architects of Trudy Culross suddenly padded through the arrival lounge, pushing luggage carts and gazing about apprehensively for a glimpse of their firstborn, I knew a moment of sheer panic. What if they didn't like me?

It was worse than that. They didn't even know me. True, I was an altogether leaner version of what had left home. My hair was much longer, redder. I was browner. Maybe my face was a bit older. But I stood there as my mother bustled through the exit doors into the scented darkness, looked into her winter-pale face and realized as her sharp green eyes stared at me . . . and through me . . . and beyond me . . . that the change was much more drastic than even I had anticipated. She has since said she was confused by the journey, the heat, the strangeness of her surroundings, but my mum, just for a moment, looked at me as if I was a total stranger.

Thank God for Colin, who came bowling out ahead of his long-suffering dad, picked me up in a bearhug and swung me round to the amusement of the Balinese onlookers, who had probably never seen anything approaching his tall frame. Personally, I'd never been as glad to see anyone as I was to see those three as we rattled back to base in my landlord's jeep.

Late into the night, we sat on the front porch, exchanging news – Mum almost beside herself with excitement (I could practically see her blood pressure soaring), while all the time Dad sat smiling quietly, embarrassed by the depth of pleasure he felt at just seeing me again. My announcement that I'd be sharing a room with Colin gave Mum food for thought. She stood uncertainly on the front porch of her little *losman*, nightie in her hand, saying things like, 'Er, but you *can't* share a room with Col . . . ' And then, more gently – as if somewhere along the road I'd completely lost my marbles as well as my sense of what was 'proper' – 'He's your *brother.*'

'Yes, I know. And I haven't seen him for ages. And we've got a lot to catch up on, so he's sharing my room.' And then, as she continued to look shocked: 'Mum, I've shared more rooms and more mattresses with more strangers than I care to think about. There's nothing wrong with sharing twin beds

361

– that's more privacy than most of the world gets. Now – get some sleep. We've got a long day tomorrow.'

And do you know something, she went like a lamb! Mark you, she was no sooner safely tucked up in her bed than she was out of it again – hopping up and down on the front porch, yelping about this horrible disgusting *thing* next to her pillow and how she couldn't, wouldn't – not for anything – sleep in that awful room. By this time, Colin had reappeared out of our bathroom and Dad had wakened up, so we all checked out this thing which had scared her so. Admittedly it was a big one – maybe three inches long. And it was particularly dark and shiny, its antennae long and very active. But. . . .

'Look, Mum, it's just a cockroach,' I said, placing an upturned glass over it, slipping some paper under it and removing it to the garden. 'The whole island is alive with them. And snakes and rats and spiders and lizards. So you might as well get used to it.'

'Never!' croaked Mum, who, according to Pop the next day, sat guard over both of them all night. And that after twenty-six hours of straight flying.

Trying not to laugh at her distress, Colin and I strolled back to our little room and, once we'd got settled in our beds, we talked our heads off. Eventually, he grew still, began to snore and I was left awake, to wonder what the coming days would bring.

I'd arrived in Bali a week earlier, after a horrendous trip across Java, through unseasonal monsoon rains which washed away roads, which affected the bus connections and brought all kinds of vegetation down on to the tracks, creating havoc with the trains. I seemed to walk around permanently in sodden wet clothes and caught the first cold I'd had since leaving Europe. Still, the hassle all felt worthwhile, the morning my bus finally left Muslim Java, with its predatory, lascivious males, and crossed into gentle, Buddhist Bali with its civilized, sweet-natured people.

I'd had a sleepless night, avoiding the unwelcome attentions of various Muslim passengers, whose hands kept coming into contact with parts of my anatomy under cover of darkness. But some sense of order and propriety was restored as dawn broke and I settled back for a bit of shut-eye – knowing instinctively that, now I was in Bali, I could finally relax.

A couple of hours spent in Kuta, the main town, was enough to convince me that this was *not* a side of Bali I wanted to introduce my folks to. Mostly because it wasn't Balinese. It had been overrun and totally ruined by a certain type of Australian – drunken, rowdy, trouble-loving yobs who abuse Bali in much the same way as their British counterparts abuse Ibiza.

What I was looking for was a stretch of silver beach, fringed with shady palm trees and bordering a safe, inviting, secluded bay. Somewhere quiet, natural and unspoilt – a little bit of paradise which, until now, my folks had only ever seen on the 'Bounty' adverts. I know, I know – I was asking for the impossible. But in a little place called Candydasser, I found it just the same.

Next morning, after a lovely breakfast of toast, marmalade, coffee and fresh fruit, the Culross tribe headed out on the first of three local buses which would take us to our destination. Piled in with the beautiful, delicate Balinese women in their colourful sarongs and cummerbunds, their jewellery eye-catchingly intricate and their hair bound up with flowers.

We meandered through rice fields and mango groves, through banana and pineapple plantations, dawdling at the foot of cloud-draped mountains; passed small, flower-decked shrines by the roadside; heard the merry clash of cymbals and the tinkling of temple bells long before we saw the temples; crossed rickety wooden bridges over fast-flowing streams; crept through gentle valleys, filled with the scent of exotic flowers; saw parakeets fly up from forests of bamboo, to settle in palms heavy with coconuts.

Hour after hour, mile after mile, there were scenes to delight the eye. While at every stop along the way, locals noticing these pale faces on the bus would hop aboard and travel on a mile or two, simply for the opportunity to meet us. It was my mother who fascinated them. Her shock of silver hair, her green eyes, white skin and freckles, proved an unfailing

363

magnet. So that everyone wanted to talk to her and ask questions (they were amused to discover Colin and I were brother and sister). If we were stationary in a market place, for instance, Mum would suddenly realize that just the sight of her elbow or hand protruding from the window would prove too much of a temptation. Sooner or later, one of the women selling fruit would step up to the bus and Mum would feel curious brown fingers trying to pluck the freckles from her skin.

Dad, meanwhile, was in another world. Many times I glanced at him over my shoulder and always he was staring intently through the windows. When finally we reached Candydasser and Colin was unloading our luggage, I turned to my father and said, 'Well, Pop – what d'you think?'

We stood together in the dusty road, as the bus disappeared in the haze. Then he looked down at me, his face a picture. 'Trudy, it was worth it – the money, the flying, your mother's fussing, everything – just for that bus ride. Fabulous.'

I'd dragged them ten thousand miles to see Bali but, for once, it looked like I'd done the right thing.

I had booked us into a pretty little *losman* which nestled in a palm grove just a few feet above the beach. It had two rooms – each with twin beds and its own loo and shower – a steep, thatched roof and a riot of colourful plants creeping right up to the front porch. The windows looked out on a perfect view – the garden, the pale curve of sand and the bright green of the shallows. Further out, we could see breakers crashing against the coral reef, which was draped like a necklace across the entrance to our little bay and beyond that, the azure blue of deep water sparkled in the sunlight.

There were one or two other *losmans* in the grove, but they were deserted and Candydasser was as private as any beach could hope to be. Life was reduced to a simple routine of sleeping, eating, talking, walking and listening to music. Although, since there was no electricity, I was very mean with the batteries. The days began when the sun came up and pretty much ended with the sunset; after which we would walk along the dusty road, piercing the darkness with our torchlight as we headed for one of two eating houses, where the decor was basic, but the food was delicious.

Slowly, slowly, my parents relaxed; my father went for a swim morning and afternoon, while Mum sat in the shade of a palm tree – unable to swim and trying not to mind the fact that she was missing all the fun. Then came the day we decided she should 'go aquatic' and the beach echoed with the sound of laughter as we all thrashed around in three feet of water – Mum sinking slowly from view and taking at least one of us with her, each time we attempted to set her afloat.

Still, at the end of two hysterical hours she was doing it – bobbing around with the rest of us in the shallows. Coughing and spluttering each time she met a wave head on, but swimming, just the same; her face alight with the novelty of the experience and the knowledge that, at sixty-one, she'd mastered something else.

On one of our very first evenings there, when the folks, still jet-lagged, had gone early to bed, Colin and I took a hurricane lamp, a bottle of whisky and strolled barefoot along the beach. It was a beautiful night – the breakers glittering in the moonlight and the palms silhouetted black against a sky full of stars. We talked for hours about his life back in London, his flat, his girlfriend, his job.

He wasn't happy, hadn't really been very happy when I'd left London. I could sense he was on the verge of making some decisions and changing the direction of his life. But that was a big step – one he hadn't quite plucked up the courage to take. I sympathized, for how long had it taken me to finally make a break? Sometimes, you've got to go all the way to the bottom before you start heading up, and right then, Colin wasn't unhappy enough, depressed enough or frustrated enough to change his life. It was coming, though. It was coming.

I told him a bit about what had happened to me since we'd last met in Corfu, but, strangely enough, after months of wishing I had someone to share things with, I found that I didn't really want to talk to him about my travels. Didn't want to go into detail about what had been happening to me or what I planned to do next. And not just when I was around Colin.

As the days passed, it became obvious to me *and* my folks, that I didn't want to talk much about anything at all. It really was wonderful to see them and it gave me a warm, contented feeling to just sit with them, listening to their idle chat and enjoying their company. But I – who had been to so many places, seen and done so much – simply had nothing to say. And I couldn't understand it.

Not only that but, more and more, I found a need to remove myself from my family for a couple of hours each day, actually found myself sneaking out of the *losman* before dawn, so that I could walk the beach alone or sit, quiet and still, with my thoughts. After months of craving company and spending endless hours staring into space wondering about my family, I'd been reunited with them. Only to discover that I needed to keep some kind of 'distance' between us. It just did not make sense.

Not until the morning I was swimming alone and saw my mother walking towards me down the beach. She'd obviously walked the length of the bay to find me and suddenly I was irritated that she should intrude on my privacy like that. Impulsively I raised my hand and gestured for her to go back and leave me alone; saw her falter for a moment, then turn around and walk away. Part of me felt rotten, part of me didn't. Something was happening between my parents and myself – maybe something long overdue – and all I knew was that I had to go with my feelings, even though I didn't understand them.

In the end, it was dear old Mum who provided the answer. As I headed back to the *losman* after my swim, I found her sitting quietly in the sand waiting for me. She'd been in Bali for four days and in all that time, she'd hardly taken her eyes off me – checking me out – and I knew the moment of truth had come. Even so, her question completely floored me.

'Trudy . . . ' she began. And then, without any preamble, 'Something's happened to you. Have you been in prison?' Her eyes were steady as they looked into mine. Obviously, she'd steeled herself to hear the worst.

I laughed then. Couldn't help it – probably because I realized that whatever I had to tell her was tame, compared to what she had imagined.

'Look Mum, a lot has happened to me. An awful lot – and some of it not pleasant to repeat. But no – I haven't been in prison. What on earth gave you that idea?'

'I don't know,' she said, her face worried and puzzled at the same time. 'But you're so – different. Oh, you still enjoy a joke and we're having great fun. And you've never looked better. But there's something . . . you're keeping things to yourself. It's as if you had a secret.

'Sometimes I watch you and your face is so quiet and serious – so *contained* in yourself. I said as much to Dad. Though, of course, he thinks I'm imagining it all. But I'm not, am I? Something happened. Something serious. And I thought, now, what could have happened that would have this effect on Trudy? It's as if you'd been – locked away.

'I'm just glad it wasn't what I thought,' she finished, as she got slowly to her feet. 'But whatever it is, you're different. Older. I don't know . . . '

And then, as if she was still trying to put her finger on the spot: 'You don't seem to need anyone any more. Back there – you waved me away when you were swimming. Oh, yes – I got the message!' and she smiled at my discomfort. 'It's all right – really. But you never would have done that before . . .' There was no accusation in her tone or any sense of hurt. Just the acknowledgment that I wasn't her little girl any more. Not anybody's, come to that. My own person at last, beyond anyone's influence.

Trust Mum to come up with the explanation for my strange behaviour. She'd sensed that the insecure child in me had disappeared and with it, the desire to please. My mother – probably unaware of my lifelong efforts to win approval – was now very conscious of my new emotional independence. I was still a loving daughter but I was no longer a particularly obedient or dutiful one. She'd sussed that. And something else besides . . .

Early next morning, I was roaming the beach again – watching the sun creep over the edge of the mountain to bathe the

367

bay in rosy light. As usual I chatted to the Balinese women collecting coral along the tide line; paused to watch the fishing skiffs dash through the breakers, their sails fluttering like jewelled butterflies. But that morning, my mind was working overtime.

Had I been in prison . . .?

I'd toyed with Mum's question over and over, realizing it was important. That somehow, with her usual intuition, she'd found the key to what had changed in me.

Prison. I imagine the worst thing about being locked up isn't so much the lack of communication with other people – it's the business of having to be alone, of having nothing to divert your attention so that, sooner or later, you're forced to tune into your own heartbeat, your own breathing – yourself. Having to face your weaknesses and shortcomings and listen to your petty, sordid little thoughts; trying to hold fast as your fear gets the better of you. Unless you like yourself a lot, it must be hard to be in prison, in solitary. Because, unless you can live with yourself, it's hard to be alone.

It had been impossible for me, so I'd gone to impressive lengths to ensure I always had company. Bruno, the ever-watchful barman – and, of course, my little black book – could vouch for that. So in a way, this journey HAD been a bit like being in prison, as I'd found myself completely isolated.

Time after time, I'd tried to dump the responsibility for myself on some man – ready to be whatever kind of woman was required, if only he would carry the load. But eventually I'd had to face the fact; I was woefully inadequate at sustaining myself and, until I learned to do that, I was useless to anyone.

But now, thank God, that was all over. At last, I had learned to function alone – and that meant enjoying my privacy, discovering pleasure in solitude. Silence and tranquillity were mine to savour . . . now that I could listen to my heartbeat, my breathing and feel no fear at the thought of being alone. Now that I could listen to my most wretched, snivelling, secret thoughts and still forgive myself for having them.

All these pieces – so many emotional fragments – they all finally came together as I sat on that empty beach, feeling enormously grateful. For the woman who had known me longest (and knew me best) had flown halfway round the world to sit in a quiet place with me and hold up a mirror. And I had looked into it . . . liking what I saw.

Mum and I didn't discuss it again – there was no need. She knew I hadn't been in prison and that mattered a lot. As to what had really happened, she guessed she'd hear the whole story when I had the courage to tell it. She's glad I'm telling it now.

At the end of a week of R & R, the tribe moved on again. By now, we'd hired a little white Suzuki jeep of our own and we wandered as the spirit moved us, through this island of mists and mountains, fierce sunrises and spectacular sunsets. We meandered along with no schedule and nothing planned; stopping here to watch thousands of bats flying home in the dawn to their sacred cave, much revered by the locals; taking time out there to watch the famous Monkey Dance performed on the steps of an ancient temple.

Another time, we spent the afternoon swimming in the ornamental pools of what had once been a royal palace – enjoying the icy cold mountain water, while shoals of tame goldfish played hide and seek with us. Each evening, we would rest at one of the many *losmans* or guest houses along the way – sometimes going to sleep in rooms sumptuously decorated, other times relaxing in places which were incredibly simple, their shower rooms open to the sky and filled with plants, so that it felt like bathing in a tiny, secluded garden.

Then came the day we arrived in Lovinia Beach and my parents decided to set up camp. Lovinia Beach wasn't the prettiest spot on the island but then, as I already knew, travelling isn't about places, it's about people. And the people here were wonderful.

The only other guests at the place turned out to be a crazy gang of deep sea divers, taking a well-earned break after a stint in the Java Sea. A Kiwi called Dave and a couple of Singaporeans called Johnny and Sam – they played as hard as they worked. And they were playing very hard indeed, when we got to Lovinia Beach. Within hours, they'd adopted my folks, made Colin an honorary member of their drinking club and I knew I'd found what I'd been looking for – the perfect spot for my folks to enjoy their last few Balinese days.

I think the highlight for both of them was when we rented a little dug-out canoe and the seven of us headed a couple of miles offshore, to a place Dave knew was particularly good for snorkelling. We finally dropped anchor and the boat bobbed about in the morning sunlight, my dad tentatively fixing a mask to his face, as he gazed into the crystal-clear depths below.

Dad knows everything there is to know about marine and tropical fish. He's lovingly bred them ever since I was a little girl, so that I knew my Neon Tetras from my Siamese Fighters long before I could count to ten. But Dad had never seen these wonderful creatures in their natural habitat and watching his face as he prepared to slip into the water, I knew he was in for the treat of a lifetime.

Mum, by now a swimmer for all of two weeks, had no intention of treading water beyond what had been the safety of her little bay. She knew as well as I did that we were in unprotected water and there probably were sharks about. And, though she'd willingly cleaned out fish tanks and checked temperature gauges in an effort to understand Dad's hobby, she felt, understandably, that sticking a piece of rubber in her mouth and blindly following my Dad was really going overboard. Still, I'd seen what was down there and knew how beautiful this underwater world was. I couldn't bear for her to miss it.

So, I cajoled her into the water and she floated with her arms locked around the wooden pole which rested in the water, stabilizing the canoe. Gently, Johnny persuaded her to put on the face mask. 'It's easy, Mama,' he laughed. 'Just hold your breath and put your face in the water. You'll see plenty fish!'

Game to the last, she pulled on the mask and dipped her head underwater and the look in her eyes when she surfaced a few seconds later was one I'll never forget. She was thrilled to death. Ten minutes later, she'd had her first snorkelling lesson and, plucking up all her courage, she slipped one hand into mine, loosened her grip on the stabilizer . . . and we were off. Doggy-paddling around the canoe to begin with, but gradually widening the circle as one thing after another caught her sharp eyes and we went chasing after schools of parrot fish and shoals of flat faced angels. It was the first time my dear old mum had ever dipped her silver head below the waterline and she'd chosen to do it in one of the most vibrant, colourful, exotically populated oceans in the whole world.

Yes, I think that was the highlight of the trip for them. But there was another moment when it all came together for me.

It was our last evening at Lovinia Beach and the Balinese family who ran our guest house wanted to give a special feast for the folks. That evening, there were sixteen people sitting round the table, with my mother in pride of place at its head. By now she was tanned, had lost a little bit of weight and was looking very pretty in a pale blue dress.

She'd been wonderful all day, the smile never leaving her face. Not even when they dragged a poor squealing piglet along to the front porch for her approval, then whipped it round the back of the kitchen, where they promptly cut its throat. The pig's blood-curdling yells moved Mum to say she wouldn't be able to swallow a single mouthful – no matter how deliciously barbecued it was. But when the pig was brought to the table, surrounded by tomatoes and lettuce and with a rosy fruit in its mouth, Mum stayed wonderfully cool.

An enormous salver of rice was brought to the table and placed before the honoured guest and, smiling regally, Mum leaned forward with a large silver spoon. But before she could touch the rice it began to erupt like a miniature volcano and suddenly, inches from her face, two absolutely enormous cockroaches broke through the tip of the rice pile. Antennae waving frantically in the air, they looked like two flash gangsters gate-crashing a smart Italian wedding and my heart sank into my boots as I caught Dad's eye and we both remembered the roach scene on that very first night. Mum was about to embarrass us all – and I could hardly blame her.

I closed my eyes in despair and waited for her hysterical screams to echo all over Lovinia Beach. Nothing happened, so I opened my eyes in time to see Mum digging into the mountain of rice with her spoon. With one deft movement – one effortless flick of the wrist – she turfed the insects out of our dinner and they flew through the air, shiny shells clattering as they made contact with the wall.

Beaming happily, her host insisted, 'See? Rice very fresh. Cockroaches only live in fresh rice!' while Mum, quite unperturbed, gave a smile which oozed understanding and calmly began to fill up her plate.

I was more than pleased with her; more than proud of her. That night, I loved her to bits for being such a trouper. But then, all three of them had made this part of my journey something I would never forget.

Two days later, I left them in a pretty little *losman* surrounded by cool, shady gardens. In thirty-six hours, they were heading back to London, while I was retracing my steps through Java to Singapore.

'Have you any idea at all how much longer you'll be gone?' Dad had tentatively asked, the evening before I flew. I knew better than to tell him that part of me never wanted to go home again – that I'd happily stay on the road forever. And if Mum guessed, she was too shrewd to comment.

'Look, Pop don't worry about me. You can see I'm well. You can see I'm happy, can't you? Honestly, I'll be home before you know it. So start saving – the first round's going to be an expensive one and it's on you!'

Next morning, wearing a white cotton sheath dress and high heels, my nails and lips bright with colour, I kissed them goodbye right there in the gardens – no more airport farewells. Anyway, this time I had no doubts about it, I'd soon be seeing them again.

As he'd done the last time we parted, Dad hugged me tight and said nothing. Mum gave me a kiss and a little blessing with her eyes. I walked away a few steps, then turned back and smiled at her, remembering the very last thing she'd said to me when I'd flown out of London . . . 'Whatever happens, remember, you're my daughter.'

I hadn't understood it then. I'd begun to understand it now. And she wouldn't have to remind me of who I was ever again. Because, at last, I knew.

Chapter Seven

Sad at the thought of home

The moment I touched down at Auckland airport, I knew coming to New Zealand had been a mistake. Admittedly, the journey had started badly, with me almost missing the plane in Singapore. My welcome at Kiwi immigration wasn't exactly rapturous and, long after the other passengers had disappeared, I was still answering questions in a vain attempt to gain entry.

It was the passport that did it – crammed with stamps which had amassed over the last year, it proclaimed me to be a busy traveller. And what they wanted to know was: did that also make me a busy girl?

I'd been on the move a long time . . . surely that cost a lot of money, so where did my money come from? queried one.

'Seventeen years' hard labour, back in London – you should try it sometime,' I answered with a thin smile.

I'd spent quite a time in India. Was that *all pleasure* or was there any *business*? wondered, another. And slowly I began to get their drift. Either I was a drug runner or I was a well-paid whore – probably both. The Java stamps didn't help my case; Siobhan had told me back in India that Java – like Bombay – was a favourite stop-off point for hookers looking for quick money. And I wasn't exactly dressed like your average traveller. Just a few hours earlier, I'd been running around in the steam heat of a Singapore day – my sleeveless cotton shift, caught around the hips in a large bow, and my high strappy shoes perfect for there and then. But hardly right for here and now. No doubt about it, in the eyes of the assembled gentlemen, I was a fast lady. And a highly undesirable alien.

'Ahem . . . Madam . . . I notice this ticket was bought just yesterday,' began yet another of my interrogators. 'How long ago did you decide to visit our country?'

'Yesterday.' Well, it was the truth. I'd dropped by the travel agents the previous morning, still undecided whether to head up to the Philippines or across to New Zealand. But recent reports of tourist hotels being blown up willy-nilly in Manila had bothered me . . . and the prospect of Fiji had been the clincher. Drawn by the lure of the South Pacific – maybe even a visit to the legendary island of Tonga – I'd decided to pay a call on the Kiwis in passing. At three o'clock that same afternoon, I'd picked up my tickets en route to the airport and I'd flown just after seven. An impulsive decision, which I was already beginning to regret.

'I must say, I find that surprising,' he went on. And to give him his due, he really did look surprised. 'Most of our visitors don't just drop by. Trips to New Zealand are planned months in advance . . . '

I sighed dramatically. 'Really? Well, if this is the kind of reception they get, I can't think why they bother.' And then, thoroughly tiring of the whole thing: 'Look here, I'm on my way to Fiji – my ticket's valid all the way to America – and frankly, I've just about had it with your country already. It's freezing, the rain's pissing down outside; I was fumigated before I even stepped off the plane. To put it bluntly, I'm not terribly impressed. So, if you've got any doubts about letting me in, that's fine. Stick me on the next plane to Suva and see if I care.'

I was almost disappointed to find myself standing on the rainswept airport steps ten minutes later, looking for transport into town. It had not been an auspicious beginning.

Once I'd booked into a guest house, I headed for Auckland's shopping centre, anxious to buy myself some reasonably warm clothes. Two tracksuits, gloves, a pair of white leather baseball boots and a couple of scarves later, I handed over my trusty plastic card – and collided with problem number two. I'd been one step ahead of my creditors for months, now. But here in NZ, they were waiting for me and my card couldn't cough up the price of a cup of coffee.

It took ten minutes of fast talking to convince the store manager that I was a little rich bitch on a world tour – having to tolerate the minor technical hitches, such as this one, which got in the way of me having fun. He soon saw the sense in not carrying heavy clothes when one spent one's entire life in warmer climes; saw the necessity of protecting one's anatomy from frostbite or worse, should one suffer the inconvenience of arriving in the middle of a Kiwi winter; convinced himself that I was indeed the victim of another computer cock-up and allowed me and my winter woollies to pass unchallenged: Still, it was just a little too close for comfort.

One large lunch, one man-sized dinner, one good night's sleep and, twenty-four hours later, I was horribly ill. I still don't know what was wrong but, as I lay in my little room, shivering and throwing up in turns, it did occur to me that I might be reacting to the 'normality' of my new environment, which was horribly familiar to me. All the way from the veneered dressing table and wardrobe at the foot of my bed to the fish and chip shop at the end of the street. They might just as well have had 'made in Dundee' written all over them.

Too late, I realized I'd wandered more than halfway around the world only to set foot in a country which was the mirror image of Scotland in the Fifties. I'd gone through another time warp and, for the next month, I would be forcibly reminded of my girlhood with every single mile I travelled. Yes, New Zealand turned out to be a very big mistake.

Not that there weren't some pleasant moments. Like meeting Chas, the night before I left Auckland. I was in my usual dressed-up-and-dining-out mode, when he came into the restaurant with a friend. A conversation eventually started up and Chas – all of twenty-two, with reddish-blond hair and an open, honest face – admitted that he hadn't seen much of this country he'd grown up in. He was a junior officer in the merchant navy, home on two weeks' leave. And was there a chance he could tag along with me?

The question was put half in jest and, equally in jest, I said he could come along if he presented himself at my guest house at seven the following morning, which was when I was moving out for my bus north to Cape Reinga. He was on the doorstep just after six-thirty – his little blue Ford Anglia ticking over in the drive and his holdall slung in the boot.

Chas was a sweetheart. Full of life and fun, courteous and shy in the manner of nearly all New Zealand men. Honest and vulnerable and lonely, too, in spite of a houseful of brothers and a teacher-mum who sounded like a bundle of laughs. What Chas really wanted was a girl. And until the right one came along, he figured I would do. But I figured the rules would have to be spelled out sooner or later, so soonest was fine by me. On that first day, as we travelled north, Chas had told me all about Billy, a boyhood friend who lived and worked on his dad's sheep farm. The farmhouse sounded very stylish, with endless rooms where Chas was sure we'd be put up for the night. Well, the story *sounded* okay. And Billy did turn out to be every bit as nice as Chas said, if a little (all right, completely) uncommunicative. And it certainly was a sheep farm – there were thousands of the bloody things, stretching from our parked car as far away as the eye could see. And the farmhouse was beautiful, large and airy and spacious.

Unfortunately, we ended up spending the night in Billy's place – a small shack on the edge of their property. The tumble-down front porch, decked out with bits of ragged washing, the sheepdogs lying on the overstuffed sofa and the mould on mostly everything in the larder certainly gave it that 'frontier, homesteader' feeling. While the offer of his one bedroom (and, of course, its one bed) left me in no doubt that the boys were being boys and the moment of reckoning had come.

For about twenty minutes, we sat around uncomfortably in the living area, while I listened to them talking non-stop about Billy's one reason for living – the massive motor bike which took pride of place in the room and was propped up against the mantelpiece. Even I could see it was a beautiful thing – a long, low black machine absolutely awash with shiny chrome. A futuristic bit of hardware which was really a work of art – a machine which Billy had designed and painstakingly built but one which had never been let loose on the road.

Eventually, of course, I had to go to bed and half-amused,

half-annoyed, I clambered into the old brass affair and waited for Chas's next move. Would he read the symbolism in the T-shirt, knickers and knee-high socks in which I was most unseductively attired? Or would he still go for broke, I wondered, as he silently came into the room and began to undress.

I suppose men do feel a sense of obligation when it comes to making their pitch, since to display a lack of interest or sexual desire could be regarded as less than flattering to a lady. So I will assume that the events of the next ten minutes were a sign that the last thing Chas wanted to do was to cause me offence by falling asleep.

Naturally, I thanked him for his generous offer but explained in no uncertain terms that, while I enjoyed the prospect of a travelling companion, I had no need of a bedmate. I didn't mind sharing a room but I'd been duped into sharing the bed. No, I wasn't angry but I wasn't pleased, either, and it mustn't happen again. Understood? And poor Chas, understanding, stood down.

Sleep claimed both of us then, but not for long. Suddenly dragged back to consciousness by the scream of tyres and choking exhaust fumes, I sat up in the rickety bed just in time to see Billy fly through the bedroom door astride his gleaming metal monster. Straight past the bed he rode, screeching to a stop under the window and reversing out of the room to roar around the living area, before parking in a belch of smoke in the kitchen. Chas and I looked at each other through a blue fug, our laughter suddenly erupting in the uncanny silence.

Once we'd got the sleeping arrangements under control, we two had a great time, wandering ever northwards until finally we stood together on the cliff top at Cape Reinga. Great mates by now, we huddled for warmth beneath the lighthouse and watched the Tasman Sea to our left, beat up against the Pacific Ocean on our right – the two great bodies of water meeting at the base of the cliff we stood on and coming together with a mighty, shuddering crash, as wave after wave did battle. And then, having seen what we came to see, we turned the little Ford Anglia's nose around and headed south again.

Two weeks after leaving Auckland, we poodled back into that

little town again – happy to have had the time together, but sad that it was coming to an end. Next day, I was travelling south to Wellington and Chas was heading back to his ship.

Just on the outskirts of town, he stopped to make a phone call and returned to the car with an invitation to dinner at his place. I figured it wasn't such a hot idea – not being exactly the kind of girl a twenty-two-year-old should take home to Mum. But then I figured we'd become good friends, despite the fourteen-year age gap and, if Chas could cope with his family's raised eyebrows, so could I.

Deciding against the tracksuit, baseball boots and other youthful traveller's trappings, I left Chas watching my land-lady's telly while I went to my room and turned back into who I really was. The white silk cheongsam strewn with tiny pink flowers had been tailor-made for me in Singapore. It fitted. Nails painted, hair styled, make-up applied, Chas's travelling companion presented herself for inspection.

'Christ, I'm glad you didn't look like that back at Billy's place,' he gulped. 'Or we never would have got out of bed.'

His brother gulped too, when I walked through the door. So did his mother *and* his mother's teacher friend, as I strolled into the kitchen and shook hands all round. Mother of Chas wasn't much older than me – something she worked out in five seconds flat, by dint of some shrewd questioning. It took her two minutes more to glean, with a mother's intuition, that her son was mildly infatuated.

Then followed a further nerve-racking three minutes, during which I was led off by big brother for a drink and poor Chas was debriefed in the kitchen by an anxious Mama. Still, once she'd reassured herself that young Chas had *not* been chewed up and spat out, or in any way interfered with by Yours Truly, she was the perfect hostess – treating me like one of the family in that way which is so typical of New Zealanders.

'I must say, you're not quite what I'd expected,' she admitted as she waved goodbye at the end of what had been a lovely evening. 'I thought Chas was bringing home some pale little slip of a Scottish thing with a pony tail and ankle socks, badly in need of a home-cooked meal.'

'Well, she was right about the home-cooked meal!' Chas murmured as we walked off to his car. 'You really pigged it. Although it beats me, how you managed to eat anything in that dress . . . '

Ah, Chas . . . you've still got a lot to learn about women. And I hope you have loads of fun finding out.

Next day I was on a coach heading south towards Hawke's Bay and here – thanks to New Zealand's highly organized tourist office – I got myself fixed up as a house guest on a farm. I got a taste of sheep farming, staying with the lovely Mogey family and learning a little about the New Zealanders' way of life – not to mention their taste for fine wines, good food and after-dinner conversation. John Mogey and I conducted most of ours lying on our stomachs in front of a roaring fire – a good bottle of New Zealand red at our elbows. John would hold forth on everything from the nuclear bomb to the Japanese taste for reindeer (he loved a good argument), while his wife Lynne – sensing I was partial to a lively debate myself – happily sat back to enjoy the heated exchanges.

On to Wellington and then across the Cook Straits to the little town of Picton at the tip of South Island, where I fell in with a lovely family of Maoris and spent a lively evening or two around yet another roaring fire – sampling the local brew and listening to their colourful chatter and richly embroidered legends, while outside, the beginning of winter rattled and howled at the doors and windows of the little hotel.

I moved on down the wild coastline to Christchurch, headed inland to the majestic waters of Lake Tekapo and travelled on through the Southern Alps. Life became one long round of buses and bus stations – my days an endless game of catching the coach, while my mind turned into a timetable repository. The country became a moving picture beyond a sealed perspex window, as we swept through hills and valleys, forests and lakes; deserted farming crofts marooned in seas of golden corn; snowstorms of sheep on emerald green fields. Day after day, I looked out on New Zealand . . . and Scotland stared defiantly back, reminding me of my origins and mocking my futile attempts to keep on running. Finally, I was forced to accept the logistics of my situation.

If you walk out of your front door, turn right and keep on going, you will eventually end up back outside your front door. And that was precisely what I had done. Maybe I *was* on the other side of the world just then, but I was also on the homeward leg – the last but one stretch. Unless I made a drastic change in direction, my own front door was now only a few thousand miles away and the thought made me very uncomfortable. But it wasn't until my one hundredth coach deposited me at the foot of Mount Cook, that I began to understand why.

I was afraid. With good reason, I figured. And it was Mount Cook which brought my fear floating to the surface.

That first evening, I'd arrived just before sunset at the Hermitage; a lovely old hotel fashioned of wood and stone, it stands on the edge of a windswept plain, gazing out over a sea of rippling bronze grass. Hemmed in by towering hills and dwarfed by the sheer grandeur of this valley, the Hermitage stands in the shadow of the mighty Mount Cook. Erupting spectacularly, straight out of the valley floor, the mountain soars in a proud, unbroken vertical – scything through cloud to pierce the vivid blue of the sky. Cloaked in blinding white snow – crowned in flurries of silver vapour, like the breath of some invisible dragon – it stands defiant. Daring anything and anyone to conquer it. And many have tried.

That evening, I walked through the wide valley – still but for the whistle of wind through grass and the high, plaintive call of a homeward-bound bird. The silence was eerie in this deserted place; the mountain somehow beckoning – appearing so near and surely within my reach, if only I could top that first rise. . . .

I had never stood at the foot of anything so grand before and for the first time, I began to understand why a mountain is something human beings feel obliged to climb, despite their fears. 'Because it's there,' mountaineers have been quoted as saying, when asked why they commit such madness. The answer had never made sense to me, until that afternoon.

But Mount Cook is very definitely 'there', beautiful and dangerous, silent and mocking, full of quiet ridicule for anything as transient as humanity. Standing there, I had a sense of being all alone with this dreadful mountain. Yet I knew that wasn't the case.

The papers had been full of it for the last couple of days: two teenage climbers were lost on the mountain, missing, now presumed dead – the weather closing in so quickly that rescue parties had been called off the mountain that very afternoon, forced to abandon their search. Now, as the last rays of a bright, harsh sun turned the mountain's face into a mask of glittering diamonds, I wondered about these two boys. Felt almost linked to them telepathically as my eyes scanned the relentless whiteness, half-expecting to see some sign of life far above me.

I'd read once that freezing to death is a very pleasant way to die and now I was sure it was so. Found myself thinking that, if a person had to die, then surely meeting that fate on the icy splendour of Mount Cook was a noble – even joyful – way to go?

When I see them on paper, my thoughts seem very morbid now. But standing motionless in the gold of that evening, I wasn't particularly sad for the missing climbers. I recalled how many sordid, sad little routes to death I had seen; the lepers in Egypt, the junkies in Goa. Recalled the death train in Bombay, the tragic sights in Calcutta – all miserable ways to take one's leave of life.

Were these boys still alive high above me? And if they were, had they passed that stage of being afraid? I could only hope so and, standing there, I said a little prayer for them. I hadn't prayed since I was a young girl. Yet it felt perfectly natural to utter the words now, in the middle of nowhere, for two boys I'd never met.

I suppose it was thinking of the boys' fear that made me start to examine my own. During the next two days, while the weather closed in and I waited in vain for it to clear, I had lots of time to think. For hour after hour, I gazed quietly out at the mountain – buffeted by rain, shrouded in mists – and I worked out what was going on and why New Zealand, with all her memories of home, saddened me so.

I wasn't constantly on the move because I loved travelling – although part of me certainly revelled in the freedom and the excitement of each new day. I was on the move because I was afraid to go home, afraid of heading back to London to discover I hadn't really changed; terrified at the prospect of returning to my old life, only to find myself slipping into old ways.

I had learned to be alone among strangers. Discovered a curious pleasure in eating, sleeping, travelling and just *looking* at things by myself. But how would I cope with doing all these things solo, when I was back among friends? Would I begin to feel lonely, all over again? And if it got desperate, would I start turning the pages of my little black book? Would Bruno find me back on his bar stool, twirling this way and that, with one eye always on the door, in search of unwary talent?

Once I'd had friends, but where were they all now? Amy gone to pastures new; Hannah in love, her days and thoughts taken up with someone else. Nadia and Graham, Rui and Simon, Peter and even Colin had simply got on with their lives. The tiny space I had once occupied for each and every one of them had probably long ago been filled in and smoothed over. And so I'd moved on – aiming for nothing and heading for no one – because I'd been afraid that there was nothing and no one to go back to.

Being alone is so much easier than being lonely. . . .

Well, the weather lifted finally and I headed out again making for Queenstown, since it seemed as good a destination as any other. And in Queenstown I mooched around, doing all the things travellers do. But now that I wasn't such a carefree traveller, none of it brought me the same pleasure. The days were overcast, the temperature dipping, the rain a constant drain on my optimism.

One day I decided to treat myself to a jet boat ride along Skipper's Canyon. I shot along the canyon with half a dozen other yelping passengers, heady with the thrill of it all – my hair nearly torn from my head in the screaming wind and a bright orange lifebelt strapped to my back. It was a bit like going on a funfair ride and as silly a way as any to kill an hour.

Travelling upriver, we turned a bend and slid into quiet

water. Letting the engine idle, the boatman pointed to the high, dark canyon wall which rose straight out of the river, further upstream. About twenty feet or so above its surface, an angry fall of water thundered out of a narrow, dark crevice.

'Keep your eyes on that!' he yelled over the thundering water and, even as I wondered what was going on, something shot out of the crevice and seemed to hang in space for an instant, before it plunged with a mighty splash into the foaming water beneath. Even as it landed, I could hear screams and I held my breath as I realized that the object had been a raft of some sort and it had overturned in the river.

Even as we craned our necks to see what happened to its occupants, another raft shot out of the hole, closely followed by a third.

'That's the end of the white water expedition,' our man went on. 'See that hole in the rock face? That's the end of the Devil's Elbow. Quite a ride, should any of you folks fancy it!' And we were off again, bouncing along the waves back towards the jetty. Me thinking I wouldn't allow myself to be propelled through the air like that for anything – knowing it had scared me just to watch it.

Knowing too, that if I wanted to get to grips with my fears, the Devil's Elbow was probably as good a place to start as any. . . .

One minute I was safe – knees together, legs braced, numbed toes digging into the soft, fleshy crease where the dinghy walls met the floor. Next minute, I was gliding through the air and down into the depths, my eyes following the giddy whirl of rocks and sky and hissing foam, even as I sank beneath the churning waves.

Deafening noise, frantic drumming on my helmet . . . tingling heat along my skin as icy water sucked and pummelled and bundled me along. My eyes were tightly closed – mustn't lose the contact lenses. The last breath I took was still trapped between my teeth and my chest felt tight. Another sharp blow to the right of my helmet, then a grating sensation as my head scraped the river bed or a rock face or something. I didn't even know which way up I was . . . and my chest . . . was this what it felt like to drown?

A sudden blast of cold air on my stinging face and a sensation of light on my eyelids, as my life jacket catapulted me back to the creamy surface. Thank God, I was face up, even if I *was* travelling backwards. *'Remember – if you end up in the drink, it's arms crossed over chest, legs straight out in front, feet together to push away from rocks.'*

Visions of my vertebrae being splattered across a wall of rock set me thrashing wildly until I'd twisted around enough to see where I was going. 'Shit, shit, *shit!*' Did I yell it or just think it, as I bounced along in a tunnel of grey water, a wall of foam rising up on both sides. Off to my left, the wet glistening stone of the chasm whipped by and dead ahead – no more than fifty feet away – a slim, smooth monolith reared up. The dreaded Shark's Tooth, around which the water boiled and snapped in fury, before it divided and went charging on.

'Which way will I go?' I wondered distractedly (as if I had a choice) when something skimmed past my left shoulder. A paddle. *My* paddle? I panicked, suddenly fearful for the first time as I remembered the instructor's warning.

'Remember – anyone goes in the drink, it's a fine. Anyone loses their helmet, it's a fine. Anyone loses their paddle, it's a fine. Anyone not completing the journey, it's a fine . . . '

Dazed, I heard yelling as if from a long way off, yet when I raised my head, the dinghy was almost on top of me. The instructor stood up, wrestling with the tiller and motioning frantically with his head to the far wall of the chasm. I knew he was yelling for me to swim, although above the noise, I could only make out the mouthing of the words.

He had to be joking! I was caught up in a whirlpool of water, its pressure so great I could barely raise my arm. Swim? *How?* Then another voice, closer, said: 'Hold on baby' and I looked up into a bearded face, eyes calm beneath the scarred red helmet. I felt his gloved hand clutching the collar of my wetsuit and we flew together down the white water – me and the little grey dinghy.

I was a cork, a leaf, a paper boat. A freeloader, going to

hell in a borrowed helmet. A non-paying passenger on the biggest roller-coaster in the world – twenty miles long and downhill all the way. And there was no time to be afraid. I knew I was almost on the Shark's Tooth but I didn't feel any panic. Just a light sensation in my head, tightness in my lungs and, louder than all the other sounds, the frantic beating of my heart.

Hands clawed at my back and I felt my body being lifted up. Instinctively I thrust my weight forwards, as someone else grabbed my backside and I toppled face down into a few inches of wet slop and the sweet smell of rubber. Face resting against the fragile skin of the dinghy floor, I could feel water bubbling furiously against my cheek and I turned my head in time to see the Shark's Tooth, hugely outlined against the ice blue sky, whizzing past just inches from my plimsolled feet.

Laughter all around me, self-congratulatory but tinged with hysteria. 'Jesus! That wuz close!' chortled a Kiwi voice as Red Helmet bounced me unceremoniously back into my so recently vacated position – fourth man, back right. I laughed the loudest and longest and I was still laughing as the dinghy slipped into quieter water and nosed up on to a ribbon of pebbles and smooth dark stone.

No time to rest, no time to think. Diving out, we pulled our dinghy clear, then waited to see how the others fared. There were four rafts facing the white water and the Shark's Tooth was one of the toughest stretches. Our instructor was new and had to earn his stripes – so we were first. Now the second raft made it through the heaving channel. And the third. But the fourth was a long time coming and it glided through like the *Marie Céleste* with no sign of life on board.

For a long second, all of us watching were silent with surprise. Until we focused on the flailing arms and legs, the bobbing blue and yellow helmets and a face turned towards us – frozen for an instant in an expression of disbelief, before it disappeared.

Galvanized, we ran and tumbled over the escarpment, adrenalin making us sure-footed as goats on the slippery stone as we flung ourselves thigh-deep into the iciness of a river which cast breathless, panting bodies up on shore like spent fish.

More wild laughter and back-slapping while we rounded up rowers and paddles. Then a sudden cry as someone checked behind a rock for a paddle and found one of the team wedged tight behind a stone outcrop, trapped just inches below the waterline.

He was big, hefty and it took three others to pull him out. Draped about them he looked half-drowned and still seemed to be choking – his face purple as water streamed from his ears, his mouth, his nose. But everyone's blood was up and the chasm rang with whoops and yells and cries of 'Let's go for the big one!' In the midst of the bravado, his terror went unnoticed as he was dumped on a rock to recover.

Quietly, I watched while he shook and trembled. Definitely in shock. But right now, we were in the navel of New Zealand. One hundred feet down and only one way out for both of us.

Moments later we'd cast off again. The sun came out, smiled coldly on us, strafed the water and the rocks with her hard glare and turned the froth and spray into a million points of rainbow light.

Everyone sang and so did I. I felt drunk as a skunk, high as a kite and thrilled with the terror and excitement of it all. I laughed to remember the sleepless night, the missed breakfast, the nerves which led up to this run. Now I couldn't wait for the next stretch of white water. Wanted to feel again that elevator in my stomach as we skimmed and soared over white and blue, ricocheted off smooth stone, zig-zagged the jagged rocks.

I'd survived a ducking – the worst was behind me now and I was calmer; thinking straight at last. So I jumped to it when the boss yelled: 'Fourth right!' and issued my commands. I pushed and pulled, reversed and froze like I'd been doing it for ever, instead of for the first time. Eagerly I put my back into the strokes, kept up the rhythm without any effort, although we'd been hauling for hours.

Little by little, we became a team. Nine bodies in a boat, indistinguishable behind parkas and lifebelts, beneath helmets and harness. But at the end of five hours, I knew I'd recognize these features anywhere, so often had we exchanged quick glances, smiles and winks of reassurance and support.

Laughing gleefully, swearing with the best of them, I was ready for the Devil's Elbow – that last long run through a cave only four feet high and five feet wide.

'When we hit the Elbow, keep your heads low, your elbows in and watch that pinpoint of light at the end of the tunnel. There's a twenty-foot drop at the end of it, so for chrissakes, hold on to the ropes. And be ready to paddle the second we hit bottom. . . .'

And that's what I was doing now, winding my fingers around and around the freezing cord and jamming my feet even further into the crevices of the dinghy as we shot through the cramped, dark tunnel. I gasped as the pinpoint of light became a gaping maw and I yelled – we all did – as we were launched heavenwards in a torrent of furious water to fly through the air like a wingless grey bird.

The belly landing jolted my spine as I unwound fingers, grabbed the paddle and rowed as if my life depended on it. Which, in a way, it did. Then we were in smooth, fast-flowing water and the instructor yelled 'Fourth right – out *now* and hold this mother-fucker'. I was over the edge, up to my crotch in freezing water, straining against the flow until other hands took up the task.

And all the time I gazed backwards, staring up with a mixture of pride and disbelief at the black hole way up in the rock face – so high, with its beard of white water trailing into the boiling, steaming cauldron below. As I watched, another dinghy torpedoed out to drop with a sickening lurch like a giant blue pebble.

Did I really do that? The idea made me tingle all over, although my breasts were aching with the cold, my hands and feet beyond all sensation. None of it mattered in the face of what I'd just been through. What I could do again, if I wanted to. And if I could do that, was there anything I couldn't do, once I stopped being scared of it?

I was embarrassed now to think of my fear – the stomach cramps and diarrhoea which had plagued me since dawn. I'd been silent on the drive to the rapids, fumbling with my wetsuit until the instructor, in despair, had dressed me, the way you would a child. Staring at the river in grim fascination, I'd expected every moment to hear myself chickening out; even when I'd stepped warily into the dinghy, I couldn't believe I'd go through with the trip.

Now, five hours later, here I was, looking at the most exciting rapids in New Zealand from the finishing line. No wonder my smile was as wide as wide can be. . . .

Staggering to the bank, I dragged off the wetsuit, my freezing jeans and jerkin and bundled myself into a spare set of clothes. Going in search of the promised tea and whisky I came face to face, or rather, feature to feature, with Red Helmet – looking different now. The light beard belied the dark hair and the fact that he was balding. He wore gold-rimmed glasses and they made him look older, somehow. Yet the quiet grey eyes and the slightly chipped front tooth were unmistakable. This was the man who probably saved my life.

I wanted to hug him and thank him for saving me, for calming me; I felt there was a bond between us, after what we'd just been through. Felt close to all of them for, although they looked different now, I still recognized the features of the other men from my crew. I soon realized some subtle change had taken place. No longer united by a common danger, we'd become strangers to each other again – Red Helmet for one, looked almost embarrassed by the intimacy of these last few hours, as he smiled self-consciously at me and then turned away.

I didn't even get the chance to thank him, which made me sad for a moment. But accepting the inevitable, I turned away too. Contemplating the hills, the trees, the green and purple of the landscape, I knew I would never stop being surprised, pleased and sometimes disappointed by people – and even I was no exception.

That day I had pleasantly surprised myself. Tomorrow, I was flying back to Auckland and the day after that, I would take off for the Fijian islands. Heading home, albeit the long way round . . . and London was getting closer all the time. When I got there, what would I turn out to be? The nicest surprise I'd ever had or the biggest disappointment of my life?

Chapter Eight

Dancing with death again

The urgent clatter of a ship's horn echoed across the water, shattering the peace of the afternoon. Lying on my back, eyes closed against the sunlight and head cushioned on a piece of silver-bleached driftwood, I heard the noise above the strains of Sibelius' Violin Concerto. So I turned the volume up and went back to dreaming as the music flooded the headphones of my Walkman.

It was the end of my second week on Plantation Island and I'd quickly fallen into the routine of this tiny place. Now I knew that, half a mile back along the beach, Rosie, the entertainments boss, would already have lined up her troops. Willi would be playing his guitar while the rest of the welcoming committee would be chanting a Fijian song, swaying in their colourful sarongs and clapping in rhythm. Tall, statuesque Rosie, with her beautiful almond eyes and smiling mouth, would be standing by the water's edge, arms draped with colourful garlands of hibiscus and frangipani, with which to welcome this latest ferryload of overwhelmed guests. Mostly middle-aged, pasty-faced and overweight, they would be racing up to the cocktail bar any moment now, swarming over sands made immaculate each dawn by an army of Fijians who rake the beach, removing tidelines, sharp stones – even fag ends – to leave it tidier than any Axminster.

From her prime spot on the beach – just in front of the honeymoon bungalows, a little to the right of the windsurfing school and an order's throw from the bar – the lovely Kitty would be raising herself up on tanned elbows and gazing out from beneath her beach brolly to examine the latest arrivals.

Mostly they weren't our type. Too old, too fat, too rich, too married. But once in a while, the ferry would cough up something interesting. Fairly young and tall, often European – mostly taking a little time out from travelling and fair game for the fun house.

The fun house was actually the dorm – home for budget-minded travellers like myself, who passed this way. Enjoying all the five star facilities of the complex – its restaurants and bars, its tennis courts and water sports – we nevertheless kept ourselves apart from the richer, older residents. Holidaymakers who island-hopped their way around Fiji on expensive package tours, they mostly stayed for three or four days en route to Singapore or Sydney. Hugging the front porches of their beach bungalows by day and downing their Fijian Firecrackers and Plantation Punches by night, each of them living in splendid isolation in their little patch of paradise, they would watch us 'fun housers' go by with more than a little envy. For, although they had the money, we were the ones having the prime time . . . and the dorm was where it all happened.

The evening I'd arrived in the little six-seater sea plane, I'd walked into this long, low bungalow – pleasantly surprised by the layout. Three of the four walls were lined with sofas, upholstered in brightly striped cotton, while a double line of sofas, set back to back, ran down the centre of the room. There were two doors in the fourth wall. Opening one, I found four shower stalls, two loos and a line of four wash-basins. While the other door opened on to a little room which had six sofas ranged round the walls. I soon learned that this little room was the inner sanctum; the club; the sleeping quarters of the 'in crowd' – those travellers who had been around longest and pretty much ruled the roost.

The sofas turned into comfortable beds at night. And the occupants turned out to be of both sexes. Up until a couple of weeks before, there had been separate sleeping quarters for the men, but a hurricane had made off with the thatched roof – and most of the sofas – of the male dorm, so bunking up had become the name of the game.

No one at the reception desk had advised me about these

rather adventurous sleeping arrangements and the first I knew of it was when a singularly large and noisy male charged through the door, walked along the line of sofas and collapsed on the bed opposite my own. John was big and bluff – an Arctic fisherman taking his yearly four weeks off, playing and drinking hard and always in the middle of the action. He snored a lot and talked in his sleep but I got used to it after a couple of nights.

The main dorm slept thirty-six bodies and since the ratio of male to female was seventy/thirty, it's hardly surprising I thought I'd died and gone to heaven. For it really was quite something to surface from sleep and lie in that half-dreaming, half-wakened state, idly watching some beautiful man as he dozed an arm's length away from my appreciative gaze.

And, of course, as travellers came and went, the view constantly changed. One morning I woke to find a curly-headed Canadian propped up on one elbow, smiling across at me. His pleasant 'good morning', delivered with a delicious French accent, being the perfect way to start the day. Another morning, I surfaced just after dawn, my eyes lingering on the unforgettable sight of two long-legged Swedes on the sofas opposite. I'd turned in early the night before, without meeting my latest bedmates. But there they were, both quietly slumbering, their white-blond mops falling over unlined, boyish faces. Completely naked beneath their single sheets, they were something to see – tanned limbs splayed out carelessly, chests rising and falling as they gently snored, oblivious to the scrutiny.

Forget modesty in a place like this. When thirty-six bodies rise and shine side by naked side, pyjamas look oddly out of place. Intimacy was in and personal privacy was OUT as, morning and evening, the same old rugby scrum developed around the washbasins, showers and loos, amid much pinching of towels and shampoos (not to mention bottoms). But although the comments filling the air were ribald, they were also good-natured. And while the level of nudity I encountered on my trips between bed and bathroom was enough to promote meltdown under normal circumstances, it left all of us curiously unaroused in this environment.

I'd be lying if I said I didn't find the situation even mildly erotic. Of course I did. But believe it or not, sexual shenanigans were rarely on the agenda with the fun house crowd. At first I couldn't understand it – imagining that this kind of intimacy, in such a beautiful setting, was bound to create a real hothouse atmosphere. Then I realized that, by removing our clothes, we had also effectively removed a lot of the mystique; in shedding our inhibitions, we also managed somehow to shed our sexual desire – at least with each other.

The dorm crowd was like one big family – into midnight feasts and pillow fights, sing-songs and arguments; the idea of sexual couplings seeming unhealthy to the point of being incestuous.

Which was why the daily ferry, not to mention the half-dozen six-seater planes which buzzed in and out each day, always created a stir. 'Don't screw your friends' was the dorm's unwritten rule. Heeding it, those fun housers with a keen sexual appetite were constantly on the look-out for the speciality of the day – a screwable stranger. Unless, of course, he moved into the fun house and became a member of the family. And the lovely Kitty, with her waist-length auburn hair and her soft Canadian accent, was a girl with her eye permanently on the changing menu.

Although this casual nudity was the order of the day inside the dorm, the Fijians are a modest people and even going topless wasn't allowed on the beach which fronted the complex. This was one of the reasons I strolled on for half a mile or more each afternoon. On the far side of the island I'd found a tiny secluded bay which afforded the privacy I needed – not only to bathe in the nude, but also to spend a couple of hours each day by myself. For although I enjoyed the camaraderie of communal life, I needed more than ever to be by myself.

By now a resident for two weeks, I'd progressed to the inner sanctum – sharing that much sought-after little back room with Kitty and a motley crew of four men. Kitty, at twenty-seven, was a doctor from Ottawa who had just completed a trip through China. A figure of generous proportions was complemented by an equally generous personality and a tremendous sense of fun. I'd first seen Kitty limbo dancing

on the beach, her long hair trailing on the sand as she effortlessly bent double and slipped beneath a bamboo pole just
eight inches from the ground. She straightened up, laughter
gurgling up in her throat as she graciously accepted the
applause of her audience, and I knew instinctively she was
my kind of girl.

Now we were firm friends but even Kitty hung back each
afternoon, as I picked up my gear and headed off down the
beach. Like the others, she sensed that there were times when
I needed to escape. And really, these times – like now – were
the best times of all.

Sighing lazily, I sat up to survey the scene. Ahead of me,
the beach curved away to the left and disappeared around a
tiny headland; the complex and the dorm lay on the other side
of it. At my back, the island itself petered out in a collection of
black, shiny boulders which slid into the Pacific. To my right,
the beach ran uphill slightly until it met a palm grove – thick
with trees, despite the recent hurricane. While, to my left, the
clean fine sand ran down into pale green shallows. About
thirty yards out, the reef ended and, beyond that point, I
could see the ferry making its way through the dark blue of
the deep water, heading for our sister island.

Slipping off my headphones, I gave up on Sibelius and
tuned into the gentler sounds of waves against sand and wind
through foliage. It was hot, hot, hot. Very, very still. I was
utterly content. And tomorrow was my birthday. Next morning, determined to have a party and a half, I hopped over to
Suva, the main island, in a little taxi plane and was soon
rattling into the main town to do some shopping.

I'd arrived there three weeks earlier, hot on the heels of a
hurricane which had devastated the island's vegetation. I
hadn't been impressed with the main town, the buildings run
down and neglected and the shops run by a whole Asian
community, which seemed oddly out of place here.

So I'd moved off to a tiny atoll at the north end of the
island, ending up in a little bungalow on a deserted complex.
Then had followed an unpleasant few days, during which I
was almost eaten alive by mosquitoes and took my life in my

hands every time I strolled from my bungalow to beach or restaurant. Hurricane Hilda had played fast and loose with practically every palm tree on the place and there was a very real danger of having my skull split in two by silently descending coconuts. Each tree had to be carefully navigated, angles of descent worked out and suitably wide berths given to each trunk, should its fruit decide to suddenly plummet earthwards.

As if that wasn't bad enough, the only other guest turned out to be a shy, wealthy Kiwi – a bachelor in his early forties. While my 'hostess', the owner of the complex, was a washed-out Australian divorcee in her mid-fifties who was never more than a foot away from a bottle of whisky. She wanted to sell up, he was thinking of buying this 'honeymooners' hideaway'. And for reasons which still aren't entirely clear to me, my hostess thought that I could somehow be the deal clincher. She offered me money to go to work on him. 'Do whatever it takes, dear. I think he's probably still a virgin, so a smart girl like you shouldn't have any trouble . . . ' It took me a moment to realize which way her mind was working.

It was true that he watched me all the time but, in all fairness, he wasn't exactly spoiled for choice – it was either me or her. Presumably she figured that a surfeit of sex would fry his brains so much he'd have signed on the bottom line without a murmur. I felt too sorry for her to be insulted and she got her answer next morning as I loaded my gear into the little boat and we skimmed out over the shallows. Over my shoulder, I could see her sitting on her verandah, her two dogs at her feet and her bottle of Johnnie Walker at her elbow. My proposed victim had come down to see me off, his trousers rolled up awkwardly as he pushed my boat off the sand with a last shy smile and wandered aimlessly back up the beach. Ah, well . . . it was her hangover, her atoll, her problem, I'd decided, as I'd headed back to Suva and then flown on to Plantation Island.

In the supermarket, I bought loads of crisps and cheeses and half a dozen bottles of wine, for the inner sanctum booze-up. Then, figuring there just might be some mail for me – maybe even a birthday card from home – I strolled off to the Post Office.

There was one letter, my name scrawled across the envelope in handwriting I didn't recognize, and I was full of anticipation as I headed back to the airport and my flight to Plantation. It wasn't until we were airborne and winging out across the shiny blue of the Pacific that I opened it, eager for news. *'You won't have heard yet, but Brian's dead. Cancer. In the end, he was desperate to die and it was the best thing. You wouldn't have recognized him. I know you'll be upset and I'm sorry to break the news to you this way. I can't believe how much I miss him. . . .*

There was more, but I couldn't read it. Instead, my eyes blurred with tears and I fixed my gaze on the little perspex window, remembering how happy I'd been just moments before. Brian, dead . . . He hadn't been one of my closest friends, but he'd been a very old one. A man I'd known since my teens who was only a few years older than me. Feeling immensely sad – and somehow almost guilty that I felt so well – I watched as the shark's fin shape of Plantation swam into view. Lying on a bed of shimmering blue, her edges fringed with white and wearing a headdress of jade green feathers, she was such a beautiful island; a beautiful place to have a birthday. And it was a beautiful day to be alive. Poor Brian. . . .

The news had certainly taken the edge off my celebratory mood and, dumping my shopping in the deserted dorm, I avoided the usual morning meeting place and headed off instead for my private bit of beach. I leaned against my piece of driftwood and stared out at the ocean. About five hundred yards offshore, *Black Magic* rode lazily at anchor, her scarlet sails neatly furled and the sun glinting on her chromework. I could just make out the dinghy, trailing at her stern like a puppy dog, and I knew that Seth was home.

The sun was still high and I knew it was a little early for my daily workout but I was too sad to sit still with my thoughts. Slipping on my swimsuit, I stepped into the warm water and walked through the thigh-deep shallows until I came to the edge of the reef. Then I plunged into the deep water and struck out for the yacht. I still wasn't much of a swimmer and I was still afraid of water but every day, I swam from the beach to Seth's floating home and every day my strokes were stronger and I was a little less afraid.

Even though one of the rich tourists had taken me to task over it. A very handsome, blonde Australian woman in her late forties, she was living in one of the luxury complex bungalows with her husband and another couple. One morning, as I walked past her place to my private bay, she called me over.

'I see you swimming out to Seth's yacht every day,' she said pleasantly, squinting up at me in the sunlight. 'You're not scared, are you?'

Misunderstanding her, thinking she was referring to Seth's reputation with the ladies, I laughed and said she shouldn't listen to the bar gossip – Seth was a real gent.

'Oh, I don't doubt it. That isn't what I meant – ' And then: 'Look, I don't want to scare you, but have you any idea of what's out there?' and she jerked her head in the direction of the water. 'Back home, we don't take any chances – you wouldn't catch me dead swimming off that reef. I just thought I ought to mention it, in case it hadn't occurred to you . . .'

But it had occurred to me. Lots of times, I thought, as I settled into a steady rhythm. I knew enough to know that reefs were the favourite haunt of reef sharks and poisonous snakes, dangerous corals and a host of other unpleasant inhabitants. And for sure, no one else ever swam here in deep water, although the shallows were alive with the dorm crowd. Even now, I don't know why I did it – why I made that twenty-minute swim each day – for I certainly knew the risks I was running.

I guess it was the old 'Why does a man climb a mountain?' story. 'Because it's there', mocking his unnamed fear. And when he conquers a mountain, I suppose his fear is conquered, too. All I know is, I waded into that water day after day with my heart in my mouth. Kept my head down and struck out blindly, breathing steadily to control my nerves, concentrating on my stroke for the same reason. Sometimes thinking about what slid through the depths beneath me but mostly trying not to.

Never looking at *Black Magic* for more than a second at a

time, since she often seemed to be beyond my reach. Sensing, as the welcome clinking sound of her rigging carried to me on the breeze, that I was almost safe. Knowing, as the bottom rung of her ladder loomed up before me, that I was nearly home and dry. And then there was that moment when I clambered up her black wooden hull, popping my head above deck to yell, 'Permission to come aboard, cap'n?' That sweet sense of achievement when I sat on her prow, legs dangling in space as I surveyed the endless distance between myself and the beach. While down below, Seth broke out a couple of beers, Ella Fitzgerald played on his tape deck and *Black Magic* twisted and turned coquettishly, flirting with the wind and tide.

Seth was a big man – a gentle giant. He could have been a youthful sixty-year-old or a forty-five-year-old who'd had a misspent life. He looked old – a real sea dog – but he acted young, so I had no way of knowing his real age. Not that it much mattered. Seth was Australian, with salt and pepper hair, striking blue eyes, wide, muscular shoulders and a beer gut. He was dressed permanently in pink; washed-out, oil-stained and sun-bleached. But pink just the same. I couldn't decide whether he'd actually invested in a pink wardrobe, or whether this was the result of a laundry session gone wrong. But I figured it took a lot of guts to walk around in pink outfits all day long and Seth was certainly no wimp.

He lived on *Black Magic* and chartered her out around the islands. And yes, he was a man for the ladies but he never said a wrong word or made a wrong move around me. I think he genuinely enjoyed my company and had surmised, just by watching me around the place, that I wasn't on the look-out for a man. What's more, he never commented on my swimming sessions, seeming to understand that there was a reason behind them. Except one particular evening, he'd invited a few of us on board for supper and we'd all been on deck, having a drink while he cooked. The moon had been high, the night still and warm and the water gleamed with phosphorescence. Unable to resist it, I'd slipped over the side for a couple of gentle circuits of *Black Magic* before dinner. He'd held the ladder steady while I'd climbed back on board then, without a word, he turned on a powerful flashlight which was permanently set up on deck. Curious, we all watched as he trained it down into the water and it penetrated the depths for maybe twenty feet or so.

I don't know whether they were attracted by the light or whether they'd been there all along, but the sea was full of massive shapes, gliding silently around the yacht. Layer upon layer of them, dozens and dozens of shapes sliding through the dark. He gave me a long look, then switched off the beam, knowing he'd made his point. I still swam out to *Black Magic* every day, but I never again went into the water after dark.

On my birthday afternoon, we talked about more serious things. About running away (I suspected Seth was outrunning a past even more eventful than my own), about life. And about death. I felt better for the chat and, by the time I'd slipped overboard again, Seth was all set for my party that evening and so, at last, was I.

Half an hour later, back on my little strip of beach, I took off my swimsuit, strapped my Walkman to my waist and slipped on a Dire Straits tape. Then I strolled down to the shallows, turned the volume up full and danced like a dervish. Tiny fish fled in all directions as I jumped around in the surf – completely naked, completely alone and totally tuned to the insistent beat which pounded in my head. I could feel the warm water against my ankles, the sun hot on my breasts and legs. Brian was dead and that was tragic. But I was alive, with everything to play for – just as Seth had said. It was my birthday. I was thirty-seven and still in one piece, admittedly, against all the odds. As I laughed aloud in sheer good spirits, yet another little plane took off from the tiny airstrip behind the screen of palm trees. It catapulted out past the edge of the island, then turned sharply back towards me as it began to gain height – although it was still low enough for me to make out the pilot through the window. Laughing, I waved wildly, blowing him kisses and, dipping his wings, he buzzed me as the plane shot over my head.

A week later, Kitty and I relinquished our sofas in the end room and made our way back to Suva. From there, we flew on to the tiny island of Roratonga and rented the prettiest little house, treating ourselves to the unaccustomed luxury of separate beds (and bedrooms), a shower room with hot water and a *kitchen*. I hadn't cooked for myself – or anyone else, come to that – in an age. But the fridge and the cooker were too much of a temptation. While women the world over were complaining that they were tied to the kitchen sink, we willingly immersed ourselves to the elbows in ours and came over all domesticated for the next few days.

Bouncing into town on our little rented moped, we toured the shops for fruit and vegetables, dragging home all manner of weird and wonderful fish on which to demonstrate our culinary expertise. Old recipes were dredged up from the recesses of travel-logged brains, while improvisation became the name of this latest game.

One day, Kitty cooked for me, next day, I prepared some gastronomic feast for her. Far into the evenings, we amused each other with tales of our travels, our men, our countless mistakes, while the tapes I'd carted all across the world played on Kitty's ultra-smart, state-of-the-art travelling cassette player.

By far the most screechmaking entertainment turned out to be the nightly cockroach hunts. The cheeky beggars had taken to dining in the fridge and, although we checked it out from top to bottom, we couldn't for the life of us see how they got in. Still, there they were each night, perched on top of the butter, sawing frantically at the meat – annoyed at being interrupted and furious at finding themselves turfed out of the best restaurant in town. They were big buggers, too – although that was hardly surprising, when you consider the amount of food they were getting through. And as we chased them round and round the kitchen, our yelps and screeches must have carried for miles.

Throughout all of it, the rain fell in a heavy curtain relentlessly for three days and nights. But since we hadn't come to sunbathe or sightsee, we were unperturbed. Instead we cooked, ate, chatted and hunted and waited for the rain to stop, knowing that, when it did, we would begin one of the most exciting adventures yet. For the waters round Roratonga are known to be among the clearest in the world, with perfect visibility to a depth of a hundred feet. And Kitty and I had come here to learn to scuba dive.

A crazy idea, really, when you consider how afraid of water I still was. Yet our teacher – a tiny Aussie with a shock of red curly hair and a walrus moustache – seemed unconcerned when I admitted that I couldn't dive, had only recently learned to snorkel and had no intention of sticking my head below the surface of any ocean, unless I was wearing my contact lenses, without which I was as blind as a bat.

Finally the rain eased, although the sky was heavily overcast and the wind was high, as we turned up at Charlie's scuba school that first morning. Kitty and I were joined by a large and incredibly powerful looking Canadian girl, who turned out to be a longshoreman back home, and the three of us settled down for a morning's schooling, during which we learned about air tanks, weight belts and depth gauges . . . and a dozen different ways to die.

Charlie's delivery was chatty and not without humour, but by lunchtime, no one was laughing. My head full of stories of Rapture of the Deep, air bubbles in blood vessels and all sorts of other nasties, I followed the others in search of a lunch I really didn't want to eat – knowing that, at long last, I'd probably bitten off more than I could chew and that scuba diving might prove to be my Waterloo.

Already I was beginning to panic – which meant that I'd broken the first rule, before I'd even set foot in the water. And the panic took a stranglehold on me immediately after lunch. That's when Charlie, having graphically described what our fate would be if any of us fouled up, went on to outline the kind of things we had to do, in order to win our diving certificate.

Talk of diving fifteen feet to retrieve face masks, snorkels and other items, went straight over my head, since I'd never dived for anything in my life. Swimming for so many yards without face mask or snorkel . . . removing all gear, leaving it on the ocean bed, then diving back down to put it all back on . . . coming up from a depth of one hundred feet with nothing but a lungful of air . . . I sat through it all, calmly resigned to the fact that I'd never have the nerve to do any of it. But it was the talk of 'breathing buddies' which really did my head in.

This particular party trick was obviously designed to help a diving partner who had run out of air. The idea was that I should remove my mouthpiece and pass it over to someone else, who would then breathe with it, while I sat there – presumably unconcernedly – holding my breath under tons of water. The very idea struck me as ludicrous and I had awful visions of battling to the death with anyone who was foolish enough to try it with me, since I just wasn't the stuff of good buddies.

So you could say I had a lot on my mind, later that afternoon, as we loaded our gear aboard Charlie's van and bumped off down to the beach. Not for us the reassuring tiled walls of the municipal baths. We were having our first lesson in the open waters of the Pacific. Casting a jaundiced eye over the unfriendly water, I wriggled into my uncomfortable wetsuit and snapped the weighted belt around my middle. Since I invariably screwed up the simplest mechanical things – like setting an alarm clock – the mere idea of connecting my mouthpiece to my air tanks and my air tanks to my air gauge thingy, quite wore me out. So much responsibility!

By the time I was duck-walking down the beach behind the other three – my depth gauge bumping against my boobs and my curiously dry mouth totally devoid of the spit I needed to smear on my mask – I'd lost all desire to conquer the ocean. All I really wanted was a good, stiff drink.

Following Charlie's example, I walked into the water until it was lapping my backside. Then I got down on all fours, clenched my teeth despairingly around the mouthful of rubber and submerged myself face down in the water. For a second or two, I was so afraid, I didn't draw breath at all and when I did inhale the sound echoed eerily in my head. I realized my eyes were tightly closed and I opened them to see Kitty's flipper kick out just a foot in front of my face. They were off – sliding through the sandy gloom like ungainly seals and, unthinking, I kicked off, too.

It was one of the most incredible moments of my life, when

I realized I was actually moving in and through this strange, silent place which I'd only ever floated on top of. A world I'd only ever looked down on was now unfolding all about me. Effortlessly, I was skimming over a fine, sandy floor: *'Try not to put your hands on the sea bed. Waken a sleeping Manta Ray and you'll get a nasty wound . . . '*, gliding past waving scarlet fronds: *'Keep clear of the red stuff. It's Fire Coral and it burns like buggery . . .'*, craning to peep into gulleys and crevices: *'Remember, every nook and cranny could be home for a Moray or worse. So keep your eyes peeled . . .'*

It was fascinating and I was trying to enjoy the experience, knowing I'd never be mad enough to don a wetsuit again, when I suddenly swam straight into Kitty, who had bumped into Sue, who was the only one who'd been keeping an eye on our Charlie, halting obediently as per his command.

Then followed a ludicrous forty minutes or so, during which Charlie threw my snorkel, then my mask, then one of my flippers, into twenty feet of water and I paddled about like some retarded labrador retriever – trying my damnedest to dive, but suffering the ignominy of recovering sweet FA as I continually popped back up like a cork. Thank God for Kitty who eagerly dived for all of my belongings as well as her own – a tribute to all those years of giving dolls' tea parties under water (well, that's what she told me afterwards).

Then there were the forward somersaults and the reverse ones. Three in each direction, please, and executed underwater while Charlie watched, presumably checking our co-ordination, maybe even our sense of direction. The other two managed it but I wiggled and jiggled comically, going ass over tit more by luck than design – totally unable to tell which way was up or how many somersaults made three. Coughing and spluttering, I catapulted to the surface, while Charlie gazed at me in the manner of one who'd lost a quid and found a bent penny. I figured, as scuba teaching went, he'd had it too easy for too long. Now he was about to earn his money.

Exercises over, we submerged again and slipped back inland. By now, my heart had stopped pounding and my breathing was less erratic. Even so I dragged myself out of the water, totally exhausted, and staggered up the beach –

glad to be on dry land and determined never to repeat the exercise.

So I guess it was that old fear of failure that had me climbing back into the wetsuit next morning, although the sea was even more angry and the sky even darker than it had been the day before. This time, I slid into shallow water with hardly a trace of nerves and, seconds later, we were all heading into deeper water and I was swimming straight for Waterloo.

In my own defence, I have to say I managed to do more stunts in the next hour than I would have dreamed possible. To my amazement, I mastered the art of clearing a water-filled face mask *without* losing my lenses. Just as I managed to swim for a set distance underwater, minus air and face mask – and *still* didn't lose the lenses. I removed my mask and replaced it. Removed my tanks and replaced them. All of my movements robot-like, since my brain had long ago disengaged.

Suddenly the heavens opened and a torrent of rain cascaded down, shattering the watery ceiling some twenty feet above our heads. I suppose everything was worth it for that weird sensation alone. . . .

Anyway sitting there, cross-legged in a circle on the ocean bed, we were put through our paces, and suddenly it was 'buddy' time. I watched with mounting apprehension as Charlie removed his mouthpiece and handed it to Sue, who let hers fall from her mouth as she breathed in this new air supply. Charlie sat on, guru-like, as she took several mouthfuls, before returning the rubber hose. It looked easy, but I still didn't like it.

Sue then repeated the exercise with Kitty, and, finally, Kitty turned to me and held out her hand for my mouthpiece – her eyes behind the mask questioning, since I'd been adamant over supper the previous evening that I'd never part with my precious piece of rubber. Sensing my hesitation, she pulled her mouthpiece from her face and I distinctly saw her exhale. Even then, I doubt if I'd have done it for anyone else – certainly not Miss Longshoreman – but mechanically, I took the piece from my mouth and passed it over. Then sat there, letting my breath out little by little and wondering how the hell I'd get the thing back in without swallowing half the Pacific with it.

It was all over in a couple of minutes. I'd had Kitty's air, she'd had mine and nobody had been asphyxiated after all. Then, just when I thought it was safe to stop worrying, Charlie took off his gear, laid it in the sand, shot to the surface, then duck-dived back down to re-dress – jamming the air into his mouth, while he squirmed around for the rest of his stuff. Miss Longshoreman went next and, after her, Kitty swam to the surface and I watched her floating for a second above my head, her auburn hair streaming out like a fan. Then she dived straight and true, the bubbles escaping from her nose and mouth as she floundered around next to me, searching for her air supply.

Oh dear, oh dear, oh dear . . .

Well, I got the gear off and laid it in quite a neat pile. Hit the surface and gazed back down at the little circle of bodies beneath the ocean. Dived. And dived again. Dived a fourth time and a fifth. But no technique, no chance and, on six occasions, I shot back to the surface like a blow-up rubber doll, while the current carried me further and further away from my rubber wardrobe and the old panic began to take hold. In the end, they had to come and get me – Kitty toting my tanks, Miss Longshoreman trailing my flippers and mask – by which time, energy all but spent, I was swallowing pints of water and my throat was red raw.

For long moments, I argued with Charlie in the water. All of us bobbing around on the surface, while the wind got higher and the rain beat down – Charlie's language getting more colourful, the more I refused to strap on the tanks. The prospect of going back underwater really scared me, yet I knew we were too far out for me to be able to swim back unaided. So eventually I calmed down, shut up and slid back in behind them, acknowledging that, whatever I'd been in a previous life, I sure as hell hadn't been a little fishy.

I can laugh about it now. Maybe I even laughed about it that night – finding some consolation in the fact that, although I'd lost face, at least I hadn't lost my precious lenses. But there was no way – no bloody way – they could talk me into joining them on day three. I had had enough.

Well, Kitty got her certificate, although she burst every blood vessel in her eyeballs in the attempt – the blue of her eyes staring evilly out of vampirish scarlet whites. Miss Longshoreman also collected hers. I got an 'I've dived in the Pacific' T-shirt and learned another lesson. Which was that, while there's nothing wrong with failure, there's everything wrong with simply not trying. So I was glad I'd given it my best shot.

Tail tucked between my legs, I flew out of Roratonga with Dracula's daughter a few days later. Kitty was half-sad, half-excited, knowing that our next stop, Tahiti, was her last port of call. In just four days, she'd be doing the rounds of old friends in Ottawa, wandering through the hospital wards or chatting to next-door neighbours, as if she'd never been away.

I remember we were talking about that – the anti-climax of being home – as our plane took off and climbed up into the dark and angry sky. Yet long before we reached Tahiti, the chances of either of us seeing home again had become extremely unlikely . . .

Kitty had fallen asleep first and I stared out of the porthole, watching the rain lash the illuminated wing just below me. Then I must have dozed, too, and the next thing I knew, a terrific noise – more a bang than an explosion – reverberated above the sound of the engines. In the same instant, the whole plane plummeted forward and sideways and, in that split-second fear takes to arouse one from sleep to absolute, nerve-twanging consciousness, I knew we were in trouble.

I'd made a lot of flights over the years. Had often hit bad weather; thunderstorms and sheet lightning. Knew that unmistakable sensation when a plane hits an air pocket and falls like a stone for long, heartstopping seconds.

But, sitting at the back of the plane, I could see jackets and holdalls, magazines and bouquets of orchids tumbling from the overhead storage. Knew that we were in a dive – and a steep one at that.

I felt a stomach-clenching fear which was all the worse for being sudden and severe. I'd been scared a lot of times, but until that moment, I'd never been in the grip of blind terror. I'd let out one small cry when I'd heard the first bang, yet after that, I was quite silent. So was Kitty – although the man sitting next to her garbled incoherently and started yelling for a stewardess and I heard a woman crying hysterically a few rows behind.

'Ladies and gentlemen – everyone – fasten your seat belts immediately, please – ' The stewardess's voice came over the intercom, depressingly agitated. And above the sound of a hundred frantically pinging 'fasten seat belt' and 'no smoking' signs, was the clunking of several hundred belts.

'Much bloody good they'll do us, if we're going in the drink,' I thought, as I began to fasten mine. But even as I struggled with the metal, there was a second loud noise, which seemed to vibrate through the whole aircraft and, nose first, we plummeted out of the sky again.

Convinced now that we were going to crash, I became curiously detached from all of it as the plane began to level out. I leaned back against the head rest and gazed quietly out of the window at the teeming rain. We were definitely losing altitude fast. I knew by the pain in my ears. The question was: was the pilot controlling the descent, or were we on a collision course?

As if in answer to my unspoken query, a man's voice suddenly cut through the noise. A voice oozing with calm and completely unruffled. The voice of our captain, reassuringly middle-aged and, hopefully, experienced.

'Good evening, ladies and gentlemen. I'm sorry you've had to travel on such an unpleasant night – ' he began sympathetically. 'We have headed into a bout of unexpectedly severe weather and you may have noticed a slight reduction in our altitude.' *Try five thousand feet and still dropping.* 'This is because we have decided to fly below the front, to ensure your comfort.' *And the lower we fly, the less far we have to fall.* 'You may have noticed some noise a few moments ago. This is quite normal and is a result of our reduction in speed.' *Mostly due to the fact that we have lost our tail.*

Oh, he was good. He was very, very good. But I wasn't fooled for a minute. Neither was anyone else. Yet the passengers grew quiet, order was restored and three-hundred-odd souls limped on through the wicked night – all of us thinking of friends and families; the things we shouldn't have done and the things we should have said.

Throughout those few awful minutes, Kitty and I hadn't exchanged one word. But I glanced at her now and with a tremulous little smile, she slipped her hand into mine. We stayed like that for the next hour or so, while wild stories circulated round the plane about a ruined undercarriage, problems in the hold, a dicky wing, an engine failing.

Personally, I couldn't get over the irony of my situation. Fancy travelling around the world and risking life and limb countless times in a madcap search for answers, only to get the answers and end up dead – hanging around in the Pacific, waiting to become some shark's lunch. Life's a bitch and then you die, right?

It was with a very real sense of having forfeited yet another of my nine lives that I stayed on in my seat, long after we'd squealed down the runway and taxied into Tahiti airport. Later, standing in the immigration queue, I watched as the aircrew swept through the arrival lounge. All of them pale and drawn – the captain staring dead ahead, almost as if he didn't want to look at us patiently waiting; the soon-to-be Polynesian tourists, who'd come dangerously close to taking their last holiday snap.

Part of me wanted to step out of the line and thank him, since I knew – we all did – that we owed our survival to him. But the great pretence was already underway. The cover-up. The public insistence that nothing untoward had happened on a perfectly routine flight – and to say 'thank you' would have blown the gaffe. So I thanked Kitty instead, for holding my hand and not being a wimp.

We were in and out of Tahiti in twenty-four hours flat. Unable to stand its Frenchness, its cutesy, chic sophistication; its expensive street cafés and awful snobbery. We didn't like the fact that we had to pay New York hotel prices to lie on the floor of some guy's living room – along with a dozen other travellers; or the fact that Gauguin's museum contained everything *but* a single Gauguin painting.

So we caught a ferry to one of the neighbouring islands and spent a pleasant couple of hours afloat, reminiscing about the past weeks and congratulating ourselves on the fact that we were alive to talk about them at all.

Kitty, on her last day of freedom, had been determined to see me safely housed *somewhere*. Almost as if leaving me apparently without a roof over my head was somehow a bad omen. The little island looked entrancing as it loomed out of the heat haze. Richly green, pounded by surf and with a high mountain soaring up inland, like a great grey witch's hat. We asked around at the harbour and heard that there were five brothers on the other side of the island who maybe rented rooms. So we hitched a lift in a passing jeep, the friendly local dumping us by the roadside a couple of miles further on, and pointing to a dirt track.

At the end of it, we found the five brothers and yes, they did have rooms. Although mine wouldn't be ready for an hour or two. So I dumped my luggage, and Kitty and I strolled along the shady road – the only one on the island, as it turned out – towards a little restaurant the boys had told us about. The proprietress was happy to cook us lunch, insisting we could have anything we liked, just as long as it was barbecued parrot fish. With it, we had altogether too much to drink and I took photographs of the lovely, limbo-dancing, red-eyed Kitty and she took photographs of li'l ol' wine drinkin' me.

Much later, we wandered back along the dusty road screened from the sea by flame and pink-flowering hibiscus and frangipani bushes heavy with perfume. A few yards from the tarmac, the surf bounded up on a thin ribbon of beach and, just offshore, a tiny atoll floated in a bright blue sea. Beyond that, the purple and lavender of distant Tahiti shimmered on the horizon.

By now, the sky was slightly streaked with pink, the sun was slowly sinking and it was time for Kitty and me to say goodbye. We heard the worn-out engine of the pick-up truck long before it rattled round the bend. There were four boys in the cabin and, while they were happy to give Kitty a lift to the harbour, the only berth was in the back, they explained apologetically. The back, wouldn't you know, was full of fish. Hundreds of them in shiny rainbow colours, slipping and slithering all over the floor.

While the engine idled, we gave each other a last hug – both of us travellers for too long to say the usual, trite things, like: 'You must look me up in London,' or: 'My place is yours, whenever you come to Ottawa.'

Instead: 'You're some gal. Try to keep in touch,' she smiled. 'Sure . . . I'll look out for you at limbo competitions,' I answered. And then she was up and on the truck, sitting astride the mound of fish, her smile wide as she waved . . . at which point the truck lurched forward, she lost her balance and went flying – completely disappearing in amongst the livestock. So my last memory of Kitty isn't so much a vision as a sound – rich, deep, uproarious laughter, which lingered in the warm air, long after Kitty herself had disappeared.

Chapter Nine

I'll follow the sun

For the next couple of weeks, home was a delightful little thatched roundhouse, one of several in the compound – five of them bedrooms, the sixth a kitchen and all of them raised up on stilts. A series of bamboo poles planted in a large circle formed the outer structure and the wooden floor of the room was lashed to these, so that it cleared the ground by at least two feet.

The poles were linked by a latticework of palm fronds, which created a low wall and gave the occupant a little privacy, but above this, the little round room was open to the elements, protected from the worst of the heat and the rain by a high, pointed thatched roof. This in turn overhung the circular roof beam which ran around the tops of the poles, so that although there were no curtains, the deep fringe of dried grasses offered a little more privacy. And there was, of course, no door.

The only piece of furniture in the room was a mattress on the floor and suspended above it was a mosquito net. But by now I had the knack of turning a few square feet of space into a home and within the hour, I had transformed the place. The mattress was draped in a colourful lungi and the pillows wrapped in bright scarves so that, shrouded in its gossamer net, my bed began to look impossibly romantic – like something out of a Turkish harem.

My multi-coloured wardrobe of skirts and petticoats was hung from the circular roof beam, together with my ribbons and belts, while my wealth of Fijian coral beads, my bright shiny Indian bracelets, my earrings and toe rings were nestling happily in a massive shell I'd found, its mother-of-pearl glinting warmly by my bedside.

Once I'd set up my Walkman and my trusty speakers, I stood back to admire my little room – filled now with colour and soothing flute music – thinking that Siobhan, that home-maker *extraordinaire*, would have been proud of me.

Satisfied with my handiwork, I went off to explore and discovered 'mod cons' which were straight out of *The Swiss Family Robinson*. The communal bathroom was built in much the same way as my bedroom, except that the floor wasn't raised up. Instead, the earth had been covered with smooth pebbles, through which the water drained away. The wash-basin was incredible, fashioned as it was from a massive shell into which a hole had been drilled and a little metal drain inserted. The shower was a slim metal pipe standing in the middle of the room and the decor consisted of a riot of flower-ing plants which grew unchecked up the latticework walls. In the midst of this jungle bathroom, the white porcelain loo looked oddly out of place.

The kitchen, too, was like something out of a castaway film set, with its sink shored up on tree trunks, its cupboards made of roughly hewn bamboo and bright yellow parakeets perched cheekily along its latticed walls, heads cocked to one side as they waited to clear up stray crumbs of food.

Aware of my presence as I wandered around their home, yet too shy to approach me, the five brothers went about their business. They were building still another roundhouse, larger than all the others – probably destined to be the equivalent of my living room back home – and as they worked, they chatted away in a combination of French and their local dialect.

Aged between eighteen and around twenty-eight, they were all very solidly built and attractive boys. Their bodies tanned and youthful, yet with that smoothly rounded *soft* look to their physiques – fleshy and almost womanly – which is so typical of these island people.

Their father had died some years before, their mother lived on mainland Tahiti and the five brothers lived here harmoniously enough, each with his own bedroom and his own allotted tasks.

By the end of that day, I'd wormed my way on to the work rota, offering to cook for the boys. Although, when one of them handed me a couple of dozen little fishes, threaded like beads on to a ribbon of palm frond, and gestured for me to turn them into dinner, I knew a moment's uncertainty. I wandered out of the compound with them, crossed the hot tarmac and ducked through the curtain of bougainvillea edging the opposite side of the road. Before me, the pebble beach stretched down to the water's edge about ten feet away and the waves slid in gently, chuckling as they washed over the smooth stones.

Settling comfortably on my haunches, my skirts pulled high above my knees to avoid the odd rogue wave, I unthreaded the little silver fishes and began to gut them with the only utensil I'd found in the kitchen – a small, bent fork. Carefully I tossed the innards into the shallows, while all around me, landcrabs as big as saucers meandered across the pebbles and scuttled along the water's edge. And as I worked, I gazed about me, loving the beauty, the tranquillity of the place.

Banners of brilliant pink were unfurling across an evening sky which was already streaked with silver and, on the distant horizon, I could make out the purple outline of Tahiti, shrouded in a heat haze. The air was heavy and warm in spite of a gentle breeze, which flirted through the trees, so that palm leaves hanging low over the water rocked and dipped their fronds into the waves.

It was Saturday night in Polynesia. Soon, it would be Saturday night in London, too. I smiled as I thought of how the other half were living. Imagined the crowded, smoky bars, the noisy nightclubs, the smart clothes, the clever chat and knew I wasn't missing much. All alone in the gathering dusk, I worked away with my fork and my little fishes – happily planning a menu for my five hungry neighbours and feeling not the slightest desire to be anywhere else doing anything different.

Early next morning, the sun slid unhindered into my bedroom and after a quick shower, I sat on my doorstep, gazing up at the mountain which towered above the whole island as I enjoyed my breakfast of fresh fruit. Then I wandered out of the compound and across the road to the beach. The boys had suspended a hammock from two trees at the water's edge and I passed a pleasant hour swaying gently above the waves in the early morning warmth, enjoying the breathtaking view.

About a hundred yards offshore, a small palm-decked atoll nestled in the sun. Even from here, I could see the white fringe at the water's edge and guessed it had a sandy beach – the perfect place to take my clothes off and indulge in some uninterrupted sunworshipping. The problem was getting to it, since swimming across was out of the question; the channel of water which divided both islands looked much too deep and fast-flowing. Yet when I mentioned to Tui, the middle brother, that I would like to visit it, he immediately offered to row me out there each day, in exchange for my services as a cook.

And so my days took on a new routine. I'd spend the mornings doing chores – like the washing. Filling the old oil drum with water, I'd pile in all my laundry and climb into the drum after it. Then, standing thigh-high in the cool sudsy water, I'd sing along merrily, pounding out the rhythm as I trod the clothes clean. Each day I straightened up my little room, turfing out the roaches and spiders which had gatecrashed in the night and disturbing tiny lizards which had crawled into the cool darkness of my clothes. Then I would walk the mile or so to the cluster of shacks and stores which made up the village, strolling back home with that evening's dinner offering.

In the early afternoon, I would climb into Tui's little canoe and he would row me out to the little island, over water which was deep and fast-flowing but which was crystal clear, so that I could gaze down fifty feet or more into a wonderland of light and shadow, teeming with colourful life.

The atoll was smaller than a football pitch and on my first visit I'd walked around it in less than ten minutes. But it was deserted, it was sandy and it was a real sun trap. This was where I spent my afternoons, catching up on my diary or writing letters home, playing music or just snoozing lazily in the heat. Then, as the sun dropped lower in the sky and the shadows grew longer, I would slip into my clothes and wait for Tui's tiny figure to appear on the distant beach, pushing his boat into the water.

I'd been on the island for four days and was heading for the village on my usual shopping expedition, when Tui's ramshackle old jeep screeched to a halt beside me and he shyly offered me a lift. We'd only been driving for a couple of minutes when a second jeep came rattling towards us and stopped as it drew level, causing Tui to slam on his brakes with a wide smile. The two drivers were soon hanging out of their windows, deep in animated conversation, and so entranced was I by the scenery just outside my window, that it was a few seconds before I even thought to glance at this other person.

But when I did, this latest addition to the local scenery fairly took my breath away. For he was no shy and gentle Polynesian; no simple, naïve local. He was haughtily French, his eyes green in a lean, tanned face, his dark brown hair curling over his collar and tumbling across his forehead. A good-looking man, probably in his late thirties, who noticed me in the instant I became uncomfortably aware of him. And, if his eyes were anything to go by, the effect was mutually devastating. I know I looked away quickly and gazed out at the ocean, feigning disinterest, although I was absolutely tingling inside. Amazed at the discomfort and confusion I felt, I wouldn't allow myself even a parting glance, as suddenly Tui stepped on the gas and we took off in a cloud of dust.

'He . . . was *gorgeous*,' I kept thinking to myself, as Tui began a stilted conversation and I tried to reply in my usual, horribly fractured French. I had gazed at him for less than a minute but after that chance encounter, I couldn't get the man out of my mind. During the next few days, he suddenly appeared everywhere I went and I seemed to be forever catching glimpses of him in the distance. Each time I experienced all the painful symptoms of girlish adoration – embarrassing in one of my age and experience, so it would have been some consolation to know I was having the same disconcerting

414

effect on him. But he ignored me to such a degree that I began to think I'd imagined that look of naked interest in his eyes.

Once, he drove past me as I was strolling along the road. I recognized his jeep as it came towards me, yet he increased his speed as he drew level and drove on with no hint of recognition. Another time, he strolled into the baker's shop as I was walking out and again, although his eyes looked straight into mine, there wasn't any sign of acknowledgement in his gaze. I suppose I was just as cool; just as distant. Just as bowled over. And just as afraid.

For it had been months and months since I'd felt attracted to anyone; a long time ago that I'd slipped the little silver bracelet from my ankle and given it to Martin. Ever since I'd fallen for that man, sex with strangers had lost its attraction, since sex without emotion wasn't what I wanted. Yet here I was, excited half to death by the mere presence of a man; tormenting myself with images of how it would be to have him make love to me . . . and I didn't even know his name.

A couple of evenings later, I had been sitting on my doorstep as usual, peeling some potatoes in preparation for dinner. Watching as the last rays of the sun turned everything a warm gold, so that even the boys looked like burnished sculptures as they worked together on the roof of the latest house, just yards away. Dusk had fallen fast and I had gone into my room to light my hurricane lamp, when the jeep drove into the compound. So the first I knew of our visitor was when Tui suddenly appeared out of the darkness to explain shyly that there was no need for me to cook that evening, since the brothers had been invited out to dinner. I could just dimly make out a figure lurking behind Tui, but now this person stepped forward into the pool of light which my lamp cast over the ground. It was the Frenchman.

It took me a moment to realize that I was being included in the invitation, although when I looked into his face for confirmation, Tui's friend looked less than happy about the arrangement. Almost angry, in fact, and for a moment I was completely thrown. Of course, I refused dinner, insisting I'd rather stay at home. Although I didn't know what the hell I'd do with myself all evening – with none of the boys for company, no batteries for my radio, only the light of the hurricane lamp to read by and not even the nightly cooking ritual to occupy me.

Really, it was ironic that the only man I'd fancied in ages not only didn't fancy me – he couldn't even be civil when we met. That's what I was thinking as both men walked away. Then suddenly, the Frenchman turned back, moved near to me and stroked my cheek very gently, although he didn't utter a word. He was so close, I could smell him – a wonderful odour of wood and perspiration, which lingered on in my memory long after he was gone.

Suddenly, I didn't mind that I was being left behind; wasn't troubled by their laughter as the men piled into the two jeeps and roared out of the compound, leaving me all alone in the dark. Because now I knew that my instincts hadn't misled me. The Frenchman was every bit as smitten as I was. And even more determined to deny it. I couldn't help wondering why.

The answer was an obvious one and I got it next day from Tui, who innocently replied to all of my casual questions about his friend. Claude *was* French and had lived here for the last nine years. He had been part of a French government scheme to generate new industry on the island but he had chosen to stay on after his tour of duty was completed. He had married a Polynesian girl, fathered three children and had become a leading light in the village, highly regarded by the locals – particularly Tui and his brothers, who treated him like a local hero.

In other words, this lovely man was as straight as a die and the last thing he was looking for was trouble. No one could understand that better than I and from then on, I tried very hard to put him right out of my mind. It worked, too . . . until the Night of the Rat.

I knew very well that whole families of them lived in the compound and rats weren't exactly new to me. Each night, once I'd turned out the oil lamp and settled down in bed, I'd hear the creatures scuttling along the circular beam which held up the roof. On that particular night, I'd hung my clothes up over the beam as usual and, without thinking, I'd also draped my white leather belt across it. As usual, I heard the busy scuffling as the first rat capered sure-footed around the circuit. Then he must have stepped on to the belt, which slid from the beam, making him lose his foothold.

I heard his frantic scramble as he tried to regain his balance; heard the dull thud as my belt landed on the floor and a second, heavier one, as the rat hit the deck just behind it. At which point, he went nutty, careering around the room and becoming more and more frantic, as he bumped into things. Lying there in the pitch black, minus my lenses and unable to see even my hand in front of my face, I wondered at his inability to see where he was going. Didn't all rats have big red eyes, all the better to see with . . . and long yellow teeth, all the better to bite with . . . and weren't they all infected with rabies?

Growing more frightened by the minute, I tried to light the lamp, hoping to scare him away, but I dropped all the matches in my haste. In the darkness, I heard him slamming into the music tapes and scratching furiously at my bag. Heard him bump into the shell and scatter all my jewellery. I was just thinking he was so terrified, he'd probably bite anything he came in contact with, when he blundered into my mattress – which was on the floor, of course – and bounded across my legs. He was heavier than your average cat and that was enough for me.

Diving up out of the bed, I got caught up in the mosquito net and panicked myself half to death, trying to find the way out of the net and my room. It wasn't until I was bounding across the compound to the first bungalow, which happened to be Tui's, that I remembered I was stark naked. Then followed a real pantomime, during which I woke Tui up and refused to let him light the lamp, since I was starkers. That amused him no end, as he threw out a towel with which I could cover my embarrassment. After which, both of us headed back to my room to find – surprise, surprise – Mr Rat was nowhere in sight.

Even so, I was thoroughly jittery by now and spent the rest of the night with the lamp lit, sleeping fitfully in its friendly glow.

417

I must have wakened just before dawn and, turning off the lamp, I lay on my back, watching as the outline of my roof and the silhouette of my clothes gradually became visible in the thin, silver light. I'd slept badly, had unpleasant dreams – didn't feel good at all. In fact, I felt rotten. Anxious, alone and *lonely*. Something I hadn't felt for ages. I tried to think of nice things – tried to remember Martin's hands, his eyes and his laugh. It didn't work. So I conjured up Claude instead; recalled his handsome face that first day in the jeep and remembered how he'd touched my cheek the other evening. Then I gave my imagination free rein and made love to him in my mind and, making love to him, I must have fallen asleep again.

. . . I was lying on my side in that sleeping/waking state, that delicious limbo in which you can hear without listening and see with your eyes closed. I could feel the room was lighter but not yet bathed in sunshine and I sensed, more than saw, the movement at the foot of my bed. I accepted, the way a dreamer does, that someone was in my room. Someone had made a mistake; that's what I thought in my sleep as, without the least apprehension, I raised my head, expecting to have a conversation with one of the brothers who, in this latest dream, was coming back to reclaim what was, after all, usually his bed.

For a moment, I didn't recognize the figure which hovered beyond the mosquito net and sleepily I asked, 'What do you want?' There was no reply and then I began to think that perhaps I wasn't dreaming after all. Which was when the figure moved around to the side of my bed, leaned forward and slowly raised the edge of the mosquito net.

Claude's face swam into view, just as I had imagined it earlier, and I relaxed, knowing this *was* a dream. Then he kissed my lips and the kiss was real enough to make me draw back in fright; but only for an instant, as I understood that Claude's face was actually inches from my own. I didn't have to think. Didn't need to question what I did next. All I knew was that I had willed him to come to me and suddenly, inexplicably, he was here.

Quietly, he slipped into bed next to me; kissed me gently,

then more urgently, before losing his control completely and making love to me like a man possessed. While I gave myself up gladly to the thing I wanted more than anything in the world right then; revelling in the long missed sensation of a warm body next to my own, the long forgotten pleasure to be had from giving pleasure. I lost all track of time as we rolled over and over in the bed, exhausting each other with our unspoken demands. . . .

Then it was much later, the room was filled with sunlight and I lay on my back, pinned down by the comforting weight of Claude's body. Our faces an inch apart, we studied each other, smiling yet silent. Both of us knowing that, while taking something we each desperately wanted, we'd given something we both desperately needed. Neither one a user and neither one used.

Raising himself up on his elbows, he kissed me gently one last time, then he slipped out of the bed and looked at me for an instant before he lowered the mosquito net. A second later, he was gone and it was only when I wound my arms about my body – sleepy, satisfied and totally content – that I realized we hadn't spoken a single word to each other. Not from the first moment until the last. In fact, the whole encounter was almost surreal and already part of me had begun to wonder if I'd imagined it all as I flipped over on to my stomach and buried my head in the pillow. And there it was – a beautiful hibiscus blossom, freshly picked and blushing prettily against the sheet. Delicately veined and glowing with early morning colour, it lay there, a gift from my phantom lover and a reminder of a wonderful moment in time.

Slipping out of bed and fastening a sarong about me, I sat down in my open doorway and breathed in the lovely morning. The flower lay cradled in my lap and, smiling at the secret we two shared, I tucked the blossom into my hair and sat there, feeling beautiful.

I saw Claude one more time after that. It was on a Sunday morning, the day before I sailed back to Tahiti, and I decided I wanted to go to church. More and more, I had tended to do that on my journey. Not because I was having any revival of Christian beliefs but because I enjoyed being a part of the community atmosphere which always existed at church gatherings.

The church services in this part of the world are wonderful – the congregations a sea of vivid colour and the singing rich and powerful, harmonious and energetic at the same time. The women wear white dresses and the most exotically decorated straw hats, while the men vie with each other in their white trousers and wonderful, wildly printed shirts.

Determined to get in the spirit of things, I put on a little white blouse with a pin-tucked front and puffed sleeves and wore both of my white cotton petticoats, which reached nearly to my ankles. Tui insisted I wear the straw hat which his mother donned for her church outings and I wound a silk scarf around the crown, just to brighten it up.

Although I'd long ago given up wearing shoes, I unearthed my white cotton espadrilles, tied the laces together and slung them over my shoulder. Then, happy as a sandboy, I set out on the two mile walk to the church. It was a lovely old building, built like a wedding cake, glistening with whitewash and standing on a spit of land, with the ocean lapping on three sides. It was enclosed by a white picket fence and a smartly painted five-barred gate and I stopped just outside it to put on my shoes.

The air was filled with the sound of voices as the singing rose and fell – sometimes low and sad, at other times loud and joyful enough to split the rafters. I was late for the service on purpose, knowing that, this way, I would draw less attention to myself. So I walked down the deserted garden path, climbed the wide steps, crept in through the open doors and slipped unnoticed into the back row of the congregation. Still, I aroused the curiosity of my nearest neighbours, who were soon engaging me in friendly conversation – seemingly oblivious to the booming voice of their preacher as they talked to me and about me.

I stayed in my seat at the end of the service, while the congregation queued up at the doors. I couldn't think why it was taking them so long to leave and it wasn't until I joined the queue that I realized the preacher, his elders and assistants had formed a line from the door down the front steps to the garden. And they were shaking the hand of every single member of the congregation. Feeling a bit of a fraud, I soon found myself having my hand pumped up and down by a succession of friendly, smiling individuals . . . and one in particular was smiling more than most.

For an instant I panicked, afraid that he might think I'd engineered this meeting to compromise him, but I needn't have worried. Claude could obviously tell from the look of complete bewilderment on my face that he was the last person I'd expected to see in church. Sensing my embarrassment, he took both my hands in his, asked me in French how I was and then explained to the next man in the welcoming line that I was a visitor to the island, staying with Tui and his brothers.

Then he relaxed his reassuring grip on my hands, gave me the sweetest smile and allowed me to pass along the line. I felt his gaze following me as I moved on, glad that we'd had this chance to take our leave of each other. Married he might be; a caring husband and father he certainly was and nothing we had done would change that. But he was a man too, and just for a little while, he had been his own person, choosing to share himself with me.

Even more important, meeting him had confirmed something I had always known about myself, which was that I like men and I will always want them in my life. I had learned to stand alone and now I didn't need anyone to prop me up, but I still wanted to share myself with some man, some day. I'd discovered how to be happy by myself, but I didn't want to make a career of being alone, any more than I wanted to make a virtue of being celibate. Ever since I'd stopped using sex as a weapon to hurt or as a commodity to barter, lovemaking had become as special for me again as it had been all those long years ago, when I'd first met Rui.

Moments later, I was out of the gate and back on the road, my shoes slung over my shoulder again and my bare feet pounding out a steady rhythm on the warm tarmac. On my left, the mountain gazed down benevolently, casting deep lilac shadows over the palm groves. While on my right, the ocean sparkled and sang and in the distance, my little green atoll danced and shimmered in the heat haze.

The air was filled with the smell of frangipani and the sound of birdsong, the sky was blue and the morning felt gloriously clean. My smile was wide, my heart was light, as I skipped and twirled my way along the road, hugging to myself the delicious secret – that I was in love again. But not with Martin or Claude or Hafez – or even the incorrigible Rui. Somewhere on this long and magical journey, I'd fallen head over heels in love with life.

I had taken wing – flown free for a while – but any time now, I would have to come down to earth. Back in the everyday world, my wings would be well and truly clipped and I might never get the chance to fly again. The question was, could I hold onto these good feelings, once I'd been permanently grounded? Keep my optimism through whatever bad stuff lay ahead?

Even now, I didn't know the answer. I could only hope the strength I *thought* I'd gained was constant. Could only pray the truth I thought I had discovered, was real.

The next day, I left the tiny island with its quiet Frenchman and its five shy brothers and, forty-eight hours later, my plane took off from Tahiti.

I'd slipped quietly into my seat, anxious not to disturb the blonde woman who slept soundly next to me but, when she surfaced an hour or so after take-off, she introduced herself to me. Karen was a bubbly, animated Californian who was heading home after a month's business mixed with pleasure in Australia and, in the hours it took us to slip into American airspace, we told each other all kinds of things, the way strangers on planes sometimes do.

Karen was no air-head but a capable businesswoman, but even at this first encounter, I could tell she was spinning out. She was full of the kind of nervous energy, brittle humour and easy laughter which people hide behind when they are terribly hurt and angry. So I was hardly surprised when she confided that her marriage had recently broken up. 'Still . . .' she shrugged it off, 'it's all history now. He's been gone three months and already I can hardly remember what he looks like. Amazing, huh?'

My heart sank at the news as I remembered how I'd been three months after Rui had disappeared. Still wandering around in a daze, unable to believe that we were all washed up; expecting him any minute to walk through the door or ring me to say 'Can we try again?' Wanting him and needing him, yet unable for the life of me to conjure up his face in my memory. In deciding to get divorced, Karen had entered a gruelling marathon and, watching her determined, hurt little smile, I knew she was still on the starting blocks.

By the time the plane was in a holding pattern over Los Angeles, Karen had persuaded me that what I *didn't* want to do was stay in that mad, bad and horribly polluted city. Instead, she'd offered to take me home with her and, since by now I was really enjoying her company, I accepted her invitation.

The moment we left the airport, I was glad of her company, as I experienced reverse culture shock in all its awful glory. Stretch limos, smart clothes and sour faces surrounded me on all sides. The sound and the smell of money was everywhere, while mean-mindedness and bad temper, those sidekicks of affluence and success, seemed to fill the air around me. I can't tell you how much I hated it or how desperate I was to get out of that place.

But even when I reached the sanctuary of Karen's lovely little house in Santa Barbara, the assault on my senses continued. All sorts of previously unconsidered things offended me now; like the huge amount of meat Karen doled out to her two deliriously happy dogs. Huge, well fed monsters, they licked her half to death in a rapturous welcome, before settling down to the kind of food that children in Calcutta could only ever dream about.

Idly, I read the wording on the doggy biscuit box – noted how well balanced this doggy diet was; how carefully the vitamin, mineral and protein intake had been accounted for. But I really baulked at the 'special offer' printed on the lid. If Karen – or anyone else – took the trouble to collect six box tops and then forwarded them, together with forty dollars, to the manufacturer, she would receive, by return of post, a custom-made, personalized dog tag for her much loved pet. No ordinary dog tag, this, but a gold-plated, deluxe version 'for the dog who had everything'. Forty dollars to dress a dog up in gold . . . the very idea of it made me want to throw up and I couldn't help thinking how much good forty dollars could have done, in some of the miserable hovels I'd visited. Really, it was obscene.

For days, I reeled around like this – very aware of Karen's natural generosity towards me and mindful that her friends had welcomed me warmly into their privileged group. But grateful as I was for all the hospitality, I was depressed by the wretched waste that was part of Western life. Grimly I watched the self-indulgence and listened to the 'I'm all right Jack' philosophy which was part and parcel of the great American dream.

It saddened me to remember that this was how the other half lived – saddened me even more when I reminded myself that I was very much a part of it. Oh, maybe initially I would hold out, but sooner or later, I'd become yet another avid consumer. Another addition to the world of the 'haves' – choosing to forget the thousands of people I'd seen who had nothing.

It was true, too. Within days I'd begun the consumer process, visiting first of all Karen's expensive hair salon to have my wayward mop controlled. Then had come the shopping expedition, since I realized I couldn't fly into New York looking like a native. The white, raw silk business suit had been just the thing for winging into JFK airport; the little black silk dress with the big price tag, just the thing for dinner in Manhattan. Shoes had proved a bit of a problem, since my feet had grown wider after months of walking everywhere unshod and they didn't take kindly to being squeezed into the black, Italian leather slingbacks.

But Karen and I persevered and within days, the transformation was complete. By the time I said a last goodbye to my newest friend, I was unrecognizable as the woman who sat next to her on the plane from Tahiti. And no one who watched the tanned, sophisticated woman boarding the flight to New

York would have believed that, just weeks before, she'd been a barefoot islander, naked but for the beads at her neck and the flower in her hair.

I think it would be fair to say that Henry C. Stone was surprised when he heard my voice on the other end of the line. He'd heard from me twice in the last one and a half years – the first time from a rooftop in Athens, the second from a hotel room in Bombay.

'Hey, Red – where the hell are you?' he yelled down the phone, practically going into orbit when I said I was sitting in a hotel in the Avenue of the Americas – just a taxi cab ride from his office. 'I'll be there in twenty minutes. Sit tight!' he laughed and I stood there, holding on to the receiver, long after it went dead.

For the hundredth time, I asked myself if I was doing the right thing, knowing even as I pondered the question that Henry was one more loose end I had to tie up. Restlessly I paced around the room, nervously checking my reflection in the heavy gilt mirrors and wondering what he would make of this re-styled me; hardly daring to think how I might feel about him.

Henry C. Stone . . . I'd thought I loved him once. Convinced myself that he was the sort of man who could make my life complete, since he was living the kind of life I had wanted for my own – stylish, sophisticated, social, successful. I'd been hugely intrigued by him for all sorts of reasons but mostly because he was smarter than me, more single-minded. If anything, even *more* determined than me to get everything he wanted out of life. I'd regarded all of these things as desirable qualities and they made him, for me, a desirable man.

Since our last meeting in New York, I'd often wondered how much of the feeling I'd had for Henry had been real and how much of it imagined. Had I genuinely been in love with him? Or had it been just one more example of me trying to lose myself in a man – any man – all that long time ago, when I sensed my life was falling apart? Any moment now, I hoped to have the answer.

425

My first glimpse of Henry was strange. After all, apart from my folks, his was the first familiar face I'd seen in a long, long time and I was thrilled to see that same old smile. Enjoyed the hug and the chaste kiss on the cheek – suddenly experienced a real feeling of reality as Henry stood quietly holding me. Proof positive that the dream was over and I really was going home. But as to how I felt about him . . . it was impossible to say.

Over the next couple of days, we met for lunch, rendez-voused for drinks in the evenings and lingered over dinner. But physically, I kept my distance from Henry – returning each evening to my hotel, as I tried to work out how much he meant to me *without* letting sex cloud the issue. On the fourth evening, we slept together and it was good and when he suggested I move into his apartment for my last few days, it seemed a logical next step.

Living with him was pleasant enough. We took walks in Central Park, raided the nearby supermarkets for the kinds of delicacies I hadn't tasted in ages. Took in a movie; went to a couple of parties. But all the time, I watched myself watching Henry. Studying this man who had been getting on with his life, while I had been living mine. One and a half years had passed . . . and I wasn't the only one who had changed.

Henry's large loft apartment yielded up lots of clues. The wardrobes were bulging with even more expensive suits – all of them making statements about Henry's taste and his bank balance. The fridge, on the other hand, was even emptier than I'd remembered, the kitchen obviously hardly used. Henry might well be sleeping here, but he was doing most of his living somewhere else.

The telephone rang incessantly and I soon got tired of pick-ing it up and taking his messages, so ignored it after the first day. Yes, of course, lots of the callers were women. It would have been naïve of me to expect anything else.

The mail was also interesting. All these letters addressed to Henry C. Stone III. He'd dropped the 'Jnr' in favour of some-thing he fancied was more impressive – more in keeping with the heavyweight image he was trying to cultivate – and I couldn't help teasing him about that. But Henry wasn't amused. Wasn't amused by lots of things which had appealed to him such a short time ago – including my rather irreverent approach to his increasingly stuffy and structured lifestyle.

Oh, yes indeedy, that apartment told me all kinds of things, but the most interesting clues of all were on the walls. The last time I had visited Henry, they had been quite desolate and bare but now they were covered with etchings and water-colour sketches and oil paintings – all of them originals.

Even if the art collection hadn't arrested my attention, the number of invitations to gallery openings, artists' exhibitions and the like would certainly have registered eventually. But slowly it dawned on me that, as part of his grand plan to be the perfect man – aesthetic as well as astute, sensitive as well as successful – Henry had set himself up as a patron of the arts, a latter-day patron saint of struggling artists. I think I would have minded less if I thought he liked it more – art, that is. But I got the uneasy impression that, while he might not be exactly buying it by the yard, he was collecting *art* for a purpose other than pleasure or even investment. He was making another statement about who he intended to be, if he wasn't that person already.

I remember one particular gallery we visited together . . . I recall that I didn't like any of the artist's work. Mostly executed in oils, I found his images harsh and unsympathetic. Honestly, I know nothing about art but, in the manner of the most humble lay person, I know what I enjoy looking at and I know that sense of communication when some stranger's vision makes me pause, when his interpretation of a thing makes me consider it in a new and different light. This artist didn't do it for me. Even now, I can't believe he did it for Henry, either. So, while it's undeniably bitchy of me to men-tion that there just happened to be a blank, empty wall in Henry's apartment and this particular painting was, if nothing else, approximately *the right size*, I think there's little doubt that the practical aspect of the purchase was certainly an issue.

Noticing how Henry lingered in front of the canvas, I dou-bled back to see what I had missed. It was garish. Lots of reds and oranges, with livid streaks of green – lurid, heavy-handed and cold. I glanced at Henry's face as he studied the catalogue. *Buy! Buy! Buy!* I could almost hear the harsh staccatto ringing in his head. He was going to buy this? Surely not.

But Henry was a man with a mission – a space to fill, one and a half yards by two and this worked out at just over three thousand dollars a square yard. As he glanced around for assistance, I couldn't stop myself from saying: 'Henry . . . you're not serious. You don't really like this, do you?'

'Sure. It's exactly what I've been looking for and I know just where I'm going to put it!' he replied enthusiastically, although this last piece of information came as no surprise to me.

'But . . . Henry, it's *awful*,' I persevered. 'Are you sure you can live with that, day in and day out? I mean, it isn't even very well executed, is it?'

'What's wrong with it?' he queried, cocking his head to one side – which might very well have improved the image. 'I like it. Anyway, a sunset is a sunset is a sunset. It's a lot of colour, Red; what's to execute?'

I couldn't believe the evidence of my own ears and that's when I completely blew it. 'Henry . . . for God's sake!' I hissed. 'For a start, it isn't a *sunset*, it's a *sunrise*. There's a helluva difference, you know – ' Then I stopped short as I caught the perplexed, guarded light in Henry's eyes and realized with a shock that he *didn't* know.

'Look – can't you see how cold it is, in spite of the reds and oranges? Don't you feel the chill? That's a morning sky for you – invasive and challenging. That's a threatening dawn if ever I saw one.'

Aware that the chilly atmosphere had seeped out from the painting and was now threatening to engulf both of us, I heard the control in his voice as he said, '*This*, Red, is a sunset. I like it and I'm buying it. And since I'm the one who's going to live with it, what the hell's *your* problem?'

I was silent then. Realizing as he went off to find the artist that I hadn't really *had* a problem until then. But now, it loomed large. We tried to be nice to each other for the rest of that evening. Told jokes and planned how we would spend the next day. But that night, I slipped out of Henry's bed and wandered through the loft to gaze down from the windows at a city which never slept.

I have seen some beautiful sunsets; watched the soothing dusk creep across many a friendly evening sky from Rhodes to Rajasthan. Just as I have been wide-eyed and bushy-tailed through many dawns, gazing out from trains and boats and planes to watch the display. To witness the spectacle of a rising sun sear its way into the fading greys and silvers of a dying night. Henry was now the proud owner of a badly painted sunrise. It worried me that he didn't know it.

Of course, I could hardly blame him; I don't suppose anyone in Manhattan ever caught a glimpse of that huge burning globe. Instead, their days went from black to grey, from light to bright, before growing dark again. The whole city was blind – perpetually cocooned in a haze of heat and pollution.

Henry was a wonderful man, exciting and challenging in so many ways. But he was already thirty-eight and there was still so much he didn't know. Such a lot he didn't want to learn. With that ten thousand dollars, he could have flown to the Greek islands and spent a couple of weeks just getting on speaking terms with nature. He could have lived the simple life, enjoyed the simple things. Could have sat through a dozen sunrises and a dozen sunsets and still gone home with change in his pocket. But no. Henry was too busy to take time out. Too wrapped up with his telephones and his computers, the German exchange rates and the Tokyo stock market to even notice that his office lacked a window and he rarely ever saw the light of day.

And as I sat there, watching the dark sky go grey, I finally tied up the loose end that was Henry C. Stone III. He was a special man, in many ways. I was still attracted to him, fascinated by him – convinced that he would go on from success to success. And once I'd been anxious to share it all but not any more. Given time, maybe I could fall in love with Henry again, but I doubted it. For how could I share myself and my life with a man who had never seen a sunrise?

Two days later, I was packed and ready to leave. Henry took me down to the terminal but he couldn't see me off at

Newark airport, since some important clients were due in from Chicago and Henry – the firm's man of the moment – had to make his pitch. It hardly mattered, since we'd said everything we had to say, made half-hearted plans for Henry to visit London in the autumn; talked about the possibility of spending Christmas together; gone through all the 'miss you, kiss you' routine, since to say what was really on our minds would have been painful for both of us.

I was sad when he disappeared into the crowd and the coach pulled out into Manhattan's busy streets. And as we shouldered our way through the New York traffic I took a good long look at this city I'd once thought I might settle down in, knowing I wouldn't be visiting it again for a very long time.

As my plane took off and rose up into the evening sky, dusk was already falling like a veil over Manhattan. I glanced down from the porthole at the clamour and glitter of Henry's kind of town and decided he was welcome to it.

The seats next to me were empty and, with no chance of chatting the hours away, I plugged in my headphones and concentrated on the music. I smiled as Albinoni's 'Adagio' filled my head, flooding me with memories of Bruno and his wine bar and a grubby little hotel room in Bangkok.

Slowly, slowly, that insistent little voice at the back of my mind now whispered the reality of my situation. I was going home. Home to no money, no job and maybe few friends. Home to examine the remnants of my old life and, hopefully, pick up a few of the pieces. Home to the rain and the phone bills and the noisy upstairs neighbour. Home to a small basement flat, a little white dog . . . and (the acid test) being by myself.

Had I learned anything at all? Was I sane again, whole again – *normal* – and had the world turned me into a woman I could happily live with? I couldn't help thinking that the answer was 'yes' to all of that but even so, the nervous tension began to tighten across my stomach. That was okay too, since I knew now I was allowed to be afraid. Patiently, I reminded myself that nothing which lay ahead of me could be as difficult as some of the stuff I'd left behind. Just as no one out there could inflict the kind of damage that I'd once chosen to inflict upon myself.

Still I worried and fretted about the future. I was my own person now, satisfied and content. This was something to savour, something I didn't want to lose. This was happiness . . . could life in London steal it from me?

'*Remember – anyone goes in the drink, it's a fine. Anyone loses their paddle, it's a fine. Anyone loses their helmet, it's a fine. Anyone not completing the journey, it's a fine . . .* 'The voice of Our Leader suddenly came at me out of the jumble of memories and I smiled to recall how his words had terrified me then. Well, I'd paid more than my share of fines and this was one journey I'd no choice but to complete. It did occur to me, though, that there could be a worse training for life than a week spent white water rafting in New Zealand. . . .

'God . . . I have been so lucky,' I thought, as I gazed out of the window. Watching as a dying sun shot the clouds through with flaming red, then rosy pink, then palest mauve, as it took its leave. It was a beautiful sunset, scrawling its delicate signature in streaks of violet as it slowly disappeared.

Then the dove grey sky was empty, save for that first star, winking palely down at me. I had often looked for it at the end of my day and each time I spied its friendly light, my mind slipped back through time. Carried me to a gently curving beach just as dusk slipped over the headland and left me in a hollow of fine sand, with the night breeze sighing in the palms, a warm wind blowing off the ocean . . . and Martin sitting quietly by my side.

Memories . . . so many of them. And no one and nothing could take them away. All these wonderful places and all these marvellous people, who would linger on in my imagination – filling my dreams and stepping into my waking thoughts, whenever I wanted to relive the moment.

Unbidden, they came to mind now . . . desert walks with Amer, train rides with Siobhan, fun and games with Chas, middle-of-the-night heart-to-hearts with Kitty. Which memory would come to my aid when life became unbearable?

And suddenly, there it was – filling my head and my heart with optimism, laughter and a pure burst of joy. The memory of me – all alone with the sky, the sea and the fishes – naked as the day I was born and dancing like a dervish in the waves. Fiji, on my birthday. In that magical moment when I *knew* I had made it through.

ALISON RICE

Travel Tips and Holiday Hints

Small print in English is as small as small print in Arabic, and not quite as pretty. Alison Rice explains the finer points of getting about for today's traveller.

Don't put your home address on your luggage on the outward journey – it pinpoints an empty house for an eagle-eyed thief

Self-caterers bound for Yugoslavia should pack a jar of coffee. The local stuff doubles as insect repellent.

If you're taking two bikinis with you, make sure they're the same shape – no funny white bits!

Buy an insurance policy that has a manned 24-hour telephone number for emergencies

Use toothpaste as an emergency antiseptic

Pay as much as possible of the cost of your holiday by credit card. Then you're covered if the tour operator goes bankrupt

From choosing the right holiday, knowing what to pack, advising on insurance and giving a complete country-by-country break-down of what to expect around the globe, *Travel Tips* is an invaluable part of your hand luggage.

Alison Rice is a regular columnist for *The Observer* and *Mail On Sunday*, a frequent presenter on local and national radio and a seasoned traveller.

MYRA LEWIS with Murray Silver

Great Balls of Fire

It was more than thirty years ago when 'The Killer' arrived in London with world-wide single sales nearing an astonishing 25 million for 'Great Balls of Fire' and 'Whole Lotta Shakin' Goin' On'. But the star's reputation took a nosedive as soon as he alighted from the plane. A stray reporter had asked the age of his young wife.

Now his biographer, Myra Lee Lewis was the child bride and 13-year-old cousin of the piano-pounding bad boy who unwittingly sparked off the international furore that nearly wrecked his career.

He's been alive and kicking ever since. 'Jerry's living life quicker than we can film it', once complained Adam Fields, producer of the movie based on this book and eight years in the making. Dennis Quaid stars as Lewis and had the wild man himself as his creative consultant.

Five years was all Myra needed to research the man she loves and knows so well.

GREAT BALLS OF FIRE is the most frank, personal and singular inside story of rock and roll's last and first – living legend.

'The man is a rock'n'roll classic.'

Dennis Quaid

A Selected List of Fiction Available from Mandarin Books

While every effort is made to keep prices low, it is sometimes necessary to increase prices at short notice. Mandarin Paperbacks reserves the right to show new retail prices on covers which may differ from those previously advertised in the text or elsewhere.

The prices shown below were correct at the time of going to press.

☐	7493 0118 X	**The Wire**	Nik Gowing	£3.99
☐	7493 0136 8	**A Kiss of Fire**	Masako Togawa	£3.50
☐	7493 0144 9	**A Question of Guilt**	Frances Fyfield	£2.99
☐	7493 0112 0	**Night Soldiers**	Alan Furst	£3.99
☐	7493 0034 5	**Questions of Identity**	Bob Cook	£2.99
☐	7493 0076 0	**The Crystal Contract**	Julian Rathbone	£3.99
☐	7493 0110 4	**Ice**	James Follett	£2.99

TV and Film Titles

☐	7493 0101 5	**My Left Foot**	Christy Brown	£3.50
☐	7493 0055 8	**Neighbours I**	Marshall/Kolle	£2.99
☐	7493 0057 4	**Dealers**	Gerald Cole	£2.50
☐	7493 0115 5	**Capital City**	Michael Feeney Callan	£3.50
☐	7493 0132 5	**Great Balls of Fire**	Lewis/Silver	£3.99

All these books are available at your bookshop or newsagent, or can be ordered direct from the publisher. Just tick the titles you want and fill in the form below.

Mandarin Paperbacks, Cash Sales Department, PO Box 11, Falmouth, Cornwall TR10 9EN.

Please send cheque or postal order, no currency, for purchase price quoted and allow the following for postage and packing:

UK — 55p for the first book, 22p for the second book and 14p for each additional book ordered to a maximum charge of £1.75.

BFPO and Eire — 55p for the first book, 22p for the second book and 14p for each of the next seven books, thereafter 8p per book.

Overseas Customers — £1.00 for the first book plus 25p per copy for each additional book.

NAME (Block letters) ....

ADDRESS ....

....